T0327718

NEOLIBERAL RESILIENCE

Neoliberal Resilience

LESSONS IN DEMOCRACY AND DEVELOPMENT FROM LATIN AMERICA AND EASTERN EUROPE

ALDO MADARIAGA

PRINCETON UNIVERSITY PRESS

PRINCETON & OXFORD

Published by Princeton University Press
41 William Street, Princeton, New Jersey 08540
6 Oxford Street, Woodstock, Oxfordshire OX20 1TR

press.princeton.edu

Library of Congress Cataloging-in-Publication Data
Names: Madariaga, Aldo, author.
Title: Neoliberal resilience : lessons in democracy and development from Latin
America and Eastern Europe / Aldo Madariaga.
Description: Princeton : Princeton University Press, [2020] | Includes
bibliographical references and index.
Identifiers: LCCN 2020011578 (print) | LCCN 2020011579 (ebook) | ISBN
9780691182599 (hardcover) | ISBN 9780691201603 (ebook)
Subjects: LCSH: Neoliberalism—Latin America. | Neoliberalism—Europe, Eastern.
| Economic development—Latin America. | Economic development—Europe,
Eastern. | Democracy—Latin America. | Democracy—Europe, Eastern. | Latin
America—Economic policy. | Europe, Eastern—Economic policy—1989– | Latin
America—Politics and government—1980– | Europe, Eastern—Politics and
government—1989–
Classification: LCC HB95 .M33 2020 (print) | LCC HB95 (ebook) | DDC
320.98—dc23
LC record available at https://lccn.loc.gov/2020011578
LC ebook record available at https://lccn.loc.gov/2020011579

British Library Cataloging-in-Publication Data is available

Editorial: Hannah Paul, Josh Drake
Production Editorial: Terri O'Prey
Jacket/Cover Design: Karl Spurzem
Production: Erin Suydam
Publicity: Kate Farquhar-Thomson, Kate Hensley
Copyeditor: Jay Boggis

Jacket/Cover Credit: Shutterstock

This book has been composed in Arno

Printed on acid-free paper. ∞

Printed in the United States of America

10 9 8 7 6 5 4 3 2 1

To Malú, Domingo, and Matilde

CONTENTS

PREFACE

BETWEEN LATE 2019 AND EARLY 2020, Chile went through the most extreme moment of political turmoil since Pinochet's dictatorship. During the last two weeks of October 2019, the world saw images of Chilean streets crammed by protestors, metro stations on fire, crowds looting supermarkets, and military forces deployed throughout the country—an image that revived the troubled 1970s in everyone's memory. This came as a surprise to many who saw Chile as a poster child of free markets and democratic stability. In fact, liberal elites worldwide have exhaustively cited the Chilean example in order to justify neoliberalism and market-conforming economic reforms. Much of this praise is based on objective improvements: almost uninterrupted economic growth, controlled inflation and fiscal accounts, rapidly falling poverty rates and Latin America's highest income per capita; a stable party system, strong institutions, low corruption levels, and low levels of civil unrest—all of which helped the country lead economic and political freedom rankings. For ordinary Chilean citizens, however, the rise in Santiago's metro fare that sparked the protests came as the straw that broke the camel's back. In fact, the motto quickly became "it is not about 30 pesos [the amount of the fare rise equivalent to less than USD 5 cents] . . . it is about 30 years."

Against this backdrop, one must think about what lies beneath Chile's "awakening" and what it means in terms of the troubled relationship between neoliberalism and democracy. The key to understanding "Chile's awakening," as many have observed, is its extreme inequalities. The best-known part of this are Chile's extreme socioeconomic inequalities embedded in the country's neoliberal development model, which has produced stark income and wealth concentration, privatized social services, and extreme urban segregation. Equally significant, although less known, are Chile's stark political inequalities and outright deficits in democratic representation, which are also directly connected with neoliberalism as I demonstrate in this book.

Chile's transition to democracy was, to put it mildly, peculiar. Chile returned to democracy with a political constitution written by Pinochet and voted for under a state of siege. Through a series of institutional mechanisms that I carefully analyze—among which, electoral laws and malapportionment, unelected veto players, congressional supermajorities for key legislation—the Pinochet Constitution granted a quasi-permanent veto power to the pro-Pinochet business and political elite. Chile's political system not only blocked representation for those who demanded more transformative changes, but also helped demobilize society, disconnect parties from their voters, and ultimately detach the political elite from the general public.

We now know that this constrained democracy was not a peculiarity of the Chilean case but a core part of the global neoliberal political project. Limiting democracy has been the best way of safeguarding neoliberalism from its opponents. And for more than thirty years, this was successful in Chile. In this context, the country's months-long "awakening" shows the limits and long-term effects of a constrained democracy and the perils of Chilean-style neoliberal modernization, providing important lessons for those countries that have followed its example.

After months of intense demonstrations that included a constitutional "state of emergency," the toll is as encouraging as tragic. October 25 2019 will be remembered as "Chile's largest march," when close to a fifth of the country's population—between 1.2 and 1.5 million in the capital alone—protested to the chant of "Oh, Chile has woken up!" demanding that the military return to the barracks as well as substantive policy and political changes. Demonstrators were able to force into the public debate several topics that were outside the government program of right-wing president Sebastián Piñera but that remained longstanding demands among the population, namely, reforms to Chile's privatized and highly segregated pension, healthcare, and education systems, and a referendum to decide whether to change or maintain the current Constitution passed during Pinochet's dictatorship. As this book goes to press, Chileans are deciding on the future of their political and institutional system as never before in the country's republican history. Moreover, if the "approve" vote wins, it will be the first time that the country's political constitution has been written by a constitutional assembly either partially or entirely composed by people elected especially for that task. It is not hard to foresee the possibility of a profound transformation of the country's political and economic order under these conditions.

At the same time, however, following the October events repression by the police and military has reached levels unseen in democratic times. Thousands of protesters have been wounded and tens of thousands arrested. Four international independent human rights organizations visited the country (the United Nations High Commissioner for Human Rights, the Interamerican Human Rights Commission, Amnesty International, and Human Rights Watch) confirming "regular" and "serious" human rights abuses against protesters and detainees and urging the government to reform the police.[1] As of January 2019, the National Institute for Human Rights presented more than one thousand judicial actions against the country's security forces, including allegations of torture, rape, and murder.[2] As of today, police abuses continue while protests maintain their frequency and radicalness. In this scenario, rightwing groups have been calling on the government for firmer action against rioters and to boycott the constitutional referendum under grounds that the state cannot guarantee social order. They also appeal to middle- and lower-class voters who fail to see the connection between the change of the Constitution and the rapid amelioration of their immediate socioeconomic conditions and play on their fear that transforming the country's core institutions will only worsen their already fragile situation. Consequently, four months after the start of the protests, in February 2020 no significant advances had been made in the "social agenda" of reforms while new laws condemning protestors and increasing repression capacities were under way.

It is clear that Chile has finally woken up after a long neoliberal night. What is less clear is the future it has woken up to. Although it seems unlikely that the

1 For the respective reports, see "Report of the Mission to Chile," 30 October–22 November 2019," United Nations Human Rights, Office of the High Commissioner, https://www.ohchr .org/Documents/Countries/CL/Report_Chile_2019_EN.pdf; "Chile: Deliberate Policy to Injure Protesters Points to Responsibility of Those in Command," Amnesty International, https://www.amnesty.org/en/latest/news/2019 November chile-responsable-politica-delib-erada-para-danar-manifestantes/; "IACHR Condemns the Excessive Use of Force during Social Protests in Chile, Expresses Its Grave Concern at the High Number of Reported Human Rights Violations, and Rejects All Forms of Violence," Inter-American Commission on Human Rights, http://www.oas.org/en/iachr/media_center/PReleases/2019/317.asp; "Chile: Police Reforms Needed in the Wake of Protests," Human Rights Watch, https://www.hrw.org/news/2019/11 /26/chile-police-reforms-needed-wake-protests.

2 Naomi Larsson, "Beaten, Mutilated and Forced to Undress: Inside Chile's Brutal Police Crackdown against Protesters," Independent, January 26, 2020, https://www.independent. co.uk/news/world/americas/chile-protest-police-violence-nudity-human-rights-a9294656 .html.

country will rapidly fall into chaos and ungovernability, it is equally unlikely that its leaders will respond in a timely and effective manner to the demands from the street. The quest for a middle ground may bring light—a revitalized democracy and a new development model under a new social and political pact—but also more shadow—renewed democratic constraints shielding neoliberalism and extending its morbid consequences. In this fluid but highly consequential scenario, this book offers keys to understand the mechanisms underpinning the resilience of neoliberalism and what we can expect from attempts at radically altering them through democratic means.

Beyond this unexpected turn of events, and thinking about the parallelism between the Chilean story and that of other countries at the other end of the world, it is good to remember how the interest in the relationship between neoliberalism and democracy came about.

In many ways, I started writing this book in 2008 when I visited East-Central Europe for the first time. I had just finished a fixed employment contract at the United Nations Economic Commission for Latin America and the Caribbean (ECLAC) in Santiago, Chile, where I worked analyzing social policy in Latin America and got more acquainted with the organization's history and discourse on dependency and development. There, I understood that the concern over social policy should not overlook a bigger and more fundamental concern for economic structures as a crucial element determining the possible patterns of economic and social development. This got me interested in other economic policies, notably industrial policy. In August of that year I travelled with my friend Mario Acuña, to Prague, Cracow, Bratislava, Budapest, and Zagreb. I was quickly intrigued by the strange feeling of new and old, progress and decay, hope and despair. This experience, and encouragement from Manuel Riesco, motivated me to enroll in a Masters program at the Central European University in Budapest in 2010–2011—with the benefit of hindsight, a life-changing experience.

In Budapest, I became aware of the relationship between Latin America and Eastern Europe in terms of development, and the possible links with Latin American ECLAC-based structuralist and dependency schools. A couple of years later, while on parental leave for the birth of my son Domingo, I came across a book by Ivan Berend on Eastern Europe's history of economic dependency, its embrace of communism as a way out of it, and its return to the periphery of capitalism after the fall of communism. I remember feeling it was a closing of a circle—or perhaps the start of a new one.

This book was made possible by the help, encouragement, and support of many people. I would like to start by thanking the three people who have been crucial sources of inspiration and support for this project. Wolfgang Streeck believed in this project from the first moment. His critical scholarship and engaged research have been a constant source of learning. Becoming acquainted with Béla Greskovits's work on the political economy of policy reforms and development and his comparison between Eastern Europe and Latin America made all this start to happen. Béla's writings with Dorothee Bohle have provided a key benchmark for comparativists of capitalist diversity outside the capitalist core. Not least, Doro's advice and encouragement, and her perceptive criticism, have been a constant source of intellectual challenge and stimulus.

Parts of this book were presented and received valuable feedback at different stages at the REPAL Conference (2013), the University of Tallinn (2013), the European University Institute (2018), the Max Planck Institute for the Study of Societies (2018), the Polish Academy of Sciences (2018), and the Political Economy Research Group (PERG) at the Central European University (2018). A number of people read parts of the argument at different points in time, and some took the time to read and comment on entire chapters and even the whole manuscript: thanks to Bruno Amable, Juan Bogliaccini, Dorothee Bohle, Tomás Bril-Mascarenhas, Lászlo Bruszt, Juan Carlos Castillo, Sebastián Etchemendy, Carlos Freytes, Béla Greskovits, Juan Pablo Luna, Antoine Maillet, Daniel Mertens, Cristóbal Rovira Kaltwasser, Eduardo Silva, Alex Spielau, Tomás Undurraga, Wolfgang Streeck, Anna Ząbkowicz, and Zbigniew Żółkiewski for their insightful comments and suggestions. Others took the time to share impressions on the content and form of this work at different stages, including Sabina Avdagic, Jens Beckert, Martin Höpner, Julius Horvath, Guglielmo Meardi, Eduardo Olivares, Gabriel Palma, and Ben Ross Schneider. Many other people contributed directly or indirectly to the final product. My younger brother Andrés Madariaga provided truly invaluable support and research assistance for chapter 3; Carlos Sandoval, Sebastián Zarricueta (INE Chile), and Leandro Cabello (ECLAC) helped with data issues, while Ewelina Laskowska helped with Polish translations. Marcin Serafin, Lukasz Pawlowski, and Alo Raun helped navigate the vagaries of Polish and Estonian politics and society. Sofia Rivera provided superb editing assistance.

During my field research in Eastern Europe and Latin America, several people helped me get in touch with scholars and public figures, contacts that helped me gain access to other high policymaking positions. For this I thank Daniela Astudillo, Zosia Boni, Michal Boni, Jorge Cauas, Ingrid Gerling, Rosario Montero, Marcin Serafin, Lukasz Pawlowski, Alo Raun, Alan Sikk, Aleks Szczerbiak, Liisa Talvig, and Miguel Torres. Nicolás Cherny was kind enough to give me access to the Archivos de Historia Oral (AHO) interview archive at the Gino Germani Institute in Buenos Aires. Sharing fieldwork in Argentina with Raimundo Frei was an experience in itself.

Some of the material presented here has appeared in two published articles: "Mechanisms of Neoliberal Resilience: Comparing Exchange Rates and Industrial Policy in Chile and Estonia," *Socio-Economic Review* 15 (3): 637–660; and "Business Power and the Minimal State: The Defeat of Industrial Policy in Chile," *The Journal of Development Studies* 55(6): 1047–1066, with Tomás Bril-Mascarenhas. Although this book expands and revises this material and puts it in the context of a different theoretical focus, I thank the journals involved and my co-author Tomás Bril-Mascarenhas for their permission to reproduce extracts of them here.

This book is partly based on my PhD studies at the Max Planck Institute for the Study of Societies in Cologne, Germany, between 2011 and 2015. During my stay at the Max Planck, I benefited from the good friendship and excellent scholarly advice of a number of colleagues. Special thanks to Jens Beckert, Helen Callaghan, Matías Dewey, Lea Elsässer, Nina Engwicht, Timur Ergen, Irina España, Felipe González, Martin Höpner, Annette Hübschle, Daniel Mertens, Markus Lang, Marcin Serafin, Christine Trampusch, Christian Tribowski, Armin Schäfer, and Wolfgang Streeck for their support. Jürgen Lautwein and Susanne Hilbring provided superb financial and library resources. The first draft of the book was completed at the Centro de Investigación y Docencia Económicas (CIDE) in Mexico City, which provided excellent research facilities and a friendly academic environment. Many thanks to Blanca Heredia and my colleagues at the Programa Interdisciplinario sobre Política y Prácticas Educativas (PIPE) for making my stay in Mexico a most pleasant one. Research funding for this project came from the Max Planck Society and in the later stages, from the Center for Social Conflict and Cohesion Studies (COES) (ANID/FONDAP/15130009) and from a ANID-Max Planck Society joint research project (ANID/PCI/MAX PLANCK INSTITUTE FOR THE STUDY OF SOCIETIES/MPG190012). The Max Planck Institute for the Study of Societies and the Max Planck Partner Group for the Sociology of Economic Life funded a short research stay to present my book in September

2018 in Cologne, Budapest, and Warsaw. Finally, I thank Sarah Caro and Hannah Paul from Princeton University Press for supporting this project and guiding me through it.

My deepest gratitude goes to my family, who encouraged me to leave home to explore new horizons, but always with an eye towards returning and telling my story. To my parents who taught me the importance of hard work and most especially, to my wife Malú, and my children Domingo and Matilde, who provided the inspirational touch. They are what keep me in motion.

Mexico City and Santiago, January 2019 and February 2020

NEOLIBERAL RESILIENCE

1

The Puzzling Resilience of Neoliberalism

As you will understand, it is possible for a dictator to govern in a liberal way. And it is also possible for a democracy to govern with a total lack of liberalism. Personally, I prefer a liberal dictator to a democratic government lacking in liberalism.

—F.A. HAYEK TO A REPORTER QUOTED IN FARRANT, MCPHAIL, AND BERGER 2012, 521

DURING THE LATE AFTERNOON of September 7, 1986, a militarized cell from the Chilean Communist Party tried to kill General Augusto Pinochet. Pinochet was known worldwide for having participated in the bloody putsch against the democratically elected president Salvador Allende in 1973, and as the leader of the repressive military dictatorship that ensued and that backed the first large-scale experiment in neoliberal policymaking in the world. On that September afternoon, the Communist cell attacked Pinochet's convoy with heavy artillery as he was returning from his country house near Santiago. Five agents of Pinochet's guard were killed and another eleven severely wounded. Pinochet escaped almost unscathed.

Although this was without doubt his most remarkable escape, it was far from the only challenge Pinochet survived. Years before the assassination attempt, in the mid-1970s Pinochet explicitly broke the pact of succession in what was then a military *junta*, successfully maneuvering to oust the other members of the junta and instituting a series of regulations that made him the dictatorship's strongman. It was a true "coup inside the coup" (Valdivia 2003). Not only this: he devised a constitutional formula for government succession that secured his long-term oversight of Chilean politics even in the event of a return to democracy.

Two years after the assassination attempt, in October 1988, a united political opposition—with the help of international pressure—defeated Pinochet in a referendum, forcing a return to democratic rule after seventeen years of dictatorship. However, even as the new authorities took office, Pinochet managed to remain commander-in-chief of the army for another ten years, controlling the process of democratization through the constant menaces of a military takeover. Ten years later, in September 1998, Pinochet was captured in London and faced extradition to Spain, where he was charged with the murder of Spanish citizens during his dictatorship. After two years of legal procedures, the British authorities released Pinochet, alleging that the former strongman— now 84 and with visible signs of physical and mental deterioration—could not stand a trial. But when Pinochet returned to Santiago, he stood up from his wheelchair, greeted his fanatic followers with his walking stick, and walked out of the airport, to the astonishment of the local and international press. He lived comfortably in his mansion in Santiago until he died seven years later.

The association between a political system based on permanent repression and a public philosophy premised on the idea of individual liberty has puzzled scholars ever since the Chilean experience under Pinochet. Some of the most ardent supporters of neoliberalism have felt compelled to excuse, on theoretical grounds, such an embarrassing historical coincidence. After advising the Chilean military junta in 1975, Milton Friedman argued that economic liberalization was a precondition for political liberalization, and that political freedom was in turn necessary for the long-term maintenance of economic freedom, therefore highlighting the temporary nature of Pinochet's rule (Friedman 1982). Others, however, have felt that the two are much more intertwined than commonly thought. Thus, for Friedrich Hayek a limited dictatorship was a better safeguard for individual liberty than an unlimited democracy (Farrant, Mcphail, and Berger 2012). In this book I argue that the connection between neoliberal economics and less-than-liberal political regimes is not only a philosophical digression but is in fact rooted in history. Pinochet's story conveys, if somewhat cruelly, the idea that neoliberalism's durability is not just about good or bad economic policymaking: the countries where neoliberalism has survived the longest are those that designed their democratic institutions in such a way as to constrain the possibility of switching to other policies. In this sense, the Chilean neoliberal trajectory was not a peculiarity, but part of a political project with diverse historical experiences supporting the idea that protecting free markets—and its beneficiaries—required encroaching on democracy.

This book joins several recent works that show the connection between constrained democracies and the neoliberal political project (Slobodian 2018; Maclean 2017). We know now that since its beginnings, the neoliberal thought collective found democracy—a political system giving voice to the masses and incentivizing the competition for their vote—to be the main threat to its political project. Not only this: as Slobodian convincingly argues, neoliberalism "developed precisely as a response to the growth of mass democracy" (2018, 34). Unlike these works, this book is not an exercise in the history of neoliberal thinking about democracy; rather, it studies the politics behind neoliberalism's continuity over time—its *resilience*—as a process intimately connected with the gradual erosion of democracy. It tracks neoliberal resilience and democratic erosion in four Latin American and Eastern European countries with diverse trajectories: Argentina, Chile, Estonia, and Poland. I argue that neoliberalism remained resilient where it was able to reduce the representative component of democracy, maintaining free and competitive elections but bending the policy outcomes of those elections to the maintenance of neoliberalism. Neoliberalism survived in its purest form in those countries where it was *protected from democracy*.[1]

Resilience, a concept commonly associated with engineering science, psychology, and community studies, denotes the capacity of an object, person, or group to withstand external perturbations (Madariaga 2017, n. 1; Schmidt and Thatcher 2013, 13–16). The typical response of a resilient body is to alter some of its properties in order to accommodate the external perturbation without changing its core composition and nature. In the case of neoliberalism, the concept of resilience has been used to describe neoliberalism's "continuity . . . over time, its dominance over competitors, and its survival against powerful

---

1. A review of *The Calculus of Consent,* one of the key books of James Buchanan, the founder of the Virginia school of neoliberalism, in the journal of the Cato Institute praised it precisely for offering guidance on "protecting capitalism from democracy" (MacLean 2017, 81). We will come back at the key role of Buchanan's thinking in this story of neoliberal resilience in chapter 2.

challenges and rivals" (Schmidt and Thatcher 2013, xvii).[2] Books about the resilience of neoliberalism (particularly those published after the 2007–2008 crisis) tend to focus on overarching trends; I instead establish the limits of neoliberalim's resilience through a clear operationalization of its policy goals and concrete policy alternatives (see Crouch 2011; Duménil and Lévy 2011; Grauwe 2017; Kotz 2015; Mirowski 2013). I identify which countries maintained their neoliberal trajectories over time, when they departed from neoliberalism's core dictates, and whether those departures were enduring or not. In addition, unlike the focus of most works on advanced capitalist economies, I argue that to analyze the resilience of neoliberalism it is important to look outside the capitalist core, particularly at the history of over three decades of neoliberalism in Latin America and Eastern Europe. As will become clear, the specific conditions under which neoliberalism was adopted in these regions facilitated the connection between resilient neoliberalism and constrained democracy.

I demonstrate that connection in three ways. First, I study the actors and coalitions that supported the establishment of neoliberalism and defended its continuity over time, using a mixed quantitative and qualitative strategy (chapters 3 and 4). Second, I investigate the mechanisms that eroded democracy and allowed these actors to maintain their grip on public policy changes (chapters 5, 6, and 7). Here, I contrast cases where neoliberalism remained resilient (Chile and Estonia) with cases where it was contested and even temporarily replaced (Poland and Argentina). Finally, I consider the consequences of the continued resilience of neoliberalism for the future of democracy. By doing this, I engage with the current literature on the crisis of democracy, the rise of populism, and their relationship with neoliberal economics, reflecting on how different experiences of neoliberal resilience pose different threats and paths toward democratic erosion.

Neoliberalism's resilience—and contestation of the neoliberal project— radically altered these four countries' patterns of democratic competition and representation, generating specific paths toward democratic hollowing and/ or backsliding.[3] Understanding the specific paths by which neoliberalism eroded democratic institutions, and how domestic political actors reacted to those erosions, is crucial to understanding how populist movements are tak-

2. For a different usage associated with the resilience of societies to neoliberalism, see Hall and Lamont (2013).

3. For the formulation of the hollowing of democracy, see Mair (2013). Greskovits (2015) provides an insightful discussion differentiating democracy's "hollowing" from its "backsliding."

ing root today, and whether populism threatens democracy or has the potential to cure it (see Mair 2013; Mudde and Rovira Kaltwasser 2013b; Rovira Kaltwasser 2014).

The rest of this introduction proceeds as follows. First, I define what I understand by neoliberalism and state the problem of neoliberalism's resilience in length, the puzzlement that arose after the events that followed the 2007–2008 financial crisis, and justify my focus on the Latin American and Eastern European experiences. Second, I develop the book's argument about the connection between neoliberalism's resilience and the erosion of democracy. In turn, I show how this argument contributes to the existing literature on neoliberalism. Finally, I describe the book's methodological aspects and structure.

The "Strange Non-Death" of Neoliberalism[4]

What Is Neoliberalism?

Neoliberalism is an oft-invoked but ill-defined concept (Boas and Gans-Morse 2009; Cahill and Konings 2017; Crouch 2011; Connell and Dados 2014; Maillet 2015; Steger and Roy 2010). While it is useful and necessary to understand some of the most pressing problems of contemporary societies and economies, the polysemy of the concept makes it necessary to define clearly what we understand by it before undertaking an empirical study. In turn, I analyze three common definitions of neoliberalism, their respective foci when analyzing neoliberalism's continuity or resilience, and justify my own choice.

One first definition of neoliberalism understands it as a *policy paradigm*, that is, as "a framework of ideas and standards that specifies ... the goals of policy ... the kind of instruments that can be used to attain them, ... [and the] nature of the problems they are meant to be addressing" (Hall 1993, 279). Following this, Cornel Ban refers to neoliberalism as a "set of historically contingent and intellectually hybrid" (2016, 10) economic ideas, including prescriptions from neoclassical economics, monetarism, and supply-side economics, that aim at increasing the power of markets—and the corporations operating in them—in the allocation of goods and services and the reduction of discretionary government interventions to make them credible with market actors. Neoliberalism does not preclude State intervention, and often even requires it; however, it gives business (epitomized as impersonal "markets") the power to decide which interventions are desirable and which are not.

4. See Crouch (2011).

For less developed economies, neoliberalism has been associated with promoting policies that "get the prices right." In other words, they open markets, eliminate price distortions and regulations, and bar discretionary government intervention in the economy through tariff protections, industrial policies, and state ownership of companies (see Plehwe 2009; Saad-Filho 2005; Williamson 1990b). Authors working with this definition of neoliberalism tend to look at the factors affecting the survival of neoliberal ideas over time when analyzing neoliberalism's resilience (Ban 2016; Blyth 2013; Mirowski 2013; Schmidt and Thatcher 2013).

An alternative to this approach conceives neoliberalism as a *policy regime*: it is the set of policies in the neoliberal paradigm that are embedded in the interests of specific societal groups or classes in specific national contexts (Cahill 2014; Crouch 2011; Streeck 2014; Wylde 2012). This definition of neoliberalism requires an understanding of the societal actors and coalitions who benefit from it and give it their political support. It seeks to explain neoliberalism's resilience in terms of the political-institutional characteristics and incentives of party systems that make coalitions more or less prone to maintaining neoliberal policies over time (Flores-Macías 2012; Madariaga 2017; Roberts 2015), and business-state relations that increase the influence of neoliberal businesses in policymaking (Bril-Mascarenhas and Madariaga 2019; Bril-Mascarenhas and Maillet 2019; Culpepper 2010; Fairfield 2015a; Hacker and Pierson 2010).

Yet a third treatment of neoliberalism comes from Marxist analyses that understand it as a transnational class project (Duménil and Lévy 2011; Harvey 2007). Authors following this tradition trace the links between the ascendance of neoliberalism to a worldwide hegemonic paradigm, the parallel reconfiguration of class relations beyond national states into supranational business networks following the crisis of advanced capitalism in the 1970s, and the establishment of neoliberalism as state policy (see Carroll and Sapinski 2016; Cox 1987; Robinson and Harris 2000; Sklair 2001). Recent accounts putting emphasis on the history of neoliberal ideas trace the origins of the neoliberal political project to the postwar period—some even as early as the dissolution of the Habsburg empire after World War I (Jones 2012; Slobodian 2018; Mirowski and Plehwe 2009). Here, the issue of the resilience of neoliberalism is studied in two ways: first, in terms of the operation of globalized free markets in which processes of financial liberalization and deregulation since the 1980s have enabled transnational financial capital to restrain domestic political actors from changing neoliberal trajectories (see Appel and Orenstein 2018; Campello 2015; Kaplan 2013; Roos 2019); second, through the "encasement"

(Slobodian 2018, 13) of the world economy in a world order of institutional governance and international law affecting states' sovereign policy decisions (see Chwieroth 2009; Gill 2002; Pop-Eleches 2009).

These three definitions of neoliberalism and its resilience broadly correspond to three disciplinary fields in comparative and international political economy: discursive institutionalism, historical institutionalism, and critical international political economy. In spite of coming from different epistemological traditions, they are in fact three facets of the same phenomenon, and all are necessary to fully understand it (see Madariaga 2020). At the same time, while neoliberalism's class roots and the history of its transnational diffusion are crucial to understanding its worldwide dominance, this dominance has relied on the experiences of a few countries that have become neoliberalism's standard bearers. Although international pressures have provided an important engine for neoliberalism and have constituted a "container of last resort" against challenges to it, it is domestic actors and institutions that have played the key role in neoliberalism's durability in those countries (more on this on chapter 2). Moreover, it is impossible to understand the resilience of neoliberalism as a set of ideas and policy recommendations without understanding how those ideas are appropriated by domestic political actors in their concrete political struggles. In other words, while acknowledging the importance of neoliberalism's transnational class dimension and its ideational architecture, I focus on how these are translated by and embedded in national institutions through the struggles of specific national business actors, political leaders, and state bureaucracies.

Going beyond existing research, I analyze not only how neoliberals struggle to institutionalize their preferred policy solutions as state policy, but, more fundamentally, how they strive to alter the very rules of the democratic political game to increase their political clout and reduce that of their opponents.[5] From this perspective, a resilient neoliberal policy regime is one that is able to institutionalize neoliberalism's basic premises in the very functioning of its democratic polity, making changes ever more difficult over time. When this is not the case, neoliberalism remains prone to challenge. In the extreme case, neoliberalism is not just contested over and over again, but it is replaced by an alternative policy regime that, with new supporters, can eventually reproduce itself.

---

5. For power resource theories inspiring this idea, see Korpi (1985), Rueschemeyer, Huber, and Stephens (1992).

Neoliberalism in Crisis? the Global View

Ever since the subprime crash in August 2007 and the fall of Lehman Brothers one year later, the future of neoliberalism has been at the forefront of scholarly debates. The depth of the Wall Street crisis (and its many repercussions extending to the European debt crisis and the Greek bailouts) created the illusion that this was *the* crisis of neoliberalism, compounding expectations of a revival of Keynesianism, a "New" New Deal switching to more progressive policies, or the start of a slow but progressive disintegration of capitalism as we know it (Appel and Orenstein 2018; Duménil and Lévy 2011; Kotz 2015; Steger and Roy 2010, 131–36; Kuttner 2018; Mason 2017; Streeck 2016; Wallerstein et al. 2013). These expectations were encouraged by past episodes of paradigmatic shift following major economic crises and the idea that these dynamics of pendular movement through crises is innate to the development of capitalism (Blyth 2002; Gourevitch 1986; Hall 1993; Duménil and Lévy 2011; Grauwe 2017; Kotz 2015). Nevertheless, despite these early predictions, neoliberalism has survived. As Mirowski has ironically put it, "neoliberalism is alive and well: those on the receiving end need to know why" (2013, 28).

To understand the puzzling resilience of neoliberalism, I take two positions. First, instead of looking at big ruptures and crises, I claim that we can only understand how neoliberalism survives if we analyze the way it overcomes constant challenges and alternative paths. This implies switching from a punctuated equilibrium or critical juncture view of political development, to one focused on gradual changes and reproduction mechanisms (Pierson 2004; Streeck and Thelen 2005). Second, I argue that the resilience of neoliberalism thus understood is better explained by studying the history of over three decades of neoliberal resilience at the capitalist periphery.

Despite the universal character of neoliberalism and its policy recipes, the actual practice of neoliberalism in the core and the periphery of global capitalism has been quite different (Appel and Orenstein 2018; Boas and Gans-Morse 2009; Connell and Dados 2014). In the advanced capitalist countries, neoliberalism has progressed gradually as a more or less successful challenge to postwar political and economic institutions; hence the frequent characterization of "actually existing neoliberalism" as an "always-imperfect realization" of neoliberal theory (Cahill 2014; Connell and Dados 2014, 120). In fact, at least until the 2000s, it was still believed that neoliberalism represented just one of at least two successful *varieties* of advanced capitalist political economy (Amable 2003; Campbell and Pedersen 2001; Hall and Soskice 2001; Iversen and Soskice 2019). Students of advanced capitalism have thus concentrated on dem-onstrating the slow transformation of neoliberalism into the dominant policy and political practice it is today (Crouch 2011; Blyth 2013; Streeck 2014). In this sense, more than the resilience of neoliberalism per se, what they study is the gradual erosion of the postwar compromise (see Glyn 2007).[6]

At the periphery of global capitalism, particularly in Latin America and Eastern Europe, the implementation of neoliberalism was a different story: fast and sweeping, amounting to a complete restructuring of state-society rela-tions with profound consequences for institution building and public policy. Moreover, the fact that neoliberal reforms were implemented alongside the reconstruction of liberal democracies facilitated the connection between neo-liberal economic policies and the political project behind them.[7]

Despite the rich experience and research on radical neoliberalism outside the capitalist core, as Connell and Dados lament, "the most influential ac-counts of neoliberalism are grounded in the social experience of the global North" (2014, 118). This book brings Latin America and Eastern Europe back into the core of the debates about the future of neoliberal capitalism and de-mocracy. Interestingly, recent events seem to be bringing neoliberal experi-ences in the advanced and nonadvanced worlds closer together. In fact, re-search on the survival of neoliberalism at the core of the capitalist economy and its impact on representative democracy has given place to scholarly debate over the ascendance of right- and left-wing populism; the relationship between neoliberalism, austerity politics, and the rise of populist forces; and the parallel erosion of fundamental democratic values and institutions (Brown 2015; Eichengreen 2018; Dumas 2018; MacLean 2017; Mair 2013; Levitsky and Ziblatt 2018; Kuttner 2018; Przeworski 2019). The Latin American and Eastern Euro-pean experiences shed light on these global political-economic phenomena.

Neoliberalism in Latin America and Eastern Europe: The Empirical Puzzle

Latin America and Eastern Europe underwent rapid and thorough processes of economic and political liberalization in the final decades of the twentieth

6. Early accounts of this dynamic in individual countries can be found in Crouch and Streeck (1997). For a thorough analysis centered around industrial relations, see Baccaro and Howell (2017). For detailed and compelling studies of the gradual liberalization of Germany and France, see Streeck (2009) and Amable (2017), respectively.

7. More on this below.

century. The economic crises of the 1980s heralded the collapse of decades-old economic development models that spearheaded these countries' quest for modernization and industrialization in a context of economic and political "underdevelopment" (Berend 1996; Edwards 1995; Przeworski 1991). In this context, neoliberalism was understood as a development project able to put an end to these countries' manifold economic and political ills.

Given the wholehearted commitment to radical market reform, countries like Chile and Poland became poster children of the "new development orthodoxy" (Rodrik 1996, 12–13) and were taken as benchmarks of good practice for other nonadvanced political economies in an era when neoliberalism became the only game in town (Åslund 1994; Edwards 1995; Sachs 1990). According to the eminent Hungarian anthropologist Karl Polanyi, explicit attempts at building a market society tend to generate societal "counter-movements" to shelter that society from the effects of free markets (Polanyi 2001). In Latin America and Eastern Europe, these counter-movements came in waves, some accompanied by massive social protests, and many market-reformed countries shifted over the years towards less orthodox development alternatives (Bohle and Greskovits 2009; Frieden 1991a; Greskovits 1998; Orenstein 2001; Roberts 2008; E. Silva 2009). Steep and repeated economic crises, the disintegration of industrial and social tissues, growing unemployment, and rising inequality forced authorities to slow down the pace of reform or undertake outright policy reversals—alternative development projects that challenged neoliberalism's capacity to survive. However, a handful of countries maintained and even reinforced neoliberalism despite these challenges.

Figure 1.1 depicts this process. It shows the Index of Economic Freedom, a measure constructed from a series of indicators assessing policy goals dear to neoliberalism (such as the free movement of capital and minimal government intervention in the decisions of private actors) for the countries under study, as well as the average for their respective regions.[8] Most countries follow a

8. This indicator is based on policy orientations and outcomes. Other indicators of market reform show the progress of institutional reform, among which, the Economic Freedom of the World Index by the Fraser Institute, the liberalization indexes by Morley, Machado and Pettinato (1999) and Lora (2012) for Latin America, and the EBRD Transition Indicators for Eastern Europe. These indexes make it hard to assess Eastern Europe, where all countries were building capitalist institutions from scratch during the 1990s and 2000s, and therefore show continuous progressions rather than discontinuities over time. The index here presented has several shortcomings, including a lack of coverage of the 1980s and early 1990s. It should therefore be taken only as a representation of the research problem, and not as a proof of its existence, nor as a case selection technique.

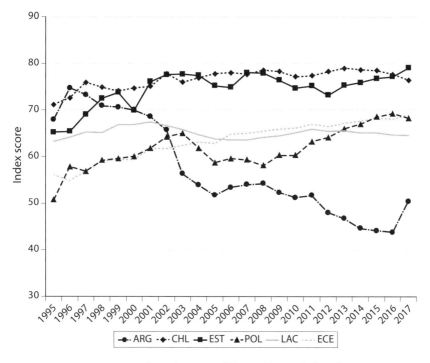

FIGURE 1.1. Latin America and Eastern Europe, Index of
Economic Freedom for Selected Countries 1995–2017
Source: Author's elaboration based on data from Heritage Foundation,
http://www.heritage.org/index/.
Legend: ARG= Argentina, CHL= Chile, EST= Estonia, POL= Poland, LAC= Latin America
(average 10 countries), ECE: East-Central Europe (average 11 countries).

pattern of ups and downs over the years, but regional averages remain relatively stable over time. In Eastern Europe, the upward trend has moderated after a period of strong liberalization in the run-up to the entry to the European Union (2004–2007).

Taking these trends into consideration, the trajectories of Chile and Estonia are polar opposites to that of Argentina. While the first two have remained "mostly free" (70–80 points in the index scale) throughout the period and have the highest scores in their respective regions, Argentina descended dramatically from "mostly free" (70–80 points) to "repressed" (40–50 points) in just a few years. At the same time, Poland remained close to the Eastern-European average, except for a downturn in the 2000s. How have Chile and Estonia remained neoliberal over time? What do they have in common, and in what respects have they differed from other countries that show either moderate variations (Poland) or more significant shifts (Argentina)?

How Neoliberalism Survives

Policy and Polity: The Two Sides of Neoliberalism's Resilience

In an early assessment of the adoption of neoliberalism in the advanced world, Herman Schwartz suggested that the actors pushing neoliberalism were "engaged in a strategic politics that attempt[ed] to change the rules of the game rather than just seeking their preferred outcomes in the context of extant rules" (Schwartz 1994, 529). Schwartz's observation closely describes conditions at the outset of the dual transitions to democracy and market capitalism in Latin America and Eastern Europe during the 1980s and 1990s. As O'Donnell and Schmitter observed in those years, "actors struggle not just to satisfy their immediate interests and/or the interests of those whom they purport to represent, but also to define rules and procedures whose configuration will determine likely winners and losers in the future" (O'Donnell and Schmitter 1986, 4:6). Theoretically, this resembles what Tsebelis called a "nested game:" a situation in which "the actor is involved not only in a game in the principal arena [that of neoliberal *policies*], but also in a game about the rules of the game [that of the neoliberal *polity*]" (Tsebelis 1991, 8).

The core argument of this book is that to understand the resilience of neoliberalism one needs to distinguish between these two component parts of neoliberalism: *policy* and *polity*. The *policy* part stems from the economic program of neoliberalism, while the *polity* part originates in its political program, which seeks to change the institutions of democratic organization that enable and constrain the kinds of policies that can be pursued.[9] In other words, neoliberalism entails not only political dynamics in which actors try to implement their preferred economic policies, but also those in which actors try to implement their preferred political institutions and other organizational aspects of the underlying democracies.

I identify three concrete mechanisms that constrained democratic representation in Latin America and Eastern Europe, making changes to established neoliberal policies more difficult (see chapter 2). One is the reduction and blockade of the power resources of those actors that could challenge neolib-

---

9. For a discussion of these concepts under similar considerations, see Hajer (2003) and Palonen (2003).

eralism with alternatives; the second is the increase of the power resources of businesses interested in the continuity of neoliberalism; and the third is the institutionalization of neoliberal policies in a way that made them more difficult to reverse.

Liberal democracies offer channels for the representation of diverse actors in the policy process. The most important one is elections, where parties vow to gain the votes of their constituencies and enact the policies they favor. In the political arena, neoliberals attempt to reduce the power resources, opposition, and representation of groups losing from neoliberal policies. I call this *opposition blockade*. Neoliberals use two features of democratic polities to reduce the political clout of actors opposing them and to block their representation. First, neoliberals use electoral systems to decrease the opposition's direct representation in politics. Second, neoliberals employ executive power and non-elected veto players to prevent changes when the opposition does gain representation.[10]

Conversely, business plays a key role in democratic capitalist societies: it is responsible for employment opportunities and wages that define the overall levels of welfare. Business can form part of the support base of democratically elected governments, particularly when parties have corporations as their core constituencies. Although most of the time business is associated with more conservative political projects and supported by right-wing parties (Gibson 1996; Luna and Rovira Kaltwasser 2014), fractions of the business class have also been linked to support for more progressive development models (see Swenson 1991; Schneider 2004b). Businesses can also make themselves heard in policy discussions without needing to join government coalitions. As the literature on business power has consistently shown, corporations can influence policy toward their own preferred outcomes—even under governments with completely different policy preferences (Culpepper 2010; Fairfield 2015a; Hacker and Pierson 2010). In this sense, building a business base that will support neoliberal policies, constrain alternative policy agendas, and/or actively participate in policy design is crucial for neoliberalism's survival. As I will demonstrate, reformers have used privatization as a way of allocating economic

10. A third source of opposition blockade deals with labor market institutions and organized labor. Although I include this in analytical terms in chapter 2, for reasons of space I do not analyze this mechanism in detail in this book. This dynamic of labor acquiescence and protest to market reforms and the outcome in terms of neoliberalism's resilience has received considerable attention in the literature. See, e.g., Crowley (2004), Drake (1996), Etchemendy (2012), Murillo (2001), Ost (2005).

resources to individual firms, business groups, and whole economic sectors that are expected to support the continuation of neoliberalism. I call this mechanism *support creation*.[11]

Finally, there are ways to constrain authorities' room to maneuver, independent of their partisan affiliations and of the power of business. Even politicians with the right partisan orientations can succumb to popular or business demands and reduce the scope of neoliberalism. If this happens, relevant policies can be delegated to state bodies whose staff is insulated from the pressures of partisan politics, shielding neoliberalism both from " 'acting minorities' and 'lunatic majorities' " (Rugier cited in Amable 2011, 17). As neoliberals realized early on, in liberal democracies where political constitutions define what the polity can and cannot do, the best way to insulate neoliberalism is to enshrine its basic principles—and even concrete policies—in the Constitution itself (Amable 2011, 17; Bruff 2014; Gill 2002; Slobodian 2018). I analyze two ways of accomplishing what I call *constitutionalized lock-in*: independent central banks and fiscal spending rules. The complex interplay between these three mechanisms—opposition blockade, support creation, and constitutionalized lock-in—explains both the resilience of neoliberalism in Chile and Estonia, and its moderation and/or outright reversal in Argentina and Poland.

Regarding the operation of these mechanisms, I wish to make three caveats. First, it is important to note that these are not the only mechanisms that can account for neoliberalism's resilience. Taken together, they point to ways of twisting or undermining the functioning of democracy, altering the polity with the aim of reducing resistance to neoliberalism from alternative political projects. These mechanisms coerce; they blockade. A different set of mechanisms that increase the resilience of neoliberalism relate to what Michael Burawoy (1982) called the "manufacturing of consent." These include mechanisms that increase the legitimacy of neoliberalism among the broad public, acting not at the level of specific interests but at the level of cultural understandings and ideas (see Boltanski and Chiapello 2005). For example, certain authors study the "governmentality" of neoliberalism, explaining its policies as a device that shapes individuals' dispositions and thus their compliance with neoliberalism's tenets (Amable 2011; Brown 2015). Alternatively, Baker (2009) has studied how the importation of new goods, cultural patterns, and lifestyles— thanks to trade liberalization and increasing globalization—has transformed

---

11. In chapter 2, I discuss in detail the relation between support creation and the mechanisms of business structural and instrumental power prevalent in the literature.

reluctant working and middle classes into avid consumers and supporters of neoliberalism in certain Latin American countries.

These consensual or legitimation mechanisms also affect the functioning of liberal democracy, and the two types of mechanisms—coercive and legitimating—may well connect in diverse ways (see Brown 2015). One might even argue, following Max Weber, that acting on interests and coercion alone is not enough to sustain neoliberalism in the long run. In fact, over time even the most coercive institutions tend to be used, adapted, and incorporated by new actors who, distanced from their origins, may regard them as unavoidable— even legitimate. It is, however, beyond the scope of this book to study these interactions, and therefore I concentrate on the first set of interest-based coercive mechanisms.

A second caveat is that although I make the case that the resilience of neoliberalism has rested conspicuously on the above-mentioned mechanisms, these may not be exclusively "neoliberal." In other words, since these mechanisms imply the reduction of democratic representation of alternative political projects, they may well be used for increasing the probability of survival of other development projects in other contexts. Whether or not they are characteristically neoliberal only history will tell.

Finally, the argument of this book should not be understood as implying that those regimes where neoliberalism did not take root are more democratic today than those where it did. This would be the wrong conclusion. The causes of democratic decline extend well beyond democracy's economic underpinnings. In fact, all the Latin American and Eastern European countries that experienced dual economic and political transitions in the 1980s and 1990s continue to face substantial economic and political challenges today. Instead, I argue that in those cases where neoliberalism survived, the reduction of democracy and its representative dimension can be directly linked to neoliberalism's resilience.

Beyond the Rise of Neoliberalism: Alternative Explanations

Much of the vast literature on neoliberalism has been devoted to understanding its rise and varied economic success from diverse perspectives, including broad theoretical syntheses (see, among others, Blyth 2002; Bönker 2001; Haggard and Kaufman 1992; Hall 1993; Campbell and Pedersen 2001). Recent debates have shown the diversity of political-economic regimes that "neoliberalizing" forces generated. For example, Fourcade-Gourinchas and Babb

(2002) revisit the old debate about the pace of reform and how this affected the depth of neoliberalism, Etchemendy (2012) analyzes this diversity as a function of how different "liberalizing coalitions" coalesced, while Bohle and Greskovits (2012) and Pop-Eleches (2009) emphasize the strategic and divergent responses of domestic political elites to challenges such as International Monetary Fund (IMF) stabilization programs, the ethnic composition of new democracies, and EU accession. Similarly, Ban (2016) shows how domestic characteristics such as ideological legacies and institutions, and the timing of integration with the global flow of neoliberal ideas, affected the way neoliberalism was translated into local political practice. There are, therefore, varieties of neoliberalization depending on a series of political, institutional, and ideological factors located both inside and outside national economies (see also Thelen 2014; Baccaro and Howell 2017).

These works are extremely valuable in that they spell out the forces putting neoliberalism in motion and, therefore, make room for hypotheses about the mechanisms through which neoliberalism reproduced itself in specific national contexts. However, in their concentration on emergence and path creation, scholars have overlooked the dynamics of resilience and path reproduction, which are the focus of this book (see Bril-Mascarenhas and Madariaga 2019; Madariaga 2019). A historical process may be set in motion and reproduced by entirely different forces (see chapter 2). To understand the resilience of neoliberalism, we need to focus specifically on mechanisms of reproduction.

Another set of approaches has concentrated on reactions against neoliberalism. In Latin America, scholars like Roberts (2008) and Silva (2009) have shown the importance of social movements and popular protest in challenging neoliberalism, opening the way to an era of paradigmatic "left-turns" in the region (see Levitsky and Roberts 2011; Weyland, Madrid, and Hunter 2010). The absence of popular revolt in the more "patient" Eastern European societies has prompted Greskovits (2007), Bohle and Greskovits (2009), Appel and Orenstein (2018), and Hanley and Sikk (2016), to explain the emergence of new populist forces and their illiberal rhetoric as an attempt to represent masses disaffected with neoliberalism. Although few would claim that an entirely new and well-defined development project has emerged from these contentious experiences (but see Appel and Orenstein 2018, 160–69; Bresser-Pereira 2011; Wylde 2012), many authors see in these reactions the emergence of a "post-neoliberal" order (Grugel and Riggirozzi 2012; Rovira Kaltwasser 2011).

Exploring these challenges allows us to build helpful counterfactuals that illuminate not only the context of threats to neoliberalism, but also the circumstances in which neoliberal policies have been able to survive and thrive. Now, where these works focus only on the challenges, we miss an opportunity to study cases of neoliberal resilience. In fact, while they imply a generalized break with neoliberalism, recent events, particularly in Latin America, have shown instead that the "left turns" were much more contingent than previously thought (see Luna and Rovira Kaltwasser 2014).

Unlike the many works studying neoliberalism's manifold implementation in concrete national experiences, a few scholars have focused on the sources of neoliberalism's continuity. I review these in more detail because they present arguments about neoliberalism's resilience that compete with the one here presented. One set of works follows the different strands of "discursive institutionalism" by understanding neoliberal resilience in terms of ideology. The most thorough presentation of this argument is that by Schmidt and Thatcher (2013), who summarize existing research on ideational continuity and point to three characteristics making neoliberal ideas resilient: first, their generality, malleability and plasticity; second, the gap they allow between theory and reality; and third, their persuasiveness in public discourse. As to the first, it is unclear how these characteristics make neoliberalism more resilient. One could have ascribed the same characteristics to Keynesianism, given the many ways in which it was translated and adopted in actual practice (Hall 1989). If anything, the notion of neoliberalism's generality as a capacity for resilience argues the opposite. But when does neoliberalism stop mutating into yet another specific form of that general form? In other words, when does neoliberalism stop being neoliberalism and become something else? What is the limit demarcating neoliberal resilience from its opposite? Claiming that neoliberalism is resilient because of its adaptive capacity and plasticity has led some to make general claims about the survival of neoliberalism without establishing the boundaries that distinguish it from its opposite. Recognizing this, I focus on two specific policy domains, exchange rate and industrial policies, and operationalize them thoroughly in order to make this distinction clear (see chapter 3).[12]

The second argument is that the constant failure of neoliberalism in practice (rather than producing paradigm change as in the passage from Keynesianism to neoliberalism) reinforces itself because proponents can claim it has not been properly implemented. Like the last point, it is not entirely clear what

---

12. Chapter 3 also gives an extensive economic and political justification for the choice of these two policy domains as the foci of analysis.

it is about neoliberalism that gives it this special characteristic vis-à-vis other sets of ideas. For Mirowski, the answer lies in psychological theories of "cognitive dissonance" which demonstrate that the "confrontation with contrary evidence may actually augment and sharpen the conviction and enthusiasm of a true believer" (2013, 35). In other words, by rejecting real-world evidence true neoliberals have doubled down on their beliefs and worked even harder to silence alternative ideas (Mirowski 2013, 356–58). But cognitive dissonance does not by itself warrant the survival of neoliberalism, and, more to the point, we know, thanks to the work of discursive institutionalists, that many of those adopting neoliberalism were not true believers but supported neoliberalism only contingently (Schmidt and Thatcher 2013, 24–25). More fundamentally, this mechanism seems to belie the previous one: on the one hand, neoliberalism is resilient because it is general and malleable, and therefore, can accommodate and incorporate critique; on the other, neoliberalism is resilient because it can preserve its purity by contrasting its principles to its actual implementation. If we believe in politics, we are forced to ask what compels policymakers that are not true believers to maintain neoliberalism despite being proved wrong in practice, and here is when ideational approaches fail to provide a compelling answer.

Schmidt and Thatcher's third mechanism of neoliberal continuity is as surprisingly simple as it is hard to sustain: some ideas are just more resilient than others because they lend themselves better to convincing rivals in public discourse. In practice, this has led to reducing the importance of discourse *tout court*, as public deliberation and the battle of ideas have been less studied than internal characteristics of neoliberalism like its "seeming coherence" (Schmidt and Thatcher 2013, 26) and "completeness" (Schmidt and Thatcher 2013, 31) at the moment of succeeding over other ideas. Take for example Blyth's argument that austerity prevailed because it is an "intuitive" and "appealing" idea (Blyth 2013, 7). Thus, despite the intention, one is left with the feeling that the triumph of neoliberalism is a purely rhetorical artifact.

What lies behind this is a critique of the lack of clear conceptualization and empirical testing of the ideational mechanisms of neoliberal resilience.[13] In this book I do not question the fact that ideas are important components of politics, and that they provide basic meanings and instruments for political

13. For a thorough critique of "ideational" accounts of neoliberal resilience, see Cahill (2014). For an exercise in testing ideational versus other explanations of neoliberalism's continuity, see Madariaga (2020).

actors to pursue their preferences and intentions. I agree, moreover, that political entrepreneurs provide discourses, frameworks, and interpretations of situations that make sense for coalition formation purposes. However, this is not the same as stating that "ideas and discourse [are] the explanatory variable for their own resilience" (Schmidt and Thatcher 2013, 31). In fact, Schmidt and Thatcher concede that the weaknesses of ideational approaches warrant a closer look at "the interests of key actors and the institutional framework within which neo-liberal ideas are formed, developed, disseminated, debated, and adopted" (Schmidt and Thatcher 2013, 414). After all, as Slobodian reminds us, "[f]rom the beginning, the doctrine of neoliberalism reflected an intermingling with the needs of its patrons in the business community" (2018, 21). This book examines who these "patrons" were, and how they retained their power to control the trajectory of neoliberal resilience.

A second set of works that provides an alternative explanation to this book's puzzle points to international influences and pressures. Decades ago, Barbara Stallings (1992) lamented that the analysis of policy adoption and continuity had turned to domestic factors just when the globalization of the economy meant international forces increasingly influenced domestic policy choices. Following her lead, a number of authors have highlighted how financial liberalization has led to policy diffusion-*cum*-imposition and placed significant constraints on the ability of domestic political coalitions to pursue policies conflicting with neoliberalism (Appel and Orenstein 2018; Maxfield 1998; Polillo and Guillén 2005; Simmons and Elkins 2004; Roos 2019). Other authors, particularly for the case of Eastern Europe, have focused on the power of international institutions and what Bruszt and McDermott call "transnational integration regimes" (2009). Along these lines, a number of works analyze the influence that the prospects of accession to the European Union had on Eastern European states in terms of liberalizing both their economies and polities and adopting specific institutions and policies (R. A. Epstein 2008; J. Johnson 2016; Schimmelfennig and Sedelmeier 2005; Vachudova 2005).

There is a prolific research tradition that, while taking international pressures seriously, grants significant freedom to domestic actors at the moment of deciding on whether, how, and when to give in to these pressures and implement international policy blueprints (Bruszt and Greskovits 2009; Campello 2015; Kaplan 2013; Pop-Eleches 2009; for a classic, see Cardoso and Faletto 1979). As Anna Kowalczyk convincingly argues, "instead of simply imposing their projects on societies worldwide the transnational capitalist classes must build alliances, overcome fractional conflicts and provide material concessions to some members of societies in order to build and reproduce their hegemony" (2019, 2). Hence, while international norms and pressures are exerted evenly across cases, their actual implementation in local contexts varies greatly, generating a diversity of arrangements and patterns of policymaking (Ban 2016; Bohle and Greskovits 2012).

Several works concentrating on the international level in isolation fail to acknowledge this. For example, Appel and Orenstein (2018) claim that after the 2007–2008 crisis, alternative development models emerged in Eastern Europe that reflected the breaking up of the "competitive signaling" mechanism driving neoliberalism in the region since 1990. But their argument about the discrediting of neoliberalism in the region runs contrary to overwhelming evidence that neoliberalism came under question only for a short time after the crisis, and that the most striking feature of the crisis from the policy point of view is not neoliberalism's dissolution but its resilience. More importantly, their focus on the international dimension leads them to present the breakup with neoliberalism as a unified "exit" response, overlooking the widely different experiences among Eastern European countries and the potential conflict among domestic elites that the emerging "alternative" projects generated (see Becker and Jäger 2010; Bohle and Greskovits 2012; Myant and Drahokoupil 2012; Myant, Drahokoupil, and Lesay 2013). In the case of this book, the very fact that countries like Argentina, Chile, Estonia, and Poland, once poster children of global neoliberalism (with the analogous international pressures), have shown a diversity of experiences of neoliberal resilience and contestation makes the case for concentrating on the domestic level, where these pressures are received, translated, and used as a political weapon.

Without making the international context the main focus of this book, I do account for the constraints that the international economy and its institutions have placed on domestic policymaking in two ways. First, I consider international financial institutions and economic dynamics as a *constraint of last resort* defending neoliberalism against attempts by national democratic governments attempting to escape from it (see chapter 2). Following Slobodian (2018), I treat this "encasement" as directly related to neoliberalism's secular quest to bind democratic governments. Second, I view international pressures as a context that affects domestic decisions especially coalition-building strategies and possibilities (Jacoby 2006; Stallings 1992). Since regions like Latin America and Eastern Europe were submitted to different types of international pressures at different times; comparing them controls for these contextual effects and argues for the existence of global rather than idiosyncratic or regional mechanisms in explaining neoliberal resilience.

The key innovation of this book is to put a special emphasis on the relation between neoliberalism and democracy, and the mechanisms that link them. My results uncover a direct connection between the successful development of neoliberal capitalism and the limitation of democracy through institutional design. This link shines new light on the relationships between capitalism, democracy, and development, a timely topic in the comparative analysis of developing political economies (Collier and Collier 1991; Haggard and Kaufman 2008; Rueschemeyer, Huber, and Stephens 1992).

Research Design and Plan of the Book
Empirical Approach and Methods

This book is based on a small-N study drawing on the tradition of comparative-historical analysis (Skocpol and Somers 1980; Mahoney and Rueschemeyer 2003). I use a combination of comparative methods and within-case process tracing. While the comparative method helps identify relationships and controls for omitted causal factors in small-N research, within-case methods help to strengthen the validity of the comparative exercise by examining causal links in the individual cases (Mahoney 2003, 363–65; Collier 2011, 824). This research design has become standard in academic practice when analyzing institutional development and change (Hall 2003; George and Bennett 2005; Blatter and Haverland 2012; see, e.g., Bohle and Greskovits 2012; Etchemendy 2012; Haggard and Kaufman 2008). The cross-regional span of the comparison in this study is less common even among comparative studies and constitutes a true innovation, revealing the global scope of mechanisms of neoliberal resilience.

The more or less contemporary political and economic liberalization of Latin America and Eastern Europe during the 1980s and 1990s marks a common point of departure for comparing national as well as regional trajectories of neoliberal resilience. Despite the different structural specialization of the two regions and different forms of integration into global commodity chains, they share an equivalent position in the international political economy in terms of their dependence on capital flows and their peripheral incorporation into transnational integration regimes, presenting a similar set of enabling and constraining factors for development projects led by domestic political agents (Bruszt and Greskovits 2009; Bruszt and McDermott 2009).

In terms of case selection, I use a combination of most similar and most different cases (Seawright and Gerring 2008). The universe of cases is composed of middle- to high-income countries in Latin America and Eastern Europe that enacted radical economic reforms in concert with major political transformations in the last decades of the twentieth century. Argentina, Chile, Estonia, and Poland present underlying similarities and differences in the outcome of neoliberal resilience, and furthermore form paired comparisons. All of them share the fact that the adoption of neoliberalism followed inflationary crises and combined exchange rate stabilization and structural reforms that dismantled previously interventionist states and industrial policy. In the case of Latin America, Chile is the quintessential case of neoliberal continuity despite the many nuances introduced over the years (Madariaga 2020). For the opposite outcome, I select Argentina, a country with a number of economic, social, and political similarities with Chile, but where neoliberalism failed to take root after three successive attempts. In other Latin American countries, like Colombia or Mexico, neoliberalism was adopted more gradually, while in countries like Brazil and Uruguay it was adopted only half-heartedly and quickly abandoned (see Madariaga 2020).

In Eastern Europe, the Baltic States represent the most advanced neoliberal reformers (Bohle and Greskovits 2012). Among them, Estonia is the prime example of neoliberal continuity, especially after its deflationary approach to the 2007–2008 crisis. For the opposite outcome, Poland and the Czech Republic were orthodox neoliberal states at the beginning of their transition, but gradually moderated their initial orthodoxy (Bohle and Greskovits 2012). I select Poland in place of the Czech Republic because the latter was not in a situation of economic crisis at the time of the transition nor did it suffer from hyperinflation, and because in Poland and Estonia—but not the Czech Republic—the fall of communism followed a pattern of negotiation between old communist and new democratic elites. Moreover, many authors have recognized that the Czech Republic, as well as other countries initially considered "gradual reformers" (such as Hungary), had by the mid-1990s already surpassed Poland's progress in economic reforms, even though Poland was a more prominent example of shock therapy transition (see Bohle and Greskovits 2012; Schoenman 2014; Stark and Bruszt 1998).

Data collection for this book came from a variety of sources including official economic data, specialized secondary literature, a selective analysis of official documents and newspapers, and interviews with local analysts and policymakers. Interviews were conducted when access was possible and when the questions that arose during the research process merited them. I conducted a total of fifty interviews in the four countries. A handful of interviews from Argentina were facilitated by the Archivo de Historia Oral (AHO), at the Gino Germani Institute. In order to protect the integrity of interviewees, quotes from interviews are reported anonymously.

Plan of the Book

Chapter 2 presents the theoretical framework, focusing on the policy and polity parts of neoliberalism: that is, the connection between neoliberalism and democracy. It also conceptualizes how the mechanisms of opposition blockade, support creation, and constitutionalization help produce neoliberal resilience. Chapters 3 and 4 deal with the policy part of neoliberalism in Latin America and Eastern Europe. They demonstrate the resilience of exchange rates and industrial policy in Chile and Estonia in contrast to resistance to similar policies in Poland and Argentina, as well as the coalitions that have come together to support or oppose them in different periods (chapter 3 analyzes this resilience, or lack thereof, quantitatively, while chapter 4 follows a qualitative perspective). Chapter 3 further provides a justification for the selection of these policy domains and an operationalization of concrete policy alternatives, as they are associated with neoliberal or alternative development projects.

Chapters 5, 6, and 7 are devoted to the polity part of neoliberalism, and to tracing how exactly the resilience of neoliberalism rested on the erosion of democracy. Chapter 5 focuses on support creation: the increase of power resources through privatization for those business actors expected to defend the survival of neoliberal policies. In Chapter 6 I analyze opposition blockade with respect to the political expression and representation of parties opposed to neoliberalism. I study a number of sources used to block these parties, including electoral rules, executive powers, veto players, and lustration (in the case of Eastern European countries). Chapter 7 focuses on the locking-in of exchange rates and industrial policies in institutional frameworks, up to and including the constitution, that reduced partisan influences on them and made future changes and reforms more difficult. I concentrate on two such experiences: the establishment of central bank independence and fiscal spending rules.

In the concluding chapter I consider the outcomes of this study in terms of understanding the politics of neoliberal resilience and its implications for the future of democratic capitalism. In this context, I reflect on the apparent paradox that the cases of neoliberal resilience are those that show a more stable democracy and less thoroughgoing penetration of populist political dynamics than in the cases of neoliberal contestation and discontinuity. Could neoliberalism, and the limited democracy it promotes, be the savior of democracy? Or has it instead opened the path to the ultimate demise of democracy as we know it? Is the current wave of populist forces a threat or a corrective to neoliberalism's democratic deficits?

2

Explaining the Resilience of Neoliberalism

MUCH OF THE LITERATURE on neoliberalism has been devoted to explaining its rise, worldwide spread, and diverse institutionalization in different contexts. However, the most recent analytical challenge, particularly after the 2007–2008 crisis, is to understand neoliberalism's resilience. If we believe, as the historical-institutionalist scholarship has convincingly argued, that the mechanisms giving rise to a certain phenomenon are usually not the same as those underlying that phenomenon's reproduction, then we need to concentrate on finding those latter mechanisms in order to explain the resilience of neoliberalism (see Collier and Collier 1991; Mahoney 2000; Thelen 1999).

In this chapter I explain neoliberalism's resilience by developing an analytical framework with concrete mechanisms of reproduction. Until now, research has differentiated between the impacts of neoliberalism on economic policies (policy) and on political institutions (polity). Examples of the first include works devoted to understanding the interests and ideas behind the diverse institutionalization of neoliberal policies across the world (Ban 2016; Etchemendy 2012; Maron and Shalev 2017; Prassad 2006; Teichman 2001). Examples of the second are analyses of how neoliberalism has translated into different organizations of the polity, the subjects that interact in it, and the institutions that define "which political action is possible in a capitalist society" (Gill 2002, 48; Amable 2011; Brown 2015; Biebricher 2015; Crouch, Porta, and Streeck 2016). I claim that these two constructions of neoliberalism correspond to two different neoliberal schools of thought—in retrospect, perhaps the two most influential ones: the Chicago School, where neoliberal policy emerged, and which had a great influence on new development theories and practices; and the Virginia School, which developed ideas on modifying the constitution of the polity in order for it to protect neoliberal principles.[1] To understand neoliberalism's resilience, we need to consider that it is institutionalized on two levels. First—the "Chicago" part of neoliberalism—are concrete policies and the development program contained in the diverse economic theories behind it. Second, the rules of the game establishing what kind of policies can be pursued and which actors have the legitimate power to participate in those decisions—what I call the "Virginia" part of neoliberalism.

These two schools of thought developed, in tandem, a conception of neoliberalism as a set of policies that grounded developing countries' expectations of making the leap to the next level of development, and as a set of institutional constraints on representation and government action. Moreover, I explain how the Virginia school of neoliberalism was crucial to the survival of the Chicago part. I develop three ways by which neoliberalism reduced the range and scope of democratic politics, thereby increasing its chances of survival: by creating support among business elites and empowering them through the privatization of state assets; by blocking opposition from political actors critical of neoliberalism and therefore, potentially against it; and by insulating key policymaking areas from the discretion of governments.

Neoliberal Policy and Polity: From Chicago to Virginia

The history of the rise and spread of neoliberalism has occupied more and more pages of scholarly debate in the last decades. Its origins are ineluctably placed in the early decades of the twentieth century amid the socialist calculus debate, the demise of free market capitalism and the Gold Standard during and after the Great Depression, and the rise of Keynesian economics to the canon of economic rationality and political management (Boas and Gans-Morse 2009; Cahill and Konings 2017; Connell and Dados 2014; D. S. Jones 2012; Mirowski and Plehwe 2009; Slobodian 2018). In this story, there are a number of important names and places contributing to the neoliberal "thought collective" (Mirowski and Plehwe 2009), and authors recognize diverse phases

---

1. A third "neoliberal" school recently discovered and studied by Slobodian (2018) is the Geneva school, which vowed to institutionalize neoliberalism's principles at the level of international institutions, governance, and law. I will discuss this in connection with Virginia due to the fact that they share a similar preoccupation with the binding of democratic polities through higher institutional orders.

in the creation of neoliberalism, but two names and institutions are crucial to understanding neoliberalism's resilience and the development of the two paths described below: the University of Chicago with Milton Friedman, and the University of Virginia with James Buchanan.

According to Daniel Jones (2012), Friedman and Buchanan made early thinking about neoliberalism (in authors such as Hayek, Von Mises, etc.) politically and economically palatable. Thanks to them, neoliberalism matured as an intellectual and political movement and became ingrained in public discourse. These thinkers became respected public intellectuals, but at the same time they were "policy propagandists" and "belligerent" parties in the "life or death struggle" between socialist/collectivist and free market/libertarian ideas (D. S. Jones 2012, 97; 120).

Contrary to visions of neoliberalism as always liberalizing, it is now widely recognized that the state is a key component of the neoliberal project. This is so not only because neoliberalism needed the state to create the conditions for its rise, but also because neoliberalism transformed the sense and mission of the state to one of the promotion and defense of economic liberty before anything else. In doing this, the state not only created and enforced the conditions that enabled private enterprises to operate in more or less free markets, but also, and more importantly, allowed the creation and maintenance of a politico-economic order which actively defended itself against impulses to overthrow it, through state-directed coercion insulated from democratic pressures (Bruff 2016, 109–10; Brown 2015; Gill 2002). In what follows, I develop in more detail what I understand by the policy and the polity parts of neoliberalism.

Neoliberal Policy and Development

Following their belief in the self-correcting mechanism of perfectly competitive markets and their superior resource allocation efficiency, the chief objective of economic policy according to neoliberals was to set markets free, and set prices that would liberate the potential of private entrepreneurs.[2] They

2. It is important to note, as will become evident throughout this book, that this quest for freer markets and transparent prices went hand in hand with increasing market power, oligopolization, and state intervention. Phillip Mirowski (2013) has referred to this as the "double truth" doctrine of neoliberalism, while others have coined the idea of an "actually existing" neoliberalism to contrast it with the theory of competitive markets devoid of state intervention and regulations that features in academic debates (Cahill 2014).

linked this directly to the problems of economic development. In a journal article in 1958, Milton Friedman put it in the following terms:

> What is required in the underdeveloped countries is the release of the energies of millions of able, active, and vigorous people . . . an atmosphere of freedom, of maximum opportunity for individuals to experiment, and of incentive for them to do so in an environment in which there are objective tests of success and failure—in short a vigorous, free capitalistic market (Friedman quoted in Strassmann 1976, 67).

This implied releasing the full potential of consumers and producers in free markets from the distortions of government intervention and securing price stability so that those markets could function effectively. These ideas and the consequent policy implications would stand at the heart of neoliberalism's development agenda. It was, in fact, no surprise that Chicago's preoccupation with development issues from early on confronted two topics that were seen as the crux of price distortions in developing economies: trade and finance, which crucially affected the two policy domains studied in this book: industrial policy and exchange rates (see Strassmann 1976, 67).

Since the work of authors such as Arthur Lewis, Raul Prebisch, Albert Hirschman, and Paul Rosenstein-Rodan, among others, the canon in development economics had been to question the wisdom of comparative advantage and free trade as a guide to the development of less advanced economies and to advocate for "big push" strategies of industrialization and structural change involving heavy state intervention and selective protection (Sánchez-Ancochea 2007). Neoliberals' reaction was to fight this and replace it with their own vision that favored free markets and eliminated discretionary state intervention. They attacked the industrialist development planners and the developmentalist gist of international institutions such as the World Bank, supporting instead, from early on, the specialization of underdeveloped countries in primary product production and exports (Plehwe 2009).

These debates can be traced back to the early neoliberals in post–World War I Vienna and were developed within the Mont Pelerin Society in the early 1950s. In the latter case, Chicago had a key impact on them. Jacob Viner, one of the leaders of the first Chicago generation, was among the first to criticize the state of the art in development economics and engage in open debates with the structuralist school, alongside other Mont Pelerin members like W. Röpke, P. Bauer, and T. Schultz. A Chicago colleague, Harry Johnson, was among the key figures of the new trade theory, or what some have called "the counter-revolution in development theory" (Toye in Colclough 1993, n. 4). Although it was not his main area of study, Milton Friedman remained a strong advocate of unilateral trade liberalization both in the United States and abroad (Strassmann 1976, 68). In the context of the U.S. presidential race of 1964, as an advisor to the failed Republican candidate Barry Goldwater, Friedman wrote: "As libertarians, our strategic objective is free international trade" (Friedman quoted in D. S. Jones 2012, 200).

The reduction of tariffs and subsidies—and the elimination of other non-tariff restrictions—became an influential position in international circles starting in the 1950s and 1960s, particularly at the World Bank, through the revisions of the dominant theory of trade by authors such as Anne Krueger, Jagdish Bhagwati (a student of Johnson's), and Bela Balassa (a Viner protégé). Research by these authors showed a close connection between exports and growth: they argued that free trade policy could have an important role in improving export performance, and that there was an inverse relation between higher trade protection and export success (Colclough 1993). In the words of Bhagwati and Srinivasan, "there is little empirical support for those who would argue that restrictive regimes generate dynamic gains that offset their static inefficiencies" (Bhagwati and Srinivasan 1978, 14). Wary of the difficulty of advocating a unilateral and across-the-board reduction of tariffs, subsidies, and other protections, as advocated by Friedman, these authors resorted to secondary solutions such as price or market-based mechanisms instead of non-market ones (like import/export quotas), and maintaining uniform tariffs and rates of protection instead of setting them selectively, which for them represented the inexcusable government discretion promoted by the then development orthodoxy (see Colclough 1993).

An important part of the neoliberals' quest for free trade was based on the work of another revered Chicagoan and Nobel prize winner, Georg Stiegler. Stiegler's theory of regulatory capture explained the existence of tariffs and other protections for specific industries—or any regulation, for that matter—not as a development device driven by economic needs, but as a reflection of the power of different interest groups, with negative consequences for economic growth and efficiency. This theory was expanded to comprise a theory of the "rent-seeking society" as a generalized behavior of economic actors in systems where administrative allocation (i.e., discretionary state intervention) rather than market allocation was prevalent (Krueger 1974). This idea of the

rent-seeking society became essential to understand—and criticize—the activities of governments as advocated by the early development thinkers. It was
subsequently extended to comprise all sorts of government intervention and
regulation of the economy, including selective support to certain industries,
the imposition of regulations and protections, the promotion of infant industry, and the use of public enterprises for economic purposes—the core of late
industrialization strategies.

Chicago led the way in expanding a second area of the new development
theory: price stability, the role of finance, and the importance of exchange rate
policy. In his controversial address to the American Economic Association in
1967, Friedman explained: "Our economic system will work best when producers and consumers, employers and employees, can proceed with full confidence that the average level of prices will behave in a known way in the future—preferably that it will be highly stable" (Friedman quoted in D. S. Jones
2012, 207). Hayek was more concise when he stated that the chief duty of every
economist was, plainly, to fight inflation (Hayek 1973, 9). Friedman is known
for his work on monetary theory, based on his study (with Anna Schwartz) of
the Great Depression, and how monetary profligacy helped deepen it. The idea
of a stable supply of money (the basic tenet of the new doctrine of "monetarism") influenced the New Classical Macroeconomics of Robert Lucas and
others, which rejected all government intervention in terms of monetary
policy for being ineffective and inflationary, and which promoted central bank
independence (more on this below).

In the case of less advanced economies, the idea of price stability and free
markets, and the critique of soft money and state-owned development banks
as advocated by development economists, became fashioned under the notion
of "financial repression." Two Stanford graduates with Chicago connections,
Edward Shaw and Ronald McKinnon, were the key figures behind it. According to them, "financial repression" refers to a situation where state regulations
reduce the transmission of deposits into loans (and more generally of savings
into finance capital), where high inflation and artificially low interest rates
reduce the returns on capital, and where capital cannot freely flow to the activities where it would gain greater returns (McKinnon and Grassman 1981; Mishkin 2007). Thus, the urge to liberalize domestic financial markets. More generally, neoliberals saw in the Keynesian capital controls of the postwar era one
of the key reasons behind speculative attacks harming price stability, and thus
they strongly advocated the liberalization of capital accounts (Chwieroth

2009, 70–71). They also saw exchange controls and financial repression as important activities of rent-seeking governments in less advanced countries, since they believed that state-directed credit favored inefficient firms and cronies (Chwieroth 2009, 80–81; Mishkin 2007). In this sense, neoliberals had a taste for the capacity of financial markets and capital flows to both enhance economic development and growth, and to discipline rent-generating governments and rent-seeking interest groups.

The relation between monetary policy and capital flows, and the key role of exchange rates thereof, was formalized by Harry Johnson and Nobel prize winner Robert Mundell. Both worked with prominent neoliberals at the LSE and Chicago, including Friedman himself. Johnson developed what later became known as the Monetary Approach to the Balance of Payments (MABP), a theory describing the mechanism of price adjustment under different exchange rate situations and their effect on the balance of payments, a chronic problem generating stop-go cycles in developing economies. On the staff of the IMF since the early 1960s, Mundell, along with Marcus Flemming, another IMF staffer, derived what became known as the Mundell-Flemming theorem or the trilemma of monetary policy in an open economy—an important contribution to MABP. The trilemma detailed the optimum use of monetary and fiscal policy under diverse conditions of openness to capital movements and exchange rate regimes. The MABP would first be used by Latin American neoliberals in their application of fixed exchange rates under free capital accounts in the 1970s (Ardito Barletta, Bléjer, and Landau 1984; Foxley 1983), while the trilemma would be consistently considered in the conditionalities attached to IMF loans (Polak 2002, 20). Authors such as Boyer (2011, 136) argue that, although not explicitly recognized, both Johnson's and Mundell's contributions to monetary theory in the open economy derive directly from Friedman's seminal contributions on the exchange rate debate.

In sum, Chicago neoliberalism was most influential in what would become the new orthodoxy in development theory (see Rodrik 1996). As I showed here, and as I will analyze in more detail in chapters 3 and 4, exchange rates and industrial policy became key policy domains of Chicago neoliberalism. However, as will become more and more evident throughout this book, the continuity over time of neoliberalism cannot be explained by the "good economics" behind Chicago policies. Rather, we have to look at the development of neoliberal theories on democracy and constitutionalism: neoliberalism's polity part.

Neoliberal Polity and Democracy

Unlike the Chicago focus on positive economics, the Virginia school had a strong normative orientation and was focused on the organization of society.[3] As Buchanan emphasized in his book with Richard Wagner criticizing Keynesianism, "[t]his book is an essay in political economy rather than in economic theory. Our focus is upon the political institutions through which economic policy must be implemented" (J. M. Buchanan and Wagner 1977, 4). Not only this: there were strong internal disputes between the two currents, and Buchanan expressed his overt criticism of the Friedmanites' overemphasis on policy, complaining that that economists "feel no moral obligation to convey and to transmit to their students any understanding of the social process through which a society of free persons can be organized without overt conflict while at the same time using resources with tolerable efficiency" (Reisman 1990, 1; see MacLean 2017, 40–41).

Virginians found inspiration in the early neoliberals, and particularly, in the writings of Friedrich Hayek. Early neoliberals saw themselves not so much advocating for market-enhancing economic policies or the market in itself, but on "redesigning states, laws, and other institutions to protect the market" (Slobodian 2018, 6). It was Hayek who first paid systematic attention to this in *The Road to Serfdom*, where he explored the dangers of the reliance on government and the need to revitalize old liberalism in its defense of economic liberty, not only as a just foundation for the economic order but as the best form of organizing society (MacLean 2017, 39). Hayek therefore highlighted not only the type of policies needed for a free society, but also the important role that prevailing political institutions played in making this possible (Hayek 1973, 1978). According to Slobodian (2018), this quest for finding legal-institutional fixes to protect markets from democracy involved both nation-states and ultimately the world order.

Two issues emerged from these discussions: the first concerned democratic representation and majority rule, in relation to how institutional rules empowered different groups in society; the second, how representation of those groups, and the incentives behind its institutional setting, translated into con-

---

3. Friedman certainly contributed as well with his writings in *Capitalism and Freedom*, where he states the essential coincidence between economic (market) freedom and political freedom, and the fallacious distinction between the two as separately concerned with individual freedom and material welfare.

crete government policy. In *The Constitution of Liberty,* Hayek made his frustration with these two basic principles of representative democracy clear:

> There are at least two respects in which it is always possible to extend democracy: the range of persons entitled to vote and the range of issues that are decided by democratic procedure. In neither respect can it be seriously contended that every possible extension is a gain or that the principle of democracy demands that it be indefinitely extended (Hayek 1978, 104).

Hayek's remarks were universal and, furthermore, reasonable when set against the possibility that democracy turns against basic civil freedoms. However, in the tradition of classic liberalism that he vindicates, these basic freedoms were narrowed to economic liberty and private property. The basic problem was, therefore, that representative government could destroy capitalism—and the proprietor class—unless constitutional reform ensured and protected economic liberty against the will of the majority (MacLean 2017, 81). Hence, the task of researchers at Virginia became "to expose the foibles of government as the best way to protect the market (and property) from popular interference (the majority)" (MacLean 2017, 77). In other words, they needed to discover how to override popular decisions when they controverted the superior principle of economic liberty (Slobodian 2018, 15).

Limiting Democracy

The neoliberal fear of democracy stems from the well-known hypothesis of the tyranny of the majority. Neoliberals fear that a government with unlimited power would use that power to respond to the interests of the specific groups and constituencies that support it—the majority—against the will of those that do not—the minority (Hayek 1973, 12; J. Buchanan and Tullock 1967, 253; see Przeworski 2019, 16–19). The worst part of this power was taxation, which Buchanan saw as a "legally sanctioned gangsterism" (MacLean 2017, xxii) that violated the liberty of individual taxpayers.

Neoliberalism's quest for limiting democracy targeted the identification, in modern democracies, of majority rule as *the* doctrine of popular sovereignty (J. Buchanan and Tullock 1967, 260). Buchanan and Tullock's analysis of majoritarian rule explains how the 50 percent +1 can secure benefits by coercing the other 50 percent −1 to follow their preferences, and by imposing costs on them. For the authors, a morally justifiable constitutional order—one that respected individual liberty—should ensure that no individual would be coerced or forced to do what she had not agreed upon. Any other type of decision-rule, even a qualified majority rule, implied a higher overall redistribution than necessary among individuals and a bias toward coercing the minority into higher taxation. They would contribute more than they wanted and receive less for it.

Neoliberals therefore became fully aware that the ability of the propertyless majority to coerce the proprietor minority depends on how political institutions were designed. As Hayek put it, "[w]hat we call the will of the majority is thus really an artifact of the existing institutions" (Hayek 1973, 11). The conclusion was that it was necessary to alter the way political institutions confer power to different groups. This idea sounds more eloquent in the words of Walter Lippman, one of the fathers of the Mont Pelerin Society. In a newspaper article in 1961 Lippman argued that "The crux of the question is not whether the majority should rule but *what kind of majority should rule*" (Lippman quoted in J. Buchanan and Tullock 1967, 249, italics are mine). This explains why Buchanan and Tullock argue for the unanimity rule, which, they reason, is equivalent to giving the minority a veto power to prevent the imposition of costs on them that they do not agree with (J. Buchanan and Tullock 1967, 259).

In making their case, Virginians resorted to the teachings of James Madison and his approach to "constitutional democracy" as a way to create checks and balances limiting the power of majority governments and their possible effects on minorities (see Gill 2002). Interestingly, as Dahl observed, Madison never expressed the same such "anxiety . . . over the dangers arising from minority tyranny" (Dahl 1956, 9). In fact, as Nancy MacLean has convincingly argued, the outcome of Virginia proposals would be no less than to "restrict what voters could achieve together in a democracy to what the wealthiest among them would agree to" (2017, 2).

Insulating Policymaking

Neoliberal resistance to bureaucracies and deliberate state action dates back to the writings of Karl Popper (in *The Open Society*) and Henry Simons, Milton Friedman's mentor (D. S. Jones 2012, 37–49, 93). In Hayek's formulation, this preoccupation was conflated with the idea of the impossibility of planning (due to the planner's inability to know all individual preferences) and the unintended consequences of state intervention, echoing also the early works of von Mises. This quickly led scholars to concentrate on constitutional "limits on the potential exercise of political authority" (Buchanan quoted in D. S. Jones 2012, 131).

Neoliberals' fascination with rules stems from their realization that politicians are self-interested individuals, not benevolent despots that would apply the "good economics" of Chicago-type policy. In the words of Hayek, "even a statesman wholly devoted to the common interest of all the citizens will be under the constant necessity of satisfying special interests, because only thus will he be able to retain the support of a majority, which he needs to achieve what is really important to him" (Hayek 1973, 10). In other words, the ingrained bias of representative majoritarian democracies toward higher taxation and spending means that economic policy "cannot be left adrift in the sea of democratic politics" (J. M. Buchanan and Wagner 1977, 175).

At the same time, neoliberals distinguished between constitutional rules and ordinary rules (Buchanan and Tullock 1967; Hayek 1978; see Gill 2002). While the latter could be subject to political struggles over their definition, the former should be a quasi-permanent body of rules stipulating what is possible in the realm of politics, establishing what kind of policies can be subject to the realm of partisan considerations and changing government majorities. Given that for Virginia the basic instruments of economic policymaking in a democratic society were prone to interfere with what they considered to be basic individual liberties, economic policy should be constrained by constitutional not ordinary rules. In this vein, the idea of constitutionalizing certain rules is crucial since it "involves not only the idea of hierarchy of authority or power but also that of a hierarchy of rules or laws, where those possessing a higher degree of generality and proceeding from a superior authority control the contents of the more specific laws that are passed by a delegated authority" (Hayek 1978, 178). The idea was to reduce the discretion of governments when enacting economic policies by subjecting their decisions to a set of rules established in the constitution, thereby restricting their possible actions.

While Virginia neoliberals focused on the "economic constitution" of nation-states, neoliberals from the Geneva school used the same type of reasoning to promote the "encasement" of the world economy through a web of governance and international law (Slobodian 2018). Thus, the ultimate corset for democratic politics would lie in the international arena, where international institutions would be able to punish domestic governments and bring them back into compliance with the principles of economic liberty.[4]

4. Slobodian (2018) has uncovered a crucial if hitherto unknown part of the history of neoliberalism, which leads to a better understanding of its global reach and the role of international regulations and institutions in constraining democratic governments as directly linked to the neoliberal political project. The latter, however, has received considerably more attention than the constitutionalization of domestic political economies, which is the focus of this book

In sum, Virginians reflected that the "good economics" of Chicago neoliberalism was not secure in a democratic political system, and that these systems must be radically altered to protect economic freedom. Crucially, Virginians proposed increasing the veto power of the proprietor minority, decreasing the influence of electoral majorities, and constraining policymaking through the establishment of rules binding authorities. These are the crucial mechanisms through which neoliberalism remained resilient over time.

Mechanisms of Neoliberal Resilience: Toward a "Market-Compatible" Democracy"[5]

As Virginia neoliberals were clearly aware, the most important issue for the resilience of neoliberalism—and for that matter, the resilience of any policy regime—is democracy. By definition, democracy is a form of political organization characterized by the fact that those in power cannot expect to stay there forever, and that political institutions enhance competition for votes and effective representation of those votes. This implies that development projects and the underling policy regimes may change at every new election or economic crisis, jeopardizing neoliberalism's hegemonic pretense. It is important, therefore, to understand the extent to which neoliberalism's resilience rests on undermining democracy.

Representative democracy can be seen as constituted by two dimensions: competition for office among distinguishable political alternatives, and effective representation of voter demands through public policy (see Dahl 1956, 1972).[6] These two dimensions juxtapose with others that reinforce the same idea: the distinctions between, for example, the constitutional and popular aspects of democracy (Dahl 1956; Mair 2013), democracy's legitimacy and efficacy (Linz 1978), the input and output legitimacy of democratic govern-

---

(see, e.g., Chwieroth 2009; Pop-Eleches 2009; Roos 2019; Schimmelfenning and Sedelmaier 2005; Vachudova 2005). In the next chapters I will discuss the role of the EU, the IMF, and the World Bank, although this will not be the main focus.

5. Wolfgang Streeck has used this term based on a speech by Angela Merkel to the German parliament where she complains about the slowness of legislative procedures and urges that the speed of the Bundestag accommodate that of the market (Streeck in Crouch, della Porta, and Streeck 2016, 500–501).

6. These two dimensions are of course, sustained by certain institutional prerequisites associated with civil liberties such as freedom of speech, freedom of association, freedom of press, and the like (Dahl 1989; Lipset 1981; O'Donnell 2007).

ments (Scharpf 1999), or responsibility and responsiveness as the two goals of political parties in government (Mair 2009).[7] Although the literature tends to emphasize the processual or competition dimension of democracy, even these "minimalist" definitions of democracy often need to assume the more normative representative dimension in their account (see O'Donnell 2007; Dahl 1989; Przeworski 2019). For example, Adam Przeworski, a well-known advocate of minimalist definitions of democracy, argues that "[p]olitical forces comply with present defeats because they believe that the institutional framework that organizes the democratic competition will permit them to advance their interests in the future" (Przeworski 1991, 19). However, he also points out that a "stable democracy requires that governments be strong enough to govern effectively but weak enough not to be able to govern against important interests" (Przeworski 1991, 37). The challenge for competing democratic projects is to maintain the balance between effectively representing the citizenry, and ensuring that this competition is meaningful enough to present real alternatives and moderate enough not to encourage extremist positions that put into question the very foundations of the democratic order (see Levitsky and Ziblatt 2018; Przeworski 2019).

Two characteristics derived from these dimensions make it difficult to sustain extreme policy regimes in representative democracies: the dynamics of party competition and the empowerment of the lower echelons of society. Following the seminal works of Hibbs and Tufte, students of partisan politics have long shown that more often than not, government turnovers are followed by policy swings (e.g., Boix 2000; Franzese 2002). Moreover, when government turnover is underpinned by economic crises, policy regimes tend to suffer punctuated changes that reflect not only government and policy shifts but also more fundamental changes in the underlying makeup of societal power and the prevailing economic policy paradigms (e.g., Gourevitch 1986; Pempel 1998; Hall 1993; Blyth 2002). A key explanation for these swings is the incentives offered by democratic political institutions and the competition they generate for representing the contrasting demands of distinct groups in society. Most important, democratic regimes allow the propertyless masses to

---

7. In some of these debates there is an even finer distinction between efficacy and efficiency or between output and outcome (see Linz 1978; Scharpf 1999). As will become clear below, in the representative dimension of democracy I include the normative aspects relative to both the capacity to govern effectively and to respond to key constituencies, as opposed to the pure procedural and constitutional aspects of holding elections and establishing checks and balances.

influence political decisions and use "politics against markets" (Korpi 1983; Esping-Andersen 1985). This is in fact the key reason why conservatives feared democracy would unleash the tyranny of the majority against the privileged few, and according to Linz and Stepan (1996, 12–13), it explains why postwar western democracies were essentially mixed economies (see also Przeworski 2019, 18–19). In this line, Linz and Stepan argue that "democratic consolidation *requires* the institutionalization of a socially and politically regulated market" (1996, 13 itallics added). In other words, there is an implicit tension between the resilience of neoliberalism and democracy.

If political democracies have ingrained mechanisms for facilitating power turnovers, either through regular elections or following acute economic downturns, and if the underlying incentive structures produce a bias toward regulated markets and mixed economies, any study trying to understand the roots of neoliberalism's resilience will wonder how and why neoliberalism has survived under democratic regimes. The answer is that it has introduced particular mechanisms that alter the functioning of representative democracy, transforming it into a "market-conforming democracy" (Streeck in Crouch, della Porta, and Streeck 2016, 500; Crouch 2004). Research into the history of neoliberal ideas tells us that this was neoliberals' key objective from the beginning (MacLean 2017; Slobodian 2018).

Students of authoritarian reversals usually locate assaults on democracy either in the erosion of its competitive/constitutional dimension—free and fair elections, checks and balances, and so forth—or in the underlying infrastructure of civil rights and freedoms (see Linz 1978; more recently Levitsky and Ziblatt 2018). In the case of neoliberalism's resilience, the assault on democracy comes mainly through the reduction of different aspects of its representative dimension: that is, limits to the effective representation through government policy of those groups demanding alternatives to neoliberalism. Students of "post-democracy" (e.g., Crouch 2004; Mair 2013; Bruff 2014; Scharpf 1999) and its associated phenomena have concentrated on one aspect of this process: the delegation of policymaking to independent state agencies insulated from partisan considerations, either at the national or transnational level—what I call constitutionalized policy lock-in. In addition to this, two other mechanisms have increased the resilience of neoliberalism: support creation, or the generation of supportive constituencies among business, and opposition blockade, which reduces the representation of political parties challenging neoliberalism.

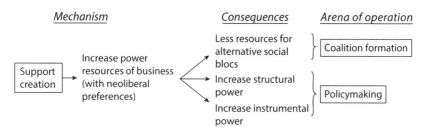

FIGURE 2.1. Support Creation
Source: Author's elaboration.

Support Creation: The Political Economy of Privatization

Support creation consists of using privatization as a way to alienate state assets and empower specific firms, economic groups, and/or sectors expected to support the continuation of market reforms.[8] Support creation acts on the business support base of neoliberalism, increasing its power *vis à vis* democratically elected governments—particularly businesses with preferences for neoliberal policies.

This affects the representation of alternative development projects challenging neoliberalism in two ways (see figure 2.1). First, it reduces the scope of societal alliances. Historically, progressive political projects under capitalism have relied on the support given by certain segments of the business community even if only reluctantly (see B. R. Schneider 2004b; Swenson 1991; Paster 2013). By increasing the power of businesses with neoliberal preferences, neoliberals prevented the formation of progressive coalitions, or what I call "alternative social blocs," that were prepared to challenge neoliberalism. Support creation works, for example, by reducing long-term support and campaign funding to these alternative groups, and/or channeling it to supporters of neoliberalism.

Second, the shift in power toward business reduces the representation of alternative development projects in the arena of policymaking by altering the

8. Another source that will not be dealt with here is liberalization in general, and the liberalization of specific markets in particular (see Schamis 1999). For example, the privatization of public policy and public utilities (especially pension funds) is yet another way of strengthening the power resources of business groups supporting neoliberalism. For a study of Chile's privatized pension system under these lines, see Bril-Mascarenhas and Maillet (2019).

responsiveness of elected authorities to their constituencies. As the literature on business power has convincingly argued, democratically elected authorities are constrained by the capitalist "market prison" (Lindblom 1982). Due to their ability to determine the economic fate of countries (and therefore the electoral prospects of governments) businesses have a variety of channels to either include or eliminate certain policies from the agenda (structural power), or to influence the policymaking process (instrumental power) (Culpepper 2010; Hacker and Pierson 2002; Fairfield 2015b). While the two work through different mechanisms, they have a similar outcome: altering the policy decisions of elected governments and bringing them closer to the preferences of business.

Many authors working on businesses' structural power point to the elimination of financial barriers, the structuring of international bond markets, and the liberalization of capital accounts as key mechanisms increasing the structural power of businesses, particularly those in the financial sector (Campello 2015; Kaplan 2013; Maxfield 1998; Roos 2019). In fact, as Mair (2009) convincingly argues, democracy's current ills are reflected in the persistence of governments changing from responsiveness to domestic constituencies to responsibility to international (financial) markets. This is consistent with the idea of support creation. In fact, as I analyze in detail in chapters 3 and 4, finance is one of the key business actors demanding and defending neoliberalism.

Following Bril-Mascarenhas and Maillet (2019), my focus is rather on how state assets have been used to create structural power, which was subsequently made available to business. Neoliberalism has remained resilient thanks not only to the freeing of markets (i.e., financial deregulation), but also, and more fundamentally, thanks to the constraining of democracies. Unlike financial liberalization, privatization not only acted on business structural power by increasing the danger of capital flight threats; it directly created a business support base for neoliberalism. Therefore, it not only *released* the potential of free markets and the "market prison" mechanism: it *created* that potential by increasing the importance of private property in the economy and by consequently reducing the importance of state-owned enterprises, historically one of the state's most important sources of autonomous funding (see Roos 2019, 57). By focusing on privatization instead of financial liberalization, we can observe how this mechanism prevented the formation of a business base for alternative development projects, and constrained coalition formation and the emergence of alternative social blocs and political projects.

Neoliberal Arguments for Privatization

A modern capitalist economy needs a functioning private property regime. This argument is as old as capitalism, and central to its many interpretations. However, after the Great Depression, following the teachings of the early development thinkers, developing countries began to experiment with increased state involvement in the economy. This experiment rested on the finding that the increased role of the state in the process of capital accumulation led to a part-industrialization, part-modernization revolution among many successful late developers (Gerschenkron 1962; Kurth 1979). State intervention and property-ownership thus increased significantly in Latin America under Import-Substituting Industrialization (ISI) and, needless to say, in Eastern Europe under state socialism (Hirschman 1968; O'Donnell 1973; Berend 1996).

Neoclassical economists warned of the dangers that too much state involvement in the economy could bring in the long run. As we saw above, while Hayek concentrated on the futility and perversity of state intervention, Stiegler and Krueger elaborated a theory of rent-seeking, identifying state intervention and ownership with corruption and cronyism. Studying the working of enterprises in state socialist economies, the eminent Hungarian economist János Kornai (1986) found similar mechanisms in what he called "soft budget constraint" economies. In sum, neoclassical economists came to see government action as both economically inefficient and politically damaging, concluding that "the best way to limit rent-seeking is to limit the government" (David Colander cited in Schamis 2002, 15). It therefore comes as no surprise that privatization figured prominently in the Washington Consensus development agenda and in the market reform efforts carried out under the auspices of international financial institutions (see Williamson 1990b).

Privatization as Support Creation

Discussions about the need for, and best form of, privatization focused on technical details, obscuring the political dynamics behind it. Recognizing this, several works on the political dimension of privatization have convincingly argued that far from dismantling rents, market reforms often create new ones. This is particularly true when state assets are appropriated noncompetitively, when public monopolies are transferred to private hands intact, and when there is a lack of proper regulatory frameworks (Schamis 2002, 4).

Observers of privatization processes in Eastern Europe had a clear under-standing that these processes implicitly or explicitly included political goals, and that the formation of a proprietor class stabilized and consolidated the new capitalist formations (Berg and Berg 1997; Rutland 1997; Greskovits 1998; Eyal, Szelényi, and Townsley 1998; Schoenman 2014). They even saw privatiza-tion as a support for democracy, since "[o]nly citizens of a property-owning democracy possessed the incentives, and the material means, to formulate political demands and mobilize support for their interests and views indepen-dently of the state" (R. Martin 2013, 27). While some concentrate on showing that political privatization results in corruption, cronyism, and reform failure (Staniszkis 1990; Hellman 1998; Manzetti 2010), others argue that the very success of market reforms can be linked to specific business groups and indi-viduals targeted as beneficiaries of privatization's largesse. The proceeds of this privatization would then allow these business groups and individual entrepre-neurs to expand and/or consolidate their current economic activities, and enable them to serve later on as crucial supporters of the new economic policy regime (Etchemendy 2001, 2012; Schamis 2002). Following this, we under-stand privatization as supporting specific economic actors and as causally linked to the continuation of neoliberalism over time.

Opposition Blockade: Democracy by Neoliberal Design

Opposition blockade is in many ways the opposite of support creation and consists of the reduction of power resources of those actors presenting chal-lenges to neoliberalism. Gill (2002, 48–49) speaks of the "lock-out" of forces challenging neoliberalism. The actors locked out of the political arena need not be actual challengers but presumptive ones, based on their past political behavior. It is now common knowledge that since at least the 1980s, left-wing parties that once advocated some sort of social democracy have become active agents of neoliberalism (Mudge 2018). However, as I show in chapter 4, at the moment of the installation of neoliberalism and market reforms, they tended to actively oppose neoliberalism even if more often than not they ended sup-porting it. A similar story can be said about organized labor as an opposition to market reforms.

Opposition blockade acts on two arenas: coalition formation and political representation (see figure 2.2). In the first, it reduces the power resources of organized labor—for example, through the elimination of corporatist struc-

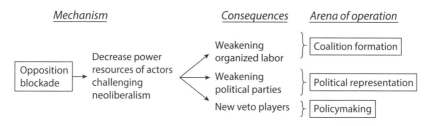

FIGURE. 2.2. Opposition Blockade
Source: Author's elaboration.

tures, the assault on union rights and collective bargaining, and the increase in flexibility of labor markets—preventing labor from being an active force in the consolidation of strong social-democratic and/or national-popular alternatives.[9] In the second arena, opposition blockade utilizes political institutions to prevent the configuration of political majorities against the continuation of market reforms. This type of opposition blockade acts on the political expression and representation of opponents of neoliberalism, mainly (but not only) through left-wing parties. I focus on the latter mechanism, in which neoliberals block opposition in order to prevent government turnover from becoming a challenge to the neoliberal order.

Neoliberal Arguments for Restricting Democracy

The dual transition to democracy and free markets in Latin America and Eastern Europe created a series of dilemmas attributable to the simultaneity of these processes and the possibility of them going wrong (see especially Offe 1991). These dilemmas were famously presented as a "J-curve" (Przeworski 1991, chap. 4; see Fish and Choudhry 2007; Gans-Morse and Nichter 2008). Due to the benevolent operation of free markets, economic liberalization was expected to significantly improve economic conditions and, therefore, provide support for democracy—but only in the long run. In the short term, liberaliza-

9. Theoretically, the relation between neoliberalism and the blocking of labor unions can be traced to the writings of Olson (1965). The "national-popular" was a category emerged in the Latin American social sciences to refer to the type of coalitions of the postwar era between a myriad of subaltern groups—including but not restrained to the urban working class—and the national bourgeoisies, that struggled to overcome the particular development problems that each country presented. See Faletto (1979).

tion (of domestic prices, trade and capital flows) and deregulation would generate a slump in domestic production and employment along with a dramatic increase in prices, worsening economic conditions in the immediate aftermath of economic reforms. In the context of liberalized political competition, this could easily lead to the deterioration of confidence in democracy and growing support for antireform and antisystem parties—thus the initial drop in the slope of the curve that gave it the characteristic J shape. As Appel and Orenstein put it, "[n]eoliberal reformers were almost certain to be voted out of power with the onset of transitional recessions" (2018, 1).

The ensuing instability and policy reversal would empower representatives of the *ancién regime*, compounding the real threat of an authoritarian and state-interventionist setback. In this context, even the milder "gradual reform" strategy was seen as potentially destabilizing to ongoing economic and political liberalization, subjecting the population to a lengthy process of adjustment that would eventually turn the tables against those reforms (see Balcerowicz 1995, 262–64). Strategically, the debate was therefore how to overcome the initial period of economic recession and low popular support without jeopardizing the long-term prospects of economic reform and democratic consolidation. This debate elicited a number of works analyzing reform strategies, and the institutional arrangements that would maximize them.

Some argued that, given the expected transitional recession, the greatest threat to liberalization would come from groups who lost in the process (see, among others, Haggard and Kaufman 1992, 1995; Nelson 1989; O'Donnell and Schmitter 1986). Therefore, efforts had to be devoted to blocking these groups from derailing the process of economic reforms. On the one hand, labor was expected to use collective action and massive strikes to prevent liberalization. On the other, it was believed that an unconstrained dominance of the left would induce leftist parties to fragment into factions "likely to engage in efforts to outbid each other with more and more extreme promises to the electorate" (O'Donnell and Schmitter 1986, 4:63; see Haggard and Kaufman 1995, 170–71). Democracy was a key problem here: it could reduce the costs of collective action and mobilization at the same time it was providing incentives for politicians to respond to those societal pressures (Lijphart and Waisman 1996c, 236; O'Donnell and Schmitter 1986). An unconstrained process of political liberalization could create the perfect storm: strong civil society actors pressing against reforms and strong political actors—notably from the left—wanting to represent them, thus "sabotag[ing]" economic and political liberalization (Przeworski 1991, 180).

This scenario warranted two opposing reform strategies: "either cooperating with opposition parties ... or destroying them" (Przeworski 1991, 181). These became known as the "social-democratic" and the "shock-therapy" strategies, respectively. While the first incorporated the broadest possible set of actors in the shaping of reforms, increasing their representativeness at the expense of alleged technical soundness, the second undermined the opposition to reforms, therefore increasing their "technical soundness" at the expense of their representativeness (Przeworski 1991, 183; see Bresser-Pereira, Maravall, and Przeworski 1993; Manzetti 2010). Put differently, while the social-democratic strategy emphasized managing political liberalization and economic liberalization simultaneously, the shock-therapy strategy concentrated on economic liberalization at the expense of political liberalization.[10]

The victorious shock therapy approach disentangled two periods (see Haggard and Kaufman 1995; Nelson 1993; Roland 2002). In the first, when societal pressures would be most pressing, new democracies least stable, and economic reforms most painful, democracy should be sheltered from pressures from below and reformers insulated. Only in the second period, when economic reforms had already started to show the expected results, could new democracies increase participation and representation in order to secure support for the new status quo from the large mass of losers from the first stage (Nelson 1993; Roland 2002; Santiso 2003). As Joan Nelson put it, in this second stage "consolidation of economic reforms requires a new consensus on the general nature of societal goals and the means for pursuing them" (Nelson 1993, 442).

Extending "Democraduras" to Make Neoliberalism Resilient

In their path-breaking book on transitions from authoritarianism, O'Donnell and Schmitter envisaged a number of transitional paths toward consolidated

---

10. *Nota bene* that a third strategy was also possible but given much less attention: that of political liberalization first, economic liberalization later. This is highlighted by Linz and Stepan (1996, chap. 21) as the "Spanish way": devising a set of—legitimate—political rules of the game that gave higher legitimacy to the economic reforms emerging from that initial political pact. For Linz and Stepan, placing the prime engine of democratic legitimacy on economic performance, as in the prevailing discussion in Latin America and Eastern Europe, meant in practice "invert[ing] the legitimacy pyramid" (1996, 435–39). Observers of the Latin American and Eastern European transitions highlighted, however, that differently from the Spanish case, the context of acute economic crisis in these regions made this option unavailable.

democracies. They called "limited political democracy" or *democradura*[11] an intermediary situation in the long-haul process of democratization, where political liberalization was "coupled with old or new restrictions on the freedoms of particular individuals or groups who are deemed *insufficiently prepared or sufficiently dangerous* to enjoy full citizenship" (O'Donnell and Schmitter 1986, 4:9, italics are mine). They found two characteristics to be important in identifying *democraduras*: first, conditions and institutions that restricted party competition and electoral choice (such as banning certain parties or ideologies, fixing high costs for their formation, rigging franchises, or overrepresenting particular interests); and second, establishing a series of veto players designed to circumvent the accountability of elected leaders to popular demands by placing certain issues out of their reach.

O'Donnell and Schmitter (1986, 4:42–43) expected *democraduras* to wither over time for reasons linked to the same problems that had led to the initial liberalization of authoritarian regimes: limited participation and accountability, corruption and complacency coming from sheltered competition for office, and so on. Democratization would ensue in phases, where each new phase would lay down "more inclusive and tolerant rules of competition and toleration" (O'Donnell and Schmitter 1986, 4:44; see also Haggard and Kaufman 1995, 10). Apart from these subsequent waves of political liberalization, Linz and Stepan included a key yardstick to measure complete democratic transitions: "when the government *de facto* has the authority to generate new policies, and when the executive, legislative and judicial power generated by the new democracy does not have to share the power with other bodies" (Linz and Stepan 1996, 3).

Far from a transient state in a process of democratic consolidation, *democraduras* became a permanent state. What neoliberals did in practice, therefore, was to extend the first phase of economic and political transition through to the institutionalization of those rules that excluded the losers of economic reforms from constituting powerful majorities and influencing the policy process.[12]

11. The term comes from the conjunction of the Spanish terms "democracia" and "dictadura," but also, from the Spanish "dura," hard. While "democradura" (literally, "hard democracy") implied political liberalization within some authoritarian constraints, the opposite "dictablanda" (or "soft dictatorship") implied the maintenance of dictatorship with some political openings.

12. This is far from surprising if one takes into consideration the lineage of the liberal idea

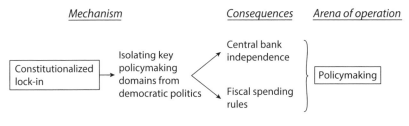

FIGURE 2.3. Constitutionalized Lock-In
Source: Author's elaboration.

Locking-in Neoliberalism: Constitutionalizing Rules, Avoiding Discretion

Theorists of path dependency coined the concept of "lock-in" to illustrate how established institutions constrain future policy choices. Because of the existence of "increasing returns" and "positive feedback" dynamics, the introduction of certain institutions at one point in time constrains the choice of other institutions later on, reducing the plausible set of options for institutional and policy change (Mahoney 2000; Pierson 2000; 2004). These authors foresaw diverse mechanisms leading to lock-in. For example, power mechanisms whereby those who benefitted from existing policies would have a de facto veto power over reforms, or economic mechanisms in which sunk costs associated with investment in new institutions would prevent future changes. In our case, the *institutional* lock-in establishes rules that isolate certain policy domains from partisan competition and later constitutionalizes them, making them even more difficult to change.[13]

Constitutionalized lock-in acts on the arena of policymaking influence by reducing the possibility of governments and political parties representing alternative policy preferences from altering existing neoliberal policies (see figure 2.3). Two modern institutions are central to the possibility of locking-in neoliberal policy alternatives in exchange rates and industrial policy, the policy areas studied in this book: independent central banks and fiscal spending rules. While the first insulates the price stability goal of exchange rate policy

---

of political representation, which dates back to Lockean possessive individualism where representation was bound to owning private property (Gill 2002, 58; see also Amable 2011).

13. The inspiration for the concept comes from the notion of "lock-in" in Gill (2002) and of "constitutionalized monetarism" in Streeck (1994).

from political considerations, the second limits the use of public expenditures to support industrial policy schemes and specific economic sectors.

Neoliberal Arguments for Binding Democratic Governments

As we saw above, the responsiveness of elected governments to particular constituencies and interest groups was a key preoccupation for neoliberals in the 1970s and 1980s. Classical economic policy instruments such as monetary and fiscal policy were seen as the main cause behind chronic inflation and fiscal deficits in representative democracies. In the case of nonadvanced political economies, these malaises were exacerbated by the predatory behavior of local business elites, state capture, and cronyism. Students of the political business cycle demonstrated that elected governments have incentives to use economic policy instruments for partisan purposes, inflating the economy before elections to increase support for incumbents and afterwards in order to deliver to their constituencies (Alesina and Summers 1993, 152).

In an influential article, Kydland and Prescott (1977) argued that discretionary economic policy could never deliver the expected benefits because rational economic agents adjust their expectations and behavior following changes in government policy. In other words, by anticipating government policy, economic agents undermine the very bases under which policy estimates are conducted, thereby altering policy outcomes and producing suboptimal results. As a consequence, stable and predictable policy rules are preferable to discretionary policy.

Neoclassical economists offered concrete alternatives to overcome the problem of government discretion. In the case of monetary policy, they argued that elected authorities might delegate power to an independent agency that will not have electoral or partisan motives (see Barro and Gordon 1983; Rogoff 1985). Such an agency in charge of monetary policy, they asserted, would need a reputation of always favoring price stability over other policy goals like full employment, growth, or the promotion of domestic industry. It might do so in two ways: first, through legal and institutional devices forcing officeholders to abide by price stability rules; and second by directly appointing individuals with an "inflation-hawk" reputation. The result was the birth of independent central banks.

In a similar fashion, several authors argued later for the need to establish clear fiscal rules in order to eliminate the inherent spending and debt biases of the democratic political process (Hagen and Harden 1995; Alesina and Perotti

1999). Again, the policy recipe favored rules over discretion. A fiscal rule can be defined as "a permanent constraint on fiscal policy, expressed in terms of a summary indicator of fiscal performance, such as the government budget deficit, borrowing, debt, or a major component thereof" (Kopits 2001, n. 2). Fiscal rules are currently seen as "the most straightforward approach to controlling [the] behavior [of elected authorities] and they seem attractive for simplicity and transparency" (Hagen 2002, 265). Hagen (2002) mentions three means to establish rules for fiscal policy: setting spending limits or targets before and during parliamentary debate; designing political institutions that increase competition and accountability; and establishing procedural rules centralizing the budget process and empowering those agents whose interests are more aligned with fiscal conservatism.

Despite the fact that fiscal rules have become more and more fashionable, their effectiveness in actually constraining government discretion is still under debate (see Hagen 2002; Schuknecht 2005; Price 2010). But they can also be used as a way to signal to businesses—in particular, financial markets—a government's intention to maintain fiscal conservatism, thereby reducing speculative attacks and promoting stability and growth (Kopits 2001, 9–10; also, Schuknecht 2005).

Constitutionalized Lock-in as a Reduction of the Policy Space

There is ample evidence that the operation of independent central banks and fiscal spending rules have reduced the operation of political business cycles, in particular limiting the policy options of left-of-center governments (see, among others, Way 2000; Maloney, Pickering, and Hadri 2003; Ozkan 2000; Rose 2006). It is therefore no mystery that constitutionalizing monetary and fiscal policy implies a reduction in the partisan influence over policy, favoring the neoliberal tenets of price stability and fiscal conservatism, and forcing the adoption of neoliberal alternatives in exchange rates and industrial policy (this was, in fact, the explicit neoliberal rationale). Scholars have consequently begun questioning the accountability of these delegated institutions and how they erode representational democracy (Clark, Golder, and Golder 2002; Haan and Amtenbrink 2000; more generally Bruff 2014).

A number of recent studies have shown that, in practice, these institutions seem to provide less of a constraint on governments than previously thought. One strand of literature suggests that policy convergence—or the erosion of partisan differences—is actually the result of different institutions of the political economy, or that the effect of independent central banks and fiscal spending rules is only positive when reinforced by other constraining institutions and veto players (Clark, Golder, and Golder 2002; Stasavage 2003). Conversely, other authors put the emphasis on agency, showing, for example, that central bankers actually have room to enact their own preferred policies instead of always favoring inflation-averse results (Vaubel 1997; Adolph 2013). From this perspective, to understand the outcome of policy decisions it is more important to know *who* uses the rule rather than *how* the rule is institutionalized. In other words, although central bank independence and fiscal spending rules effectively reduce the influence of elected governments on key policy domains, they may not necessarily preclude partisan behavior on the part of elected authorities. Did these institutions provide effective constraints on government discretion in Latin America and Eastern Europe? If yes, did they do this thanks to their own institutional mechanisms that prevented non-neoliberal policies, or did they merely open yet another channel of influence for business interests?

In chapters 5, 6, and 7 I will analyze the operation of each of these three mechanisms and test their causal relevance by deriving empirically observable implications of each mechanism, and using evidence from different sources to confirm whether and how they helped actors interested in the continuity of neoliberalism maintain control over the trajectory of public policy and prevent challenges from alternative policies and actors. But before undertaking this analysis, in chapters 3 and 4 I delineate the actors supporting and opposing neoliberalism, particularly in the case of exchange rates and industrial policies.

3

Neoliberal Policies and Supporting Actors

AS LATIN AMERICAN AND EASTERN EUROPEAN countries sought to reform their political economies during the crises of the 1980s and 1990s, neoliberalism became a development project providing concrete answers in a
number of policy domains. In general, these answers aimed at liberalizing and
deregulating markets, privatizing state companies, reducing the space for deliberate state action, and making market price signals the true driver of economic decisions among private economic actors (Williamson 1990a). By taking these neoliberal steps, policymakers thought, countries could shed the
interventionist economic models they thought were at the root of many of the
economic and political ills affecting them (Åslund 1994; Edwards 1995; Sachs
1990). Albeit offered as a set of necessary economic reforms, neoliberalism
produced winners and losers among domestic actors and was therefore supported and opposed by diverse sectors of society. Ultimately, implementing
and maintaining neoliberal reforms depended on support from those actors
benefitting from them (Greskovits 1998; Schamis 2002; Haggard and Kaufman
1995; Etchemendy 2012).

But who were these actors that supported and defended neoliberalism? The
literature is undecided.[1] I undertake therefore an empirical analysis based on
quantitative and qualitative data to discover the patterns of support and opposition to neoliberalism in two concrete policy domains: exchange rate and
industrial policies. Establishing these relationships empirically is crucial for
establishing causal links between the mechanisms theorized in chapter 2 and

---

1. See more below.

the resilience of neoliberalism, and more broadly, to the understanding of neoliberalism as a political project based on the gradual and purposeful erosion of democracy. In fact, if the actors who benefitted from the erosion of democracy are not the same as those that demanded and defended neoliberalism in the first place, then the causal link between the two is difficult to sustain. In other words, chapters 3 and 4 help connect economic and political actors with their policy preferences and political behavior.

My analysis also examines the dynamics of policy continuity and change. One major drawback of existing accounts of neoliberalism's resilience is an over-reliance on stylized facts and generalized trends, leading to overarching claims that often fail to capture the complexity of these processes, as well as a lack of analysis of concrete policies/domains that reveal neoliberalism's resilience—or lack thereof (see, e.g., Crouch 2011; Appel and Orenstein 2018). Analyzing patterns of support and opposition to concrete policies reveals whether these countries maintained their neoliberal trajectories over time or switched to (short-lived or more durable) alternatives as they contested or even dismantled neoliberalism.

Chapters 3 and 4 offer three connected steps to respond to these concerns: first, a categorization of concrete policy alternatives with regard to their affinity to neoliberalism, which clearly establishes the spaces where we can evaluate its continuity; second, an analysis of what types of actors supported and defended these neoliberal policy alternatives over time; and, third, an account of the patterns of support and opposition that surrounded policy changes and that either maintained countries on a neoliberal trajectory or drove them away from it.

This chapter gives a quantitative assessment of these dynamics. Using a regression analysis based on historical data from the countries here studied, it investigates which economic actors demanded and supported the implementation and continuity of neoliberal policies and which political actors were more inclined to supply these policies. The chapter indicates that it was the financial and internationally competitive business sectors, together with right-wing governments, that were the actors most clearly associated with price-stability driven exchange rates as key components of neoliberal development projects.[2] These economic sectors were also associated with opposition to industrial policies. In the case of noncompetitive business sectors, data show mixed results: no relation with exchange rates and an important association

---

2. See below for the categorization and definition of different fractions of the business class.

with industrial policy drives when controlling for financial and institutional constraints. Following secondary literature in this regard, I argue that the support of noncompetitive business sectors for neoliberalism or alternative policies depended on a series of contextual conditions, including the share of external capital in the sector, macroeconomic conditions (for example, steady economic growth versus crises and inflationary episodes), and the availability of a coalition partner in terms of political support.

This quantitative assessment is complemented in chapter 4 with a qualitative analysis digging deeper into the underlying coalitional dynamics and concrete policy options derived from them. Chapter 4 analyzes therefore how actors joined forces, forming true "social blocs" pushing forward and defending neoliberalism against alternative development projects, and how these social blocs related to the resilience of neoliberalism in terms of policy continuity and change. As we will see throughout this book, the strength of different business sectors and their capacity to lead ample coalitions or social blocs able to pursue development projects, either supporting neoliberalism or presenting alternatives to it, are of crucial importance for understanding the politics of neoliberal resilience.

Exchange Rates and Industrial Policy for Development

I focus on exchange rate and industrial policies as key policy domains for analyzing development projects in nonadvanced countries, and particularly for understanding the resilience of neoliberalism. Although many other types of policies (taxation or social policy, for example) could have been chosen—and have been thoroughly studied by other scholars—this choice is warranted for both economic and political reasons.

In the case of exchange rates, both scholars and policymakers have stressed their central economic significance. Broz and Frieden, for example, contend that "[t]he exchange rate is the most important price in any economy, for it affects all other prices" (Broz and Frieden 2006, 587). In fact, exchange rates simultaneously affect exports and imports, real wages, consumption, savings, price levels, and, more broadly, economic growth and development (Bresser-Pereira, Oreiro, and Marconi 2014; Guzman, Ocampo, and Stiglitz 2018; Frieden 2016; Rodrik 2008; see discussion in Klein and Shambaugh 2009). Exchange rates reflect the relative price between imported and exported goods, and the relation between domestic and foreign exchange; thus, the policies that define the behavior of exchange rates set basic incentives for different types of economic actors. For example, exchange rates have a key influence on tradable industries because they directly affect the international price of their products. Thus, exchange rates define the ability of these firms to compete either in international markets or domestically and, ultimately, a country's trade balance with the rest of the world. And the trade balance is intimately linked with the development prospects of less developed countries. Exchange rates also affect inflation and consumption by making imported goods more or less expensive, thereby impacting real wages and the purchasing capacity of the population, as well as the imported components of domestic production and therefore, productive investment.

The strategic importance of exchange rates is even more pronounced in developing open economies with substantial financial and trade liberalization (Frieden 1991b; Ffrench-Davis 2010). A key historical problem for governments in these economies has been how to balance their need to import the capital goods that they do not produce with the need to earn foreign exchange to pay for those capital goods by exporting their less sophisticated goods, and how to upgrade their productive structures in the process (ECLAC 2012; Bresser-Pereira, Oreiro, and Marconi 2014; Gereffi and Wyman 1990). The inability to earn enough foreign exchange through exports—often due to the adverse terms of trade and productivity dynamics associated with less sophisticated goods—has typically led developing economies to become saddled with crippling external indebtedness as they search for ways to pay for imported goods. As debt inexorably rises, countries face stop-go cycles and balance of payments crises because they are usually not able to repay debt and external capital flows out of the country. In this context, exchange rate policies are a crucial instrument to adjust trade balances, capital flows, and balance of payments disequilibria, because they can change the prices of imported and exported goods and can set incentives that either promote or limit capital flows. Consequently, exchange rate policies have been at the center of the most diverse development models, and also became a central preoccupation for neoliberal development thinkers. Making a comparison with inflation—widely recognized as one of the most daunting macroeconomic problems in nonadvanced economies—a former Brazilian minister of economy put it bluntly: "inflation cripples, but the exchange rate kills" (Bresser-Pereira 2006, xvii).

Conversely, industrial policy schemes—defined as any "government intervention to promote particular patterns of industrialization" (Kosacoff and Ramos 1999, 38)—have been key components of late and "late-late" development strategies (Gerschenkron 1962; Kurth 1979; Gereffi and Wyman 1990; Amsden 1992; Wade 1990; Auty 1994; Khan and Blankenburg 2009). In its different variants, industrial policy has a direct relation to the idea that what you produce and export critically defines your capacity to earn foreign exchange, increase productivity and wages, and promote innovative industries (Hausmann, Hwang, and Rodrik 2007; Palma 2009; Paus 2004). And although industrial policies have historically had a bias toward traditional manufacturing industries, over time they have broadened their scope to include other sectors like agriculture and services (see Ornston 2012; Thies 2014). There are a myriad of specific instruments to promote industrial policy, including expenditure-related ones such as direct subsidies and transfers as well as trade-related ones such as tariffs and nontariffs measures, not to mention tax exemptions, investment incentives, and subsidized credit (see Schrank and Kurtz 2005; Kosacoff and Ramos 1999).

Because they are policy domains that can turn key actors into winners and losers, exchange rate and industrial policies are central to my analysis—they have the potential to generate a plethora of policy preferences and political strategies. Importantly, when it comes to exchange rate and industrial policies, business is not necessarily united in favoring neoliberalism, as it is in the case of other policy domains such tax policy, fiscal policy, or even social policy (Fairfield 2015b; Hacker and Pierson 2002; see Bril-Mascarenhas and Madariaga 2019). Choosing any of these other policy domains handicap any analysis of neoliberalism because they make it easier, *a priori*, to conceive of an allied business class favoring its continuity. As we shall see in the empirical analysis below, this has indeed not always been the case, and on several occasions certain business sectors have supported alternative policies instead of neoliberal ones.

Equally important, there is no consensus among experts and the general public as to what types of exchange rate and industrial policy solutions should be preferred—particularly in the case of exchange rate policy. Contrast this with other areas of economic policy like trade, where the ideational consensus around the benefits of (relatively) free trade has led to a broad preference for it. In fact, a well known analyst of exchange rates agrees that there is no generally agreed "welfare baseline" when distinguishing between different exchange rate alternatives, which increases the probability that "exchange rate policy is *entirely* the result of political economy factors" (Frieden 2016, 8; see also Klein and Shambaugh 2009). In the case of industrial policy, while the Washington Consensus produced an important and widespread rejection of state intervention, this consensus was short-lived. By the 2000s, different variants of state assistance to economic sectors were already being approved, and the same Washington institutions that had previously ruled out industrial policy from the feasible set of options started to accept and promote different forms of state intervention and industrial policy concerns (see Bril-Mascarenhas and Madariaga 2019; Kurtz and Brooks 2008; Schrank and Kurtz 2005). Taking these two policy domains as the focus of analysis, therefore, reduces the possibility that different societal actors prefer specific policy alternatives because of a broad ideological consensus.

In order to identify which concrete exchange rate and industrial policy options lie behind the neoliberal project—and which are associated with alternatives to neoliberalism—I operationalize different policy alternatives as either contributing to neoliberal or alternative policy goals (as discussed in the literature), thereby illuminating the relationship between economic and political actors and the neoliberal policy alternatives in exchange rate and industrial policy they choose. Using Hall's (1993) distinction between policy paradigms, concrete policy alternatives, and their parameters, I identify three policy paradigms in exchange rate and industrial policies according to the degree of discretionary state intervention they allow (tables 3.1 and 3.2): neoliberal, embedded-neoliberal, and developmental (for the labels, see Bohle and Greskovits 2007; Kurtz and Brooks 2008).

Exchange rate policy alternatives strive for either price stability/credibility[3] or competitiveness (Broz and Frieden 2006; Frenkel and Rapetti 2010; Frieden, Ghezzi, and Stein 2001; Frieden 2016). Neoliberal alternatives lead to price stability and foster investment and capital flows. They include fixed exchange rates (especially when more appreciated), and floating exchange rates when combined with inflation targeting, which allows monetary discretion but commits to maintaining a low level of inflation (see Mukherjee and Singer 2008). Although fixed and flexible (pegged and floating) exchange rates are commonly understood as polar opposites, I consider them as part of the same overall goal. In fact, Milton Friedman himself viewed them as closely related policy alternatives, given their reliance on market mechanisms and underlying focus on a sole policy target: price stability (Hanke 2008). In spite of what

3. It is worth noting that no actor would reasonably seek "price instability" as a policy goal (see Bearce 2003). The choice therefore needs to be seen in the context of the trade-off between alternative policy instruments putting emphasis on different policy goals.

TABLE 3.1. Exchange Rates and Policy Goals

Policy goal (paradigm)	Policy alternatives	Description	Government discretion
Price stability (*Neoliberal*)	"Dollarization" ("euroization")	A country stops issuing its own currency and adopts a common currency with other nations or one issued by some other country.	−
	Currency board	Explicit legislative commitment to fix the nominal exchange rate at a certain parity. The authority guarantees full convertibility of foreign exchange.	
	"Tablita"	Authorities precommit the future path of the exchange rate given the expectations of evolution of the economy.	
	Free float	Commitment of the monetary authority not to intervene, leaving the nominal exchange rate to be determined by the market.	
Price stability and competitiveness (*Embedded-neoliberal*)	Crawling peg (Backward-looking)	Authorities peg the local currency to a foreign currency—or to a basket of currencies—but adjust the rate gradually over time in a series of small corrections (usually to account for past inflation).	
	Exchange rate bands or Crawling bands	Authorities set an exchange rate target and margins for exchange rate flotation, intervening to maintain a certain parity, but allowing flexibility. The margins can be adjusted over time.	
	Adjustable peg	Authorities commit to defend a particular parity but reserve the right to change it under certain circumstances, usually to maintain export competitiveness.	
National competitiveness (*Developmental*)	Managed float	Authorities are not committed to defend any particular rate, but nevertheless intervene in the market at their discretion, to maintain their desired exchange rate level.	
	Multiple exchange rates	Authorities impose restrictions on foreign exchange transactions. Different regimes and/or parities are devised according to the type of agents and operations.	+

Source: Author's elaboration based on data from Bubula and Ötker (2002), Frieden, Ghezzi and Stein (2001), Frenkel and Rapetti (2010, 11–13).

TABLE 3.2. Industrial Policy and Policy Goals

Policy goal (*paradigm*)	Policy alternatives	Description	Government discretion
"Get prices right." No market intervention or only to protect/enhance market competition (*Neoliberal*)	Neutral state	Industrial policy reduced to market regulations. The role of industrial policy is replaced by other policies like liberalization and international integration.	−
	Business-friendly	The role of industrial policy is to reduce costs, i.e. flexibility of labor markets, reduction of taxes, and other business support measures.	
"Align prices." Tackle market imperfections through functional interventions (*Embedded Neoliberal*)	Horizontal promotion	Rests on the recognition of recurrent market failures that can be specific to certain sectors (e.g., SMEs). Provision of an array of public measures understood as a common infrastructure that levels the playing field but does not privilege any sector in particular.	
	Open-economy industrial policy	Low but not necessarily uniform tariffs, fiscal and credit incentives for exports, FDI attraction, pro-export bias.	
"Alter" prices. Actively induce a pattern of industrialization through selective interventions (*Developmental*)	Developmental state	Strategic use of protectionism, selective subsidies, redistribution across economic sectors, importance of state bureaucracy.	+

Source: Author's elaboration based on Kosacoff and Ramos (1999), Román (2003), Schrank and Kurz (2005).

is commonly believed, Friedman lamented that he was seen as adamantly opposed to fixed exchange rates—a belief that he attributed to the title of his seminal article on the matter, "the case for floating exchange rates"—when in reality he viewed them as equally plausible options (Boyer 2011, 149). He opposed, on the contrary, the use of fixed-but-adjustable regimes giving discretion to governments to change the exchange rate parity.

On the other end of the policy spectrum, we find exchange rate regimes that allow precisely this: wide monetary discretion and protection against imports. These include managed flotation (especially when aimed at keeping depreciated exchange rate levels) and multiple exchange rate regimes that discriminate between different sectors, allowing authorities to decide the level of exchange rates that each sector faces (see Bradford 1990; Frenkel and Rapetti 2010). Between these two poles, so-called intermediate exchange rate regimes try to tackle both policy goals—price stability and competitiveness—at the same time (see Williamson 2002). This is the case, for example, with exchange rate bands, crawling pegs, and adjustable pegs.[4] Given that the orthodoxy has tended to highlight either fixed or floating regimes as the desirable options, I treat the adoption of intermediate regimes as a departure from neoliberal exchange rate alternatives. In fact, the common neoliberal wisdom is that monetary policy can have only one objective: price stability.

One can also follow this classification for industrial policy alternatives. Neutral or neoliberal industrial policy measures are intended to let market forces and natural competitive advantages lead economic growth by themselves. These neoliberal industrial policy alternatives can also include state efforts to regulate markets (in neoliberal terms, establishing clear rules of the game for markets to operate freely) such as sanctions for monopoly practices, or efforts to reduce costs through "business-friendly" measures. At the other end of the continuum, we find "developmental" industrial policy regimes that involve a "set of 'price distortions'—that are needed to redefine, through structural change, the path of economic growth" (ECLAC 2012, 32). These imply the selection of specific economic sectors (generally from natural-advantage primary sectors to more advanced manufacturing industries) for public investment and/or forced state redistribution. Such interventions are usually considered to be "industrial policy proper" (Chang 1996). The intermediate position (embedded-neoliberal) is characterized by policy measures intended, unlike neoliberal regimes, to tackle market failures, but without an explicit sectoral bias—in contrast to developmental regimes. Most policy measures are therefore horizontal in nature. Here we find, for example, policies aimed at correcting capital markets through the provision of competitive grants for small and medium enterprises. Under embedded-neoliberal regimes I also include what authors call "open economy industrial policy" (Schrank and Kurtz 2005) or "implicit industrial policy" (Melo 2001), which imply state preferences for certain sectors but not specific activities. An example is the

---

4. A special type of crawling-peg ("forward looking" or *tablita* in Spanish) exchange rate is closer to the policy goals and operation of a fixed exchange rate than those of intermediary regimes. See Frieden, Ghezzi, and Stein (2001).

promotion of foreign direct investment (FDI) and the attempt to channel it to R&D-intensive sectors. To this end, governments use instruments like tax exemptions, deferrals, and rebates, but do not impose additional taxation on certain activities and do not involve an explicit redistribution from one sector to another. Due to increased support to "embedded-neoliberal" industrial policies by international financial institutions and the possibility of incorporating these neutral interventions under the idea of correcting "market imperfections," I treat them not as departures from, but rather as continuations of, neoliberalism.

These exchange rate and industrial policy alternatives have been articulated in specific development models in the last decades. The neoliberal Washington Consensus (WS) development blueprint advised "getting the prices right" through market-determined exchange rates, trade liberalization, and reliance on natural comparative advantages to generate the most dynamic sectors (Williamson 1990a). Originally, the WS suggested competitive exchange rates to foster exports, stressing the need for market forces (and not state regulation) to establish the exchange rate. More often than not, however, WS-oriented politicians used fixed exchange rates as the primary component of stabilization packages preceding structural reforms (Foxley 1983; Frenkel and Rapetti 2010; Thies and Arce 2009; Schamis and Way 2003; Edwards 1995, 100–101). Through fixed exchange rate regimes, they intended to use the internal deflation adjustment process to impose monetary discipline on domestic actors in order to tame inflation and provide price stability to foster investment.

The neostructuralist theories that emerged after the demise of import substituting industrialization (ISI) agree with the WS on the importance of trade openness, but stress that "what you export matters," discarding therefore the theory of comparative advantage (Hausmann, Hwang, and Rodrik 2007; Palma 2009; Paus 2004). Accordingly, while they agree with neoliberals on the need for fiscal discipline and the maintenance of macroeconomic equilibria, they disagree on the role of exchange rate and industrial policies. They insist on exchange rate regimes that allow discretion, in order to maintain competitive exchange rate levels that favor domestic industrialization and discourage growth patterns based on nontradable sectors such as construction and finance (Ffrench-Davis 2010; Frenkel and Rapetti 2010; Bresser-Pereira, Oreiro, and Marconi 2014; Guzman, Ocampo, and Stiglitz 2018). Moreover, they try to use existing loopholes in international trade regimes to foster new types of selective industrial policy schemes (see Amsden and Hikino 2000). Following the "Great Moderation" (Allsopp and Vines 2015), when policy options turned to the neoliberal side and actual alternatives faded in key policy domains such as fiscal and monetary policy, exchange rate and industrial policies thus became crucial components of alternative development projects in the non-advanced world.

Conceptualizing the Support for Neoliberalism—and Its Alternatives

Diverse authors have attempted to categorize and describe the actors who championed and defended neoliberalism. Scholars have not always agreed in their analyses. One camp is society-centered: they emphasize the types of societal actors behind neoliberal projects, usually business as a class or particular segments of it, sometimes—but not always—in conjunction with the institutional incentive structures these actors face in advancing their interests (Harvey 2007; Frieden 1991a; Etchemendy 2012; E. Silva 1996). The other camp is state centered: they emphasize either the autonomy of state bureaucracies, particularly economic technocrats, as agents of change (Teichman 2001; Maron and Shalev 2017), or the characteristics of the politicians and political parties steering these processes (Murillo 2009; Stokes 2001; Flores-Macías 2012). Evidence is mixed: while some authors point to the usual suspects—the financial sector and the political right—as standard bearers of neoliberalism, others highlight third-way social democracy and business at large, while some draw attention to generalized sentiments among the public (see, among others, Baker 2009; Stokes 2001). How can we reconceptualize the actors providing support and opposition to neoliberalism? And can we find common categories to refer to them?

Since David Ricardo and Karl Marx, analyzing the formation of coalitions in capitalist societies depends on understanding how economic structures shape interest groups with differing political demands that are represented in a variety of ways by political parties and governments. As Haggard and Kaufman put it: "The analysis of socioeconomic structure is crucial for identifying politically relevant groups and their policy preferences, and for understanding political alignments and conflicts" (Haggard and Kaufman 1995, 6; see Gourevitch 1986; Frieden 1991b; Shafer 1994).

Using this as a starting point, this chapter links policy preferences for exchange rates and industrial policy to actors' positions in the economic structure and to right- or left-wing political parties. Although purely interest-based theories have been heavily criticized (e.g., B. R. Schneider 2004a; Geddes 1994; Woll 2008), they remain an important analytical tool to find common patterns of policy support, linking economic and political actors. Importantly, this book acknowledges the critiques while distancing itself from the most relevant shortcomings of these theories, namely, the fixed character of interests as opposed to the more malleable and context-sensitive actual policy preferences (e.g., Woll 2008; Münnich 2011; Kingstone 2001; Vogel 1999), their inability to capture the "political" construction of business (Martin and Swank 2012) and their lack of consideration for the concrete channels by which business influences policy (Geddes 1994; B. R. Schneider 2004a; Fairfield 2015a).

In line with these critiques, I conceive of preference and coalition formation as a complex process of interest aggregation and representation. I claim that the coalitions pursuing a development project form longer-term alliances that can be better captured under the concept of *social blocs*. Contemporary readings of Gramsci and Poulantzas have reintroduced this concept in an effort to capture the particular role of political parties as mediators between conflicting economic interests, and a public policy formula as the outcome of this compromise (see Amable 2017; Amable and Palombarini 2009). This conceptualization highlights the dual character of the state and its relative autonomy from the capitalist class: on the one hand, the state has a strong connection and reliance on particular business interests, but on the other, it is autonomous from them because politicians are also driven by reelection incentives (see, among others, Culpepper 2010; Fairfield 2015b; Hacker and Pierson 2002, 2010).[5] Business interests and policy preferences are more often than not "political" constructions: that is, they emerge in the process of identity formation, collective action, and negotiation of an array of societal actors giving specific policy content to basic economic interests (see Martin and Swank 2012). Moreover, the interests of economic actors are not directly translated into public policy because both political leaders and state bureaucracies have their own interests, and enjoy diverse degrees of autonomy for

5. For the original discussion, see Block (1984), Laclau (1975), Lindblom (1982), and O'Connor (1973).

pursuing them. In chapter 4 I delve deeper into these processes, while in chapters 5 to 7, I analyze the concrete mechanisms enhancing or inhibiting the power resources of different actors and social blocs, focusing on three arenas that act as channels of their interests: coalition formation, political representation, and policymaking.

To operationalize the relationship between economic structures and policy preferences under these grounds, I argue that interests need not be fixed and that we can gain flexibility by changing their definition. In fact, the fixed character of interests is closely related to how they are defined. For example, if one defines interests as protectionist or liberal in terms of whether the assets of companies in an economic sector are respectively fixed or fluid, those business sectors will be treated as always having the same interests unless they switch their assets. Therefore, it is usually assumed that manufacturing sectors tend to be protectionists because they cannot move their fixed assets in the short run (Steinberg 2015; Frieden 1991b). The same thing happens if the distinction is made based on the effects of international trade (tradable versus nontradable sectors) or even with other more fine-grained definitions: concrete companies or whole economic sectors inside each category are assigned to a fixed preference based on their presumed economic interest (see Gourevitch 1986; Shafer 1994). Therefore, when authors find different policy preferences in their study or when they find preference change, they disregard interest-based accounts.

However, if we allow for variation of interests inside broadly defined sectors over time and across contexts, we can overcome the immobility of purely interest-based accounts and at the same time, offer a common starting ground to understand the business bases of support for neoliberalism. As Steinberg argues, "preferences are not constant but they are coherent" (2015, 10). I offer therefore a modified version of interest-based theories, one taking into account the possibility of changes of interests over time and across countries, and that offers a common characterization of business actors participating in coalitions striving for different development projects.

I define three business sectors that may have varying preferences and whose economic power is crucial to understanding the behavior of the policies under study: *financial*, (*internationally*) *competitive*, and (*internationally*) *noncompetitive*.[6] However, contrary to interest-based theories, I define empirically which

6. Two other business sectors that could have been included are construction and public

specific economic sectors are competitive and noncompetitive. This means that the same sector can change its policy preferences from one moment to the next as the economic situation changes or as the sector anticipates how economic policy will affect it.

I calculate an index of revealed comparative advantages (RCA)—which captures the share of one country's exports relative to those of the world—for Agriculture, Mining, and subclassifications of Manufacturing, and then re-aggregate the respective sectors based on whether they demonstrate comparative advantage (competitive) or not (noncompetitive). [7] This means that the specific economic sectors that are internationally competitive (or not) differ between countries and over time, and changes in the international economy therefore may stimulate preference change by affecting their expectations of becoming competitive or not (see Kurtz and Brooks 2008).[8] Tables 3.3 and 3.4 detail the result of the RCA analysis and, therefore, what sectors are classified as competitive and noncompetitive in each country, taking average scores for each decade. Competitive sector are those that show an RCA index greater than 1.

---

utilities. Although the link between construction and the international economy—through finance—seems readily evident after the 2007–2008 financial crisis, it was much weaker in non-advanced political economies before the 2000s. Then, it was often more related to the dynamic of domestic demand, and it developed an intimate relation with domestic companies producing intermediate goods for the sector. Conversely, the public utilities sector has become the target of strong privatization and FDI inflows. However, the sector also has a strong connection with domestic demand and was previously closely associated with state ownership as an "'outer skin' of the welfare state" (Obinger and Zohlnhöfer 2007, 184).

7. Unlike the original purpose of RCA indexes, I use this as a methodological tool to classify economic sectors and infer their policy preferences, not to make policy recommendations based on countries' alleged "natural" comparative advantages. For further reading and research that uses RCA for similar purposes, see Vollrath (1991); M. R. Schneider and Paunescu (2012). I used two-digit classifications based on the International Standard Industry Classification (ISIC) Rev.3 system, and calculated the Balassa index for simplicity because it is widely used in the literature on international trade and export specialization. For details see the online appendix in http://www.aldomadariaga.com.

8. This is consistent with several of the critiques to pure interest-based accounts of policy preferences that highlight how actors strategically update their preferences by anticipating future scenarios (e.g., Kingstone 2001).

TABLE 3-3. Argentina and Chile, RCA Index, Competitive and Noncompetitive Sectors

Sector name	ISIC Codes Rev.3	ISIC Codes Rev.2	Argentina 1980s	Argentina 1990s	Argentina 2000s	Argentina 2010s	Chile 1980s	Chile 1990s	Chile 2000s	Chile 2010s
Agriculture, forestry, and fishing	A-B	1	6.2*	5.7*	5.9*	5.8*	2.3*	4.0*	4.3*	3.2*
Mining	C	2	0.1	1.2*	1.2*	0.6	2.0*	2.5*	2.1*	2.0*
Food and beverages	D15-16	31	3.7*	4.9*	5.7*	5.7	1.8*	2.0*	1.8*	1.3*
Textiles	D17-18-19	32	1.3	1.0	0.7	0.4	0.1	0.2	0.2	0.2
Wood and paper	D20-21-22	33-34	0.2	0.4	0.6	0.5	2.0*	2.5*	3.0*	2.7*
Petroleum and fuels	D23	353-354	1.1*	1.7*	1.5*	0.7	0.1	0.1	0.5	0.1
Chemicals	D24	351-352	0.6	0.6	0.7	0.3	0.3	0.4	0.5	0.4
Rubber and plastics	D25	355-356	0.2	0.3	0.5	0.4	0.1	0.3	0.4	0.4
Nonmetallic minerals	D26	36	0.3	0.4	0.3	0.3	0.2	0.2	0.2	0.1
Basic metals	D27	37	1.1*	0.8	0.8	0.8	7.1*	6.3*	5.8*	5.8*
Fabricated metals	D28	381	0.2	0.3	0.2	0.2	0.1	0.2	0.2	0.2
Machinery and equipment	D29	382	0.2	0.2	0.3	0.3	0.0	0.0	0.1	0.1
Electrical appliances	D20-31-32-33	383-385	0.1	0.1	0.1	0.1	0.0	0.0	0.0	0.0
Transport equipment	D34-35	384	0.2	0.5	0.7	1.2	0.0	0.1	0.1	0.1
Furniture and other	D36	39	0.0	0.2	0.2	0.0	0.0	0.2	0.1	0.0
Other	D37	41	0.0	0.2	1.6*	0.4	0.0	0.0	0.0	0.0

Source: Author's elaboration based on data from World Integrated Trade Solution (WITS) database.

Note: Competitive sectors are marked with an asterisk *. To determine competitive sectors in Argentina and Chile during the 1970s, I deducted sectoral RCA from the RCA of specific products and from product export concentrations in preceding and subsequent periods using the Standard International Trade Classification (SITC). This is because the sector-level ISIC Rev.2 classification does not cover the 1970s and the ISIC Rev.1 classification, which does, is way too incompatible with later sector families. The result of the exercise is that leading products by RCA and export concentration in the 1970s period were practically the same as for the 1980s period; therefore I repeat the 1980s classification of competitive and noncompetitive for the 1970s. There were only two exceptions to this, namely, the product families of "textiles" and "basic metals" in Argentina. The RCA index for textiles in Argentina decreases markedly from the 1970s to the 1980s, as do their share in top exports. However, despite this fall, the sectoral RCA index is 1.2 in the 1980s, and products such as textile fibers and leather manufactures remain among the top export products, with about 7% of total exports. Therefore, I consider textiles to be competitive in the 1970s and 1980s periods in Argentina. In the case of basic metals, the product family makes a huge leap from the 1970s to the 1980s; related products' RCA index jump three times (just above 1.0) and its share in total exports grows two times, to above 5 percent. In spite of this, at the sectoral level, basic metals are barely competitive in the 1980s according to the RCA index (1.1). Therefore, I consider this sector to be noncompetitive in the 1970s.

TABLE 3.4. Estonia and Poland, RCA Index, Competitive and Noncompetitive Sectors

Sector name	ISIC Codes Rev.3	ISIC Codes Rev.2	Estonia 1980s	Estonia 1990s	Estonia 2000s	Estonia 2010s	Poland 1980s	Poland 1990s	Poland 2000s	Poland 2010s
Agriculture, forestry and fishing	A-B	1	–	2.0*	2.0*	1.7*	1.6*	1.3*	0.7	0.7
Mining	C	2	–	0.1	0.1	0.1	9.0*	2.3*	0.2	0.1
Food and beverages	D15-16	31	–	1.6*	1.3*	1.3*	1.5*	1.6*	1.5*	1.8*
Textiles	D17-18-19	32	–	1.5*	1.4*	1.1*	0.2	1.1*	0.9	0.7
Wood and paper	D20-21-22	33-34	–	2.3*	3.9*	4.3*	0.0	1.3	2.0	2.1
Petroleum and fuels	D23	353-354	–	1.5*	1.8*	2.3*	0.2	0.7	0.6	0.8
Chemicals	D24	351-352	–	0.7	0.5	0.5	1.3*	0.8	0.4	0.4
Rubber and plastics	D25	355-356	–	0.7	1.4*	1.8*	0.5	1.0	2.0*	2.3*
Nonmetallic minerals	D26	36	–	1.2*	1.5*	1.6*	2.2*	2.7*	2.0*	1.8*
Basic metals	D27	37	–	0.5	0.6	0.6	0.4	2.0*	1.2*	1.1*
Fabricated metals	D28	381	–	1.2*	1.7*	1.6*	0.0	1.5*	2.2*	1.9*
Machinery and equipment	D29	382	–	0.3	0.4	0.7	0.2	0.3	0.6	0.8
Electrical appliances	D20-31-32-33	383-385	–	0.7	1.3*	1.1*	0.1	0.4	0.8	0.9
Transport equipment	D34-35	384	–	0.4	0.5	0.5	0.0	0.6	1.6*	1.6*
Furniture and other	D36	39	–	1.2*	1.7*	1.6*	0.0	1.5*	2.2*	1.8*
Other	D37	41	–	107.6*	4.6*	6.7*	0.0	1.9*	2.5*	1.7*

Source: Author's elaboration based on data from World Integrated Trade Solution (WITS) database.

Note: Competitive sectors are marked with an asterisk.

The Politics of Neoliberal Exchange Rate and Industrial Policies: A Quantitative Analysis

A first step to understand the connection between different societal actors and particular combinations of exchange rate and industrial policies is a quantitative analysis using time series cross-section data of the four countries under study.

The explanatory variable of interest is the power of different economic sectors, translated in this case as their capacity to make governments supply the kind of policies that they prefer. Scholars have used different variables as measures of business power, including capital mobility, volume of sales, profits, value generated, and size and market strength (Fairfield 2015a, 415). Every measure has its own strengths and weaknesses and captures specific aspects of the phenomenon. Measures of capital mobility, such as capital account openness and foreign investment, are particularly good at capturing the structural power of business in terms of capital flight, while others associated with market share and size are better at capturing that power in terms of economic growth and employment. Given the objectives of this chapter, I use the latter: specifically, the market share/size of the financial, competitive and noncompetitive sectors as measured in national accounts data. These data have been widely used as indicators of economic sectors' economic power (see Frieden, Ghezzi and Stein 2001; Frieden, Leblang, and Valev 2010; Steinberg 2015), and have a quality that make them particularly suitable for this analysis, namely, their availability in historical series as well as detailed sectoral disaggregation, which allows for more fine-grained treatment of individual economic sectors.

As independent variables for the regression analysis I use therefore the share of each sector, Competitive, Noncompetitive, and Financial, on GDP (value added). The data spans 1970 to 2015 in Argentina and Chile, and 1990 to 2015 in Estonia and Poland.[9] In addition, I use partisanship as an explanatory variable in connection with the power of different economic sectors. Given that we are working with only four countries and a limited number of observations, the data are deeply sensitive to idiosyncratic political conditions. Therefore, I construct an indicator based on two databases that use analogous data sources—namely, a wide array of documentation, and country expert consultations—and that provide reliable assessments of region-specific

---

9. For a description of data sources as well as an explanation of how time-series data were compiled, see the online appendix at http://www.aldomadariaga.com.

political-ideological positions. The dataset for Latin America is that of Murillo, Oliveros and Vaishnav (2010), extended by Murillo and Visconti (2017), and for Eastern Europe the Comparative Political Data Set (CPDS) elaborated by Armingeon and colleagues (2018). I recoded the data to fit a right (1), center (2), and left (3) classification, considering "right" and "left" the center-right and center-left categories respectively. The Argentinean and Chilean dictatorships, not present in these datasets, were coded as right-wing.

In turn, I show the specific analysis for each of the two dependent variables: exchange rates and industrial policy.

Exchange Rates

I conduct two analyses for this variable, one for the exchange rate regime (the rules affecting the behavior of the exchange rate) and one for exchange rate level (the actual parity of the exchange rate with respect to other currencies), because preferences for the two may vary (see Broz and Frieden 2006). A correlation between them reveals that the relation between exchange rate regime and level among these four countries is low (0.31), and therefore they represent two distinct variables.

For the dependent variable, *exchange rate regime*, there are two classifications: *de jure* (those reported by countries to the IMF) or *de facto* (exchange rate regimes derived from key macroeconomic variables). I use the IMF de jure classification as reported by Ilzetzki, Reinhart and Rogoff (2017; see Bubula and Ötker 2002), because de jure classifications are more useful when analyzing government intentions and actions (Klein and Shambaugh 2009, 38).

Following table 3.1 above, I recoded the IMF de jure exchange rate classification into a binary variable taking the value of 1 if the underlying objective is "price stability" and 0 if it is national "competitiveness." I included intermediate regimes in the latter category due to their association with more heterodox exchange rate management. Table 3.5 shows summary statistics for the variable exchange rate regime.

I estimate a linear model (OLS) to capture the relation between the variables of interest. Although the variable "exchange rate regime" is binary, and therefore using a nonlinear model would be *ex ante* more appropriate for estimating the parameters of the regression, the literature has concluded that these models present methodological shortcomings when trying to control for endogeneity and serial correlation, which are crucial in time-series data (Greene 2004; Wooldridge 2002). Therefore, even when having a binary dependent

TABLE 3.5. Summary Statistics, Exchange Rate Regime (IMF Definition)

	1970s	1980s	1990s	2000s	2010s	1970–2015
Argentina						
Mean	.6	.2	1	.2	0	.43478
Sd	(.5163978)	(.421637)	(.0)	(.421637)	(.0)	(.5012063)
Chile						
Mean	.4	.2	0	1	1	.47826
Sd	(.5163978)	(.421637)	(.0)	(.0)	(.0)	(.505047)
Estonia						
Mean	—	—	1	1	1	1
Sd	—	—	(.0)	(.0)	(.0)	(.0)
Poland						
Mean	—	.2	1	1	.69231	.2
Sd	—	(.421637)	(.0)	(.0)	(.4706787)	(.421637)

Source: Author's elaboration based on data from International Monetary Fund (IMF).

variable, the utilization of a linear-probability OLS model has several advantages over a nonlinear model, particularly when it is not used for prediction. In addition, I use robust standard errors and explanatory variables that are lagged one year, which further control for these problems.[10]

Table 3.6 shows regression results for the variable exchange rate regime using country and year fixed effects. Following the literature, model I includes three controls: GDP growth (rate), inflation (GDP deflator), the trade balance (percentage of GDP). With these controls, I try to confirm the hypothesis that authorities adopt exchange rate regimes not just as a response to the specific economic situation their country faces, but also following the power and preferences of economic sectors. Model II includes an additional control, namely, the degree of central bank independence (CBI). There is a growing literature showing that the choice of exchange rate regime and the CBI may interact and that fixed exchange rate regimes and CBI are used as alternative monetary anchors (Bodea 2010, 2014; Bernhard, Broz, and Clark 2002). I use a version of the Cukierman index expanded by Bodea and Hicks (2015) to cover additional countries and years.

Models I, II, and III show that changes in the economic power of the Competitive sector positively and significantly affect the adoption of

10. For further details, other model specifications and robustness checks, see the online appendix in http://www.aldomadariaga.com.

TABLE 3.6. Regression Results, Exchange Rate Regime, Sectoral Power and Partisanship

	Exchange rate regime orientation 1=Price stability; 0=Competitiveness		
	(I)	(II)	(III)
Competitive sectors	7.749*	7.590*	7.181**
	(2.728)	(2.445)	(1.368)
Noncompetitive sectors	2.459	3.580	1.583
	(2.310)	(1.738)	(0.811)
Financial sectors	20.32	26.39*	23.71**
	(10.34)	(9.915)	(6.743)
GDP growth	2.034	1.900	1.443
	(1.303)	(0.929)	(0.777)
Inflation	0.000674**	0.000860***	0.000959***
	(0.000121)	(0.000129)	(5.96e-05)
External balance	−0.0145	−0.00724	−0.00294
	(0.0174)	(0.0107)	(0.00781)
CBI		1.711*	1.994***
		(0.663)	(0.302)
Partisanship=Right			0.684**
			(0.152)
Partisanship=Left			0.398
			(0.187)
Constant	−3.620	−5.184*	−5.301**
	(2.264)	(1.892)	(0.955)
Observations	119	114	111
R-squared	0.558	0.636	0.764
Countries	4	4	4
Year FE	YES	YES	YES
Country FE	YES	YES	YES

Robust standard errors in parentheses.
*** $p<0.01$, ** $p<0.05$, * $p<0.1$

price-stability–driven exchange rate (ER) regimes. Model II shows that controlling for CBI, a growing power of the Financial sector also increases the probability of adopting price-stability–driven ER regimes. Finally, Model III shows that controlling for partisanship, both Competitive and Financial sectors are associated with neoliberal ER. Model III also shows the effects of a deviation from the political center to the right and to the left on the choice of exchange rate regime. As we can see, moving from the center to the right significantly increases the chances of adopting a price-stability-oriented exchange rate regime, while moving to the left shows no significant results. Meanwhile, coefficients for the Noncompetitive sector remain small and nonsignificant

TABLE 3.7. Summary Statistics, Rodrik Index of Undervaluation

	1970s	1980s	1990s	2000s	2010s	1970–2010
Argentina						
Mean	−.2255868	−.3217074	−.5644011	.2103964	.1013151	−.175613
Sd	.145598	.0955779	.33404	.0693633	.251427	.3390424
Chile						
Mean	.1449255	.1151259	.0019272	.0398448	−.000703	.0623562
Sd	.1412644	.1118611	.1365537	.0497424	.1677008	.1506083
Estonia						
Mean	—	—	.2488155	−.2176788	−.1949408	−.0390081
Sd	—	—	.1960266	.235641	.0396095	.289087
Poland						
Mean	.0806613	.2065814	.3136584	−.0325624	.0943287	.1361528
Sd	.1324649	.1387045	.1235082	.0951289	.0542625	.1659463

Source: Author's elaboration based on Penn World Tables 9.1 (Feenstra, Inklaar, and Timmer 2015).

across the three models. Although statistical significance is relatively weak due to the small N, effects are large—especially for the Financial Sector—and the results are consistent throughout different alternative specifications of the model and robustness checks.[11]

The second analysis studies the effects of the power of business sectors on the *exchange rate level*. To construct this variable, I calculated the index of exchange rate undervaluation elaborated by Rodrik (2008). This index uses data from the Penn World Tables 9.1 (Feenstra, Inklaar, and Timmer 2015) on GDP per capita, purchasing power parities (PPP), and real exchange rates to measure the divergence of the real exchange rate from an estimated equilibrium real exchange rate, showing its under- or over-valuation. This index has been used by other studies analyzing the effects of the weight of economic sectors on the exchange rate level (e.g., Steinberg 2015). Table 3.7 shows descriptive statistics for this variable and figure 3.1 a graphical representation.

I regress this index on our explanatory variables of interest (sector economic power and partisanship) using the same model specifications and controls as above. The coefficients should be interpreted as follows: negative coefficients indicate that the independent variables have the effect of lowering, that is, appreciating, the exchange rate level with respect to the equilibrium real exchange rate, while positive values indicate a depreciation of the real exchange rate with respect to the equilibrium rate.

11. For details, see online appendix in http://www.aldomadariaga.com

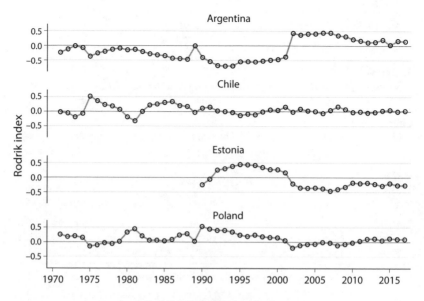

FIGURE 3.1. Rodrik Index of Undervaluation 1970–2015
Source: Author's elaboration based on data from Penn World Tables 9.1
(Feenstra, Inklaar and Timmer 2015).
Notes: Higher values correspond to higher real exchange rate=depreciated exchange rate;
Lower values correspond to lower real exchange rate=appreciated exchange rate.

Table 3.8 summarizes the results of the regression analysis. Models I and II show negative coefficients for the Competitive sector, linking this sector to the adoption of more appreciated (neoliberal) exchange rate levels. Controlling for partisanship (model III), the Competitive and the Financial sectors are significantly associated with neoliberal exchange rates. Interestingly in this case an association also appears between Noncompetitive sectors and neoliberal ER. Model III also shows that, everything else constant, partisanship has no effect on the level of the ER. Again, although relatively weak in terms of statistical significance, the effects are large and remain robust to alternative specifications of the model and robustness checks.

Overall, the analyses for exchange rates are consistent with the literature, which expects that fixed exchange rates and overvalued levels facilitate the acquisition and sale of assets overseas and preserve monetary stability, and are therefore associated with finance and exports (Broz and Frieden 2006; Frieden 1991b; Frieden, Leblang, and Valev 2010; Frieden 2016). At the same time, the stronger association between competitive sectors and exchange rate regimes over exchange rate levels may be because different industries (whether based on commodity exports and resource-based manufactures, or producing more

TABLE 3.8. Regression Results, Exchange Rate Level, Sectoral Power and Partisanship

	Rodrik index		
	(I)	(II)	(III)
Competitive sectors	−4.492[*]	−4.488[*]	−7.123[**]
	(1.811)	(1.829)	(1.819)
Noncompetitive sectors	−1.625	−2.338	−3.707[*]
	(1.220)	(1.148)	(1.433)
Financial sectors	−8.369	−11.83	−20.02[**]
	(5.357)	(5.200)	(5.137)
GDP growth	−0.501	−0.342	−1.142
	(0.488)	(0.299)	(0.579)
Inflation rate	−0.000351[**]	−0.000453[***]	−0.000541[***]
	(6.76e-05)	(7.52e-05)	(7.86e-05)
External balance	0.0271[***]	0.0282[*]	0.0300[**]
	(0.00406)	(0.00914)	(0.00745)
CBI		−0.949[***]	−1.201[***]
		(0.132)	(0.163)
Partisanship =Right			−0.0841
			(0.151)
Partisanship =Left			0.0721
			(0.0401)
Constant	2.420	3.148	4.416[**]
	(1.347)	(1.503)	(1.142)
Observations	122	115	112
R-squared	0.388	0.512	0.642
Countries	4	4	4
Year FE	YES	YES	YES
Country FE	YES	YES	YES

Note: Robust standard errors in parentheses.
*** $p<0.01$, ** $p<0.05$, * $p<0.1$.

complex products) generate differences with respect to the preferences on exchange rate *level* but not necessarily for exchange rate *regime* (see Broz and Frieden 2006). Furthermore, the analysis presents an important result with respect to noncompetitive sectors. According to the literature, intermediate and developmental exchange rate regimes tend to be associated with depreciated levels that both shelter domestic sectors from imports and boost exporters' gains in domestic currency (Frenkel and Rapetti 2008; Guzmán, Ocampo, and Stiglitz 2018). However, our analyses do not show a strong association between noncompetitive sectors and either developmental exchange rate regimes or depreciated exchange rate levels. To the contrary, it shows a mild association between noncompetitive sectors and more appreciated exchange rate levels when controlling for partisanship. I come back to this below in this chapter.

In terms of partisanship, we also found an association between right-wing parties providing price-stability-oriented exchange rate regimes, but not necessarily at particular levels. This is consistent with the literature which has found that the right favors fixed exchange rate regimes as well as more appreciated levels that ease the pressure on monetary policy and foster price stability and purchasing power, or alternatively, free floats that can work as nominal anchors within an inflation-targeting framework (Mukherjee and Singer 2008; Broz and Frieden 2006, 592; Frieden, Ghezzi, and Stein 2001; Bodea 2014). In addition, our analyses found no association with left-wing parties. This contrasts with the literature, which finds that left-leaning parties tend to prefer exchange rate regimes that allow monetary discretion, as well as undervalued levels that allow sheltering domestic producers from imports (thereby expanding employment), and flexible or intermediate regimes allowing the use of domestic monetary policy (Berdiev, Kim, and Chang 2012; Broz and Frieden 2006, 592; Steinberg 2010).

Industrial Policy

The second dependent variable of interest is industrial policy; I use data on public expenditure on economic affairs, following Obinger and Zöhlnhofer (2007), as a proxy.[12] This includes capital and current expenditure (including subsidies and transfers) directed to economic sectors. The indicator covers the central government level and is expressed as a percentage of GDP. This measure is limited because it does not distinguish between expenditure in horizontal (i.e., neutral) or vertical instruments, ignores public enterprises or expenditure outside the central government, and disregards tax expenditure (expenditures from tax exemptions instead of actual disbursement of resources).[13] As Esping-Andersen (1990) has noted, in an analysis of state involvement in public policy absolute levels of expenditure are less important

12. I also tried using data capturing the dispersion of tariff rates. However, comparable data for the countries under study are available only from 1992 onwards, and for Estonia and Poland they ceased to be available after their incorporation to the EU in 2004. Therefore, the analysis dropped the number of observations to less than half with an overwhelming presence of the South American countries in the sample.

13. The fact that it does not distinguish between capital and current expenditure is less problematic. For example, Kurtz and Brooks privilege this wider expenditure measure in order to "capture the broadest range of state fiscal interventions" (2008, 253).

than the content of the respective policies. This indicator should therefore be taken as a rough indicator of industrial policy efforts by central governments. However, there are also advantages of using this indicator, notably, that it is among the few measures available in time-series format for an important part of the analyzed period and which has a comparable basis. In my qualitative analysis of industrial policy (chapter 4), I use different kinds of information in order to expand the present analysis.

I regress the industrial policy indicator (expenditure on economic affairs as a percentage of GDP) on the three independent variables (sectoral economic power) and use inflation and GDP growth as controls. In addition, I add a measure of central government total expenditure (percentage of GDP) (model I), a measure of central bank independence (CBI) (model II), and a measure of gross domestic savings (percentage of GDP) (model III). The first is used to control for overall expenditure patterns, which could affect a government's expenditure in industrial policy.[14] The latter two are used to control for institutional and financial constraints on public expenditure, respectively. Due to the relation between fiscal deficits and inflation, CBI has been found to be strongly related with lower levels of expenditure (Bodea and Higashijima 2017). Conversely, domestic savings may have different effects on expenditure patterns: on the one hand, higher savings may offer resources for higher expenditure; on the other hand, higher savings may reflect a preoccupation with fiscal deficits and relate to conservative expenditure patterns (see the related experience of fiscal spending rules in chapter 7). Finally, model IV includes partisanship. Table 3.9 shows results for the variables of interest, using the same model specifications as above (OLS regression, robust standard errors, lagged regressors, country and year fixed effects).

Model I shows an important relationship between lower spending in industrial policy and Financial and Competitive sector power, in that order. Model II confirms these results, although adding a twist: when controlling for institutional constraints, the Noncompetitive sector is found to support higher industrial policy efforts. Models III and IV confirm this result controlling for financial constraints on expenditure and for partisanship. The Financial sector is strongly associated with lower levels of industrial policy expenditure, while the Noncompetitive sector is associated with higher levels of industrial policy expenditure, particularly when controlling for institutional and financial constraints. The effect of the Competitive sector on industrial policy spending, on

14. External debt and fiscal deficit statistics were not available for all countries/periods in the sample.

TABLE 3.9. Regression Results, Industrial Policy, Sectoral Power, and Partisanship

	Expenditure in economic affairs			
	(I)	(II)	(III)	(IV)
Competitive sectors	−0.137**	−0.106**	−0.0865*	−0.00273
	(0.0317)	(0.0276)	(0.0365)	(0.0266)
Noncompetitive sectors	0.0145	0.0579*	0.0657*	0.120**
	(0.0214)	(0.0184)	(0.0273)	(0.0352)
Financial sectors	−0.476**	−0.376**	−0.492**	−0.243**
	(0.105)	(0.0810)	(0.146)	(0.0758)
GDP growth	0.0137	0.0112	0.0366*	0.0536***
	(0.00953)	(0.0149)	(0.0120)	(0.00800)
Inflation	5.29e-06**	3.30e-06	3.31e-06	2.65e-06
	(1.33e-06)	(1.73e-06)	(2.09e-06)	(1.99e-06)
Total gov. expenditure	0.166**	0.133*	0.118	0.101
	(0.0519)	(0.0441)	(0.0618)	(0.0620)
CBI		−0.0122		
		(0.00595)		
Gross national savings			−0.00116**	−0.00128**
			(0.000344)	(0.000374)
Partisanship=Right				−0.00208
				(0.00156)
Partisanship=Left				−0.00607**
				(0.00172)
Constant	0.123*	0.0870**	0.128*	0.0997**
	(0.0445)	(0.0237)	(0.0497)	(0.0227)
Observations	118	112	118	114
R-squared	0.834	0.863	0.863	0.903
Countries	4	4	4	4
Year FE	YES	YES	YES	YES
Country FE	YES	YES	YES	YES

Note: Robust standard errors in parentheses.
*** $p<0.01$, ** $p<0.05$, * $p<0.1$.

the other hand, loses strength and significance when controlling for partisanship. Finally, in terms of partisanship, it is the left which is more associated with lower levels of spending and the right shows no effects.

These results are consistent with the literature in terms of sectoral support. The general view is that internationally Noncompetitive sectors tend to be protectionists and that state interventions have been usually directed to these sectors (see Khan and Blankenburg 2009; Auty 1994; Gourevitch 1986; Kurth 1979). In terms of partisanship, however, the results do not follow the literature, which argues that right-wing governments are associated with lower industrial policy efforts, while the opposite is true for left-leaning parties (Obinger and Zohlnhöfer 2007; Camyar 2014). Kurtz and Brooks (2008) provide a possible solution to this conundrum: they argue that higher state expenditure on industry protection can be associated with right-wing governments because they more often than not have business among their constituencies. Moreover, they argue that the presence of a strong labor movement decreases the willingness of the right to supply such policies, but it increases the left's willingness to do so. This resonates with our qualitative analysis in chapter 4.

In the end, the regression analysis shows that economically stronger Financial and Competitive sectors are associated with the adoption of price-stability-oriented exchange rate regimes and more appreciated exchange rate levels. Both are, moreover, associated with reductions of industrial policy efforts—particularly the Financial sector. This has key implications for the formation of longer-term neoliberal social blocs between these two business sectors and right-wing parties, which were found to be associated precisely with neoliberal policies. Importantly, the noncompetitive sector appears to be associated with more comprehensive industrial policy when controlling for financial and institutional constraints on expenditure, but with more appreciated (neoliberal) exchange rate levels. Meanwhile, left-leaning governments are associated with reductions in industrial policy. This indicates chances for neoliberal coalitions led both by right- and left-leaning parties with different policy emphases and diverse business support, and difficulties for the constitution of a non-neoliberal coalition supporting alternative political projects.

The Noncompetitive Sector in Context

The fact that the noncompetitive sector is not associated with developmental exchange rates and only under specific circumstances with industrial policy alternatives seems to suggest that the preferences of this sector are sensitive to the context. In other words, depending on different contexts, the noncompetitive sector might either support or oppose neoliberalism. This result seems key to understanding the conditions under which challenges to, and departures from, neoliberalism can occur. I will explore the implications of this result more closely in chapters 4 and 5. For the present, I will detail the elements of the context that could produce preference change among the sector's firms, either in support or in opposition to neoliberalism.

First, the predominance of domestic versus foreign ownership of the companies in the sector matters. Financial integration and the development of financial markets have fostered capital mobility, making it easier for investors to get out of a particular sector (Frieden 1991b, 443). Research on exchange rates and foreign investment, for example, has found that, independent of the sector they are in, multinational corporations (MNCs) prefer exchange rate regimes that make cross-border transactions easier and maintain the value of the currency for remittances to parent companies, particularly fixed exchange rates at overvalued levels—that is, neoliberal exchange rate alternatives (Frieden, Leblang, and Valev 2010; Frieden 1991b). Conversely, foreign capital through FDI has historically been seen to provide host countries with increased technology and management skills. While MNCs look for market access, location, and efficiency—that is, locational advantages that reduce costs—host countries expect that MNCs will allow a sort of shortcut to industrial and structural upgrading (Hunya 1998).

Although several authors underscore that higher FDI in Eastern Europe has led to more diverse types of assistance and incentive packages, such packages still qualify as "embedded-neoliberal" industrial policy. They do not necessarily constitute a departure from neoliberalism in our classification (see Drahokoupil 2009; Bohle and Greskovits 2012). More generally, from a global value chain perspective, the fact that multinational companies look for different types of locational advantages, including favorable policies, is not surprising (Gereffi 1995; Dicken 2010). In spite of this, multinationals have a stronger preference for decreased state intervention in industrial policy than domestic firms do, because of the higher costs and reduced benefits they accrue (Milner 1989). Moreover, there is evidence that higher FDI presence increases the productivity of domestic firms, making them more competitive both internally and externally and, therefore, less eager for state promotion/protection (see Javorcik 2004).

Research on business organization also shows that foreign companies often either seek direct relations with domestic governments or form their own business associations, thereby weakening the organizational power of domestic firms. For Eastern Europe, several authors have directly linked the transnationalization of Eastern European firms to the underlying political weakness of domestically-owned ones (Schoenman 2005, 2014; McMenamin 2004; Nölke and Vliegenthart 2009; Adam, Kristan, and Tomšič 2009). Schneider (2013) finds a similar situation in Latin America. In such cases, the existence of multinational companies is directly linked to the low organizational power of domestic businesses and their personal ties to governments. It is not far-fetched to expect that, when foreign capital enters noncompetitive sectors, these links not only reduce the sector's overall preference for industrial policy, but also make the sector less vocal and effective in demanding industrial policy measures. This was particularly the case in Estonia, where foreign ownership resulted in fewer business demands for a more developmental alternative (see chapters 4 and 5). I refer to this as the "silencing" of business demands.

A second explanation for the lack of expected results on the preferences of the noncompetitive sector, particularly for a competitiveness-oriented exchange rate, is that the threat of competition from foreign companies is just one consideration informing their exchange rate preferences. As a number of authors have stressed, the reliance of these firms on intermediate inputs and the resultant effect on their balance sheets influences their preference for overvalued exchange rate levels, which make imports cheaper (Steinberg 2015; Egan 2017; Walter 2008). This implies that noncompetitive sectors would be less inclined to support a move from fixed and overvalued exchange rates toward more flexible and undervalued levels when they are highly leveraged or rely on imported inputs. This was particularly important in the case of Argentina, where firms in the Noncompetitive sector switched from supporting alternative and neoliberal development projects and vice versa (see chapter 4).

Third, we are assuming that firms operate in one business sector alone, but this need not be the case, since business groups often diversify into different economic sectors. Although diversification could occur within economic sectors that share the competitive or noncompetitive character of the firm's sector of origin, or even as a strategy to complement assets with key inputs (e.g., energy, transportation), in the case of Latin America this strategy has quite explicitly started as a way to shelter profits coming from one sector alone. Diversification has become a key strategy for the largest, most internationalized, and most politically influential business groups (B. R. Schneider 2013). Diversification then implies that the preferences of firms cease to be strictly

determined by the characteristics and competitiveness of the sector they operate in. Chile was a good example of this (see chapter 4).

Finally, we can think of a contextual-strategic scenario changing first-order
preferences. It is possible that the lack of demand (from business) and supply
(from political parties) interact to deter noncompetitive sectors from more
active challenges to neoliberal policies. Research has shown that often business can opt for a second-order policy in order to secure support in contexts
where they do not find natural allies for their first-order preferences. For
Kurtz and Brooks (2008), for example, in order to understand the behavior
of noncompetitive business sectors demanding additional protections—or
competitiveness-enhancing policies—it is key to look not only at business-
partisan links, but also at the presence or absence of powerful unions. In Poland and Argentina, for example, noncompetitive sector firms formed coalitions with Labor–Left political parties and presented alternative development
projects replacing neoliberalism (see chapter 4).

Conclusions

In this chapter I analyzed the patterns of support for neoliberalism by different
economic and political actors. I focused on two policy domains, exchange
rates and industrial policy, due to their economic relevance for developing
economies as well as their political effects in terms of generating internal cleavages among the main actors, unlike other policies that tend to align them on
class bases and, therefore, make more obvious the desire of business for continuing neoliberalism.

I used economic structures as a starting point for thinking about the business sectors that would be ready to demand and defend neoliberal exchange
rate and industrial policies. There are many caveats. But in the following chapters I advance in several directions implied by these caveats that confirm my
analysis and dispel the problems associated with interest-based theories. I
would like to stress here the use of a comparative advantage index to determine
empirically rather than deductively which economic sectors are internationally competitive and, therefore, their policy preferences.

The quantitative analysis provides evidence that the Financial and the
Competitive business sectors demand and defend neoliberalism through their
preferences for neoliberal price-oriented exchange rate regimes and appreciated levels, and lower levels of state expenditure in industrial policy. The analysis associates the Noncompetitive sector with neoliberal exchange rate levels

when controlling for the partisanship of governments, but at the same time, more developmental industrial policy when controlling for financial and institutional constraints. In addition, right-wing parties were found to be associated with the supply of neoliberal exchange rate regimes (but not necessarily at particular levels), and left-wing parties were with neoliberal industrial policies. This quantitative assessment establishes expectations for the types of actors we should expect to find at the head of neoliberal development projects, and the policies likely to be underpinning their coalitions. It confirms the idea that the preferences of different business sectors are key to understanding support for neoliberalism, and that they can successfully pursue them under governments of different political orientation. Going forward, we shall see how social blocs coalesced along these lines in Latin America and Eastern Europe to defend or oppose neoliberalism.

4

Neoliberal Resilience and the Crafting of Social Blocs

IN CHAPTER 3, I analyzed the patterns of support for neoliberal policy alternatives in exchange rate and industrial policies of specific business sectors and political parties, as a first step to understanding what actors were behind the demand and supply of neoliberalism. In this chapter I show how the policy preferences of these major actors developed into concrete government coalitions and social blocs that supported neoliberalism as a long-term political project. I examine how business actors pursued their policy preferences and gained political influence in different historical settings, and how political actors offered compromises in exchange for their political support. These initial coalitions transformed into durable social blocs, not only pursuing certain policy preferences but defending neoliberalism as a political project, and surviving amid recurrent economic crises and government turnovers. Ultimately, the politics of coalition formation and the crafting of longer-term social blocs translated into the resilience of neoliberalism or its contestation. Hence, this analysis highlights the importance of not only the actors supporting neoliberalism, but also the experience and fate of actors who supported alternative development projects.

This chapter confirms that the strength of the financial, competitive, and noncompetitive economic sectors was crucial to explaining the resilience of neoliberalism. While the first two tended to provide stark support for neoliberalism, strong noncompetitive economic sectors generated the possibility of switching to alternative development projects, due to their demands for developmental policy and political alternatives to neoliberalism. Even when governments pursued neoliberal policies, strong noncompetitive sectors managed to extract concessions that helped them maintain their strength during neoliberal experiments and present alternatives once the right coalitional allies were in place—as I demonstrate in the cases of Argentina and Poland. At the same time, competitive economic sectors were pivotal both to provide chances for alternative social blocs to emerge and for the maintenance of neoliberalism, due to the importance of earning foreign exchange through exports in small, open, and dependent political economies (see chapter 3). In fact, their incorporation into broad developmental alliances and/or neoliberal ones, was crucial from the point of view of the sustainability of the underlying development projects. As we will see, although Eastern European cases did not have a consolidated private business class at the outset of their liberalization processes, the emerging capitalist class quickly became part of the reform coalitions' actual or expected support, either pushing for full-fledged neoliberalization or for an alternative, middle-ground development path.

The variety of differing political contexts in Latin America and Eastern Europe illuminates the formation of social blocs and policy change under diverse conditions. In Latin America, I analyze two such contexts: authoritarianism and democracy. While the first focuses on neoliberal projects with the backdrop of the military dictatorships of the 1970s, the second focuses on the period of democratization and democratic consolidation that followed those martial regimes. In Eastern Europe, meanwhile, political parties did not necessarily align on a socioeconomic right-left cleavage; this provided new possibilities for political representation and coalitional politics. In addition, the relatively arms-length integration regimes and conditionalities provided by institutions such as the IMF and the World Trade Organization (WTO) in Latin America contrasted with the deeper and more constraining integration followed by the EU in Eastern Europe, which directly affected domestic politics and the resilience of neoliberalism in these countries.[1] In fact, when it came to exchange rate and industrial policies, the Eastern European cases are more neoliberal than their respective Latin American pairs.

Taken together, chapters 3 and 4 show the key role that business played in forging coalitions that either maintained neoliberalism over time or presented alternatives that were politically as well as economically viable. The presence

---

1. For the original formulation of shallow versus deep transnational institutional integration, see Bruszt and McDermott (2009).

of business sectors with alternative policy preferences was crucial to generate competition among political parties for the representation of those demands, and at the same time, to support an alternative to neoliberalism. These results are further analyzed in chapters 5, 6, and 7 where I show the operation of the mechanisms of support creation, opposition blockade, and constitutionalized lock-in and their contribution to the resilience of neoliberalism.

The Neoliberal Project in Latin America

The quest for and maintenance of neoliberalism in Latin America took place under two very different political scenarios: authoritarian and democratic political regimes. The military dictatorships of the 1970s presented a variation of what O'Donnell called "bureaucratic-authoritarian" (BA) regimes. Unlike totalitarian or sultanistic authoritarianisms, BA regimes were characterized by a specific alliance between state bureaucracy—including the military—and the more internationalized domestic business sectors, against the peasants and urban proletariat (O'Donnell 1973; Collier 1979; see Linz and Stepan 1996). These state/business coalitions displayed a particularly virulent kind of repression in order to forestall the possibility of dissent, which facilitated technocratic policymaking and economic concentration. The dynamics of opposition and support for neoliberalism under these regimes was affected by the governance formula of the respective military juntas, whether collegial (when the military as a body was involved), or more personalistic (Geddes 1999; Biglaiser 1999). This difference affected the channels of representation of different business actors as well as the patterns of internal change and eventual regime fall. Between the quarrels among military fractions and the need of the military to resort to legitimation other than by pure force (by, for example, distributing benefits to active supporters), there was room for a narrow channel through which business actors opposed to neoliberalism could influence the decisions of the military juntas.

Later, during democratic transitions, incoming authorities faced daunting challenges in consolidating their newly representative states, especially because of economic instability (O'Donnell and Schmitter 1986; Bermeo 1990; Haggard and Kaufman 1995). The perceived need to shield democratic consolidation from authoritarian backlashes led to policy moderation and a postponement of issues such as aggressive redistribution and retaliation against the military. Eventually, the availability of a (noncompetitive) business support base for more egalitarian solutions proved crucial for left-leaning govern-ments to actively pursue alternative development projects.[2]

Neoliberalism under Military Rule

Democratic rule was suspended by military takeovers in September 1973 in Chile and March 1976 in Argentina amid general economic paralysis and dis-tributive struggles, spurred on by the exhaustion of the postwar import sub-stituting industrialization (ISI) model.

A handful of military officers against the majoritarian corporatist sentiment of the military, a set of civilian collaborators (mostly technocrats), and the most internationalized domestic businesses clustered behind a neoliberal de-velopment project in these two countries.[3] The extent to which they suc-ceeded in institutionalizing neoliberalism depended on the strength of the business sectors defending the old interventionist ISI model (see Etchemendy 2012). In Argentina, neoliberals found ways to install their demands in ex-change rate and industrial policies, but neoliberalism remained contested. In Chile, by contrast, neoliberals were not only able to install their policy prefer-ences, but also to form a social bloc able to lead a long-term neoliberal political project. The power and alliances forged by the competitive and noncompeti-tive economic sectors were central to their success.

Neoliberals in both countries came to control the key policymaking posi-tions inside the military juntas after bad initial economic results led to major cabinet shifts. Most symbolic were the replacements at the ministries of labor, bastions of an alternative nationalist-*cum*-corporatist project competing with neoliberalism. These cabinet shifts—occurring in phases during 1975–1977 in Chile and in 1978 in Argentina—turned inflation into the key economic preoc-cupation and signaled the commencement of a phase of *shock therapy*, accel-erating liberalization, state retrenchment, and privatization. Representatives of the financial sector acquired special access to policymaking in the area of banking reform and financial deregulation through their links with civilian

2. Analyzing the sustainability in time of these alternative political projects is beyond the objectives of this book. However, I venture a possible explanation connected to our framework in the conclusions to the chapter.

3. Neoliberals found an important backing in the more repressive elements of the military in a strange alliance of freeing markets and military repression. For a theoretical and empirical investigation, see Pion-Berlin (1983).

policymakers at the Central Bank and the Ministries of Economy and Finance (E. Silva 1996; Veigel 2009).

The seizing of power by the neoliberals led to the adoption of specific combinations of exchange rate and industrial policies. Particularly important was the implementation of an exchange rate-stabilization program (Foxley 1983, 113–19; Frenkel and Rapetti 2010). This constituted one of the key elements imposing discipline on the societal actors behind the alternative nationalist/corporatist project and, according to one account, represented the *coup de grâce* to ISI (Canitrot 1980; Kosacoff 1993, 25). Both countries implemented a type of fixed exchange rate locally known as *tablita* because it pre-announced a decreasing schedule of devaluations as a way to correct exchange rate imbalances before fixing the exchange rate. Chile officially fixed the exchange rate in 1979 and even envisaged the adoption of a currency board in the near future (Fontaine 2001, 396). In Argentina, the 1981 crisis arrived before the plans for this were fully accomplished.

Support for this coalition and policy formula from the competitive and noncompetitive sectors differed in both countries. Rapid trade liberalization in Chile boosted the growth of a few large firms in the country's competitive sector (forestry, fishery, nontraditional agriculture,[4] and their manufactures) (Kurtz 1999). As they grew, they successfully decoupled their fate from that of firms in the noncompetitive sector suffering the effects of exchange rate appreciation and rapid liberalization. While previously critical of the neoliberal project, these firms now openly allied with the neoliberals (E. Silva 1996; Campero 1984, 171–72, 190–91). The subsequent economic boom (1979–1981) also eased criticism by some of the more advanced firms in the noncompetitive sector (chemicals, metals) (Campero 1984, 193–94; E. Silva 1996, 194). In Argentina, on the contrary, firms in the competitive sector, particularly agriculture, weakened over time. Exchange rate appreciation due to the fixed exchange rate hit them particularly hard, while trade liberalization, which could have offset their losses, advanced only gradually in this country (Heredia 2004, 361–69; Novaro 2009, 269–70). They thus strengthened their criticism of what they saw was a too-timid reform process, eventually making them withdraw their support from the military government, which they had initially praised.

Most significant were the differences in the noncompetitive sector. In Argentina, key firms in this sector maintained dynamism during this period,

4. Traditional crops—sugar, wheat—were historically noncompetitive in Chile. During the 1970s new agricultural sectors (especially fruit) emerged, producing mainly for export.

while those in Chile sharply declined. The difference reflected the ability of the Argentine noncompetitive sector to use links to the corporatist military to maintain access to policymaking. Firms in process industries in the Argentine noncompetitive sector (steel, pulp, petrochemicals, oil) had forged their fates in close relation with the success of the state-controlled "military-industrial complex" in the previous decade, and were in a particularly good shape when the military took over in 1976 (see Castellani 2012). In the early 1970s, the Argentine "military-industrial complex" constituted one of the main industrial and financial complexes in Latin America, represented the main area of concentration of state activity in the economy, and was one of the primary drivers of technological upgrade of Argentine industry (Mallon and Sourrouille 1975, 75–76; see Katz and Kosacoff 2001). While other industry-related associations were repressed and institutional decision-making channels fragmented inside the Argentine Junta, firms and business groups in this sector could rely on their historical connections with military bureaucrats to maintain favorable policies (Canelo 2004).

By contrast, the Chilean noncompetitive sector had been weakened from the aggressive nationalizations of the Allende period and had suffered from a slump in state support during the previous decade. In fact, whereas in 1961–1962 investment in military-related industries amounted to 10.4 percent of total state investment in industry, in 1969–1970 it plummeted to only 1.9 percent (Stallings 1978, 249). Moreover, although the initial organization of the Chilean junta as a collegial structure provided institutional resources to countervail this economic weakness (Campero 1984; Martínez and Díaz 1996, 81; Valdés 2003, 16–17; Valdivia 2003, 99), the gradual concentration of power in Pinochet's hands after 1975 and his closeness to the neoliberals impeded the noncompetitive sector from participating more directly in policymaking and/or maintaining the possibility of an alternative coalition (Huneeus 2007; Valenzuela 1993; Valdés 2003; Biglaiser 1999).

In Argentina, as a result, neoliberals were unable to dismantle industrial policy in spite of their efforts. While in Chile fast trade liberalization was coupled with a significant slump in expenditures directed to subsidies and economic protections, therefore weakening even more an already weak noncompetitive sector, in Argentina capital expenditures and subsidies continued to grow despite the stark reduction in current expenditures (see Madariaga 2017, 646; Schvarzer 1981). Argentine public investment largely benefited infrastructure projects and the development of new production plants in strategic areas related to the military-industrial complex. Hence, the new policies not only followed the previous interventionist and selective pattern, but also helped to strengthen the noncompetitive sector. For example, the 1977 industrial promotion scheme supposedly devised to eliminate the industry-biases of existing policies was rather a continuation of them, benefitting the firms in the process industries previously associated with the military-industrial complex (ECLAC 1986, 15).

Thanks to this, Argentine business groups in the noncompetitive sector such as Techint and Pérez Companc were insulated from the decline of the manufacturing industry as a whole.[5] They used state investment and subsidies to consolidate their dominant positions and continued to benefit from the subcontracting of state production and services, which allowed them to take an active part in financial speculation (Azpiazu, Basualdo, and Khavisse 1986; ECLAC 1986). Thus, when internal quarrels inside the junta in 1981 made neoliberals exit the cabinet and brought corporatist military leaders back to key positions, these firms in the noncompetitive sector were ready to jump into a more developmental project (see Veigel 2009, 83; Canelo 2004, 295–98). Later on, they backed the return to democracy and the developmental project of President Alfonsín.

The financial crisis that devastated Argentina and Chile in the early 1980s sealed the complex fate of the authoritarian–neoliberal project in each of these countries. The crisis was directly associated with the boom-bust cycle that followed exchange rate stabilization and capital account liberalization (Diaz-Alejandro 1985; Arellano 1983; Frenkel, Fanelli, and Sommer 1988). GDP plummeted in both countries (falling 8.6 percent and 16.4 percent in Argentina and Chile respectively during 1981–1983), while inflation and external debt soared again. This weakened the business support of neoliberalism—especially the financial sector—and reactivated demands for rapid democratization from noncompetitive sectors, political parties, and trade unions. Meanwhile, the Mexican default of mid-1982 launched a decade of tight international financial conditions for the region, strengthening the power of the IMF and the conditionalities it attached to stabilization loans (see Pop-Eleches 2009; Bustillo and Velloso 2014). In the context of high indebtedness and pressing international conditions, exporters and producers for the internal market—and the political alliances they could forge—became crucial: the first, through their role in procuring the necessary foreign

5. Industrial output in Argentina in 1983 was only 85 percent that of 1974, while industrial employment fell by one-third (Azpiazu, Basualdo, and Khavisse 1986, 97, 103).

currency to repay debt, the second through their ability to produce substi-
tutes for imports (E. Silva 1996, 181).

In Chile, businesses in the competitive and noncompetitive sectors united
against the financial sector and the Chicago Boy technocrats, but chose to
renew their alliance with the dictatorship instead of forging a new compromise
with the emerging center-left political opposition and its mixed-economy development project (E. Silva 1996, 184–85; Campero 1993, 281–82; Huneeus
2007, 367, 372–80). Consequently, these businesses demanded a reorientation
towards a more pragmatic neoliberalism. They wanted to keep trade liberalization and deregulation, while increasing business involvement in policymaking,
debt alleviation, a higher exchange rate, higher protections for import-
competing producers, and the toleration of a certain margin of fiscal deficit
and inflation for reactivating the economy (E. Silva 1996, 157–58; 176). Amid
crumbling business support and popular turmoil, Pinochet struck an enduring
compromise with the business community led by big exporting firms in the
competitive sector (E. Silva 1996, 176–92, 203; Campero 1993, 271–72; Ahumada 2019, 95–99). He sacked orthodox neoliberals from their posts, then
appointed more pragmatic technocrats, responsive right-wing politicians, and
business representatives. From then on, the business umbrella association
CPC (*Corporación de la Producción y el Comercio*) participated closely in policy
formulation.

These new coalitional conditions allowed the maintenance of neoliberalism
under a new policy formula that required higher state intervention, but was
strictly committed to the overall goal of price stability. A crawling peg exchange rate regime was established in order to combine the neoliberal orientation toward price stability with the concerns of export competitiveness-
cum-protection from imports demanded by competitive and noncompetitive
economic sectors (see Frenkel and Rapetti 2010, 34; Morandé and Tapia 2002,
68). Although this may seem *prima facie* an outright departure from neoliberalism, a series of contextual conditions—including the space for recovery after
the deep economic slump, the strong commitment of the Pinochet dictatorship to neoliberalism, and the signing of agreements and close cooperation
with the IMF—meant that the more heterodox components of these arrangements would not prevail (see Pop-Eleches 2009, 120–122; Madariaga 2017). In
fact, although more interventionist, sector-specific industrial policy instruments were established right after the crisis (such as import restrictions and
over-tariffs for specific sectors), they were quickly scaled back as the mid-1980s
approached. The most durable industrial policies, consisting of horizontal

instruments benefitting exporters (like export drawbacks and tax rebates), were directly designed by the new consultative bodies under the control of competitive sector representatives (E. Silva 1996, 204; Kurtz 2001; Agosín 2001).

In Argentina, by contrast, the conditions surrounding the crisis precipitated democratization. A fratricidal struggle for the control of the junta between corporatists and neoliberals, and the military defeat following the failed invasion of the Falkland (*Malvinas*) Islands, strengthened the political parties demanding immediate democratization and eventually brought down the military government. New democratic elections were held in 1983, putting an end to the dictatorship and its neoliberal experiment.

The economic debacle identified with this first attempt at neoliberalism in Argentina made the business community at large seek a new compromise under democracy (Acuña 1996). A new business clique later known as the Captains of Industry (*Capitanes de la Industria*) emerged, encompassing the big manufacturing companies in the noncompetitive sector that had, thanks to the maintenance of industrial policy, successfully retained their power under the dictatorship (Ostiguy 1990). The Captains of Industry heavily condemned the consequences of neoliberalism and vowed a return to ISI, the strengthening of the internal market, continued state support for industry, and gradual instead of outright trade liberalization (Beltrán 2006; Viguera 1998). The two biggest parties competing for the presidency in 1983 (the populist Partido Justicialista, PJ, and the middle-class Union Cívica Radical, UCR) campaigned precisely on renewing the postwar ISI compromise under these premises. With the help of the Captains of Industry, the victorious candidate, Raúl Alfonsín (UCR), offered a social-democratic and developmentalist project that represented a clear departure from the previous neoliberal experiment (Novaro 2009; W. C. Smith 1990).

When he took office, Alfonsín faced the need to balance this project's preferred policies with the pressing domestic and external economic constraints that prevailed. Eventually, the Alfonsin government would become famous for its repeated and failed exchange rate stabilization programs. However, while these programs gradually moved toward using the exchange rate for anti-inflationary (price stability) purposes, the initial developmental idea was to use a high exchange rate to aid the tradable sector, in combination with an export-oriented industrial policy.[6] In fact, Alfonsín's most important stabilization plan—the Austral plan of June 1985—has been seen as a heterodox or

6. Argentina, Interview 16.

even "populist" attempt at stabilization. It explicitly avoided measures that hurt wages or contracted domestic demand, in particular by using a fixed exchange rate as a nominal anchor—then the preferred neoliberal option (Díaz-Bonilla and Schamis 2001; Fernández 1991; W. C. Smith 1990; Heredia 2006, 181–82; Machinea 1990).[7]

Meanwhile, Alfonsín's industrial policy maintained the high tariffs reintroduced by the outgoing military government, reinstated export taxes, and added a set of nontariff restrictions. In 1987, average tariffs were 39.4 percent (up from 26 percent in 1978) with a maximum rate of 102.5 percent (Kosacoff 1993, 40–42; Casaburi 1998, 14). Conversely, amid the general decline in expenditures due to inherited fiscal constraints, he maintained the industrial promotion programs that became crucial supports for continued investment (Basualdo 2006, 254). Alfonsín also introduced new industrial policy measures along the lines of export-oriented industrialization,[8] launched the integration project with Brazil (*Mercado Común del Sur,* Mercosur) with the intention of developing a joint capital goods industry and other technology-intensive sectors, and developed programs such as the *Programas Especiales de Exportación* (PEEX) that conditioned state subsidies to the achievement of export quotas in higher technology sectors, following the experience of the East Asian countries with rapid industrialization.

Due to the deterioration of economic conditions during the 1980s and the strong position of the IMF against Argentina regarding debt alleviation, the Alfonsín government had a tendency to include ever more neoliberal elements in this policy mix (Ortiz and Schorr 2006; Heredia 2006; W. C. Smith 1990; Pop-Eleches 2009). Ultimately, the failure of his social democratic-*cum*-developmentalist project amid the hyperinflationary crisis of 1989 opened the way for a new neoliberal experiment.

In addition to the role of the IMF, it is important to note, however, that there were key domestic coalitional factors behind Alfonsín's failure. Most important, his project failed to cater to the labor movement. Argentine labor was then still heavily controlled by the political opposition in Parliament, the peronist Justicialist Party (PJ). In the context of the first non-Peronist president elected under fair elections in Argentine history, labor unions' and the PJ's unaccomodating stances were important causes explaining the failure of

---

7. It is also worth noting that the economic authorities in charge of the plan were highly critical of the previous exchange rate stabilization experience. Argentina, Interviews 8 and 5.

8. Argentina, Interviews 10 and 16.

the initial, more developmental, stabilization attempts, and the subsequent radicalizing of economic conditions, especially inflation (see W. C. Smith 1990; Novaro 2009).

Neoliberalism and Democracy in the South

In Chile, a democratization process resulted in the center left *Concertación* coalition, an alliance between Christian Democrats and moderate Socialists, winning back the presidency in 1989. The ascendance of the *Concertación* triggered a recoil in the business community who backed neoliberalism under Pinochet's iron fist (E. Silva 1996, 2002; Weyland 1999a). Economists affiliated to *Concertación* parties had been the main critics of neoliberalism during the dictatorship (P. Silva 1991). As with Alfonsín's project on the other side of the Andes, they proposed an economic policy program that combined trade openness and competitive exchange rates promoting export sectors, as well as selective industrial policy measures to aid noncompetitive ones (Foxley 1984, 34, 41–42). Although it is true that the *Concertación* tempered its economic policy program in order to generate support among reluctant business elites (E. Silva 1996; Barrett 1999, 10; Arriagada Herrera and Graham 1995), its government program of 1989 maintained heterodox measures, including the establishment of a Ministry of Industry and a new framework for productive promotion (Barrett 1999, 14).

Against this backdrop, during the 1980s the business community had become an ardent supporter of Pinochet's free market reforms. The economic restructuring of the 1970s, the new export orientation of the 1980s, and extensive privatization had significantly weakened firms in the noncompetitive sector. Moreover, many firms diversified, acquiring assets in the competitive sector, the banking industry, and privatized public utilities, in the process reducing even further their demand for state intervention (see chapter 5). Furthermore, the strong economic recovery that followed the 1982–1983 crisis empowered the neoliberal social bloc to demand the continuity of neoliberalism and reduced the capacities of the new center-left governments to change economic policy, let alone their ability to create an alternative social bloc.

When democracy returned, the rightist Independent Democratic Union (*Unión Demócrata Independiente,* UDI), the political home of the closest collaborators and supporters of Pinochet, fiercely defended his legacy in Congress, and the center-right National Renewal party (*Renovación Nacional, RN*) became pivotal for negotiating key reforms, therefore moderating even more the Concertacion's initial proposals (Weyland 1999b; Fazio and Parada 2010). Meanwhile, *Concertación*-led unions followed a politics of restraint, "lower[ing] their expectations so as not to upset political or macroeconomic stability" (Drake 1996, 144). Thus, despite significant popular support and policy moderation, the *Concertación* governments of Christian Democratic Patricio Aylwin (1990–1993) and Eduardo Frei (1994–1999) faced skepticism from businesses and stiff opposition from right-wing parties in Parliament, who had benefitted from constitutional overrepresentation (see chapter 6). Meanwhile, weak noncompetitive sectors were not able to coalesce around a stronger alternative development project—as had been the initial *Concertación* program.

Economic policy developments thus pitted the *Concertación's* "two souls" against each other: one more centrist and closer to the neoliberal pragmatism of the late dictatorship years, and another more leftist and faithful to the more developmentalist policies advocated earlier during the 1980s. The benign economic situation of the first half of the 1990s (record high FDI inflows, economic growth, and a gradual reduction of inflation) made it possible to combine these "two souls" without major internal rifts. In the case of the exchange rate, the *Concertación* was happy to follow and deepen the post 1982–1983 crisis framework combining price stability with export competitiveness since it suited the neo-developmentalist ideas on exchange rate management inside the coalition. In practice, this implied a temporal departure from the preferences of the neoliberal bloc, which had now moved to demanding the freeing of the exchange rate under mounting concerns that the higher goal of price stability was now under threat (see Madariaga 2017). In fact, during the early 1990s *Concertación* economists in the Central Bank deepened the heterodox management of the exchange rate through the introduction of exchange rate bands and capital controls (see Frenkel and Rapetti 2010, 35–36; Ffrench-Davis 2003).

Industrial policy dynamics more closely characterized the struggles within the governing coalition. While trade openness was accepted, there were two distinct positions regarding international integration (Wehner 2011; Bull 2008; Ahumada 2019). The Ministry of Finance, dominated by neoliberals, privileged integration with advanced countries, which benefitted the competitive exporters of low-value-added products. The key was negotiating an entry to the North American Free Trade Area (NAFTA), which was then in the making.[9] The Ministry of Economy, by contrast, privileged integration with Latin America and the emerging Mercosur bloc. This benefitted the few export-oriented segments in the noncompetitive sector (fabricated metals, machinery). Technocrats in the Ministry of Economy and the state's industrial promotion agency CORFO (Corporación para el Fomento de la Producción) subsequently set up an array of industrial-promotion measures conceived as a way to generate support among these noncompetitive sectors and SMEs, eventually producing a business base for the *Concertación*'s more developmental economic project (E. Silva 2002; Ahumada 2019, 120–1; see Foxley 1984).

Following the preferences of neoliberals in government and intending to ally with the business community, led by the dynamic exporting firms in the competitive sector, the Aylwin and Frei administrations continued the trade policy of the dictatorship, gradually diminishing tariffs throughout the decade and signing bilateral trade agreements. As Ahumada points out, each government used unilateral tariff reductions as "a message . . . to economic agents to show its commitment to trade liberalization" (2019, 121). Chile declined the invitation to join Mercosur in 1990 and rushed to negotiate a free trade agreement (FTA) with the United States when its candidacy to NAFTA was rejected. This agreement—negotiated throughout the 1990s and signed in 2003—severely restricted the use of heterodox economic policies such as applying royalties to natural resource producers in order to finance industrial policy measures, or using capital controls to manage the exchange rate (Fazio and Parada 2010, chap. 3).[10] Moreover, the coming into being of the WTO in 1995 made it necessary to eliminate the remaining export support measures introduced in the mid-1980s (Agosín 2001). The state designed industrial promotion measures to prevent any kind of sectoral preference (Román 2003, 40; Muñoz Gomá 2001, 49, 2009; Schrank and Kurtz 2005). More important, the state did not operate as a direct provider of finance, instead ceding the admin-

9. As part of U.S. President Bush's "Initiative for the Americas," Chile got a promise that it would be able to access NAFTA. In 1994 the invitation was rejected in the U.S. congress. As a response, Chile sought to "enter NAFTA through the back door" (Bull 2008, 204) by signing individual FTAs with each NAFTA member (Wehner 2011, 85–102). Chile subsequently signed FTAs with Canada, Mexico, and the USA in 1996, 1997 and 2003 respectively.

10. When the Chilean government tried to implement a royalty—and later a tax—on natural resources, foreign companies in general—and U.S.-ones in particular—objected to the change in tax regimes as contravening parts of the U.S.-Chile FTA. This made it necessary that the new tax legislation remain voluntary, and the government had to offer hefty compensations and additional tax-invariability clauses in order for firms to enter the new system (see Napoli and Navia 2012). More on this in the following pages and in chapter 5.

istration and management of state-financed grants and credit to commercial banks, thereby heavily supporting the development of the financial sector (Bril-Mascarenhas and Madariaga 2019, 1051).

The Asian crisis (1997–1998) would upset this partial equilibrium, changing the balance of power inside the neoliberal bloc and the underlying policy regime. The crisis led to a redefinition of the actors leading the neoliberal bloc— until then, big exporters in the competitive sector and the more moderate group inside the center-left *Concertación* coalition—and the respective policy compromise. The outcome was a confirmation of the preeminence of price stability in exchange rate policy, and evidence of the continued quest for an industrial policy formula that could generate a business base of support for an alternative development project.

Politically, the 1990s and the Asian crisis triggered a process of polarization manifested in the growth of the leftist parties within the *Concertación,* the socialist party and its splinter PPD (Partido por la Democracia) party, and the rightist UDI (Garretón 2000, 84; E. Silva 2002, 346; Roberts 2011, 334). This was confirmed with the election in 2000 of the first socialist president since Allende, Ricardo Lagos, and another socialist in 2006, Michelle Bachelet. Conversely, in 1999 the right was able to force a runoff for the first time in Chile's history, another runoff in 2005, and finally to achieve the presidency in 2010. A similar polarization occurred within the business community, which turned toward its more recalcitrant sectors during the Lagos presidency (E. Silva 2002). With the passing of the decade, competitive sectors lost strength. High demand for commodity prices increased the price of copper, the Chilean main export staple, generating symptoms of *Dutch disease*, that is, a strong appreciation of the currency that severely affected noncopper exports (Fazio and Parada 2010, 99–109; Lüders 2010). In fact, toward the end of the decade the competitive sector decreased significantly in its share of GDP, and competitive exporters together with the noncompetitive sector voiced concern with exchange rate appreciation, demanding higher exchange rate levels, using capital controls if needed, to recover their competitiveness (see Scapini 2006; Díaz Cordero 2011). However, these critical voices were not enough to form a strong alternative business bloc. On the one hand, these firms were at the same time strongly committed to neoliberal policy alternatives in other domains, for example, trade.[11] On the other, the stark support for neoliberal-

---

11. For example, while in the early 1990s firms in the noncompetitive sector had been in favor of a gradual trade openness and integration with the Mercosur bloc, when the chance

ism from the peak business associations implied that these sectors' critical voices were not well represented within the business community (see Scapini 2006).

Conversely, the decade strengthened the financial sector within the business community, which reached its highest ever share in GDP. In fact, finance bottomed in 1984 after the 1982–1983 financial crisis, representing a mere 18.8 percent of GPD. It went up gradually during the 1990s and boomed again during the 2000s. Thus, while in 1990 it represented 21.9 percent of GDP, in 2000 it represented 22.5 percent and in 2010 25.1 percent, surpassing for the first time the competitive sector as the largest economic sector in terms of its share in the economy.[12] This was confirmed in 2004 when the longstanding president of the banking association (ABIF), Hernán Sommerville, was elected to lead the employers peak association CPC (*Confederación de la Producción y el Comercio*) for the first time since ABIF's entry to the CPC in 1979. The power of the financial sector was further buttressed by the expansion of the insurance industry and the emergence of new retail commerce groups at the top of company rankings, whose profits derived in large part from the provision of consumer credit (Lefort 2010; see González 2015). Against the criticisms of exchange rate appreciation, Sommerville strongly backed the functioning of the free floating exchange rate regime in place (Scapini 2006, 66).

The new balance of power affected the rather heterodox, if short-lived, policy mix of the early 1990s. In the case of exchange rates, once the Asian crisis was behind, the Central Bank rushed to ratify price stability as its main policy goal. Capital controls were eliminated, and the exchange rate was set to float freely, allowing intervention only under special circumstances (i.e., when depreciation threatened inflation targets). Further efforts were made to insulate the Central Bank from political pressures by diminishing its discretionary powers, and to bind the utilization of fiscal policy through a structural balance rule (see chapter 7). The administration of the socialist Ricardo Lagos further reinforced this by appointing hawkish technocrats to the board of the Central Bank.

In the opposite direction, during the Lagos and Bachelet governments, proponents of more progressive industrial policy regained power, thanks to

---

opened to enter Mercosur in the early 2000s, they no longer favored this option and favored instead the negotiation of FTAs with the United States and the European Union. See Ahumada (2019).

12. Author's calculations based on data from Chilean Central Bank. For details, see online appendix.

the diagnosis that the prevailing horizontal industrial policy framework had resulted in a lack of technological development that prevented further diversification of exports toward higher value-added segments (Muñoz Gomá 2001, 29–30, 2009, 45). For example, they attributed the failure to attract an Intel semiconductor plant in 1997 to a lack of incentive packages stemming from horizontal and industry-neutral instruments (Agosín, Larraín, and Grau 2009, 35). Moreover, they lamented that this framework had been unable to generate a segment of thriving SMEs or *mittelstand* supporting a developmental project (E. Silva 2002; Bril-Mascarenhas and Madariaga 2019). Progressives from the Ministry of Economy and the state industrial promotion agency CORFO extended programs, reconverted old ones, and even created entirely new programs with growing selective components (see Bril-Mascarenhas and Madariaga 2019).

The most important innovation was the use of a new tax on copper exports to support priority industrial clusters. This policy was operationalized in 2006 after lengthy negotiations in Congress gave birth to the new tax and two new public bodies: the National Fund for Innovation (FIC) where the tax's revenues were to be deposited, and the National Council for Innovation and Competitiveness (CNIC) in charge of their management. Although most of the clusters selected for support constituted activities in which Chile had already demonstrated comparative advantages (e.g., mining, salmon fisheries, fruit, etc.) and only one was an entirely new sector (the "global services" cluster), the clusters policy constituted a qualitative difference with respect to the pervasiveness of horizontal measures in the past (Agosín, Larraín, and Grau 2009; Bril-Mascarenhas and Madariaga 2019).

However, this new industrial policy framework was fiercely fought by the business community at large (particularly the competitive mining industry, national and foreign), the right wing in Congress, and even *Concertación* parliamentarians from mining regions, showing the full extent of the neoliberal social bloc and the operation of neoliberal resilience, particularly support creation. In fact, in the two periods analyzed after democratization (1990s and 2000s) willing governments that offered developmental alternatives found few economic actors supporting them, so the proposals were quickly scaled back.

In Argentina, the failure of the Alfonsín government facilitated the renewal of neoliberalism. In 1989, the country celebrated the first change of office between two democratically elected presidents in decades, amid a collapsing economy, growing social protest, and political turmoil. The victory of the PJ's Carlos Menem on a traditionally populist and state-centered platform did not

help the volatile economic environment. The new president foresaw the necessity of drastic measures if was he to survive his presidency.[13]

In a dramatic turnaround, Menem reassembled the neoliberal social bloc.
He signaled not only the government's general responsiveness to business interests but also a renewed commitment to neoliberalism. He nominated an
executive of the Bunge & Born group (the biggest conglomerate in Argentina,
broadly diversified but concentrated in the competitive sectors of agriculture
and food manufactures) to the Ministry of Economy (Etchemendy 2012, 75–
76). Bunge & Born represented the landowning oligarchy that had historically
opposed the populist alliance between domestic industrialists and the working
class that was the basis of the Peronist movement and Menem's PJ party. During the 1980s, high executives of Bunge & Born had attended the economics
course for businessmen organized by the Argentinean Chicago Boys.[14] In addition, Menem invited the neoliberal UCEDE party to take part in government. During the 1980s, the UCEDE had successfully reorganized the political
right, redeeming neoliberalism from the discredit of the dictatorial years (see
Gibson et al. 1990). Thanks to Menem's neoliberal turn, the PJ would absorb
many UCEDE adherents in the coming years (Cherny 2009, 190–91).

The Menem administration moved swiftly to implement a policy mix tai-
lored to the interests of this renewed neoliberal coalition. This was most visible
in quick-trigger trade liberalization and deregulation moves, as well as in the
Laws on State Reform and Economic Emergency, which gave the executive
ample powers to start privatization and eliminate subsidies. Moreover, the
Menem administration designed a series of stabilization plans in order to control inflation. Menem skillfully controlled the PJ party machine to create support for this new policy course, and he weakened the labor movement by di-
viding it.[15] Meanwhile, the most important opposition party, the UCR,
descended into an internal crisis after the experience of hyperinflation and
defeat in 1989.

Far from producing a stable new equilibrium, the new political configuration and Menem's policy advances produced struggles within the business

13. Several authors agree with the conclusion that the severity of the domestic and external
constraints left literally no other choice than to follow the neoliberal way (Beltrán 2006, 204;
Acuña, Galiani, and Tommasi 2007; Murillo 2001; M. Pastor and Wise 1999).

14. Argentina, Interview 15.

15. For an analysis of the characteristics of the PJ party, its relation to organized labor and
their consequences for the implementation of neoliberalism in Argentina, see Levitsky (2003,
2005); Murillo (2001); Etchemendy (2012); Spiller and Tommasi (2008).

sector (Basualdo 2006, 287–88; Beltrán 2011, 227; Etchemendy 2012, 76–77). Most important, the elimination of promotion schemes and industry subsidies dating back to the early 1970s, and the prospects of a privatization process that could transfer state assets to external capital, alienated the most dynamic fractions of the noncompetitive sector, who were dependent on state aid and the activity of state companies. They openly voiced their discontent and engaged in practices that undermined the success of Menem's initial stabilization attempts (Etchemendy 2012, 76; Corrales 1998).

In 1990 the Menem government was in an extremely fragile situation. Two consecutive stabilization plans had failed, inflation was on the verge of becoming "hyper" again, and, when his approval rate plummeted amid the alienation of his electoral base, a loss in the mid-term congressional elections loomed ominously (Heredia 2011, 185; Starr 1997, 109). Menem made a last effort to strengthen the emerging neoliberal bloc. This involved an "insurance policy" to the financial sector in terms of his commitment to price stability, but at the same time, significant concessions in terms of industrial policy to the reluctant and powerful noncompetitive sector.

Regarding the first, Menem's new economics minister, Domingo Cavallo, launched in March 1991 the "Convertibility Plan," establishing a currency board exchange rate regime. To be sure, continued high inflation and economic volatility drew support from a wide array of actors, provided that the new plan was finally able to stabilize the economy (see Heredia 2011, 192; Starr 1997; Cherny 2009). The Convertibility Law established a one-to-one parity between the Argentine peso and the U.S. dollar, requiring congressional approval for any change.[16] In the contrary direction, several measures were taken to compensate the noncompetitive sector for the expected costs of restructuring under the currency board, especially after the bold process of exchange rate appreciation that followed its introduction. The leading companies in the sector benefitted handsomely from a targeted privatization strategy (see chap-

16. There are a number of interesting notes regarding whether different actors would support, or not support, the currency board. It is known, for example, that the idea had already circulated in the Ministry of Economy previous to the arrival of Cavallo, but it was seen as too risky—especially considering the previous experience with a fixed exchange rate. It is also relevant to note that the IMF was not entirely supportive, as it was afraid that the defense of the exchange rate would erode the gains from privatization and jeopardize debt-repayment. Moreover, the Chicago Boys in government and members of the right-wing UCEDE did not support the bill in Congress because they considered it was not constraining enough as it contained some flexibility clauses. See Heredia (2011), Cherny (2009).

TABLE 4.1. Argentina and Chile, Tariff Rates 1992–2010

Year	Argentina		Chile	
	AHS	Max	AHS	Max
1992	14.17	35	10.99	11
1993	13.15	20	10.99	11
1994	—	—	10.99	11
1995	12.7	30	10.67	11
1996	14.45	30	10.99	11
1997	14.44	30	10.99	11
1998	16.73	33	10.99	11
1999	15.17	33	9.99	10
2000	15.22	33	9	9
2001	13.23	37.5	8	8
2002	14.78	21.5	6.99	7
2003	14.73	35	5.9	6
2004	11.85	35	4.89	6
2005	10.6	35	4.86	6
2006	10.74	35	2.23	6
2007	10.8	35	1.96	6
2008	9.82	31.5	1.39	6
2009	9.75	35	5.97	12.5
2010	11.43	35	4.85	15.6

Source: World Integrated Trade Solution (WITS).
Legend: AHS= Effectively applied tariffs (simple average); Max= Maximum tariff.

ter 5). Cheaper access to finance in dollars as well as economic reactivation was also important to ease criticism from the strongest groups in the noncompetitive sector (Cherny 2009, 147–48; Steinberg 2015).

Menem also combined trade openness and selective protection in the context of Mercosur.[17] Thus, while the average tariff rate decreased markedly from the previous decades and was not significantly different from that of Chile, differential tariff and nontariff protection for noncompetitive sectors such as automobiles and steel makers imposed an important dispersion in tariff rates, as is evident in the difference in maximum tariff rates between Argentina and Chile during the period (see table 4.1). Tariffs were slightly increased in Menem's second term in order to shelter domestic producers from competitive Brazilian businesses. Other additions included protective measures such as antidump-

17. In spite of a stronger neoliberal orientation under Menem, Mercosur sought to liberalize trade within the bloc but selectively protect sectors from outside competition; therefore, it remained opposite to the Chilean policy of unilateral tariff reduction. See Manzetti (1993).

ing regulations that benefitted the strongest noncompetitive segments, such as the metal industry, and transport equipment (Etchemendy 2012, 103–4), and other horizontal promotion instruments (Sirlin 1999, 109; Sánchez, Butler, and Rozemberg 2011; Baruj, Kosacoff, and Ramos 2009, 19–22).

The renewed neoliberal project in Argentina, led by the competitive and financial sectors and the populist PJ government, survived the contagion of the Mexican "Tequila" crisis in 1994–1995 and two presidential elections: in 1995 when Menem was reelected and in 1999 when the opposition took office. The Tequila effect produced a steep run from emerging markets, putting pressures on the currency board. Around 18 percent of capital in the Argentine financial sector fled the country in the first months of 1995 alone, as the Central Bank lost one quarter of its reserves and GDP contracted (Starr 1997, 97–98; see also M. Pastor and Wise 1999, 484). Unemployment rose from what had been an all-time high of 10.8 percent in May 1994, to 18.6 percent the very month of the presidential election (Starr 1997, 98; M. Pastor and Wise 1999, 484). However, the elections were framed as a decision between "convertibility or the cliff," portraying Menem as the only leader capable of steering the country through the rough waters (Heredia 2011, 205; Starr 1997, 109). Argentines elected Menem by a 20 percent margin over his closest competitor despite declining support for his government and economic program a few months earlier (Heredia 2011, 207; 209).

After the short but steep crisis, Menem redoubled his bet on the neoliberal project. He appointed Chicago Boy technocrats who had been on the fringes in the cabinet to key policymaking positions. They moved to strengthen the operation of the automatic adjustment mechanisms of the currency board, including the dollarization of domestic contracts, a renewed assault on fiscal expenditure, tax increases, and making the labor market more flexible (Cherny 2009, 119; 123–24; Novaro 2009, 512). These steps were particularly welcomed by the financial sector and received the open approval of the IMF.[18]

Following these neoliberal initiatives, the business bases of the neoliberal bloc changed in composition, with a higher weight of finance and foreign capital. First, a series of buyouts and privatizations left the financial industry much more concentrated and dependent on external capital (Castellani and Gaggero 2011, 243–47). In 2000, 90 percent of the banks represented by the banking

18. After the Tequila Crisis the IMF embraced the currency board wholeheartedly. President Menem was invited as guest speaker to open the Joint Annual conference of the WB and the IMF in October 1998, and was asked to narrate the story of Argentina as a success case (Cherny 2009, 171–73).

association (Asociación de Bancos Argentinos or ABA) were foreign (Cherny 2009, 153–54). Second, forced to adjust to the conditions of an appreciated currency, the export sector deepened its specialization in the more competitive segments: agriculture and oil (Castellani and Gaggero 2011, 280–83). Conversely, troubled with exchange rate appreciation, firms in the noncompetitive sector enacted two alternative strategies (Castellani and Gaggero 2011, 283–87; Cherny 2009, 148–49): they either took advantage of renewed capital inflows and sold their assets, or bet on the maintenance of domestic consumption through the currency board. As a result, participation of national companies in the economy fell from 50 percent in 1994 to only 30 percent in 1998 (Cherny 2009, 148).

In the aftermath of the Tequila Crisis, the political opposition began to display a common front, capitalizing on the government's sinking popularity. While labor united against the renewed assault on labor market flexibility (Starr 1997; Novaro 2009, 522–40), splinters from the PJ and other leftist parties created a new center-left conglomerate, the Frente País Solidario, FREPASO (Front for a Country in Solidarity). A new alliance (the *Alianza*) between the centrist UCR and the center-left FREPASO won the presidency in 1999.

The 1999 presidential campaign was ambiguous, as it tried to balance the conservative and leftist sentiments inside the Alianza and find the right mix of criticism and continuity with Menem (Novaro 2009, 553; Llanos and Margheritis 2006, 88; M. Pastor and Wise 2001, 67–68). Fernando De la Rúa, the new president, emphatically criticized the social costs of neoliberalism but was cautious not to compromise the continuity of the currency board. Although the new economic team were not strong supporters of fixed exchange rates,[19] the presidential campaign, amid a volatile international scenario, reinforced the idea that the currency board was untouchable (Cherny 2009, 124; see Novaro 2009). In fact, its continuity enjoyed growing support among the public, who understandably wanted to maintain high levels of consumption and avoid economic collapse (Novaro 2009, 560). The currency board was also

19. Minister of Economy José Luis Machinea had participated in the heterodox stabilization plan under President Alfonsín in the 1980s. In the early 1990s he had openly opposed the currency board, but once it was established he accepted it believing that the costs of an exit outweighed those of maintaining it. Accordingly, as a consultant to the industrials association (UIA) he tried to propose several policies (from social policies to subsidies and incentives to less competitive sectors) to help mitigate the effects of the currency board. Argentina, Interview 8.

fiercely defended by the finance-led neoliberal bloc. Before turning over power to the new authorities, Menem devised a plan to advance toward full-fledged dollarization if the crisis would deepen and threaten the continuity of neoliberalism (see chapter 7). This alternative also included an exit from Mercosur and a new trade integration agenda, following the U.S.-sponsored FTAA (Free Trade Area of the Americas) (Castellani and Schorr 2004, 72 n. 33). Noncompetitive sectors, heavily indebted in dollars, supported the maintenance of the currency board (Steinberg 2015; Cherny 2009).

However, as the economic situation worsened, positions changed. Economic slowdown eroded the already substantial current account and fiscal deficits, increasing the chances of a capital stampede and a default on external debt. What started in 1999 as timid discontent with the currency board (and nascent thoughts about alternatives) became an outright onslaught during 2001 of support for currency devaluation, the currency board replaced with a managed exchange rate regime, and conversion of dollar-denominated debt to pesos (Cherny 2009, 150–51; Castellani and Schorr 2004, 73; Beltrán 2011). The same noncompetitive business groups that had accepted neoliberalism in exchange for handsome benefits during the 1990s demanded these moves. They envisaged this as part of a new alternative development project that could restore the importance of the domestic economy, return manufacturing to prominence, and rebuild the alliance with labor (Castellani and Schorr 2004, 74–75; Etchemendy and Collier 2007; Etchemendy and Garay 2011).

As the crisis unspooled, the De la Rúa government could do nothing to appease the nervousness of international markets, and international finance—including the IMF—finally turned its back on the Argentine neoliberal project. After three successive ministers of economy and several failed negotiations with the IMF, towards the end of 2001 President de la Rúa was forced to resign, and a caretaker government led by Eduardo Duhalde (PJ) took office. Duhalde, close to the protectionist wing of the PJ and the domestic industrial bourgeoisie, signed the change of direction with his predecessor in the presidency by bringing the president of the industrials association (UIA) to the cabinet as minister of production (Cherny 2009, 228–33). As new elections approached, Duhalde dropped the currency board and confirmed the debt moratorium established days earlier by interim president Rodríguez Saa, with the support of the noncompetitive sector and the PJ majority in Parliament. The elimination of the currency board eroded the power of the financial sector, the core of the neoliberal bloc. Capital flight and debt default increased anew the importance of exporters and domestic import substituting producers for the recovery prospects (Cherny 2009, 182–83).

In 2003 Néstor Kirchner was elected. Hailing from the left wing of the PJ, Kirchner voiced harsh opposition to neoliberalism, establishing a renewed alliance with labor unions and noncompetitive business sectors that pointed toward a new version of state developmentalism (see Richardson 2009; Etchemendy and Garay 2011; Wylde 2012). He established a managed flotation exchange rate regime that was intended to keep a high and stable exchange rate which would promote domestic manufacturers of higher-value-added goods (Frenkel and Rapetti 2010, 2008). His government also maintained low tariffs and horizontal instruments, but presented new developmental industrial policy alternatives. Kirchner relaunched the taxes on exports that had been the basis of ISI and redistributed the excess revenue among his supporters (Richardson 2009). During this period, public investment increased, existing instruments were gradually shifted towards greater selectiveness, and financial markets intervention facilitated the extension of credit to manufacturing industries (Baruj, Kosacoff, and Ramos 2009; Bril-Mascarenhas forthcoming). Expenditures to support industries increased five-fold during the decade, and the government used the renationalization of pension funds to further allocate subsidized credit to productive firms (Bril-Mascarenhas forthcoming).

The 2007–2008 crisis, however, made the maintenance of Kirchner's "new developmentalism" difficult. Quarrels between the government of Cristina Fernández (Kirchner's wife and successor) and the competitive agricultural producers over export taxes marked growing criticism by the Competitive sector that had acquiesced to developmentalism in the previous years. As foreign exchange receipts receded following the crisis and the twin commercial and fiscal surpluses accumulated were slashed, the exchange rate became increasingly used for anti-inflationary purposes, with competitive and noncompetitive businesses increasingly questioning this turn. As the crisis continued, however, noncompetitive sectors began to openly support exchange rate appreciation as they worried about inflationary pressure, not to mention the consequences of a possible devaluation on their balance sheets (Steinberg 2015, 156–7). With still-ample popular support, Cristina Fernández continued as president until 2015, although besieged by inflationary pressures, economic imbalances, and a policy mix that hardly resembled Kirchner's neo-developmental one. The return of neoliberalism with Mauricio Macri in 2016 and the election of center-left Alberto Fernández in 2019 following Macri's collapse are illustrations that the discussion about development projects in

Argentina is not yet settled, and that two relatively defined social blocs in terms of political as well as economic composition regularly compete to steer the country in different directions.

In sum, competitive and financial sectors supported neoliberalism during the military dictatorships of the 1970s in Chile and Argentina, and continued their support when democratic governments were elected. Noncompetitive sectors, meanwhile, kept alternative development projects alive. Center-left governments willing to change neoliberalism offered developmental policies but were not able to present a consistent project without a strong noncompetitive business sector. Therefore, the strength of noncompetitive sectors, and the availability of a coalitional ally in government, remained necessary if there was to be an alternative to the resilience of neoliberalism. As we will see in chapters 5 to 7, the creation of support through privatization, the blocking of opposition through constraining political institutions, and the insulation of key policies from partisan considerations made this type of alliance all the more difficult, therefore increasing the chances of neoliberalism's survival.

The Neoliberal Project in Eastern Europe

Communism in Eastern Europe crumbled amid economic stagnation, decay of the state-party apparatuses, and opposition movements in a changing civil society. The first period of reforms was famously characterized by polish finance minister Leszek Balcerowicz as a moment of "extraordinary politics," during which the political constraints on reforms were lower (Balcerowicz 1995; for a similar formulation in Estonia, see Laar 2002). These political economies normalized soon enough, however, as parliamentary democratic mechanisms came to the fore, and capitalist economic relations started to take root. After the initial outburst, the politics of democratic alternation and economic growth took precedence. Instability and economic slumps generated by the liberalizing reform process itself created the need for stabilization, both economic and social. How did reformist governments withstand the protests and discontent generated by neoliberal reforms, and to what degree were they able to engage support from the emerging private business class?

Toward the end of the 1990s, EU accession overtook the agenda, altering patterns of domestic political competition and institutional change (Héritier 2005; Vachudova 2005; see Bohle and Greskovits 2012). In the case of the exchange rate, preparations for entry into the European Monetary Union (EMU) empowered central bankers and promoted discourses of "fiscal discipline, sound money and finance" (Dyson 2006, 10–11). In the case of industrial policy, EU accession generated divergent pressures. On one hand, the EU provided financial support for the development of legal and institutional capacity, strategic planning for industry promotion, and the restructuring of agriculture through programs like PHARE (literally "Poland and Hungary: Assistance for Restructuring their Economies" later expanded to cover other countries) and SAPARD (Special Accession Programme for Agricultural and Rural Development) (Suurna and Kattel 2010; Kattel, Reinert, and Suurna 2009; OECD 2005, 81–83). On the other hand, the EU established strict periods for subsidies to the new Eastern European member states, especially in sectors where they could outcompete older members (such as steel, agriculture, and food processing), which pressured governments to rapidly reduce subsidies to these industries (Sznajder Lee 2006; OECD 2005, 79–80; Héritier 2005). How did neoliberal coalitions use the process of EU accession as leverage for their project, and how did actors with alternative views react to this?

Neoliberalism and Democratic Consolidation in the East

In Poland, the reform process started with the failure of the economic and political reforms of the 1970s and the emergence of the Solidarity trade union (*Solidarność*) in the summer of 1980 (Ekiert 1996, 222–59; Kubik 1994). After several years of martial law foreclosing possibilities of quick change, and amid the radicalization of economic and political conditions, in 1988 the government announced a series of talks with Solidarity in order to negotiate the opening of the communist system. The "Roundtable Talks," as they were called, finished in April 1989 with agreements on improved worker conditions and substantive economic and political liberalization setting in motion a process that would lead to the first noncommunist government in Eastern Europe since World War II. In Estonia, then part of the Soviet Union, opposition from within the Communist Party and from outside groups in civil society was fostered by Gorbachev's mid-1980s political and economic reforms. The Baltic nations, Estonia in particular, led the demand for autonomy within the Soviet Union (Lauristin and Vihalemm 1997, 87–88; Nørgaard 1996, 1). Autonomist and independentist groups came to dominate the political scene in the late 1980s and managed to elect members to the main Soviet representative organs, paving the way for reforms. In both countries, these circumscribed political openings fueled the rise of opposition movements who called for gradual and negotiated reforms (Ekiert 1996; Berend 1996; Lauristin and Vihalemm 1997).

The deepening of the political and economic processes that followed this initial liberalization opened a period of "extraordinary politics" during which advocates of radical reform became more vocal. Soaring inflation, declining output, and widespread shortages made radical stabilization measures and institutional overhaul the only possible alternative, according to their advocates (Åslund 1994; Balcerowicz 1995). They claimed that the rapid enactment of these measures was vital to securing a decisive "leap" out of communism and to prevent being stuck in a "partial reform equilibrium" (Balcerowicz 1995; Hellman 1998; Sachs 1990). In Poland, this stance came from a minority within Solidarity who strongly criticized the pro-worker agreements at the Roundtable Talks and voiced the necessity to engage in a Latin American type shock-therapy stabilization (Orenstein 2001, 28; Balcerowicz 1994, 168). This group was backed by a handful of international advisors closely related to financial circles and international organizations. Interestingly, so-called reform communists held quite similar views.[20] In Estonia, radical reform advocates in civil society organizations called for an immediate declaration of independence from the Soviet Union, instead of the milder autonomy advocated by moderate reformers. They invoked international law to claim that Estonia was an illegally annexed state. They argued that it was necessary to form a legislative body outside established Soviet institutions, and they saw radical market reforms as a way to rapidly depart from the Soviet past.[21] Unlike in Poland, a third conservative force called the Intermovement Group tried to stop the reform process altogether. This alliance between Russian-speaking state apparatchiks, managers of state enterprises, and their workers wanted to protect the interests of the large Russian-speaking minority who felt threatened by demands for independence.[22] In what follows, I trace the rise of neoliberals in

20. Regime officials in Poland were in favor of a quick reform path in order to secure control of the political *tempo*. The program they presented at the Roundtable Talks was strikingly similar to what would later be the "Balcerowicz Plan" (S. Johnson and Kowalska 1995, 189; Kowalik 2011, 66).

21. During World War II, the Molotov-Ribbentrop pact secretly ceded the Baltic States to the sphere of influence of the Soviet Union. After the war, formerly independent Estonia became part of the USSR as the Estonian Soviet Socialist Republic (ESSR).

22. After the Soviet invasion that followed World War II, Russian speakers in Estonia increased from 5 percent of the population to around 40 percent in 1989. Most of them were imported to make up for the lack of blue-collar workers during Soviet industrialization plans. The issue of their integration into the new, independent state became crucial in the reform period (Pettai 2012, 88–95; Pettai and Hallik 2002).

these countries and how they variously succeeded or failed in shielding themselves from pressures from the "losers" of reform.

The political landscape changed completely in Poland following the Roundtable agreements and the ensuing victory of Solidarity representatives in the June 1989 parliamentary elections. Solidarity won the complete 35 percent of the seats available at the lower chamber, and all but one of the available seats for the newly established Senate. As social turmoil increased and the economy faltered, victorious Solidarity representatives convinced the smaller satellite communist parties in Parliament to support Solidarity leader Tadeusz Mazowiecki for prime minister (Howard and Brzezinski 1998, 137; Ost 2005, 48–49). In a U-turn from previous policy statements and agreements, Mazowiecki selected the radical reform advocate Leszek Balcerowicz and his team to draft an economic plan for the new government.[23] Balcerowicz prepared a shock therapy blueprint later known as the "Balcerowicz Plan" based on macroeconomic adjustment, liberalization, and privatization.

The Balcerowicz Plan included the explicit utilization of a fixed exchange rate for stabilization purposes, reflecting the preference for price stability (Balcerowicz in Bléjer and Coricelli 1995, 44–46; Poznański 1996, 176–77). The exchange rate was devalued to the level existing in the informal market and pegged to the U.S. dollar at the value of 9500 zlotys per one U.S. dollar. The exchange rate peg was viewed as a crucial element of the plan, as it was supposed to help bring inflation rates to international standards in the context of trade and financial liberalization, as well as to induce a government commitment to stabilization and market reforms (S. Johnson and Kowalska 1995, 194; see also Kołodko and Nuti 1997, 5–6; Sachs 1994, 54). This decision influenced other related economic measures, such as the need to secure a stabilization fund from international organizations in order to support the peg, as well as the need to maintain tight monetary and fiscal policies (Sachs 1994, 52–53; Nuti 2000).

The Balcerowicz Plan combined exchange rate stabilization with the elimination of industrial policy. In an interview in 1994 Balcerowicz explicitly stated:

My major concern was to avoid adopting a western type of protectionist and overregulated policy with respect to agriculture, especially of the Eu-

23. Leszek Balcerowicz was relatively distant from the core of the Solidarity movement and had not participated in the Roundtable Talks, but was known for having steered a team of economists that worked on economic reform plans during the 1980s (Orenstein 2001, 28–31; see Bléjer and Coricelli 1995).

ropean Community's CAP type, or the sort of industrial policy whereby the state bureaucracy would pick the winners by manipulating the tax system or credit policy (cited in Bléjer and Coricelli 1995, 46).

After the Balcerowicz Plan was enacted, the share of subsidies to enterprises in public spending fell from 33.2 percent in 1988 to only 17 percent in 1990 (S. Johnson and Kowalska 1995, 225). In the case of trade policy, quotas and other nontariff measures were quickly replaced by a uniform tariff, whose average rate fell from 18.3 percent to 5.5 percent during 1990 (Kołodko and Nuti 1997, 12). The only area in which the plan could not be developed as quickly was mass privatization, which reduced the business support for Balcerowicz's envisaged neoliberal regime (see chapter 5).

Support for continued reforms rested, therefore, on the relation between the government and the Solidarity trade union, and their symbolic power stemming from years of struggle against communism. In practice, Solidarity acted as a sort of umbrella over neoliberal reforms, investing its symbolic capital in the Mazowiecki government and de facto containing workers' demands (Ost 2005; Orenstein 2001; Linz and Stepan 1996, 273–74). However, the economic recession associated with liberalizing reforms, a massive drop in industrial output, a surge in unemployment, and a drastic reduction of real incomes had deleterious effects on Solidarity's main constituencies (Orenstein 2001, 48). This ushered in a period of normal politics when the symbolic power of Solidarity was not enough to deter opposition to its own government's economic reforms. Eventually, the inability of the Solidarity governments to create supporters from privatization (chapter 5) or block oppositions in Parliament (chapter 6) implied that the umbrella they offered to protect neoliberal reforms was no longer capable of stopping criticism.

Starting in 1990, opinion polls showed increasing discontent with the economic and political situation, and given the lack of responsiveness from Solidarity's political parties and union representatives, discontent turned into protest (Ekiert and Kubik 2001, 68–69; 157). Protest events increased in number, massiveness, and intensity from 1990 to 1993.[24] A majority of them were led by those sectors directly hurt by the Balcerowicz Plan: workers and managers of previously protected state-owned companies that constituted Poland's noncompetitive sectors (steel, coal and iron mining), railways, civil servants,

24. While protest in Poland did not differ greatly form high-protest events in West European countries, they were by far the greatest in a region characterized by labor acquiescence and society's "patience" (Ekiert and Kubik 2001, 113; Greskovits 1998).

and farmers (Ekiert and Kubik 2001, 109). Workers demanded higher wages and an end to massive layoffs, as well as industrial restructuring before privatization was accomplished (Sznajder Lee 2010, 43; Ekiert and Kubik 2001, 130–31; Ost 2005, 150–52). They joined the managers of state-owned enterprises (SOEs) in demanding state funds for this restructuring (Ost 2005, 150–51; Kohl and Platzer 2004, 118). Farmers' wage-related demands—price floors and guarantees—gave way to a more politicized opposition to neoliberal reforms and more violent protests as their representation switched from Solidarity to the more combative Self-Defense (*Samoobrona*) union (Forys and Gorlach 2002, 56–57; Ekiert and Kubik 2001, 136). Meanwhile, competitive companies in the tradable sector also demanded policy changes. They complained vocally in the press about the process of exchange rate appreciation produced by the fixed exchange rate, demanding currency devaluation (see S. Johnson and Kowalska 1995, 227; Gazeta Wyborcza 1991a).

An alphabet soup of political parties emerged trying to represent these demands. Personal disputes as well as the decline in support for the government led to an early breakup of the Solidarity caucus in Parliament, a fragmentation of the post-Solidarity camp, and the emergence of a competitive post-communist alternative condemning neoliberal reforms (Orenstein 2001, 38; S. Johnson and Kowalska 1995, 225–26). The Polish United Workers Party was transformed into the Social Democracy of Poland (SdRP), which together with the former Communist Confederation of Labor Unions (OPZZ), and other ex-communist organizations formed the Democratic Left Alliance (SLD) to contest the 1991 parliamentary elections. The SLD linked the output and employment drop directly to the lack of protection of agriculture and the lack of an active industrial policy, advocating more state intervention, protection of the domestic market, and progressive taxation (Markowski 2002, 62–63). Conversely, the Communist satellite agrarian party, which became the Polish Peasant Party (PSL), competed to represent farmers' discontent by stressing the need to protect agriculture in the face of integration with the West, as well as advocating an active state role in the economy—in other words, guaranteeing minimal prices for agricultural products (Gorlach and Mooney 1998, 274–75).

The breakup of Solidarity was formalized when the movement's two most prominent leaders, Lech Wałęsa and Tadeusz Mazowiecki, competed against each other for the post of president of the republic in 1990. The post-Solidarity camp fragmented into a multitude of parties and formations, which distinguished themselves mainly by resorting to a cultural cleavage between conservative-populist hybrids versus liberals (Jasiewicz 1992; Orenstein 2001, 32). While the liberal camp identified with the Mazowiecki government and the Balcerowicz Plan favored the continuity of neoliberal reforms, the conservative-populist camp concentrated mainly on social and cultural issues. Nevertheless, by voicing discontent and the need to reduce the costs of reform, these parties helped to dismantle the support for the Mazowiecki government and the continuity of neoliberalism (Ost 2005; Ekiert and Kubik 2001, 52).

Three post-Solidarity governments succeeded Mazowiecki. Jan Krzysztof Bielecki, (January to December 1991) from the Liberal Democratic Congress (KLD) who confirmed Balcerowicz in his post and tried to boost the economic reform program; Jan Olszewski (December 1991 to June 1992) from the conservative-populist side, elected under a promise to halt economic reforms; and Hanna Suchocka (July 1992 to October 1993) from the liberal Democratic Union (UW), who tried to reestablish a reform path. In the context of continued social protest, these governments offered policy concessions that gradually eroded the initial program's homogeneity and radical nature (see Ekiert and Kubik 2001, 138–39; S. Johnson and Kowalska 1995, 232).

The Bielecki government continued to back the exchange rate peg and relinquished devaluation, associating it with "economic disaster" (Gazeta Wyborcza 1991a). Any move intended to devalue the zloty was seen as a way to help exporters in general and noncompetitive state-owned firms in particular (PAP News Wire 1993). But by May 1991, the peg had already been changed from the U.S. dollar to a basket of currencies, with the implicit intention to achieve a real devaluation. The zloty devalued by 17 percent,[25] a change that was received by exporters as "nice but not enough" (Gazeta Wyborcza 1991b). In October 1991, a new change compromised the exchange rate regime altogether in a search for greater export competitiveness while, at the same time, maintaining price stability. A crawling peg regime was put in place, with the basket-related exchange rate parity subject to daily devaluations and a monthly ceiling of 1.8 percent. The change was explicitly justified as an aid to exporters, as well as a move to prevent currency runs amid expectations of a larger devaluation (Gazeta Wyborcza 1991c). In February 1992, when the Olszewski government was still settling, the government devalued the zloty another 10.7 percent, an action interpreted as a response to the "agrarian and industrialist lobbies" (Kamiński 1998, 196; see Skalski 1992).

25. The following figures are taken from Nuti (2000).

In terms of industrial policy, the trajectory of increasing concessions was similar. First, tariffs were raised again to 18.4 percent in August 1991, together with temporary import surcharges (Kołodko and Nuti 1997, 12). Second, following another failure at mass privatization, the Bielecki government created the Agency for Industrial Development (AID) to provide financial assistance to companies in distress prior to their privatization. Yet another turn occurred during the Suchocka government with the passing of a new Enterprise and Bank Restructuring Act, after lengthy negotiations with trade unions and employer associations (Orenstein 2001, 47–50; Ost 2005, 514 n. 36). State banks were recapitalized in order to roll over companies' debts, and the AID was empowered to undertake a wide arrange of measures, including giving and underwriting loans, buying equity stakes, coordinating restructuring programs, overseeing liquidations and managing enterprises postliquidation, and helping to organize and hold shares in regional development agencies (King and Sznajder 2006, 772). The new act gave workers a substantive role in restructuring and privatization. Concessions were also given to farmers. While systematic subsidies were denied, interest rates were lowered for agricultural inputs, a new Agency of Agriculture Market was created in order to regulate food prices, and the Social Security Fund for Peasants was created (Pleines 2008, 106; 110; S. Johnson and Kowalska 1995, 215). In sum, different forms of industrial policy started to emerge as a response to the demand from noncompetitive business sectors.

These concessions notwithstanding, post-Solidarity governments found themselves under increasing distress and parliamentary deadlock due to the politicization of demands and the attempt by the ex-communists to represent them (see S. Johnson and Kowalska 1995, 233). In May 1993, the Suchocka government fell after a vote of no confidence supported by populist post-Solidarity parties, marking the end of orthodox neoliberalism in Poland.

The elections of October 1993 brought the ex-communist SLD and PSL parties into a government alliance, reflecting a rejection of arms-length neoliberalism and opening up a period where political and socioeconomic actors tried to present an alternative development project (see Blazyca and Rapacki 1996, 87; Orenstein 2001, 37–38). I stress here—in contrast with Estonia and in parallel to Argentina—how the SLD/PSL governments tried to build a new social bloc out of those actors opposing neoliberal reforms, and the contours of such formation in terms of the resulting policy mix.

It has often been argued that this change in government did not truly mark a new direction in Poland's development. Two arguments are often invoked (see Szczerbiak 1998; Grzymała-Busse 2002; Markowski 2002; Tavits and Letki 2009): first, that the new government majority was more an unexpected consequence of the electoral system (which transformed the ex-communists' one-third of the votes into a two-thirds parliamentary majority) than a true rejection of neoliberalism; second, that the ex-communist parties had moderated their critical stance and embraced market reforms, modern social democracy, and prudent macroeconomic management. As to voters' intent, the election in 1995 of SLD leader Aleksander Kwaśniewski as president of the republic against high-ranking Solidarity leaders (including the legendary Lech Wałęsa, as well as the ex-minister of labor and working class hero Jacek Kuroń, and former prime minister Jan Olszewski) is further proof of a conscious rejection of Solidarity-led neoliberalism in favor of an alternative development project. Moreover, while it is true that the SLD government sought prudent macroeconomic policy and international integration, the changes in exchange rate and industrial policy contrast markedly with the previous period in Poland and the continuity path in Estonia. In this sense, I concur with Mitchell Orenstein that "the backlash against shock therapy was politically effective in Poland insofar as it stopped or delayed the implementation of additional reform legislation" (2001, 42).

The SLD/PSL government's economic plan—the "Strategy for Poland"—was a direct challenge to Balcerowicz's shock therapy. Its author, Grzegorz Kołodko, who was both minister of finance and deputy prime minister, opposed the fixed exchange rate and advocated a managed exchange rate regime emphasizing national competitiveness (Gazeta Wyborcza 1991a; Kołodko 1993, 16; Kołodko and Nuti 1997, 13; 27). The choice of exchange rate regimes during these years was also affected by the prospect of future accession to the European Monetary Union (EMU). In contrast to neoliberal views that saw the necessity to rapidly stabilize exchange rates through contractive monetary and fiscal policies, Kołodko envisaged a gradual transition, with emphasis on fiscal and monetary policy coordination, and "gradual preparations and [a] soft landing" to avoid a recession (Kołodko and Nuti 1997, 45–46; see Orłowski 1996; Gomułka 1998). Kołodko engaged in heated battles with the governor of the Polish National Bank (NBP), Hanna Gronkiewicz-Waltz, who advocated a neoliberal use of the exchange rate to reduce inflation (R. A. Epstein 2008, 55–56). Gronkiewicz-Waltz had diminished the rate of devaluation of the existing crawling peg, thus forcing exchange rate appreciation. She even put forward the idea of establishing a free float, to the delight of the emerging private financial sector (Gazeta Wyborcza 1995c; Gazeta Wyborcza 1995b).

Because the government still held the reins of monetary policy, Kołodko forced an agreement with the NBP to establish an exchange rate bands regime and demanded high exchange rate levels (see chapter 7). In other words, exchange rate policies clearly diverged from the stark neoliberal "price-stability" orientation of the early transition years.

The "Strategy for Poland" document also accorded important roles to state intervention in industrial restructuring, the stimulation of exports, and domestic investment (Kołodko 1993, 6–8; Kołodko and Nuti 1997, 37; King and Sznajder 2006, 774). Three ideas stand out: 1) industrial policy as regional development, which sparked the creation of special economic zones in selected regions;[26] 2) industrial policy as an instrument to enhance competitiveness as Poland gradually opened itself to the West—especially EU integration (e.g., through the implementation of export credit insurance and guarantees); and 3) industrial policy for the restructuring and privatization of SOEs with the use of social dialogue structures. While the first two components were horizontal in nature, the third was clearly selective. Moreover, in the case of industry-concentrated regions, economic zones that by definition were horizontal served selective purposes in practice (King and Sznajder 2006, 776). Much of these industrial policy efforts were dedicated to compensating the noncompetitive industries that had been critical of the neoliberal reforms of the Solidarity governments.

In the case of restructuring and privatization of SOEs, Poland abandoned both mass and case-by-case privatization for sector-based restructuring programs with the participation of trade unions (King and Sznajder 2006, 775–76; Sznajder Lee 2010, 43; Gilejko 2011, 68; Ost 2005, 214 n. 36). Therefore, while industry subsidies continued to drop, expenditure for the specific purpose of industry restructuring—including the contentious steel and coal mining industries—grew from 7.9 percent of total expenditures in economic affairs in 1991 to 13.2 percent in 1995 and to 31 percent in 1997, the last year of the SDL/PSL administration.[27] Restructured sectors also benefitted from the establishment of Tripartite Commissions, where enterprises and unions could, for the first time, negotiate wages and working conditions at the sectoral level.

Finally, while average tariff rates remained steady, there was a significant hike in maximum rates, reflecting a return to selective protection. Both average

26. Special Economic Zones were intended to attract investors, especially foreign ones, by offering tax breaks to regions with industries in need of restructuring and regions with high unemployment. In 1997 there were 16 Special Economic Zones (King and Sznajder 2006, 776).

27. Central Statistical Office (1998, 471).

TABLE 4.2. Poland and Estonia, Tariff Rates 1995–1999

	Poland		Estonia	
Year	AHS	Max	AHS	Max
1995	8	55	0.05	16
1996	10.45	369.3	0.01	16
1997	9.8	344	0.01	16
1998	8.15	324.1	0	0
1999	5.15	293.3	0	0

Source: World Integrated Trade Solution (WITS).
Legend: AHS= Effectively applied tariff; Max= Maximum tariff.

and maximum tariffs starkly differed from the almost absolute free trade conditions in Estonia (see table 4.2). In fact, when Poland entered the WTO in 1995 it decided to freeze its tariffs at the maximum allowable level, and actively made use of selective temporary tariff exemptions, quotas, and nontariff restrictions to protect specific competitive and noncompetitive industries, including food, chemicals, electronic and precision components and equipment, and the automotive sector (Kamiński 1998, 196–98).

In sum, the SLD/PSL government provided an alternative to the orthodox neoliberalism of the first Solidarity years. The presence of the PSL party in government provided channels for the representation of farmers' interests, while the slow pace of privatization and the existence of state-owned enterprises in competitive and noncompetitive sectors facilitated the emergence of business actors in favor of an alternative development project. Exchange rate policy fostered exports and protected domestic producers, while industrial policy shielded noncompetitive sectors from external competition and aided their restructuring, as well as providing export-oriented infrastructure to competitive sectors.

In the case of Estonia, the transition began in early 1990 with a gradual, negotiated, and ethnically-inclusive strategy promulgated by Popular Front leader Edgar Savisaar. However, the military intervention of Soviet troops in neighboring Latvia and Lithuania in early 1991, as well as the visibility of the anti-independence and pro-Soviet Intermovement group, tilted the domestic balance of power toward the more radical approach advocated by the Congress of Estonia, a quasi-state structure built by advocates of radical reform representing only ethnic Estonians. The sudden declaration of independence in August 1991, following a takeover attempt in Moscow, necessitated quick political and economic changes. Several ministers defected from Savisaar's cabinet in January 1992, forming a new government that supported radical reforms (D. Smith 2001, 69–70; Knöbl, Sutt, and Zavoiceo 2002). Led by technocrat Tiit Vähi, the first moves of the new cabinet were geared to ensure the financial viability of the new state and involved steep fiscal retrenchment and the introduction of a national currency.

Siim Kallas, governor of the Bank of Estonia (BOE) and advocate of radical reforms, managed to impose currency reform on his terms by reintroducing the Estonian kroon under a currency board. The kroon was pegged to the deutsche mark at the rate of 8=1, and the parity protected by law. Other reforms included massive price liberalization and privatization. Especially important, the new constitution included a balanced budget provision that forced the slashing of state subsidies. As a result, capital expenditures and transfers declined from 26 percent of total spending in 1991 to 19 percent in 1992 (World Bank 1993, 23, 292).

Support for continued reform efforts depended on the connection between market reforms, independence, and nation building, which infused the new economic institutions and neoliberal reforms with nationalist sentiments (Lauristin and Vihalemm 1997, 96–100; D. Smith 2001, 68–69; Pettai and Hallik 2002, 512–13). The threat from the Soviet-leaning Intermovement and the Soviet Union itself, as well as Estonia's distressed economic condition, crystallized the idea that independence required harsh measures and extended sacrifices (Lauristin and Vihalemm 1997, 102–3; D. Smith 2001, 81). While this may seem an idiosyncratic characteristic of the Estonian trajectory, I argue that the key to understanding neoliberal resilience in this ethnically-divided society is understanding how this "umbrella" was institutionalized and the right societal actors (dis)empowered, preventing policy backlashes. Unlike in Poland, the Estonian umbrella shielding reforms did not fold, but helped to prolong this extraordinary period in politics and the insulation of neoliberal reformers from demands for a different course.

The economic and social effects of shock therapy were similar in Estonia and Poland. Real wages declined sharply, beginning to recover only in 1994 but at levels well below those of 1990 (OECD 2000a, 234; 236). The differential drop in sectoral employment confirms that the harder-hit sectors were, as in Poland, agriculture and industry (OECD 2000a, 234, 236). However, the connection between neoliberal reforms and nationalist sentiment, not to mention ethnic political tensions, affected the emergence of protest movements. In fact, the closeness of the Declaration of Independence in mid-1991 with the approval of a new constitution only a year later, followed quickly by the first fully free parliamentary elections in September 1992, threw a nationalist veil over ongoing market reforms. Moreover, the relative concentration of non-Estonians (mainly Russians) in industry, and their participation in anti-independence movements in 1990–1991, made industry appear as an obstacle to independence, therefore facilitating policies that avoided protecting the sector (Lauristin and Vihalemm 1997, 90).[28] Moreover, it is estimated that in the mid-1980s between 85 and 90 percent of Estonian industry was under the direct control of Moscow (Mettam and Williams 1998, 373).

At the same time that the concentration of the Russian minority in industrial employment produced a rejection of industrial policy-type protective measures, the association of trade unions and protest with the pro-Soviet Intermovement actions helped to propagate a feeling that protesting amounted to supporting the Soviets and blocking independence.[29] This nationalist sentiment pervaded trade unions who embraced the independence cause instead of fighting for workers' rights (see Ruutsoo 1996, 109–10). A symptom of this was the fact that union leaders were often white-collar workers strongly identified with the more nationalist and radical economic stances.

Rejection of the Soviet past prevented the emergence of protest groups, not only in industry, but also in rural areas. Initial demands in agriculture were not intensified, as in Poland, by a stark decline in output, employment, and income, but by the more nationalistic claims of land restitution (see chapter 5). Two further issues complicated the organization of farmers' interests (Pettai 2012, 100–101): first, any appeal to the farmers as a group with special interests was doomed to be seen as causing disunity among Estonians; second, the first rural organizations were led by former managers of Soviet-era collective farms, which reduced the legitimacy of their demands.

The context of ethnic politics amid radical neoliberal reforms helped the exclusionary integration stance advocated by radical reformers prevail, as reflected in the new constitution and citizenship law that heavily curtailed the political rights of the Russian-speaking minority, harder hit by economic

28. Ethnic Estonians outnumbered non-Estonians by two to one in both total population and total employment. However, in industry, which concentrated about one-third of total employment, ethnic Estonians and ethnic Russians were virtually equally represented (Mettam and Williams 1998, 379).

29. Although less than one-third of the Russian-speaking minority supported the Intermovement group, the visibility of their demands as well as the direct support from Moscow made the anti-independence cause appear much larger and socially embedded than it actually was (D. Smith 2001, 49; 56–57; Lauristin and Vihalemm 1997, 95–97; Pettai 2012, 52).

reforms due to its concentration in declining economic sectors (see chapter 6). Consequently, in the run-up to the 1992 elections, the parties combining radical economic reforms with the exclusion of the Russian minority had an electoral advantage, among them the parties that had emerged from the Congress of Estonia such as the Pro Patria alliance (*Isamaa*) and the National Independence Party. A group of liberals and social democrats within the Popular Front (PF) who had an exclusionary view of the ethnic issue formed the Moderates Party. Integrationist parties who advocated gradual reforms were at a disadvantage: on the center-left, former prime minister Edgar Savisaar and his Center Party (*Keskerakond*)[30], and to its center the Secure Home (KMÜ) alliance uniting pragmatic ex-Communist managers and apparatchiks (the Coalition Party led by ex-prime minister Tiit Vähi) with representatives of rural associations (Rural Union). The latter party was in favor of continued reforms but with responsiveness to problems in the countryside (Pettai 2012, 101).

Mart Laar from Pro Patria, a shock therapy advocate and representative of the younger generation of Estonians free from ties with the Soviet past, became prime minister (D. Smith 2001, 83; see also Lauristin and Vihalemm 1997, 106). Laar's plans to revamp industrial policy included the introduction of a flat tax on corporate income, the elimination of previous tax benefits for foreign investors, an open rejection of selective measures, and a large-scale privatization program (Sutela 2001, 19). Not only were all kinds of support and subsidies slashed; the Estonian privatization process became known for not including a restructuring of state enterprises before selling them—as was the case in Poland (see chapter 5). By 1993, subsidies to state-owned companies were virtually non-existent (World Bank 1993, 48). At the same time, the Laar government started an aggressive policy of unilateral trade liberalization. By the end of 1993, average tariffs were a mere 1.4 percent (Feldmann and Sally 2002, 84).

The new government strongly backed the currency board. The capital account was liberalized in 1994, and new banking regulations were adopted (Bank of Estonia 1999, 19). More significantly, Laar stood back to back with Bank of Estonia governor Siim Kallas to withstand a financial crisis triggered by the dissolution of the ruble zone in late 1992 (OECD 2000a, 105–7). With Estonia's market economy still in its infancy, Laar and Kallas rejected bailouts

30. The Center Party cannot be considered left-wing by international standards, but according to local observers it is the one party that seeks support from less advantaged groups, and ever since has been considered the only alternative to neoliberalism in the electoral arena. See Pettai 2009, n. 15.

on the basis that they would produce inflation and undermine the currency board (Fleming, Chu, and Bakker 1996, 14; Pettai 2009, 77). Consequently, some state-owned enterprises, which in Poland constituted the backbone of business demand for an alternative development model, were placed in bankruptcy and filed for privatization (Fleming, Chu, and Bakker 1996, 20).

The first turning point came in 1994, when election results warned of discontent with the existing path of transformation, just as had happened with the election of ex-communists in Poland the previous year (Nørgaard 1996, 149; D. Smith 2001, 94; Lauristin and Vihalemm 1997, 108–9). Farmers increasingly grumbled about neoliberal policies, and new political parties sprang up vowing to represent them: for example, the Country People's Party, which was led by Arnold Rüütel, an ex-communist manager and former runner up in the 1992 presidential elections. This party, together with smaller agrarian parties, demanded higher subsidies and tariff barriers to protect farmers (D. Smith 2001, 95; Baltic News Service 1995c). Right-wing parties, including that of former prime minister Laar, fell significantly in their vote share, while parties advocating protection for the losers of reform such as the Center Party and the Country People's Party (running under the KMÜ banner together with the centrist Coalition Party) increased theirs (see Taagepera 1995; D. Smith 2001, 95–96).

Despite the higher vote for center-left and agrarian parties, a backlash against neoliberalism or even a substantive halt to the reform process as happened in Poland failed to materialize. There was a lack of business support for an alternative development project, and center-left parties were blockaded in Parliament (see chapters 5 and 6). Instead, developments during the period helped to consolidate neoliberalism.

The ethnic cleavage still illuminating the reality of party politics, and the exclusion of the Russian minority suppressed voter turnout for the Center Party, which, according to some, was the only party that could have provided a real political alternative. It finished third in the running (Pettai 2009, 86; Lagerspetz and Vogt 2013, 55). After the centrist KMÜ alliance, the second majority went to the pro-market Reform Party (*Reformierakond*), a merger of former Pro Patria and Moderates members led by the architect of monetary reform, Siim Kallas. The Reform Party conditioned its participation in a KMÜ-led government on the elimination of protective tariffs and subsidies for ailing economic sectors from the government program (Baltic News Service 1995e).

An alternative development project also failed to garner support from the emerging business class. First, privatization prevented the formation of a sizable base of support for an alternative economic policy program from state-owned enterprises under distress, as happened in Poland. In fact, in spite of the early banking crisis in 1992, the financial sector remained the most important business supporter of continued neoliberal reforms. According to some accounts, this dominance was crucial to the operation of the currency board and vice versa (Sörg and Vensel 2000, 128, 132): fears of a possible devaluation made authorities accelerate the development of financial and derivative markets amid demands for exchange rate insurance and swap contracts from the financial industry. At the same time, the issuance of forward contracts ensuring current exchange rate levels helped to dispel doubts about the continuity of the currency board. Conversely, exporters were ardent defenders of market reforms and were happy to see prime Minister Tiit Vähi, from the Coalition Party, pledge to continue the path of economic reforms (Baltic News Service 1995b).

Agriculture and the food industry sought an agreement with the rural parties in government to demand tighter levels of protection (Baltic News Service 1996c). The issue became most pressing during the Asian/Russian crisis in 1998–1999, which heavily affected these sectors. The agrarian Country People's Union reintroduced the issue of customs tariffs for food products and looked for allies in Parliament, especially Savisaar's Center Party, to support them amid the rejection of the Reform Party and Coalition Party and the fall of the parliamentary majority in 1997 (Baltic News Service 1996a; Baltic News Service 1998a).

The weakness of the noncompetitive sector as a whole was significant in this context. For example, chemicals and mining, both connected with Soviet-era heavy industry, were both declining at this time (see, e.g., Mettam and Williams 1998). These trends were supported by the large flows of FDI that followed privatization. The arrival of foreign capital to these declining industries further prevented the formation of an opposition business bloc similar to the one in Poland (see chapter 5). In other words, Estonia could not count on a strong business base for an alternative development project as happened in Poland. Hence, even if multiple political parties emerged to represent growing anti-neoliberal feelings, they would all end up allying with the neoliberals and no backlash would materialize.

Europeanization

The process of preparation for accession to the EU and the formal accession in 2004 marked a second stage in the consolidation of neoliberalism in Eastern

Europe. In terms of the formation of social blocs defending neoliberalism and pushing for its consolidation, it is important to understand how this common external pressure was channeled through domestic actors and how they used existing institutions and policies to advance their interests (see Bohle and Greskovits 2012; Schimmelfennig and Sedelmeier 2005; Vachudova 2005).

Overall, a basic consensus among Estonian elites favored EU accession. Therefore, accession did not have significant impacts on domestic political competition and policy change, as would be the case in Poland (Lagerspetz and Vogt 2004; Mikkel and Kasekamp 2008; Sikk 2009). If anything, EU accession acted in the direction of further institutionalizing neoliberalism and empowering the actors behind its defense, while at the same time reducing the already low opposition toward continued neoliberal policies. In fact, the mood associated with EU accession, as well as pressure from the European Commission for the harmonization of citizenship and integration laws, brought a relaxation of the ethnic cleavage, which increased the electoral chances of the left-leaning Center Party (see Lagerspetz and Vogt 2013).

Given the radical nature of Estonian neoliberalism, EU accession implied that the country had to reduce this orthodoxy in several domains, particularly in industrial policy. Ultimately, this served to lessen opposition to EU accession from left-leaning parties and a small group of reluctant businesses. For example, the need to increase agricultural subsidies as part of the implementation of the Common Agricultural Policy (CAP) dissuaded opposition from food producers, agrarian parties, and the Center Party (Sikk 2009, 476; Mikkel and Kasekamp 2008, 303). The biggest challenge was therefore for right-wing parties, who saw EU accession as a threat to Estonia's neoliberal path (e.g., Raig 2007). They assumed, however, that EU accession (together with the accession to NATO) was more than justified as a matter of national security and as a further step away from Russia, EMU accession being the key economic goal (Lagerspetz and Vogt 2004, 77; Mikkel and Kasekamp 2008, 309; Feldmann and Sally 2002, 99). One Reform Party MP put it in the following terms:

> In the nineties we had more free market and more liberal ideas than now, because the European Union is a Keynesian society. But of course, we had to follow the ideas of the EU.[31]

Overall, right-wing parties consolidated their dominance of party politics in Estonia, as reflected in the prevalence of the Reform Party, which managed to form part of all governments from 1999 on, maintaining a decisive grip on

---

31. Estonia, Interview 8.

government programs (see Solvak and Pettai 2008). A rightist party, Res Publica, was created from a merger of former Pro Patria and Reform Party members. Although it presented some of the right-populist overtones found in other countries in the region, presenting itself as a party close to the interests of ordinary people, Res Publica maintained a neoliberal policy orientation that conduced the antiestablishment vote into a neoliberal platform (see Taagepera 2006; Pettai 2004). In fact, despite the fact that the left-leaning Center Party became the biggest party in Parliament in 1999 and remained in that position thereafter, it was unable to form stable government coalitions, having to negotiate strategic deals with neoliberal parties that reduced its influence in government policy (see especially Pettai 2009).[32]

In terms of exchange rate policy, Estonia—and particularly the Reform Party—wanted to join the EMU as quickly as possible, and maintaining the currency board was, it was thought, the best way into it. This also confirmed Estonia's preference for price stability. It avoided devaluation in 1998 amid the Russian crisis, and changed the exchange rate peg from the deutsche mark to the euro in 1999, both decisions marking its preference for rapid EMU accession. With little to no opposition, all right-wing-dominated governments during the 2000s sought accession as a key priority (Feldmann 2006). Estonia was the first country of the 2004 enlargement (the others were Slovenia and Lithuania) to enter the last phase before accession in June 2004. However, despite excelling in the deficit and debt criteria, Estonia suffered from the pro-cyclical effects of the currency board and sizable FDI inflows after EU accession, systematically failing to meet the stringent inflation criterion. After several failed attempts, around 2007 the government decided to postpone EMU accession until the conditions were met.

Contrariwise, EU accession stimulated new industrial policy plans and laid the ground for a stronger drive toward selectiveness when the Center Party was temporarily in government. First, Estonia had to raise its tariffs and adopt several nontariff and quota restrictions on free trade, in line with the EU giving away its free trade regime and agreements with third countries (see Feldmann and Sally 2002; Raig 2007). Second, Estonia had to increase agricultural subsidies in line with the CAP (OECD 2002, 22–23, 25). Although the increase amounted to only a fraction of the subsidies received by older member states,

---

32. This was partly due to the effects of opposition blockade (see chapter 6) and partly due to the decision by the other main parties to sideline the Center Party. In addition to partisanship and the ethnic question, there was a strong rejection of the political style of party founder and most influential party figure Edgar Savisaar.

it was a significant jump from Estonia's previously low level. Third, the pre-accession process made possible a new industrial policy framework based on horizontal instruments to small and medium enterprises (SMEs) and export-ers (Tiits, Kattel, and Kalvet 2006, 60; Kuusk and Jürgenson 2008; OECD 2009, 142–43).

The most interesting development of the period is the foundation in 2006 of the Development Fund (*Arengufond*). Strongly influenced by the Finnish Innovation Fund, SITRA (*Suomen Itsenäisyyden Juhlarahasto*), this was a pub-licly financed development agency working under direct mandate from the Parliament.[33] The Development Fund emerged as the result of a quest to foster innovation and new sectors. The idea started in the early 2000s after exchange rate appreciation had reduced Estonia's competitiveness (see e.g., Tiits et al. 2003; Tiits, Kattel, and Kalvet 2006). It included a research unit studying pro-spective investments—including new industries—and an investment facility. Unlike the other industrial policy initiatives, the Development Fund consti-tuted a purely domestic push and had a clear selective orientation (Eesti Rah-vusringhääling 2005). It was conceived by the center-left Center Party and received especial support from its chairman, Edgar Savisaar, acting as economy minister while the party was briefly in government in 2005–2007. Savisaar skillfully managed to bring in other parties to support the project despite the skepticism of the neoliberal Reform Party, the senior party in the government coalition. In its final composition, the government allocated to the Develop-ment Fund the 3 percent equity stake it still maintained in Estonian Telekom plus a one-time budgetary allocation to cover current expenses.

The 2007–2008 financial crisis served to reinforce neoliberalism, dispelling possibilities of currency devaluation and retrenching the advancements in industrial policy. The 2007 election brought a revitalization of the ethnic cleav-age that once again harmed the electoral prospects of left-leaning parties.[34] This was compounded by fears that the left-leaning Center Party would emerge as the single election winner (Pettai 2009, 86). The Reform Party, which man-aged to remain the biggest party in Parliament after the elections, chose to

33. Estonia, Interviews 4 and 11.

34. The so-called Bronze Soldier Statue affair (the removal of a statue commemorating the actions of Soviet soldiers who liberated Estonia from Nazi occupation, located in the capital Tallinn), which was decried by Russians and cheered by Estonian nationalists, served to reignite dormant ethnic animosities. See Solvak and Pettai (2008). The five-day War between Russia and Georgia in 2008 brought back the specter of a Russian occupation of Estonia, adding to the rise in nationalist sentiments among the population.

form a quirky four-party government with the conservative Pro Patria and Res Publica Union, the Social Democrats and the newly created Greens, just to prevent forming yet another government with the Center Party, the second-biggest party in Parliament (Pettai 2009, 86). With the crisis unleashed, the Reform Party-led government insisted on EMU (European Monetary Union) accession, starting a process of internal devaluation that it hoped would mean finally reaching the inflation target (Raudla and Kattel 2011, 175). The need to maintain the confidence of external investors and thereby the prospects of a rapid exit from the crisis was continuously stressed as a rationale for strong austerity measures; meanwhile, Estonian civil society, characteristically, exhibited little response to the pressing economic situation (Beissinger and Sasse 2014; Raudla and Kattel 2011; Baltic Business News 2009b). With massive budget cuts, layoffs, and skyrocketing unemployment, Estonia became a true "poster child for austerity defenders."[35]

The recent industrial development projects were hard hit by the budget cuts undertaken amid the crisis. Soon after its introduction, the Development Fund had come under attack from businessmen connected with the financial sector, as well as the business press (Eesti Rahvusringhääling 2009a; Baltic Business News 2009a). Although the right-wing Reform Party-led government did not have enough votes in Parliament to eliminate the Development Fund altogether, its functioning was severely compromised. In 2009, the Telekom shares that had been the basis of its funding were taken back and sold, limiting the Fund's resources. According to one former manager of the Fund, this amounted to its "killing" (Eesti Rahvusringhääling 2009b). A new management team nominated by the government restructured the Fund, significantly changing its mission and functioning.[36]

In the end, internal devaluation and budgetary restraint paid off, as Estonia fulfilled the inflation criteria for EMU accession and the EU Commission announced its acceptance into the Eurozone in 2011, closing the circle of the institutionalization of neoliberalism in the country.

Unlike in Estonia, the process of EU accession in Poland revealed stark and enduring divisions on the issues of EMU accession and industrial policy-related subsidies. Big business and the financial sector voiced their preference for a free float exchange rate in the early 2000s (Polish News Bulletin 2002d)

35. The phrase was coined by economist and Nobel prize winner Paul Krugman in a blog entry that criticized the Estonian policy measures, provoking the rage of Estonian authorities. See Greeley (2012).

36. Estonia, Interview 11.

and switched to demand quick euro entry in the pre-accession period. They envisaged one of two formulas to speed up convergence: "unilateral euroization," or a currency board (see Jankowiak 2005).[37] This position was echoed by the Freedom Union Party (UW) and, after its dissolution, by the Civic Platform (PO) and Central bank authorities (see Zubek 2006, 199–200). Conversely, exporters and SOEs moved from demanding devaluation and currency intervention (Polish News Bulletin 2001b; Polish News Bulletin 2002c) to euro accession although with the caveat that it be accompanied by a high exchange rate to support competitiveness (see Polish News Bulletin 2006c; cf. Zubek 2006, 209). Their acquiescence coincided with a renewed privatization effort that increased the share of foreign capital in these industries (see chapter 5). Politically, the change of preference was defended mostly by the ex-communist Democratic Left Alliance (SLD) (see Polish News Bulletin 2002a). Farmers were by far the most skeptical about EU accession in general, the entry to the EMU, and especially the effects on state subsidies. So was the agrarian PSL party and the new conservative-populist parties Law and Justice (PiS), League of Polish Families (LPR), and Self-Defense (*Samobroona*). However, unlike in subsidy-free Estonia, in Poland EU accession implied pressures for a swift reduction of subsidies. One Polish civil servant referred to the EU's terms on reducing industrial policy as "a pistol held to our head" (Sznajder Lee 2010, 225). The chances for the reinvigoration of neoliberalism or the maintenance of an alternative to it were shaped by a decade of fluid politics and the emergence of new political formations after each election between 1997 and 2007.

In 1997 a renewed Solidarity camp came into power again. The bigger coalition partner was Solidarity Electoral Action (AWS), an alliance of smaller groupings mostly from Solidarity's conservative wing. Under the banner of "finishing the Solidarity revolution," AWS managed to unite the hitherto fragmented Solidarity camp by appealing to cultural sentiments rather than by rehashing economic questions, and capturing the vote of those outraged with the return of former communists to government (Szczerbiak 1998, 79, 2004, 62–65). By appealing to the cultural cleavage and Solidarity's history of opposition to communism, it helped to prevent the solidification of a true left-leaning political alternative (Ost 2005; see also Grzymała-Busse 2001). The junior partner in the coalition was the Freedom Union (UW) formed around those

---

37. For a review of options to enter the Eurozone see Gomulka (2002); for the "unilateral euroization" argument in particular, see Bratkowski and Rostowski (2004).

who participated in the neoliberal Mazowiecki government. They explicitly
targeted the winners of reforms for political support and campaigned over the
completion of market reforms and the elaboration of a "second Balcerowicz
Plan."

While the AWS economic program remained an unclear mix of reform and
protection, the appointment of Leszek Balcerowicz as minister of finance and
deputy prime minister set the tone for the government's economic policy orientation (see EIU Business Eastern Europe 1997; The Economist 1997). In
agreement with the Central Bank (NBP), Balcerowicz supported a new law in
1997 establishing the autonomy of the NBP, then in 2000 facilitated the change
to a free float / inflation-targeting exchange rate framework (see chapter 7).
This change represented the return of an exclusive price stability goal in exchange rates, a support to the development of the financial sector, and a commitment to reduce inflation to secure EMU accession (Polish News Bulletin
2000; Zubek 2006, 199). The new floating regime did not preclude exchange
rate intervention, but this could only happen when inflation targets were
under threat (Panbuła, Kozinski, and Rubaszek 2011, 293). In anticipation of
accession and the arrival of EU cohesion funds, the AWS/UW government
prepared to scale back industry subsidies and in 2000 founded the Polish
Agency for Enterprise Development (PARP) to set up horizontal grants, enacting at the same time an administrative reform that restructured regional
agencies and special economic zones (Ferry 2007).

Soon, however, the reform plans of the AWS/UW government were
aborted. A new wave of protest—the first since the early 1990s—was organized by the same combination of competitive and noncompetitive sectors
that led them back then: agriculture, steel, and coal mining (Forys and Gorlach
2002, 60; Pleines 2008; Gilejko 2011, 72). Protesters rallied against the planned
reduction of state subsidies and the new restructuring programs in the state
sector. The protests coincided with the effects of the Russian crisis on agricultural exports, and Polish farmers demanded higher food prices and import
barriers. The farmers' protests became increasingly vocal and politicized when
they fell once again under the aegis of the populist Self-Defense Union (*Samoobrona*) (Forys and Gorlach 2002, 61). Amid the unrest, the government's
popularity plummeted, forcing a breakup in 2000 (see Szczerbiak 2002b).

The 2001 election was marked by the dissolution of the parties in the previous government and the slowdown of economic growth due to the effects of
the Russian crisis. The election brought the center-left SLD/PSL coalition to
power again, in concert with the left-leaning Union of Labor (UP). In spite of

the SLD's recent economic moderation, it campaigned on the revitalization of domestic demand and a frontal attack on the neoliberal AWS/UW reforms (Grzymała-Busse 2002; Szczerbiak 2002c). In the opposition, the Self-Defense Union, capitalizing on farmers increasing Euroscepticism, became the third party in Congress. Self-Defense conditioned the support for EU accession on a negotiation of unlimited subsidies and production ceilings for Poland's ailing competitive and noncompetitive sectors (agriculture, steel, coal and iron mining) (Szczerbiak 2002c, 8, 2002b, 56–57; see also Jasiewicz 2008).

The SLD-led government coalition tried to point Poland toward a more developmentalist alternative in exchange rate and industrial policy. EU accession and high interest rates set by the independent NBP (Polish Central Bank) produced increasing capital inflows and appreciation of the zloty under the existing free-floating regime. The government, responding to demands from exporters and SOEs for active intervention, engaged once again in fights with the NBP for a more active management of the exchange rate. It even advanced plans for an outright change to a managed floating system in order to maintain a low and stable developmental exchange rate.[38] It unsuccessfully tried to force an agreement with the NBP, exchanging spending cuts for lower interest rates and devaluation. The recently approved independence of the NBP proved crucial for rejecting the deal (see chapter 7).

In industrial policy, the government tried to distinguish itself from its right-wing predecessor, postponing further privatization in exchange for yet another wave of state-sponsored restructuring plans (Sznajder Lee 2006, 227). The new plans involved the consolidation of SOEs under large state-owned conglomerates prior to their sale to a strategic investor (see for the steel sector Sznajder Lee 2010, 44–45; Gilejko 2011, 72). This entailed an acceleration of subsidies before the entrance to the EU limited its use. In other cases, the government blocked privatization altogether. Conversely, the agrarian PSL tried to increase benefits for the noncompetitive food and agriculture sectors during EU accession negotiations (Szczerbiak 2002c, 9). Poland got concessions from the Commission that were seen as a major victory for the government and for Polish farmers (EIU Newswire 2003). Among the ten new member states, only three entered the EU with the maximum subsidy rate or more: Slovenia, Latvia, and Poland (OECD 2005, 80).

The SLD-UP/PSL government fell victim, however, to the deterioration of the economic situation and its inability to meet the EU fiscal criteria. Three

38. Polish News Bulletin 2002a; Poland, Interview 8.

consecutive attempts to curb budget deficits failed to pass in Parliament and forced the breakup of the government (see Zubek 2006). Its fall, amid economic stagnation and corruption scandals, marked the decline of the ex-communist SLD (see Szczerbiak 2007, 207). With its sudden dismembering in the left camp, the 2005 parliamentary and presidential elections were a competition between the newest post-Solidarity formations, the populist Law and Justice (PiS) and the liberal Civic Platform (PO). The absence of a competitive ex-communist party led to the most hotly contested election since 1989 (Markowski 2006, 827), with PiS and the other two smaller populist parties, Self-Defense and League of Polish Families (LPR), representing the losers of economic reforms (see Jasiewicz 2008).

PiS's economic program combined policy vagueness with heated foundational rhetoric, economic nationalism, and Euroscepticism (see Markowski 2008, 1056; Jasiewicz 2008). PiS leader Lech Kaczynski rejected previous economic policies as "dictated by two powerful lobbies: the bankers, and the importers" (cited in Polish News Bulletin 2004). Consequently, they proposed to delay EMU accession, use monetary and fiscal policy to boost domestic demand, and maintain a high exchange rate and low interest rate to promote domestic businesses. PiS incorporated some of the slogans of Self-Defense including reforms of the "too monetarist, too liberal and too independent" central bank (Szczerbiak 2007, 211; 218–19; Markowski 2006, 821). In industrial policy, PiS hoped to maintain strategic productive sectors in state hands (Nowakowska and Wielowieyska 2005). On the other hand, PO vowed to speed up privatization and enter the EMU as soon as possible (Polish News Bulletin 2005).

PiS claimed victory in the parliamentary and presidential elections in 2005 and joined forces with the populist Self-Defense and LPR in 2006. The PiS-led government fell in 2007 after calling for early elections in an attempt to outvote its coalition partners and consolidate itself as a hegemonic party. Despite a having a mixed platform in economic policies,[39] the PiS government sought alternatives to neoliberalism in exchange rate and industrial policy. Like the SLD/PSL governments, it rejected a price stability-driven exchange rate and

39. In spite of its declarations, the PiS-led government ended up being rather conservative (Shields 2007). Policies close to neoliberalism included the maintenance of a balanced budget and the elimination of a tax on financial transactions adopted by the previous SLD government. Moreover, many of the key economic positions in cabinet were occupied by liberal technocrats. One of them, Zyta Gilowska, who served as minister of finance and deputy prime minister, had been one of the main architects of the rival PO economic program.

continually fought the NBP for a less contractionary monetary policy, threatening to curtail the bank's independence if it did not cooperate. Self-Defense leader and deputy prime minister Andrzej Lepper proposed to use the NBP reserves to provide cheap loans to domestic producers. The attempts of the PiS-led government to change the statute of the NBP failed amid opposition from the EU itself (see chapter 7).

Despite EU pressures, Poland maintained relatively high levels of subsidies and transfers to enterprises. Although firms in noncompetitive sectors eventually moved together with the SLD to promote euro accession, the PiS-led government tried to create its own business support base through the utilization of industrial policy. First, it halted privatization and proposed to consolidate state stakes in crucial sectors in order to strengthen domestic business and promote Polish brands and national champions. The latter was particularly meaningful in the banking sector, where the government attempted to merge the two largest Polish financial institutions into state hands (insurer PZU and retail bank PKO BP) with other minor state-owned banks in order to create a state-owned financial giant that could serve as a domestic investment-*cum*-development bank (Polish News Bulletin 2006a; Gadomski 2007). Interestingly, this had already been attempted by the ex-communists in 1994–1997 (R. A. Epstein 2008, 90). The government advanced plans to establish state-controlled sectoral holdings in other competitive and noncompetitive sectors such as energy, chemicals, mining, food and beverages, and telecommunications (see table 4.3) (Polish News Bulletin 2006b).

TABLE 4.3. Poland, PiS' Planned State-Controlled Sectoral Holdings 2007

Groups	Sector	Member companies	Value bill. USD	State control
Financial	Banking	PKO BP, PZU	29.2	>50
Energy	Oil/Energy	PKN Orlen/Lotos	—	—
PGE	Mining/Energy	PGE Energia, BOT, PSE	20.2	>60
EP	Energy	PKE, Elektrownia Stalowa Wola, Energia Pro	8.1	—
Grupa Centrum	Mining/Energy	Bogdanka, Elektrownia Kozienice, Enea	4.3	—
Grupa Polnoc	Energy	Energa, ZE Ostroleka	3.3	—
Chemical	Chemicals	Ciech, ZA Pulawy, ZCh Police	1.9	—
Spirit	Food&Beverages	Four Polmoses and WW Koneser	0.2	—

Source: Polish News Bulletin (2007a).
Note: Values converted to current USD using data from the International Monetary Fund (IMF).

The effects of the 2007–2008 crisis reinforced the status quo: namely, the contested nature of neoliberalism in Poland. Strong and externally controlled financial and competitive sectors and a robust, mostly state-controlled, non-competitive sector characterized a business base with no clear leading sector. Alternating government coalitions represented varying business and societal demands. This reflected a contested regime of flexible exchange rates plus a neoliberal-embedded industrial policy framework that grew in its horizontal components with the arrival of EU funds.

With the postcommunist left now disintegrated, the elections of 2007 produced a massive shift toward the liberal PO, who received the protest vote against PiS's lack of respect for liberal democratic procedures (see Markowski 2008; Jasiewicz 2008, 11). PO captured the left's vote by tempering its liberal discourse, making it more responsive to an economic-interventionist and socially-sensitive electorate and playing up liberal democratic values. PO ended up forming a government with the agrarian Polish People's Party (PSL), which even further moderated the supposedly liberal economic orientation of the new government (Markowski 2008, 1057; 1965–66; Myant, Drahokoupil, and Lesay 2013, 397). Instead of vowing for fast EMU adoption as it had sought in the past, the PO-led government stalled the exchange rate discussion and then postponed it indefinitely, citing the good effects of depreciation under the free-floating system on the export sector. Conversely, echoing the "economic patriotism" of its political competitor (PiS), it moved closer to a selective industrial policy (see Naczyk 2014). One crucial point in this turnabout was the realization that Poland could not rely on external capital for stable growth and had to promote instead a domestic business base including strong national brands. The PO/PSL coalition formed a new government in 2011 but was succeeded by the PiS in 2015, when it won an outright majority in parliament. Therefore, neoliberalism continued to be contested in Poland as anti-neoliberal political platforms endured.

In sum, in Estonia EU accession helped to consolidate neoliberalism through establishing the possibility—and goal—of fast EMU accession, reinforcing the power of the financial sector and neoliberal parties, and reducing criticism from the parties opposing neoliberalism (given the need to introduce higher subsidies and tariff barriers). Moreover, the 2007–2008 crisis and the need to slash expenditure for adopting the euro helped eliminate stronger industrial policy efforts by left-leaning parties. By contrast, neoliberalism remained contested throughout the pre- and post-EU accession in Poland. Although internationalization of the financial and competitive sectors and the inclusion in government of liberal parties—not to mention pressures derived from the EU accession process itself—gave a new impetus to neoliberalism, the persistence of a strong state-owned noncompetitive business sector as well as the alternation of left-leaning and populist parties in government, implied a constant search for alternative development projects. Neoliberalism was contested, even if, contrary to Argentina, no actual alternative development project appeared.

Conclusions

In this chapter I have analyzed the establishment of neoliberalism and the formation of social blocs supporting and opposing it in different contexts. In Latin America, neoliberalism had different dynamics under authoritarian and democratic regimes, but similar actors supporting it: financial and competitive sectors in business, and right-leaning parties in politics. The strength and bargaining power of the noncompetitive sector acted to debilitate neoliberalism and promote alternatives to it. The availability of this type of business support base supported different types of left-leaning political parties in Argentina, who attempted alternative development projects with their developmental exchange rate and industrial policies. The weakness of this business support eventually led left-leaning parties in Chile to look for business allies within the neoliberal bloc, thereby moderating their policy discourse while in government.

In Eastern Europe, protest on the part of those who were harmed by reforms, most significantly in agriculture and in state-owned enterprises in noncompetitive sectors like chemicals, steel, and mining, reduced the consensus over neoliberal reforms and left open the possibility of an alternative social bloc. Ex-communist and agrarian parties willing to represent the discontent of these actors led to the emergence of an incipient alternative social bloc in Poland. These actors tried to change both exchange rate and industrial policies from their price stability orientation to the promotion of exports and the protection of ailing industries from external competition. In Estonia, by contrast, the nationalistic and ethnic conflicts of the reform period trumped the chances of forming a more decisive center-left government, despite the presence of similar partisan supports as in Poland. This also reduced the possibilities of contestation from weaker noncompetitive sectors, such as workers and farmers.

The EU provided incentives for neoliberalism to consolidate through the backing of neoliberal policy alternatives and the strengthening of the discourse of its supporting actors. In neoliberal Estonia, EU accession strengthened price stability while at the same time providing room for accommodating industrial policy; in contested Poland, it applied pressure for a clear pathway toward neoliberalization. Two factors appear important to keeping an alternative to neoliberalism alive in Poland: the strength of the noncompetitive sector, mostly farmers and state-owned industries, and party alternation encouraging competition for the representation of these disgruntled sectors. The existence of populist parties with strong nationalist-*cum*-protectionist discourses willing to compete for the representation of the losers of reform and to maintain the link between SOEs, the noncompetitive sector, and higher protectionism, was vital to contesting neoliberalism, although it was unable to form a social bloc in favor of a clear alternative. After the 2007–2008 crisis, liberal parties in Poland had to accommodate this interventionist political competition, reducing their preferences for a return to orthodox neoliberalism.

This chapter helps to explain the contexts under which noncompetitive business sectors and left-leaning parties either acquiesced to neoliberalism under the leadership of the financial and competitive sectors—therefore reinforcing neoliberalism's resilience—or challenged it and supported alternative development projects, therefore debilitating neoliberalism and increasing the chances of its replacement. In the different cases where alternative development models were pursued (Argentina under Alfonsín, Argentina under the Kirchners, and Poland under the first SLD-led government) the strong alliance between these two actors—noncompetitive business and left-leaning political alternatives plus trade unions—seems critical. The endurance of this alliance and the policy preferences of the respective actors depended, however, on additional conditions: above all, macroeconomic conditions favorable to the adoption of competitiveness-driven exchange rates, and industrial policies requiring extensive public expenditures. Conversely, the cases where an alternative development project failed to solidify (Estonia in the mid-1990s and late 2000s, Chile during the *Concertación* governments after re-gaining democracy) show that the rise to power of left-leaning parties and/or parties willing to represent developmental projects and supply the kind of policies aligned with them was doomed to failure due to the lack of appropriate business supports. In fact, industrial policy efforts both in Chile and Estonia in the second half of the 2000s can be directly or indirectly linked to the quest for generating a new domestic business sector that would support the continuation of those policies and, eventually, an alternative development project *tout court*. I analyze this in more detail in chapter 5. The analysis of the ways by which neoliberals secured business support is therefore of the utmost importance to understand the resilience of neoliberalism.

At the cross-regional level, the role of the EU as an external anchor of domestic institutions and of political alternatives contextualizes the differences between Eastern Europe and Latin America in terms of neoliberal resilience. Given the neoliberal orientation of the EU in exchange rate and industrial policy, as well as the deep form of integration that it promotes, both of the Eastern European cases appear more neoliberal than the Latin American pair. In Latin America, the functional equivalent to the EU was the role of the IMF, the WTO, and the signing of bilateral FTAs, but these were more superficial forms of international integration, and therefore constituted less overarching pressures on domestic policy and institutional change (see Bruszt and McDermott 2009). In this vein, it is telling that neoliberal resilience in Chile required a broader socioeconomic support base and a more pragmatic policy regime than in Estonia, and that the constitution of alternative social blocs and the departure from neoliberalism in Argentina went much further than in Poland. In fact, in the case of Poland, pressures for fiscal consolidation before EU accession constrained the ability of the ex-communist SLD to steer a viable alternative to neoliberalism, ultimately alienating their societal bases of support and virtually erasing this party from the political landscape as new populist forces moved to represent those unsatisfied demands.

It would be difficult to downplay the role the IMF played in Latin American structural adjustments. Yet, this role was often less direct than otherwise believed (see Pop-Eleches 2009; Roos 2019). It played an ambiguous role as a defender of neoliberalism, firmly backing it at times—as in the case of Chile in the 1980s under Pinochet, mid-1980s Argentina under Alfonsin, or mid-1990s Argentina after the Tequila Crisis—but abandoning it in others, as it did in the events leading to the Argentinean crisis in the early 2000s. What is more, during the 2000s the Kirchners were able to rebuild a developmental alliance and political project from the ashes of Argentina's failed neoliberal experiment and against the backdrop of debt default and strained relations with the IMF. These considerations provide further backing for this book's concentration on domestic political dynamics.

Over the next three chapters I elaborate the mechanisms of support creation, opposition blockade, and constitutionalized lock-in, through which
neoliberal social blocs managed to retain control over economic policy and
deter the consolidation of an alternative social bloc demanding a different
developmental project.

5

Creating Support

PRIVATIZATION AND BUSINESS POWER

AS WE SAW IN CHAPTERS 3 AND 4, the support provided by segments of the business community was crucial to secure the maintenance of neoliberalism in time. This chapter explores the creation of business support through the privatization of state companies.

Privatization was simultaneously one of the most important and one of the most controversial aspects of market reforms. The new democracies in 1980s–1990s Latin America and Eastern Europe tended to see the need for massive processes of ownership change and proper regulatory and institutional frameworks. In this context, governments puzzled not so much about the need for privatization, but about the best strategy for achieving it. Should privatization happen along with or after stabilization policies? Should it focus on improving the efficiency of the privatized companies or on maximizing revenue from privatization sales? How could this process be related to the more general one of building support for a market economy and returning property to previous owners?

As we shall see, privatization had long-term and systemic effects beyond support for specific reforms during the transition period. As the former Hungarian finance minister László Békesi put it, "being in charge of privatization implies ... controlling the most important means for redistributing property and acquiring power in the economy and society" (quoted in R. Martin 2013, 80). In other words, privatization fundamentally altered economic and political institutions by transforming the power of business interests. This had two consequences for neoliberal policy regimes. First, reform governments used privatization to boost economic sectors expected to benefit from and support neoliberalism. Second, the transformation of corporate power generated a double impact on business demands for alternative development projects: it reduced that demand for alternative exchange rate and industrial policies, and at the same time increased the capacity of business to discipline governments that offered developmental policy alternatives (whether through structural or instrumental power). In this chapter I analyze how privatization increased the power resources of the financial and competitive sectors, and whether these sectors were actually more likely to support neoliberalism in the long term. To this end, I use two sets of evidence: first, the distribution of privatization proceeds among economic sectors, single companies, and/or individual entrepreneurs; and second, the political behavior of those actors benefitting from privatization.

If privatization is a causal factor of neoliberal resilience, we should find that:

1. Privatization processes had clear biases. These biases could be either (a) sectoral: that is, benefiting economic sectors whose preferences were closer to neoliberal reforms, particularly the Financial and Competitive sectors in each country; or (b) personal: that is, benefitting individuals and/or firms who had established neoliberal reform credentials.

2. Privatization benefited sectors and/or individuals who exerted their power in order to either (a) support the continuity of neoliberal exchange rate and industrial policy, or (b) prevent more progressive policies.

The findings suggest that the type of actors who were targeted for privatization and who supported market reforms are crucial to understanding the continuity of neoliberalism over time. Support creation contributed to the resilience of neoliberalism in Chile and Estonia, where privatization was channeled toward financial and competitive sectors, which supported neoliberalism. As we will see, foreign capital also played a significant part in privatization processes. This chapter confirms that its effects on neoliberal resilience were threefold: first, strengthening the financial and competitive sectors in partnership with domestic capital; second, reinforcing neoliberal policy regimes through foreign direct investment (FDI) inflows that stabilized domestic economies in key moments when support for neoliberalism due to economic crisis was faltering (particularly in Estonia); and third, when acquiring firms in the noncompetitive sector, foreign capital contributed to the "silencing" of this sector's potential demand for developmental measures, particularly—but not only—in industrial policy.

By contrast, in Argentina and Poland, where the neoliberal project sputtered, support-creation mechanisms failed. In these countries, privatization processes were characterized by either: 1) significant delays in privatization that contributed to the strengthening of a strong cross-industry state-owned sector, particularly in the noncompetitive sector of the economy (Poland); or 2) the alienation of state assets to noncompetitive sectors in order to win their acquiescence to neoliberal reforms (Argentina). In Poland, strong state-owned companies maintained their demand for state protection and at the same time prevented the formation of a more powerful business support base for neoliberalism. In Argentina, privatization had the contradictory effect of advancing market reforms in the short run but making them dependent on support from economic sectors that were ready to demand state protection once they had the opportunity. At crucial turning points, these groups were the basis of alternative social blocs and attempts to build more developmental policies.

With a Little Help from My Friends: Privatization in Latin America and Eastern Europe

In the mid-1970s, public enterprises accounted, on average, for three-fourths of the public sector deficit of developing countries, while budgetary subsidies and borrowing from the government financed more than half of these companies' deficits (Balassa 1987, 8). When capital markets were liberalized in the 1970s, public companies borrowed heavily abroad, amassing about one-third of the external debt of developing countries (Balassa 1987, 8). In the case of the three biggest Latin American countries (Brazil, Mexico, and Argentina), the figure jumped to over 50 percent (Balassa 1987, 8). In Eastern Europe in the 1980s, reform-communist countries like Poland and Hungary were also soaking in external debt, a phenomenon significantly driven by the indebtedness of public companies (Berend 1996, 229–32). The process was similar in both regions and was related to the quest for autonomous development models. With low domestic savings and scarce capital, foreign debt was contracted in an attempt to direct manufacturing sectors to export markets.[1]

The dual transition processes to market capitalism and political democracy in Latin America and Eastern Europe meant that the specific design of privatization mattered. Privatization objectives in these regions comprised both short- and long-term economic objectives, including: ameliorating budgetary

1. For the distinction between import-substitution industrialization (ISI) and export-oriented industrialization (OEI) and the different paths between them, see Haggard (1990).

and financial problems, improving the level of goods and services for consumers, facilitating the flow of foreign investment, eliminating hidden unemployment, creating stronger financial markets, and stimulating entrepreneurship (see e.g., Rutland 1997, 270–71; Berg and Berg 1997, 359). However, political motives underlay all of those objectives. In fact, many analysts argued that in order to secure the consolidation of nascent democracies, it was crucial to provide "guarantees" to the local bourgeoisies—including privatization (O'Donnell and Schmitter 1986; Waterbury 1989). This was most important in the Eastern European cases, which had to build their private economic sector from scratch. Reformers there expected that privatization would unleash "a series of self-reinforcing, virtuous, though self-interested, forces" (Zines, Eilat, and Sachs, cited in Schoenman 2014, 12) that could constitute not only the backbone of the market economy but also of democracy. Given the perceived danger that privatization proceeds could fall into the hands of former communist managers and apparatchiks, derailing the virtuous forces of private property and markets, the correct design of privatization strategies was essential for Eastern European reformers (Staniszkis 1990; Eyal, Szelényi, and Townsley 1998).

Our case studies show a clear pattern: rapid and progressive privatization in the cases of neoliberal resilience; delayed or aborted privatization in the cases of neoliberal discontinuity. Most significant, the cases of neoliberal resilience were clearly biased toward financial and competitive sectors, which in turn defended neoliberalism at key moments when it came under attack. Table 5.1 shows a summary of the results of this chapter. In what follows, I provide an overview of the pace and character of privatization and, later on, detailed country analyses substantiating the summary in table 5.1.

In Argentina, state-owned enterprises (SOEs) were responsible for around 8 percent of GDP and some 35 percent of the sales of the country's 200 largest companies in 1973 (see table 5.2; Castellani 2012, 97). Despite the efforts of the military junta to privatize state companies, the respective share in 1983 was only 4 percent lower. Looking at specific sectors, this may be explained by the slow pace of privatization in the oil and gas sectors, as well as the negligible advance in public services. Privatization stalled for a decade, and then gained new impetus during the 1990s. In 1998, the state owned only 1.3 percent of the 200 biggest companies in the country. After the 2001 crisis, however, the Kirchner governments cancelled the contracts of transnational public utility companies and renationalized crucial enterprises such as the oil producer YPF—historically the largest state-owned company—and the national air carrier

TABLE 5.1. Main Characteristics and Outcomes of Support Creation

Country	Period	Characteristics	Target[a]	Outcome[b]
Argentina	1970s	Peripheral privatization: subcontracting of activities of state-owned (SOE) firms to private companies	• Financial sector • Competitive sector	• Strengthening of Noncompetitive sector
Argentina	1990s	Privatization across the board using different methods	• Foreign capital • Noncompetitive sector	• Strengthening of Noncompetitive sector
Chile	1970s	Privatization of companies previously nationalized by Allende	• Financial sector	• Strengthening of Financial sector
Chile	1980s	Privatization of traditional SOEs and companies renationalized after the 1981–1982 crisis (exotic area)	• Competitive sector • Foreign capital	• Strengthening of Competitive sector • Silencing of noncompetitive sector • Creation of an "ideological" business base
Chile	1990s	Privatization of traditional SOEs, mainly in public services.	• Competitive sector • Foreign capital	• Strengthening of Competitive sector (diversification) • Strengthening of ideological business base (diversification)
Estonia	1990s	Privatization across the board using different methods. No restructuring of privatized companies.	Foreign capital	• Creation of a foreign business base • Silencing of noncompetitive sector
Poland	1990s	Limited privatization using different methods, with restructuring of privatized companies and privileging insiders (workers and company managers)	• Competitive sector • Noncompetitive sector	• Creation of a domestic business base • Strengthening of competitive sector • Strengthening of noncompetitive sector • Strategic parts of the economy remain in state hands
Poland	2000s	Limited privatization using different methods	• Foreign capital • Financial sector • Competitive sector	• Strengthening foreign capital • Strategic parts of the economy remain in state hands

Source: Author's elaboration.

[a] Refers to what economic sector was expected to benefit from the processes.

[b] Refers to the outcome of the privatization process in terms of support creation.

TABLE 5.2. Argentina and Chile, State-Owned Enterprises 1965–2000

	1965	1973	1983	1989	1998
Argentina[a]					
N	—	24 (1975)	21	18	1
% of sales	—	35.6 (1975)	31.5	32.0	1.3
Chile					
N	68 (1970)	596	48	45	38
% of GDP	14.2	39.0	24.0	12.7	9.0

Source: Hachette (2001, 113), Basualdo (2006, 157; 263; 387).
[a]Considers only the 200 biggest companies in the country.

TABLE 5.3. Argentina and Chile, Sectoral Participation of SOEs 1965–2000 (%)

	1965	1973	1983	1989	1998
Argentina					
Oil	—	79.2	56.3	—	—
Industry	—	13.3	7.4	—	—
Services	—	94.8	96.0	—	—
Chile					
Mining	13.0	85.0	83.0	60.0	45.0
Industry	3.0	40.0	12.0	3.0	3.0
Services	25.0	100.0	75.0	25.0	20.0
Transport	24.3	70.0	21.0	10.0	5.0
Communication	11.1	70.0	96.3	0.0	0.0
Finance	—	85.0	28.3	10.0	10.0

Source: Basualdo (2006, 166), Hachette (2001, 115).

Aerolíneas Argentinas. When Allende was overthrown in Chile in 1973, the presence of the Chilean state in the economy had reached a record figure: 39 percent, up from 14.2 percent eight years earlier (see table 5.2). In contrast to Argentina, privatization thereafter was steady. SOEs decreased to 12.7 percent at the end of the Pinochet regime, and to 9 percent in 2000. In 1998, state-owned companies had decreased their participation in all but one sector (mining) compared to 1965 (see table 5.3).[2] Beyond the presence of SOEs in abso-

2. State presence in mining is still significant today thanks to state ownership of the Chilean national copper-mining company, CODELCO (Corporación Nacional del Cobre)—the world's biggest copper extracting and manufacturing company. CODELCO's profits make up a significant part of the state budget, and the company is an important source of national pride. These motives were key to preventing its privatization during the military dictatorship. See

TABLE 5.4. Estonia and Poland, State-Owned Enterprises 1990–2005

	1989[a]	1991[a]	1992	1993	1996	1999	2006	2009
Estonia								
No. of SOEs	—	2,234		—	—	—	—	—
% of GDP	—	90	75	60	30	25	20	20
% of employment	—	85.1	—	—	—	31	25.2	23.7
Poland								
No. of SOEs	7,500	—	—	6,000[a]	—	—	—	—
% of GDP	75	60	55	50	40	30	25	25
% of employment	—	—	46	43	37	29.1	29	26.1

Source: EBRD structural change indicators, EBRD (2000), EBRD (2005) and http://www.ebrd.com/downloads /research/economics/macrodata/sci.xls. Percentages correspond to the inverse of the private sector share.
[a]Data comes from World Bank (1993, 47, 266, 307) for Estonia and Lewandowski (1994, 4) for Poland.

lute numbers in the two countries, what is noticeable is the within-country pace of privatization over time.

In Eastern Europe, privatization was concentrated in the early years of the transition from communism. Poland had an advantage in the creation of a buoyant private sector. Along with Hungary and Yugoslavia, it belonged to the type of reform socialism in which the shares of private ownership and economic links with the West were higher than anywhere else in the communist world (see Berend 1996). It is estimated that in 1989, around 25 percent of Polish output was produced by the private sector (compared to only around 10 percent in Estonia). This was most notably the case in agriculture, where some 75 percent of land was privately cultivated, contributing to about half of the private sector's share (Nuti 1999, 81). In Estonia, on the other hand, practically all economic activity (90 percent) was in the hands of the state in 1990 (see table 5.4). In this context, the creation of support through privatization became all the more important in order to sustain neoliberalism over time (see Blom, Melin, and Nikula 1996, 16–20; Ruutsoo 1996, 110).

Poland was the pacesetter in the jump from a command to a market economy and was also among the first countries in Eastern Europe to announce and launch a large-scale privatization program (Nuti 1999, 81; Schoenman 2014; R. Martin 2013). The Polish private sector grew significantly during the 1990s. However, most of this growth was due to the establishment of new private

---

Fontaine Aldunate (1988). The reduction of state presence in the mining sector after 1983 is therefore associated mainly with the expansion of the private sector after deregulation with the dictatorship's Mining Law.

TABLE 5.5. Estonia and Poland, Sectoral Participation of SOEs 1990–1996 (% of turnover)

	1990	1991	1992	1996
Estonia				
Industry	95	90	65	18
Housing	90	70	70	30
Services	90	70	45	11
Retail trade	90	65	19	4
Finance	—	—	—	14[a]
Poland				
Industry	83.8	75.4	61.7	48.3
Construction	74.5	40.5	15.0	12.1
Transportation	88.5	74.8	54.9	60.5
Domestic trade	40.5	—	8.5	7.1
Finance	—	—	—	46[b]

Source: Purju (1999, 229), Błaszczyk (1999, 215), OECD (1996, 73).
[a]Share of capital in commercial banks, 1995.
[b]Percent of total capital in banking sector.

entrepreneurial enterprises, not the result of privatization per se (Błaszczyk 1999). In Estonia, large-scale privatization was officially launched only in 1993, but by 1996 the process was already 90 percent completed, and, most notably, over 80 percent of industry and finance were in private hands. In stark contrast, by 1996 the Polish state sector still accounted for 40 percent of the economy—close to 50 percent in industry and finance (see table 5.5). Moreover, if one counts companies that were corporatized but not privatized, as well as incomplete privatizations, completion of privatization amounted to only about 20 percent (Nuti 1999, 82). The Polish privatization process sped up at the end of the 1990s but got derailed again during the 2000s. As we will see, beyond the difference in market size between the two countries, the key to understanding the operation of support creation is how reformers used privatization as a way to increase the likelihood of neoliberalism's survival. How, then, did these differences in the pace of privatization reflect the mechanism of support creation, and what was its effect on the resilience of neoliberalism?

Chile: Building a Strong Neoliberal Business Base

Privatization in Chile has had three stages, which roughly coincide with the three decades that followed the adoption of neoliberalism. In each stage, a different economic sector was targeted for privatization: the financial sector in the 1970s, the competitive sector in the 1980s, and the public utilities sector in the 1990s. No further significant privatization took place during the 2000s.

The first wave of privatization under the dictatorship of Augusto Pinochet (and its relation to support creation) is strongly correlated with the previous attempt at nationalization during the Allende government. Allende's nationalization policy rested mainly on two strategies: 1) aggressive takeover through stock purchases using the state promotion agency CORFO,[3] which then owned the shares; and 2) nationalization by force when business owners opposed stock takeovers. In the latter, the government took control of the firms by appointing state officials but did not legally change property rights.

When the military took over, the return of nationalized companies was the main concern of the business community (E. Silva 1996, 104). In fact, during the first neoliberal experiment under Pinochet (1973–1982), privatization corresponded not to a divestiture of traditional state companies but to the return of companies nationalized during the Allende period. The differing speeds of reprivatization depended on the method by which the companies had been nationalized—stock purchase or forced takeover—producing an enduring effect on the balance of power between different economic sectors, in favor of finance. As several authors recall, after the coup it was easier for the military to return those firms that were still legally private instead of those owned by the state through shares and for which the right devolution formula had to be convened (E. Silva 1996, 105; Schamis 2002, 56; Valdivia 2003, 131–32). These still-private firms, nationalized by force under Allende, also belonged to the groups that had more fiercely opposed Allende, had significant stakes in the financial sector, and were in favor of radical market reforms (E. Silva 1996, 104–6; Schamis 2002, 56–57).

Almost all the companies that had been nationalized by force had already been returned to their owners in 1974, and only a handful were pending privatization by March 1976 (see table 5.6 above). By contrast, around half of those nationalized through share-buying still had to be reprivatized in 1976. This was also the case for banks nationalized through stock purchases, whose shares the state sold only in the second half of 1975—that is, two years after the coup (E. Silva 1996, 104). Similarly, in 1979, only 30 percent of nationalized land holdings had been returned to their former owners (Foxley 1983, 67).

3. Authorities used several strategies to weaken companies and force owners to sell. See Larrain and Meller (1991, 189). There were also conspicuous cases of resistance to nationalization, most notably that of the biggest private company, the forestry and pulp producer *Compañía Papelera*, in October 1971. See E. Silva (1996, 47) and Schamis (2002, 56 n. 19).

TABLE 5.6. Chile, Pace of Reprivatization by March 1976

	Method of previous nationalization	
	By force (%)	Share buying (%)
Total nationalized	259	235
Reprivatized	251 (96.9)	118 (50.2)
In process	0	38 (16.2)
Pending	8 (3.1)	83 (35.3)

Source: Valdivia (2003, 137).

Thanks to their connections to Chicago Boys in the cabinet, a handful of groups with core business in the financial sector (Cruzat-Larraín, Vial, and Edwards, among others) actively participated in the financial deregulation procedures that took place at the Central Bank in 1974. After Pinochet consolidated his power, former executives of these groups and related Chicago Boy technocrats took over the key policymaking positions in government and provided a constant supply of cadres to fill higher bureaucratic posts. The acceleration of trade liberalization, the elimination of state subsidies for private companies, and the introduction of a fixed exchange rate were all linked to this transition.

Business groups that benefited from early devolution of their companies and access to financial deregulation expanded rapidly into the newly deregulated financial sector, controlling credit markets.[4] In 1978, two-thirds of non-regulated credit and close to one-third of all banking assets were in the hands of a handful of financial conglomerates (E. Silva 1996, 116–18). Amid financial scarcity and retrenchment of state credit, these groups were the only ones able to raise enough capital to acquire the privatized companies when the privatization of the rest of nationalized companies began (Rozas and Marín 1988, 50). In fact, they managed to acquire over half of the privatized state shares in previously nationalized companies, and control almost 40 percent of the assets of the 250 larger Chilean companies (Schamis 2002, 57; E. Silva 1996, 118). Hence, faster privatization benefiting these groups with core interests in the financial sector not only strengthened them earlier with the devolution of their firms;

4. The new *financieras* (deregulated credit institutions) were free to borrow from abroad, while banks faced significant constraints (high reserve requirements and limits to external financing) up until 1979, when the capital account was fully liberalized. The arbitration between external and internal interest rates was one of the key mechanisms *financieras* used to grow exponentially. See Arellano (1983), Reinstein and Rosende (2001).

it also handed them the resources to acquire a significant majority of stakes in firms nationalized through stock purchases.

The 1982–1983 crisis marked a major reversal of fortunes for the financial conglomerates leading the neoliberal bloc in Chile. Thanks to their cross share-holdings in financial and productive companies, they had engaged in massive self-lending and were therefore heavily exposed to nonperforming loans (see Arellano 1983). Outraged by the extent of the crisis and the concentration of debt in a few hands, Pinochet decided to take direct control of their assets in 1983 (Rozas and Marín 1988, 46; 58): 67 percent of bank deposits and 70 percent of previously privatized firms returned to the state, creating what became known as the "exotic area" (*área rara*) of state property (Schamis 2002, 60).

Once the crisis was over, a second wave of privatizations strengthened again business support for neoliberalism. This privatization wave had two major components. The first was the reprivatization of the "exotic area" of state property during 1984–1986. The main beneficiaries of this process were business groups in a better position to assume the debt of these firms as well as their need for restructuring: those in the competitive natural resource export sector, such as the Angelini, Luksic, Matte, and Menéndez groups, which had themselves also benefited in the first wave, although less than the finance-based ones. This change of property at the commanding heights of the Chilean economy reflects the change of leadership within the regime's business bases of support, from finance to the competitive economic sector (see E. Silva 1996; Ahumada 2019).

Big groups in the competitive sector carefully targeted firms to either complement or consolidate their dominant positions (E. Silva 1996, 195; Lefort 2010, 412–13; Montero 1996). For example, the Angelini Group, which was already present in the competitive forestry and fishing sectors, acquired Copec. Copec was one of Chile's major companies, with its core area in the field of oil production and distribution—a sector where the Angelini Group was starting to place its stakes. Copec had previously been in the hands of the Cruzat-Larraín Group, which converted it into a holding with significant investments in the forestry and fishing sectors. Thanks to this and other acquisitions, at the end of the decade Angelini was the biggest Chilean business group. Another example was the Matte Group, which was heavily involved in the competitive forestry sector and the manufacture of pulp and paper, owned the powerful *Compañía Papelera,* and supported the orthodox neoliberal experiment during 1975–1981. The Matte Group acquired Inforsa, a previous competitor within the forestry sector (E. Silva 1996, 195 n.58).

The alienation of state assets to these groups was a central coalitional instrument preventing the formation of an alternative social bloc and, eventually, preventing the break from neoliberalism during the turmoil generated by the 1982–1983 economic crisis. In fact, competitive sectors ended up favoring an alliance with the dictatorship instead of the developmental policy regime offered by the center-left opposition (see chapter 4). Moreover, following this alliance, business associations led by the competitive sector were offered access to policymaking though ad hoc commissions where key legislation on economic issues was drafted. One outcome of these commissions was a series of support measures for the export sector—such as export subsidies and tax drawbacks. They also supported the change toward a more competitive exchange rate regime (see chapter 4).

The second component of this privatization wave corresponded to divestiture proper. The newly privatized companies constituted important players in the noncompetitive sectors—oil production and refinery, basic metallic and nonmetallic industries—as well as public utilities (Rozas and Marín 1988, 61). The beneficiaries were mostly the managers of these companies, who had been appointed by the military government (Schamis 2002, 63–64). This process, therefore, generated new business groups, which were closely related to the neoliberal technocrats in government and were fierce defenders of the regime's political and economic legacy. In fact, in a journalistic investigation, Monckeberg (2001, 24) found that the controllers of many of these privatized companies became members or close collaborators of the right-wing UDI party, the staunchest defender of Pinochet's legacy after the return to democracy. Table 5.7 shows that in most privatizations carried out in this wave, we can identify one of three relationships to the neoliberal social bloc (see column D): ex-officials of the dictatorship, usually sitting on the board of the respective company; members of the UDI party; or previous executives of the Cruzat-Larraín group. A significant set of these privatizations was finished only a few months before the new democratic authorities took office in 1990, further reinforcing their "support creation" character (see Huneeus 2007, 440–41).

This second privatization component neutralized the potential interests of noncompetitive sectors in developmental policy alternatives, producing instead a sort of "ideological" business support for neoliberalism.[5] SQM (chemicals) and CAP (fabricated metals) that were leaders in the noncompetitive sector and emblems of previous Chilean state-led industrialization efforts,

5. González, Prem and Urzúa (2020) call firms thus privatized "political corporations."

TABLE 5.7. Chile, Major Privatizations 1985–1989

Company and industry	Book value of equity (1987) (USD million) (A)	Controller (% participation) (B)	Sector of controller (C)	Relation to neoliberal bloc (D)	External capital [a] (E)
ENDESA (Energy)	1,314	CChC (4.3), Matte/ Angelini (1.4)	Competitive, Construction	1, 2	25.6
CAP (Steel)	679	De Andraca, Menéndez/Angelini (8.9)	Noncompetitive, Competitive	1, 2	39.2
CTC (Telecomm.)	306	CChC (1.8)	Construction		63.4
Chilgener (Energy)	264	CChC (3.9), Matte/ Angelini (3.2), Menéndez/ Angelini (2.0)	Competitive, Construction	1, 2	61.1
Chilmetro (Energy)	206	Yuraszeck (21.0), Matte/Angelini (4.8)	Competitive, Public utilities	1, 2	25.9
SOQUIMICH (Chemicals)	102	Ponce Lerou (15.5)	—	1, 2	39.5
ENTEL (Telecomm.)	93	Hurtado Vicuña (12.5)	Public utilities	1, 2, 3	33.7
IANSA (Food)	90	Larraín-Vial (6.6)	Financial	1	50.1
Enacar (Mining)	71	—	—		
Chilquinta (Energy)	52	Fernández León (19.4), Menéndez/ Angelini (14.2), Matte/Angelini (11.5), Hurtado Vicuña (10.1)	Public utilities, Competitive	3	30.7
Lan Chile (Transport)	49	—	—		
Pilmaiquén (Energy)	44	Angelini (20)	Competitive	1, 2	

Source: Author's elaboration based on data from: (A) Meller (1996, 268); (B) (C) (E) Rozas and Marín (1988); (D) Monckeberg (2001).

Legend: 1= Regime official; 2= Supporter of UDI; 3= Ex-executives of Cruzat-Larraín group.

[a] In relation to percentage in private hands.

were two examples. SQM was left in control of Julio Ponce Lerou, son-in-law of Pinochet and CEO of the company during 1980–1983. Two prominent directors of the privatized SQM were Hernán Büchi and Sergio de la Cuadra, both ministers of finance in the Pinochet regime; other high-ranking civilian and military officials of the military government also held influential positions inside the company (Monckeberg 2001, 94–96). Conversely, CAP came under the control of Roberto de Andraca, its former CEO during the 1970s and 1980s (Monckeberg 2001, 73–81). Important officials of the Pinochet government sat on the board of directors of CAP after its privatization and well into the 1990s. The possibility that a strong noncompetitive sector would demand more progressive policies in Chile was therefore reduced not only due to the massive bankruptcy that occurred during the initial liberalization years; it was also further aided by the alienation of assets in the sector to loyal collaborators of the Pinochet regime. In addition to this, recent research into campaign donations has revealed the key role of companies privatized to close collaborators of Pinochet under extremely favorable conditions in financing electoral campaigns across the political spectrum. According to several accounts, this was a major way businesses managed to moderate the policy proposals of the center-left.[6] González, Prem, and Urzúa (forthcoming) argue that firms in this ideological business sector were more likely to provide campaign donations, and employment to politicians from across the political spectrum.

The formation of this ideological business base had a direct consequence for the resilience of neoliberalism in Chile: namely, it prevented the formation of a business support group close to the more developmental orientation of the policies advocated by the center-left *Concertación* governments in the democratization period. This in turn had the effect of tempering the policy proposals of the *Concertación*—sometimes even washing them away completely—as a way to entice cooperation from a powerful business community closely associated with the dictatorship (E. Silva 1996; Weyland 1999b). On the one hand, the inability of the *Concertación* to build a business base on its own was a significant factor preventing the formation of an alternative social bloc. On the other hand, the power acquired through privatization of a business sector strongly in favor of neoliberalism not only diminished the demand for more developmental policies; as will become clear below, it explicitly blocked them when more progressive proposals were discussed in parliament. Finally, the lack of a business sector supporting an alternative development

6. More on this later in this chapter.

project implied that in their quest for campaign finances, center-left parties usually needed to moderate their views in order to receive funding from neoliberal-minded businesses.

The general agenda-setting power of business, and the perils of not counting on a business base of its own, was most visible at the beginning of the *Concertación*-led transition to democracy. One of the main ideologues of the *Concertación* coalition and its policy orientation stated it straightforwardly:

> Convincing the business community of the center-left's ability to govern was very important. Hence, a main economic goal of the transition was to build the trust of the business community. They were suspicious of the center-left coalition; not unreasonably presuming that it would be more statist/interventionist. The product of this skepticism was that the center-left coalition was determined to demonstrate their governability. This led to a higher degree of controls in economic policy; more prudent policy aimed at assuaging the business and investment community (Edgardo Boeninger quoted in Kaplan 2013, 65).

Consulted about the space for carrying out the more developmental industrial policy proposals instituted by the *Concertación* government, a high official at the Ministry of the Economy at the beginning of democratization affirmed that:

> it was suspected that we were going to do all sorts of nonsense, so for us it was completely impossible in the year 1990 to start saying: 'look, we will privilege this sector, or that.' There was no condition whatsoever to do that."[7]

After the return to democracy in 1990, a third privatization wave took place, which essentially continued the privatization of public utilities companies that had already started in the mid-1980s. This helped to consolidate the dominant positions of business groups in the competitive sector, which used the privatization of public utilities as a strategy for diversification into a sector that offered them more stable returns, therefore sheltering them from price shocks (see Fazio 1997, 75). Consequently, the main business groups in the competitive sector (such as Matte, Angelini, Yaconi-Santa Cruz) acquired significant shares in the public utilities sector in cooperation with foreign capital (see Fazio 2000; Hachette 2001).

7. Chile, Interview 2.

Foreign capital was an important part of these processes. During the second and third privatization waves, foreign investors were encouraged to acquire stakes in privatized companies in alliance with domestic groups, thereby providing crucial financial assistance.[8] There were three main channels (E. Silva 1996, 202): first, in partnership with competitive-sector firms to face the debt of the companies reprivatized from the "exotic area"; second, participation in debt-for-equity programs by which investors acquired major stakes in traditionally state-owned companies together with former regime officials; and finally, the direct acquisition of companies in the competitive, financial, and public utilities sectors. Between 1990 and 1999, FDI inflows reached record highs and supported the development of the economic sectors that were bastions of the neoliberal social bloc: the competitive sector (43.1 percent of all FDI inflows), public utilities (25.2 percent), and finance (18.4 percent).[9]

The lack of a business support base for an alternative developmental policy regime became more visible during the government of socialist president Ricardo Lagos, the first socialist president since Allende, in 2000–2005. Since 1989 the socialists had coalesced with the Christian Democrats in the *Concertación* coalition, therefore significantly moderating their policy platform, but fears of leftist governance still plagued the neoliberal social bloc, prompting the right-of-center UDI party and the business community to lead a concerted attack on Lagos's government (see E. Silva 2002). With the lack of a clear majority in Parliament and the threat of a capital strike by business at large, Lagos saw no alternative for his political survival but to try to co-opt the leading business sectors (finance and competitive).

Remarkably, Lagos's government in the end strongly supported the continuation of neoliberalism. He not only strengthened the independence of the Central Bank by appointing a leading conservative economist to its board (in spite of his own coalition's more progressive candidates), but also backed the business-sponsored industrial promotion programs highlighting labor market deregulation and tax reductions instead of the *Concertación*'s more progressive industrial policy concerns (see Scapini 2006, 16–17). In fact, analysts of the tax on copper mining that encouraged progression towards developmental industrial policy alternatives argue that the government actively sided with the business community—most notably the competitive mining sector—in watering

8. Another key financing mechanism was the utilization of the pension funds privatized in 1980. Private fund administrators (AFPs) directed workers' savings toward capitalizing the newly privatized firms.

9. Author's calculations based on data from Chile's Foreign Investment Committee.

down the final legislation (Napoli and Navia 2012). Crucially, these moves helped the government coax support from an initially reluctant business community. This was famously reflected in the words of Hernán Sommerville, long-term president of the banking association and later of the umbrella business association, who claimed in 2005 referring to Lagos that "businessmen love the president" (cited in Madariaga 2020, 12).

Conversely, businesses' rejection and a blockade in Parliament explain the inability of the more progressive wing of the *Concertación* to push forward what has so far constituted the most aggressive attempt to establish a developmental industrial policy in the country: the Council for Innovation and Competitiveness (CNIC) and the clusters policy it intended to pursue, both financed with the tax on mining operations watered down with the support of Lagos (Bril-Mascarenhas and Madariaga 2019).

During the parliamentary discussions of the law institutionalizing the CNIC, the competitive mining industry assumed leadership in rejecting the discretionary use of mining tax revenues for industrial policy purposes, especially if those revenues entailed cross-sectoral transfers (Bril-Mascarenhas and Madariaga 2019). Thanks to their bipartisan lobby of mining-region legislators, they successfully blocked the institutionalization of the CNIC and demanded more extensive involvement of organized business in the management and oversight of the mining tax, watering down its otherwise more progressive uses. Lack of institutionalization left this industrial policy framework extremely fragile politically, as it depended on presidential decrees for its continued survival. It was thus easily dismantled with the arrival in 2010 of the business-backed government of Sebastián Piñera.

The fate of the CNIC and the clusters policy in Chile shows the perils of not having a business base of support for pushing an alternative development project. As recent party-financing scandals have shown, large mining business groups such as Luksic and SQM have a particular cross-partisan pattern of campaign finance donations, unlike most large firms and groups with financial and other links to right-wing parties, particularly the rightist UDI (see Monckeberg 2001, 2015; Matamala 2016). The fact that legislators from the Socialist Party have received hefty contributions from SQM has produced public repudiation and has shown the extent to which left-of-center parties were in need of a business support base, if only to finance their campaign expenses.

Conversely, the original design of the CNIC—having on its board not big business associations but individual businesses that had received CORFO

loans and other government assistance—demonstrates the connection between industrial policy and potential new sources of business support. In fact,
evaluations of the short-lived operation of the clusters policy show that in
those clusters where business was less developed before the intervention (for
example, the new "global services" cluster) participants in the program were
more likely to have a good impression of the program and to favor its continuation (see Zahler et al. 2014).

In sum, privatization significantly helped to consolidate the business bases
of support for neoliberalism in Chile. It boosted the financial sector's leading
position in the 1970s, which the sector used to back an orthodox version of
neoliberalism. After its fall amid the 1982–1983 crisis, privatization helped to
forge a new compromise with the competitive sector in order to support a
more pragmatic version of neoliberalism and permit the "silencing" of the
noncompetitive sector by giving state assets in the sector to loyal collaborators
of Pinochet. This process was strengthened with the massive influx of external
capital during the 1990s, in association with domestic capital. This pattern of
support creation reveals the absence of a business support base for an alternative social bloc in Chile (in the 1982–1983 crisis, immediately after democratization in the 1990s, and during the 2000s). The success of support creation
also explains the moderation of the center-left in its search for support among
the business community, the lack of demand for a more developmental policy
regime, and the active blockade of the few options to advance a more progressive industrial policy framework in the country.

Argentina: If You Can't Beat 'Em, Join 'Em

In contrast with Chile, the Argentinean case shows that when the noncompetitive sector was strong enough to either delay or oppose privatization—or turn
it to its own benefit—it maintained the possibility of challenging neoliberalism and contributed to the formation of an alternative social bloc demanding
more progressive policies. This pattern repeated twice in Argentina: during
the military dictatorship of 1976–1983, and during the democratic presidency
of Carlos Menem in 1990–1999.

Privatization ranked high in the plans of the military regime in 1976 (Canelo
2004, 289; Cavarozzi 1986, 44). Despite its efforts, however, privatization did
not progress as desired, primarily due to a powerful noncompetitive sector
that used its strong connection with nationalist military figures inside the gov-

ernment—especially those in charge of running state enterprises—to frustrate privatization attempts (Canelo 2004, 262–64; see also Biglaiser 1999, 17).

Toward the end of the 1970s, the meager advance in privatization plans was one of the biggest complaints of the liberal landed elite supporting the neoliberal Argentine military (Canelo 2004, 283–85). In order to overcome opposition and speed up privatization, Minister of Economy Martínez de Hoz came up with an innovative method called "peripheral privatization" (Schvarzer 1981, 60; Novaro and Palermo 2003, 229–30). In this process, public companies would subcontract their activities to the private sector so as to tighten their budget constraints and induce restructuring. At the same time, they were cut off from direct financing from the state budget and obliged to raise capital in the private market. The allocation of power resources to supporters was to take place through the provision of a market share in those sectors where state companies would retrench, rather than through direct divestiture. Accordingly, peripheral privatization took place in the industries where the state had the biggest stakes: oil and gas. State participation in these industries decreased from almost 80 percent in 1976 to 56.2 percent in 1983, while the state's presence in industry as a whole decreased from 13.3 percent to 7.4 percent (Basualdo 2006, 166).

This mechanism, however, did not serve to increase the power resources of business sectors within the neoliberal bloc (financial and/or competitive sectors). Instead, it was exploited by dynamic groups in the noncompetitive sector, who took advantage of their contacts with military officials in charge of SOEs (Corrales 1998, 36). Business groups such as Techint, Pérez Companc, Bridas, and Astra pushed for industrial policy plans and used them alongside peripheral privatization to consolidate their position, both by concentrating their market niches and diversifying their activities (see table 5.8).

As a result, the participation of these business groups in the profits of the 100 largest Argentine companies grew from 21.5 percent in 1976 to 65.9 percent in 1983 (Castellani 2012, 102). Moreover, those companies linked to the state through peripheral privatization had a utility/sales ratio of more than five times that of the companies not participating in it (Castellani 2004, 201). As a result, certain segments of the noncompetitive sector remained strong enough to benefit from access to policymaking. These segments supported the Argentine dictatorship's shift toward more developmental policies when the power balance inside the junta briefly changed in 1981. They also supported the return to democracy in 1983, and later on the government of social

TABLE 5.8. Argentina, Companies Privileged with Peripheral Privatization[a]

Group/ Company	Sector	Peripheral privatization	Other links to state
Techint	Noncompetitive (basic metals, machinery), construction	Oil and gas	1, 2
Pérez Companc	Noncompetitive* (oil, plastics/ rubber, machinery, construction), competitive (fishing, food) and finance	Oil and gas	1
Desaci	–	Oil and gas	1
Bridas	Noncompetitive (oil)	Oil and gas	1
Astra	Noncompetitive (Oil, chemicals)	Oil	2, 4[b]
Bunge & Born	Competitive (agriculture, food)* and noncompetitive (chemicals)	Oil	—
Garovaglio and Zorraquin[c]	Noncompetitive (petrochemicals), Competitive* (food, agriculture)	—	2, 4
Richards (Indupa)	Noncompetitive (plastics/rubber)	—	2, 4
Acindar	Noncompetitive (basic metals)	—	2, 4
Fate	Noncompetitive (basic metals)	—	3, 4
Aceros Bragado	Noncompetitive (basic metals)	—	2

Source: Author's elaboration based on data from Castellani (2004, 207–8), Azpiazu, Basualdo, and Khavisse (1986).

Note: 1= Public works contracts; 2= Buyer to state firms; 3= Supplier of state firms; 4= industrial. promotion schemes; * Indicates main sector when groups are diversified into other sectors.

[a]Doesn't include benefited multinationals: Pirelli, Siemens, Lepetite Dow and Indupa.

[b]As participant in the Bahía Blanca Petrochemical Pole through shares in IPAKO.

[c]Corresponds to the Bahía Blanca Petrochemical Pole that they controlled through IPAKO, with a significant presence of the state.

democrat Raúl Alfonsín and his heterodox stabilization and industrial policy plans (see chapter 4).

Large-scale privatization in Argentina took place only a decade later, during the administration of Carlos Menem. In the context of the hyperinflationary crisis of the late 1980s, the Law on State Reform passed in August 1989 gave the president extraordinary powers to advance the privatization of SOEs. This, together with the Law on Economic Emergency that eliminated state subsidies and the national purchase regime, constituted a critical condition required by external creditors for the negotiation of the pressing external debt problem facing the country (Basualdo 2006, 283–92).

Again, businesses in the noncompetitive sector were the thorns in the side of these plans. They now saw privatization as a double threat. On one hand, it would attract powerful and competitive multinational corporations (MNCs), some of them directly challenging their market niches. On the other, it would cut off the fruitful relationship with the state as both buyers and suppliers of SOEs at favorable prices, among other benefits. As staunch opponents of the partial privatization plans of the late Alfonsín presidency (Ortiz and Schorr 2006, 37; Beltrán 2006, 226–27), the biggest groups in this sector had supported Menem, who had promised to stop ongoing privatization, over the government's candidate in the 1989 elections (Corrales 1998, 29).[10] After Menem's political and policy U-turn, they threw everything they had against privatization, threatening to create social unrest by funding strikes, laying off workers, lobbying congress, and supporting opposition parties (Corrales 1998, 29).

As several authors have highlighted (Corrales 1998; Etchemendy 2001, 2012; Acuña, Galiani, and Tommasi 2007), privatization was the key to unraveling Menem's neoliberal project. He came to realize that he could only generate support for his neoliberal reform plans among the noncompetitive sector by letting them enjoy its benefits. The allocation of rents through privatization therefore went not to the financial or the competitive sectors, but to the powerful noncompetitive sector that threatened the existence of the emerging neoliberal policy regime and its support base. Thus, unlike in Chile, privatization in Argentina reinforced the dominance of powerful noncompetitive conglomerates by either securing them sector-dominating market shares, or by allowing them to diversify into public utilities (Etchemendy 2001, 2012).

This process was most visible in the noncompetitive oil and steel sectors, where state participation was at its highest (Basualdo 2006, 267). In the oil sector, the privatization process included the removal of price controls, the awarding of new areas of exploration (new bids, new association contracts, and revision of old contracts), and the privatization of the oil producer and major public company YPF. It threatened established groups like Pérez Companc, Astra, and Bridas, which had either concentrated or diversified to oil production using peripheral privatization and other links to the state. They therefore lobbied intensively to be considered in the process. As a result, most privatization procedures were relatively competitive, with the exception of the revision

10. In his last years in office, Alfonsín unsuccessfully pushed partial privatization as a way to show commitment to fiscal retrenchment with international donors and alleviate debt (see also Machinea 1990, 32). Menem's party, the PJ, was crucial in halting this privatization attempt.

TABLE 5.9. Argentina, Producers of Steel and Oil (% of total sector)

	Before privatizations (1988)	After privatizations (1994)
Oil		
State (YPF)	65.2	42.6
Pérez Companc	8.0	13.6
Astra	2.9	5.2
Bridas	3.1	4.3
Other domestic	1.9	11.1
Other MNCs	18.7	13.0
Total	99.8	89.8
Steel		
State	56.3	0.0
Techint	11.3	63.0
Acindar	28.0	30.5
Aceros Bragado	4.4	2.3
Altos Hornos Zapla	—	4.1
Total	100.0	100.0

Source: Etchemendy (2012, 105, 113, 119).

of old contracts, in which strict collaboration with the affected companies was the norm (Etchemendy 2012, 110–11). Consequently, these business groups significantly expanded their share in the sector (see table 5.9). In 1996, more than 70 percent of oil was extracted through these redefined contracts (Etchemendy 2001, 14).

In the steel sector, privatization proceeded similarly, with the advantage to powerful groups in the noncompetitive sector. Prominent international steel-makers such as Italy's Iretecnia and Germany's Thyssen publicly denounced the process as ridden with biases towards domestic producers (Etchemendy 2001, 17; 2012, 107). The negotiations were particularly fruitful for Techint and Astra, two other groups previously favored by peripheral privatization and state promotion.

Powerful business groups in the noncompetitive sector, including Techint, Pérez Companc, and Astra, also received significant shares of the privatized public utility companies in connection with external capital, helping them to further diversify their operations (Gerchunoff, Greco, and Bondorevsky 2003).

After the establishment of the currency board in 1991, FDI started to steadily pour into the country. Between 1990 and 1993, 44 percent of net capital inflows went to privatization proceeds (Heymann 2000 in Cherny 2009, 105). FDI

TABLE 5.10. Argentina, 13 Biggest Business Groups in 1997

Group	Sector	Sales current USD
Techint	Noncompetitive* (basic metals, oil, construction) and public utilities (gas)	7,000
SocMa	Competitive (construction, food)	2,170
Banco/Velox	Finance	2,118.3
Pérez Companc	Noncompetitive* (diversified), competitive and finance	1,621
Clarín	Media, publishing	1,651
Bunge & Born	Competitive* (food, agriculture) and noncompetitive (chemicals)	1,340
Arcor	Competitive (food)	1,070
Bemberg	Competitive (food, agriculture)	892
AGD	Competitive (food, transport)	840.6
Sancor	Competitive* (food) and finance	720
Pescarmona	Noncompetitive (electronics, construction)	658
Aluar/Fate	Noncompetitive (basic metals, rubber)	654.7
Acindar	Noncompetitive* (basic metals) and public utilities	600.8

Source: Fracchia, Mesquita, and Quiroga (2010, 327).
Note: * Indicates main sector when groups are diversified.

went first to the competitive export sector and then to public utilities (ECLAC 2002). Together, they amounted to more than 60 percent of all FDI flows during the period. In other words, while competitive MNCs concentrated in finance, public utilities, and the competitive sector, domestic groups consolidated their positions in the noncompetitive sector.

As I have pointed out before, the privatization strategy of the Menem government was crucial in order to harness support for neoliberalism during the 1990s. However, the way privatization was designed—that is, strengthening the power resources of the noncompetitive sector—was also crucial to keeping these sectors alive throughout the hardships of exchange rate appreciation and the turbulence of the Tequila Crisis (see Castellani and Gaggero 2011, 286–87). In fact, in 1997, groups with stakes in the noncompetitive sector that were diversified thanks to privatization ranked highly among the top Argentine business groups (see table 5.10).

It was precisely these groups that constituted the main critics of neoliberalism at the end of the decade. Beginning in 1999, the same groups that had accepted neoliberalism in exchange for handsome benefits during the 1990s would timidly start to voice their discontent with the existing economic policy framework, particularly with trade liberalization and the growth of the financial sector (Beltrán 2011, 241–42; 245–46, 2014, 303–4). One important constraint for not demanding outright devaluation was the high level of foreign-denominated debt that they held.[11] However, as economic conditions deteriorated in 2001, they turned from defense to offense, openly supporting devaluation, the elimination of the currency board, and a conversion scheme of dollar-denominated debt to pesos (Cherny 2009, 150–51; Castellani and Schorr 2004, 73). They envisaged this as part of an alternative policy regime that could restore the domestic economy, active state promotion policies, the manufacturing industry as the leading economic sector, and the alliance with labor (see chapter 4). By contrast, the finance industry and the competitive sector, represented by large agricultural producers, defended the continuity of neoliberalism with the maintenance of a fixed exchange rate, trade openness, and no state intervention in the economy (Beltrán 2014).

After the collapse of the Argentine economy in 2001–2002, in 2003 Néstor Kirchner from the left wing of the Justicialista Party (PJ) was elected. With his harsh anti-neoliberal rhetoric, Kirchner established a renewed alliance with labor unions and noncompetitive economic sectors trying to initiate a new version of state developmentalism (see chapter 4). This alternative social bloc established a policy regime decidedly different from the existing neoliberal one. It established an exchange rate regime of managed flotation aimed at maintaining a high and stable exchange rate (which would promote domestic manufacturers), taxes on exports that had been the basis of import-substitution industrialization (ISI), a shift of existing industrial policy instruments towards greater selectiveness, and new ways of directing subsidized credit to manufacturing industries.

This "new developmental" economic project fell on fertile ground among the noncompetitive business groups such as Techint and Aluar that had benefited from the 1990s privatization process, survived the reorganization of the sector at the end of the 1990s, and were the pillars of business criticism of neoliberalism during the 2000–2001 crisis. These groups, in turn, benefited handsomely, not only from the new policy framework that concentrated on revitalizing domestic demand and increasing state intervention but also from the specific policies enacted by Kirchner in the realms of exchange rates and industrial policy (Castellani and Gaggero 2017). Recent judicial investigations have revealed that some of these companies were deeply implicated in

11. Estimates are that nearly 75 percent of deposits in domestic banks and almost 80 percent of total credit were in dollars (Damill, Frenkel, and Maurizio 2002 in Cherny 2009, n. 61).

bribery schemes to get public works contracts during the Kirchner governments (Fontevecchia 2018).

Estonia: Buying Foreign Support for Neoliberalism

Privatization in Estonia was shaped by reformers who wanted to prevent Russians from taking over substantive power in the Estonian economy through insider buys. In the mid-1980s, between 85 and 90 percent of Estonian industry was allegedly under the direct control of Moscow (Mettam and Williams 1998, 373). Russian-speakers were concentrated in industry, especially in higher management and lower industrial positions, posing the threat that a spontaneous privatization process and insider-privilege in privatization proceeds would leave substantive state stakes in Russian hands. This possibility was exacerbated by existing Soviet legislation that gave the right of first purchase to workers' collectives (Andersen 1997, 304), and by the behavior of SOE managers who pressed branch ministries to expedite insider privatization.[12] Indeed, close observers detected an incipient process of *nomenklatura* privatization at the beginning of the liberalization process (World Bank 1993, 46–47; see Terk 2000, 28–29, 33–34).

When the moderate Popular Front (PF) came to power in early 1990, their first task was to suspend the sale of state assets until appropriate legislation was in place (Terk 2000, 67; Lauristin and Vihalemm 1997, 107). In 1990–1991, the PF launched small-scale privatization—small shops in which the majority of the workforce was of a majority Estonian composition—and a pilot program of direct sales including seven big enterprises. This process led to the formation of the Estonian Privatization Enterprise in September 1992 with a brief to begin a massive sales program. However, the pilot program sparked the opposition of the nationalists in Parliament, who saw that most of these enterprises were, in the end, sold to insiders (World Bank 1993, 42; see also Purju 1999, 203). This outcome, together with the independence scenario in 1991, heightened fears that Russian managers still in charge of SOEs would find intricate ways to get privatized companies into their hands (Purju 1999, 203). The need to divide property between the new nation state and the disintegrating Soviet Union—not least, the threat of buyouts directly concerted

---

12. Estonia, Interview 4. Interviewee underscores, however, that a majority of managers actually wanted to maintain companies in state hands, and that the issue for them was to keep them working.

by Moscow in order to reassert control over Estonia—further reinforced these fears (Terk 2000, 13; 31). In this context, neoliberal nationalists favored privatization through restitution of property rights to pre-World War II owners. This became the main method in 1991, and especially after the right-wing Laar administration took office in 1992 (Purju 1999, 204; Terk 2000, 50–51).

The result of the change from direct sales to restitution was a significant slowing-down of privatization (World Bank 1993, 41–44; Terk 2000, 13, 53–57; Alanen 1999, 438). In fact, restitution entailed many aspects that complicated the process and gave rise to heated debates. By late 1992, out of 200,000 restitution claims received, the government had processed only about 1,000 (World Bank 1993, 44). As privatization through restitution stagnated, the Parliament continued to debate other methods. After three years of discussion, it became clear that if steered in the right way, direct sales offered advantages. The Parliament also compromised by creating a compensation fund in which proceeds of direct sales were to be deposited in order to compensate property restitution rights, thus appeasing the nationalists (see Terk 2000, 58–59; Purju 1999, 205).

In June 1993, the Privatization Act was passed, and the Privatization Agency constituted. Two characteristics of the new agency should be underlined: its concentration of the decision-making process and the leeway it enjoyed in terms of methods and criteria, taking away the involvement of line ministries (Terk 2000, 76–79). The agency had to prepare programs to be approved by the government every year. However, it could decide relatively autonomously between different modes of selling companies, different ways to limit or restrict these sales, and which companies to include in each year's program. In practice, the Privatization Agency gave priority to speed over any other consideration (Terk 2000, 84, 88). Moreover, given the lack of domestic capital (despite the facilities included in the privatization law), finding a core external investor became the quickest way to proceed (see OECD 2000a, 126–36).[13] Strict sorting processes were carried out to screen the participation of foreigners, which served to avoid a Russian takeover (Andersen 1997, 309; see also D. Smith 2001, 128). Most of the sales deals for large enterprises took the form of a tender pre-negotiated with the buyer—usually foreign capital (Purju 1999, 211; Terk 2000, 158).

13. The fact that the state did not restructure SOEs before selling, and that the buyer was responsible for inherited debts, seems to have been a significant deterrent for domestic investors, in spite of what otherwise seemed to be favorable conditions (e.g., payment in installments or with vouchers).

In 1996, the OECD reported that, within Eastern Europe, Estonia was the only country where 90 percent of privatization had been accomplished (Terk 2000, 9). Insider buyouts were kept to a minimum (12 percent), and 60 percent went to outside owners, both domestic and foreign (World Bank in Lauristin and Vihalemm 1997, 107). Between 1993 and 1998, about one-third of total privatization revenue came from external capital (OECD 2000a, 131). This orientation strengthened the currency board's bias toward the transnationalization of the Estonian economy.

The privatization process in Estonia had two primary effects on neoliberal resilience. First, as in Chile, it prevented the formation of economic interests opposed to neoliberalism. More specifically, it helped to "silence" possible opposition by the noncompetitive sector, especially agriculture—a major source of the demand for continued protectionism in Poland. Second, foreign capital and related international actors displayed support for Estonian neoliberalism, especially the functioning of the currency board, by stabilizing the economy through massive capital inflows when it was put to test during crises.

The impacts of the privatization process in the agriculture sector are telling. This was one of the sectors that was hardest hit by the shock therapy reforms of the early 1990s, and it was also one of the more vocal sectors protesting against neoliberal reforms in Poland. Privatization could have formed a new proprietor class and a strong private agricultural sector, which Estonia unlike Poland, lacked. But the slow process of privatization delayed class formation and thus contributed to the sector's productive downfall.

Contrary to other industries, the main method in the countryside remained restitution (Terk 2000, 166; Alanen 1999). This made the process in agriculture particularly slow: whereas in 1996 about 90 percent of companies in other sectors had been privatized, in agriculture more than two-thirds of land was still in state hands (Terk 2000, 161, 168). As mentioned above, restitution was a long and expensive process, aggravated by the number and wide circle of claimants and the technicalities of land privatization.[14]

More crucially, the process itself detracted from the formation of interests in agriculture, and demobilized existing ones. As Terk (2000, 51) observes, the heirs of the original pre–Second World War tenants who re-

---

14. E.g., surveying of land, entry of the land parcel into a land cadaster and then into a national land registry, difficulty in calculating the exact fund that was to be physically returned, etc. (Terk 2000, 167; see also Alanen 1999, 438; 441; Purju 1999, 218).

ceived compensation were not necessarily farmers themselves. It is estimated, in fact, that around two-thirds of those individuals with land restitution claims lived in the city at the time of reform (Alanen 1999, 444; see also Terk 2000, 51). Inevitably, workers of collective farms who did have a significant stake in the future of the sector were sidelined. This not only trumped the process of interest formation, but also aggravated the crisis in the countryside. In a majority of cases, the heirs of pre-war tenants stayed in cities after getting their land parcels, leaving the land idle (Terk 2000, 169). According to Alanen (1999, 441), as of 1997 a majority of restituted farms were not actively cultivated. Other complex technicalities of the process further reinforced this. For example, the restitution process privatized only the land itself, whereas the means of production remained in the hands of former workers of collective farms, further aggravating the production crisis in the countryside (Alanen 1999, 441–42; Terk 2000, 169). In other words, although Estonian agriculture suffered from the slump in output that followed the transition to capitalism and was therefore a strong potential demander of more extensive state subsidies and protections, the delay in the formation of an agricultural proprietor class due to the complications of the privatization process significantly weakened those demands, contributing to reduce criticisms of the neoliberal reform path. As we will see, exactly the contrary happened in Poland, where the large size of private agricultural interests hurt by the transition process became crucial in derailing the neoliberal project in the early years of the transition from communism.

Conversely, the high share of foreign capital in the privatization of the noncompetitive sector lessened its political demands for higher protection, a process I have called "silencing." Although many authors mention the high percentage of external capital in Estonia's more competitive sectors (see Tiits, Kattel, and Kalvet 2006, 74–81), FDI's main contribution to neoliberal resilience was its high relative presence in the noncompetitive sector, facilitated through privatization. Table 5.11 shows FDI inward stocks as a percentage of total FDI in the economy and as a percentage of each sector's GDP in three years, 1997 (before the Russian crisis), 2000 (after the Russian crisis and before EU accession) and 2005 (after EU accession). What is more important is the relative rather than the total magnitude of FDI going to the noncompetitive sector during the 1990s. In 1997, before the Russian crisis, the share of FDI as a percent of the noncompetitive sector's value added was close to 55 percent, higher than in any other sector in the Estonian economy, even those receiving

TABLE 5.11. Estonia, FDI Stocks[a]

	% of total economy			% of sector GDP		
	1997	2000	2005	1997	2000	2005
Total	100.0	100.0	100.0	30.5	51.5	96.6
Competitive	27.5	19.6	13.7	47.5	61.3	81.1
Food product + beverages	8.5	5.1	2.7	70.1	102.1	118.8
Nonmetallic minerals	4.9	3.0	1.4	176.1	185.7	102.8
Wood, and paper products	5.2	2.8	5.0	54.5	47.2	127.4
Basic and Fabricated metals	2.3	1.1	0.8	62.8	52.3	47.9
Textiles and clothing	3.0	3.1	0.9	44.5	77.5	52.9
Furniture	1.7	1.3	0.7	39.6	55.3	45.4
Agriculture/Forestry/Fishing	1.3	1.3	0.6	7.1	13.3	16.8
Noncompetitive	9.3	3.8	2.2	53.7	46.4	39.8
Chemicals	6.1	1.9	1.0	205.8	154.3	109.8
Financial	14.6	32.2	66.7	19.1	79.2	269.5
Public Utilities	16.7	23.9	5.9	31.3	78.2	38.5
Other[b]	26.1	20.1	11.2	28.1	26.7	27.4

Source: Author's elaboration using data from FDI database from the Vienna Institute for International Economic Studies (wiiw).
[a]Although included in the sector averages, the table shows only subsectors with a share higher than 1% of total FDI.
[b]Comprises mostly retail trade and tourism (restaurants + hotels).

higher overall FDI flows like the competitive and financial ones. Even more, in the case of chemicals, total FDI stocks represented twice the sector's output (GDP). This situation was reversed only after the Russian crisis and reinforced after EU accession.

The decision to not restructure SOEs or clear their debts before selling them, leaving these responsibilities to prospective buyers, reveals the clear biases to foreign buyers in Estonia's privatization process. It also helps understand why those companies that had the possibility of buying Estonia's ailing state-owned firms were rather successful firms in their own merit, had enough capital and technological capabilities and therefore, did not demand strong protectionist measures thus "silencing" the possible opposition coming from an otherwise more protectionist noncompetitive sector. In 2000, for example, a Finnish electronics manufacturer called Elcoteq was among the twenty largest foreign investors in Estonia (OECD 2001a, 25–26). Although electronics was a minuscule part of Estonian GDP and was part of the noncompetitive sector of the economy, Elcoteq, a supplier of cellular telephone parts to communication giants like Nokia and Ericsson, could hardly count as a noncompetitive firm demanding state subsidies and protections.

Several authors, most notably Drahokoupil (2009), have argued that the competition for FDI among Eastern European states induced these countries to offer significant benefits packages to foreign investors, which could be interpreted as a demand for a more developmental industrial policy. This, however, does not invalidate the argument presented here. In the first place, this process of competition between states only started toward the second half of the 1990s, when many countries had already enacted different privatization methods. As we saw above, by this time Estonia had practically privatized its entire economy. Additionally, the type of embedded-neoliberal industrial policy that these foreign companies demanded—most significantly, tax breaks and the reduction of labor costs—contrasts sharply with the expenditure-demanding subsidies and tariff increases that domestic companies in this sector usually desired. This will become evident in the Polish case.

In Estonia, external investors not only acquired major stakes in all sectors of the Estonian economy, through privatization as well as greenfield investment. They also committed massive capital inflows to stabilize the Estonian economy when major crises put pressure on the currency board-dependent policy regime. During the Russian crisis, a large current account deficit caused by exchange rate appreciation produced fears that the authorities would attempt a devaluation (see Sutela 2001; Baltic News Service 1997b). However, massive capital inflows shortly after the initial shock dissipated fears of devaluation and quickly stabilized the economy, bringing calm after the storm (see Eamets, Varblane, and Sostra 2003). As early as 1997, one-third of Estonian output, generating over 50 percent of its exports, was controlled by foreign capital (Sutela 2001, 19). Three years after the beginning of the crisis, FDI stocks in the country had increased by two-thirds. The process was particularly significant in the leading financial sector, where FDI came to represent almost 80 percent of the sectors' GDP in 2000 (see table 5.11 above). Eighty-five percent of the Estonian banking market, 90 percent of leasing, and 30 percent of the insurance market became concentrated in two major Swedish-controlled financial groups: Swedbank and SEB (OECD 2000a, 116). This process accelerated after EU accession, when FDI to the financial sector increased to two-thirds of all FDI stocks in the country, and more than two times the sector's actual GDP (table 5.11 above).

The effect of the consolidation of external interests on the continuity of neoliberalism in Estonia could be seen more clearly during the financial crisis of 2007–2008. One unlikely external actor provided crucial support for the maintenance of the currency board and the government's deflationary policy:

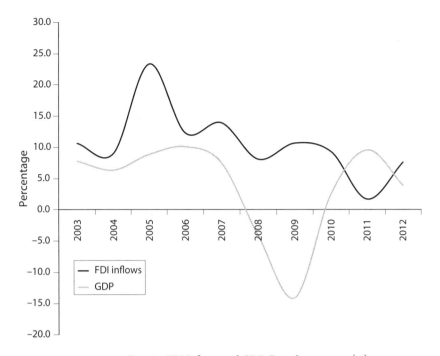

FIGURE 5.1. Estonia, FDI Inflows, and GDP Growth 2003–2012 (%)
Source: Author's elaboration using data from FDI database Vienna
Institute for International Economic Studies (wiiw) and OECD.
Note: FDI Inflows reported as percentage of GDP (value added).

the Swedish government. According to Kuokštis and Vilpišauskas (2010, 6–7), Sweden was concerned with the problems a devaluation of the kroon would bring to their banks that controlled the Estonian banking and financial systems. They feared being forced to spend Swedish taxpayer money on bailouts. In order to fend off speculators and dispel the possibility of devaluation, the Swedish Central Bank and the Bank of Estonia negotiated an agreement by which the former would support Estonia with fresh liquidity and/or the necessary loans in order to defend the currency board.[15] In addition to this, FDI appeared to be a significant element preventing a further decline of GDP during the hardship years of 2008–2009. In fact, as figure 5.1 shows, FDI maintained a constant inward flow during the worst crisis period. In 2009, when GDP dropped by 14.1 percent, net FDI inflows represented 10 percent of GDP. FDI declined in 2011, but by then the Estonian economy had already recovered from the slump.

15. Estonia, Interview 9.

In sum, the process of privatization in Estonia constituted a special type of support creation because it was heavily influenced by the concomitant process of independence from the Soviet Union and the nationalist sentiment that pervaded radical neoliberal reforms. The result of the mechanism was to forego the creation of a domestic business base, silence the possibility that ailing economic sectors (agriculture and the noncompetitive sector as a whole) would demand protections in the form of subsidies and industrial policy measures, and incorporate external capital as a key "stakeholder" and supporter of Estonian neoliberalism.

Poland: Delaying Support for Neoliberalism

Unlike in Estonia, privatization in Poland failed to create a business base of support for the continuation of neoliberalism. During the 1990s, privatization stalled, or it favored insiders accustomed to state subsidies and protection. Polish neoliberals, therefore, could not count on a strong business support base to maintain neoliberalism during the first phase of transition. Beginning in 1997, privatization sped up, especially in the financial and competitive sectors, but the state maintained significant stakes in the biggest companies in the noncompetitive sector. This both weakened the potential demand for a consolidation of neoliberalism and maintained the demand for state subsidies and protection. While during the 1990s a lack of privatization prevented the formation of a business support base, in the 2000s this base remained too weak to push neoliberalism more strongly.

The rapid events that led to the fall of communism in 1989 and put Poland at the leading edge of Eastern European transformation made Polish reformers overly optimistic about the results of privatization. The Mazowiecki government announced a massive—and clean—process, in order to oppose nascent *nomenklatura* privatization, and in September 1989 created the Office of the Plenipotentiary for Privatization. The government believed that by 1992 half of the privatization process would have been carried out (Nuti 1999, 81–82; Lewandowski 1994, 7; Błaszczyk 1999, 200). In 1990, however, recognizing a lack of progress and the need for greater human and material resources, this deadline was pushed ahead to 1995.

Polish neoliberals were confronted with a dilemma.[16] Their own preferences dictated that they should try a radical approach to speed up privatization—such as commercializing large packages of 1,000 firms at once. However,

16. Poland, Interview 5.

this entailed major technical and operational effort, as well as uncertainty about the efficiency of the process in an environment of massive concomitant changes. Most of all they feared that ex-communists in Parliament would block such processes, jeopardizing the rest of the reform plan. They opted therefore to announce a general mandate for privatization and negotiate its contents more gradually.

In August 1990, the government created the Ministry of Ownership Transformation, whose first program of privatization had two characteristics (Lewandowski 1994, 7): a multitrack method and the decentralization of decision-making. The first characteristic was no different from the situation in Estonia. Small-scale privatization was transferred to local governments, proceeded quickly, and favored insiders (Nuti 1999, 84; Meaney 1995, 287). For large-scale privatization, two methods were available: direct sales (auctions or deals) and voucher privatization. The Mazowiecki government preferred the former in order to favor external capital, but the method proved politically controversial; unlike in Estonia, many Poles were suspicious of handing over important elements of the economy to foreigners, preferring instead to promote a domestic business class (see Stark and Bruszt 1998, 94; Lewandowski 1994, 18). In fact, one Polish privatization minister recognized that he had explicitly created "as many obstacles as possible to foreign purchases of Polish companies in order to encourage a class of domestic owners" (Schoenman 2014, 93).

In 1991, President Wałęsa and Prime Minister Jan K. Bielecki gave a jolt to mass privatization through vouchers, in order to increase popular support for the program (Stark and Bruszt 1998, 95–96; Nuti 1999, 82; Błaszczyk 1999, 203). The Polish voucher program transferred privatized firms to asset management funds, which controlled them while they found a suitable investor in the name of voucher holders. However, mass privatization through vouchers also got severely delayed, this time due to opposition in parliament. The law was made effective only in June 1993, three years after the launch of the plan. One of the main points of criticism from both the postcommunists and the conservative wing of post-Solidarity parties was, again, the view that it would produce a massive transfer of Polish assets to external interests (Bonamo 1997, 577; Meaney 1995, 285–87; Ekiert and Kubik 2001, 148). Therefore, once in government, the postcommunist SLD/PSL coalition (1993–1997) reduced the scope of the program and delayed it until 1996.

Slowly, it became clear that privatization needed to be decentralized and include the interests of those opposing it, as in Argentina. Given the importance of works councils in the Polish economy in the early 1990s, not to mention workers' expectations that privatization would comprise a strengthening of employee self-management (one of Solidarity's main demands to the communist regime in the Round Table Talks), decentralization aimed at buying crucial support from the coalition of workers and company managers (Stark and Bruszt 1998, 95; Nuti 1999, 86–87; see Meaney 1995, 281; Lewandowski 1994, 18). All methods of privatization, therefore, included the significant participation of employees and managers. In the case of direct sales, for example, works councils controlled the entry of a company into the corporatization process; in the case of liquidation, employees had priority over other bidders. This meant that, in practice, employees and management had the right to veto almost any privatization proposal (Błaszczyk 1999, n. 8). The law stipulated several additional privileges for insiders. For example, in the case of direct sales, employers and managers could buy up to 20 percent of the total shares at a discount price—50 percent of the public price on the first day of sale.

The center-left SLD/PSL government brought several legislation changes aimed at speeding up the process throughout 1993–1997. All, however, maintained the insider bias and a considerable state presence (see Błaszczyk 1999, 202–4). While it reduced the veto power of works' councils over the whole process, it also increased their privileges. Under the new 1996 privatization law, employees could acquire up to 15 percent of their company free of charge, and a further 15 percent was to be reserved for farmers and/or fishermen supplying a company on a constant basis. Moreover, these benefits were extended to former employees now retired and to those on disability pensions. In 1996, a special privatization track was opened for indebted companies, and several sectors were excluded from privatization—among them strategic industries (energy, coal and defense) and a majority of public utility companies.

Decentralization made the Polish privatization experience directly opposite that of Estonia. In Estonia, the choice of method had fallen to the Privatization Agency, which could set clauses and carry out the process at its discretion. In Poland, by contrast, the choice of method and the very decision to privatize remained largely in the hands of the enterprises themselves. As a result, while in Estonia the Privatization Agency favored external capital, Polish SOEs favored insider buyouts and employee ownership. When we consider insider buyouts and a liquidation method that was also overwhelmingly insider-oriented, by the end of 1995 some 37 percent of SOEs had been alienated to company insiders, and another 54 percent were still in the hands of the state (World Bank in Lauristin and Vihalemm 1997, 107).

Two additional facts facilitated the state's continued interference in firms' decisions, even beyond those in which it had direct stakes (Schoenman 2014).

First, banks (mostly state-owned) acquired a majority stake in most companies under privatization proceeds. Second, Poland adopted a two-tiered corporate governance structure granting significant decision powers to supervisory boards that had significant representation from state agents. As a result, the state remained overwhelmingly in possession or control of the biggest Polish companies in all sectors: financial, competitive, and noncompetitive (see Gazeta Bankowa 1998; Schoenman 2014). In consequence, political parties had significant stakes in the appointment of supervisory boards, therefore controlling not only patronage resources, but, most important, the capacity of firms with loyal managers to support party finances and form part of government coalitions (Schoenman 2014, 132–37).

Johnson and Kowalska (1995, 234) describe the outcome of this privatization process in the following terms:

> Did the Balcerowicz team miss chances to build a supportive political coalition (by, for example, accelerating institutional changes)? With the advantage of hindsight, the answer is yes. Faster progress should have been made in reorganizing large state firms and restructuring the banking system. Even better, some form of mass privatization, involving the free distribution of shares to all citizens, could have created a strong political umbrella for more painful economic adjustments.

If we consider the delay in the process as well as the pro-insider bias, the picture of the business societal base for continued neoliberalism looks completely different in Poland than it does in Estonia. In fact, farmers and a coalition between workers and managers of SOEs were the more vocal groups demanding increased subsidies and protection at the beginning of the 1990s and were responsible for the slowdown of the reform process (see chapter 4). The center-left SLD/PSL government echoed these demands and put in place exchange rate and industrial policies that were in line with them, including subsidies for enterprise restructuring through social dialogue institutions, increased trade barriers for manufacturing and agricultural products, and exchange rate devaluation to promote manufacturing exports.

The choice of privatization during this first phase had a direct impact not only on the support for a broader industrial policy approach (both in terms of protection for ailing firms and support for restructuring); but it also impacted the choice of specific industrial policy programs and the performance of firms. In this sense, one could argue that the form of privatization was in itself a form of industrial policy (see McDermott 2002). For example, direct privatization included state-subsidized financing, below-market interest rates, and the possibility to defer payments, and (in one of the direct-privatization options) it mandated that at least half of workers be retained in the company (McDermott 2002, 235). According to McDermott (2002), this aided the flows of finance and know-how, and helped firms preserve and/or reconstruct productive networks, therefore maintaining their economic dynamism, productivity, and growth. Moreover, by linking the fates of banks (through debt-equity swaps privatization), large firms, and SMEs, privatization successfully linked ownership change to enterprise restructuring. According to McDermott (2002, 235; but see R. Martin 2013, 105–6), financial, productivity, and output indicators of the firms thus privatized tended to be better than national and sectoral averages, and by the end of the decade, a majority of these firms were undertaking organizational, process, and product innovations. Moreover, in the 1990s the decentralization of privatization and the role provided to local government eventually produced new forms of industrial policy based on decentralized cluster formation and regional development agencies, and constituted the backbone for the use of EU cohesion funds as industrial policy based on regional policy in the 2000s (Dornisch 1999; Ferry 2007)[17].

With the arrival of the rightist AWS/UW to government in 1997, the picture changed. It quickly developed a new law seeking to speed up the process. Already the first year in office (1998) marked a record in state revenue from privatizations of USD 2 billion or 1.3 percent of GDP (OECD 2000b, 84); by 2000 the figure reached an all-time high of USD 6.2 billion (OECD 2001b, 89, values converted to current USD). The new wave of privatization had three crucial characteristics: it was concentrated in the financial sector, albeit with important advances in the public utilities and competitive sectors; it produced a massive incorporation of external capital; and it included the largest SOEs (see table 5.12). This coincided with a renewed attempt to reduce public expenditure directed toward subsidizing restructured companies as well as the agricultural sector, and the change toward a free-floating exchange rate regime (see chapter 4).

17. Although not strictly related to industrial policy, it is interesting to note that the path of privatization focused on bank-enterprise links embedded in local institutions, and the related emergence of regional industrial policy, gave way to a pattern of corporate governance more similar to the patient capital of coordinated economies than to the equity-based financialized pattern of liberal economies (see McDermott 2002; Schoenman 2014). The consequences of this for sectoral promotion and industrial upgrading have been spelled out at large in the varieties of capitalism literature (e.g., Hall and Soskice 2001).

TABLE 5.12. Poland, Major Privatizations 1997–2000

	Sector	Controller (% of control)	Sale value (USD mill)
Telekomunikacja Polska (TPSA)	Public utilities (telecomm.)	France Telecom, Kulczyk, Polish state (35.0), Employees (15.0)	5,008.3
Bank Pekao SA	Financial	UniCredito Italiano, Allianz, Polish state (8.0)	1,287.9
PKN Orlen	Noncompetitive (fuels)	Polish state (28.4)	776.4
PZU	Financial	Eureko, BIG Bank Gdanski, Polish state (56.0), Employees (14.0)	694.4
Bank Zachodni	Financial	AIB European Investments, Polish state (4.3), Employees (12.7)	525.7
Bank Handlowy	Financial	Citibank, Polish state (6.9)	379.0
KGHM	Noncompetitive (mining)	Polish state (49.6)	310.3
Powszechny Bank Kredytowy	Financial	Bank Austria Credit AG, Bank of New York (7.9), Polish state (4.0)	308.9
Elektrocieplownie Warzawskie	Public utilities (energy)	Vattenfall, Polish state (45.0)	220.8
Polfa Poznan	Noncompetitive (chemicals)	Glaxo Wellcome, Polish state (2.7)	177.2
Orbis	Commerce (tourism)	Acor (20), FIC (10.4), Global Trade Center (5.0), Polish state (6.2), Employees (12.3)	154.1
Zaklady Przemyslu Tytoniowego Krakow	Competitive (food, beverages & tobacco)	Phillip Morris, Polish state (4.5)	133.4

Source: OECD (2001b, 84–85).

Note: Values converted to 2000 USD using data from the International Monetary Fund (IMF).

The state, however, remained in control of the noncompetitive sector, and maintained shares in privatized public utilities and the financial sector. Most significantly, this impulse was not carried further in the 2000s, when privatization suffered a series of setbacks: it slowed down during the center-left SLD-UP/PSL government in 2002–2005, was partly reversed with the PiS-led government in 2005–2007, and was even postponed by the pro-market PO/PSL government in 2007–2011. While revenue-raising privatization resumed in 2010–2013, the government was clear that a number of companies would remain in state hands for strategic reasons (Kruk 2012).

Thus, while the advances in privatization of the 1998–2002 period increased the power of the financial and the competitive sectors—at the same time facilitating the entrance of foreign capital to Poland—state concerns remained high, especially among the biggest Polish firms. This was most significant in

TABLE 5.13. Poland, 15 Biggest Companies in 2012

Size Rank	Profit Rank	Company	Sector	Controller (%)[a]	Sales[b] (current USD)
1	3	PKN Orlen	Noncompetitive (coke & fuels)	Polish state (27.5)	27,130.0
2	25	GK Grupy Lotos SA	Noncompetitive (coke & fuels)	Polish state (53.2)	10,167.7
3	2	Polska Grupa Energetyczna SA	Public utilities (energy)	Polish state (58.4)	9,383.4
4	—	Jeronimo Martins Polska SA	Competitive (food & beverages), commerce	Soc. Francisco Manuel dos Santos (PRT, 56.1)	8,877.0
5	4	GK PGNiG SA	Noncompetitive (coke & fuels)	Polish state (72.4)	8,822.4
6	5	GK Tauron Polska Energia SA	Public utilities (energy)	Polish state (30.1), KGHM (10.4)	7,597.4
7	1	KGHM Polska Miedź SA	Noncompetitive (mining, basic metals)	Polish state (31.8)	6,552.4
8	37	Grupa Eurocash SA	Commerce	Luis Amaral (PRT, 43.8)	5,090.1
9	—	Metro Group w Polsce	Commerce	Haniel (GER, 30.0), Schmidt-Ruthenbeck (GER, 15.8), Beisheim (GER, 9.1)	4,593.9
10	7	GK Orange Polska	Public utilities (telecomm.)	Orange SA (FRA), 50.7	4,344.2
11	—	Fiat Auto Poland SA	Competitive (transport & eq.)	FIAT (ITA)	4,334.1
12	—	BP Europa SE Oddział w Polsce	Noncompetitive (coke & fuels)	BP Amoco (ENG)	4,133.0
13	13	GK Energa SA	Public utilities (energy)	Polish state (51.5)	3,432.2
14	49	Kompania Węglowa SA	Noncompetitive (mining)	Polish state (..)	3,292.1
15	8	GK Enea SA	Public utilities (energy)	Polish state (51.5)	3,100.2

Source: Author's elaboration using data from Polityka, Lista 500 http://www.lista500.polityka.pl/.
[a]Information extracted from companies' investor relations website.
[b]Values converted to USD using data from the International Monetary Fund (IMF).

the noncompetitive sector, but also in other areas such as public utilities and finance (see table 5.13). In fact, Poland remained among the countries in Eastern Europe with the largest share of state assets in banking, 23.5 percent, second only to Romania (R. A. Epstein 2008, 76).

As with the Argentinean case, we can infer that continued public debate over development strategy in Poland and the shifts in economic policy orientation that each government has brought since 1997—even though not always realized in full—lies in the inability of the reform process to create a business support base for the resilience of neoliberalism, in contrast with the situation in Chile and Estonia. This reflects a situation where neoliberal policies coexist with more developmental ones, without a social bloc able to exert dominance, and with a business sector divided between supporting two different political projects (see Schoenman 2014).

Conclusions

Privatization has been crucial to strengthening the business support base of neoliberalism. As we saw in this chapter, privatization processes not only had clear biases benefitting the financial and competitive sectors, these sectors also behaved politically in ways that helped underpin neoliberalism in time. In Chile, privatization strengthened different business sectors at different times, thereby constituting an ample and strong multi-sector neoliberal business front. It helped the financial sector reach absolute hegemony among businesses in the 1970s; proved crucial to stabilize the leadership of the competitive sector during the 1980s; and in the 1980s–1990s, offered alternatives for diversification into public utilities while creating new business groups between officials of Pinochet's regime and external capital. A second noteworthy feature of the Chilean privatization process is the neutralization or "silencing" of the noncompetitive sector through privatization, creating what I call "ideological" business groups. These groups are owned or run by the very individuals who were behind the neoliberal project during the military government, preventing the formation of a business support base for alternative development projects that could strategically ally with democratic center-left governments.

In Estonia, the decision to avoid privatization to insiders and to Russian-speakers privileged Western investors. Privatization therefore served as an invitation for external capital to play a crucial role in the Estonian economy and its future development. The arrival of massive external capital into the leading financial and competitive sectors was an important factor in producing a demand for external openness and sound money. Foreign investors responded to their established interests that supported neoliberalism (most notably, the currency board arrangement) by providing much-needed FDI inflows each time they were required. The support provided to the currency board by the Swedish Central Bank during the 2007–2008 financial crisis (given the extent to which Swedish banks were involved in the Estonian economy) is indicative of the way external interests helped consolidate Estonian neoliberalism. Conversely, as in Chile, privatization played a central role in silencing potential protectionist demands among business sectors, especially in agriculture and the noncompetitive sector.

Both Poland and Argentina show privatization processes that failed to act as mechanisms supporting the continuation of neoliberalism. In Argentina, privatization did not favor supporters of neoliberalism, but instead bought the support of the noncompetitive sector opposing it. The effect was that while the strategy increased the chances for the survival of neoliberalism in the short run, it actually decreased its resilience in the longer run. Whenever economic crises affected the resilience of neoliberalism in Argentina, the empowered noncompetitive sectors sought to form alternative social blocs. This was the case both during the 1982–1983 financial crisis and the democratization period that followed the fall of the Argentine dictatorship, as well as during the 2001 crisis.

The Polish story is different from the Argentine one but still reveals important similarities. The need to maintain the pace of reforms and neutralize the coalition between workers and managers of state-owned firms (mainly in the noncompetitive sector) strengthened the case for insider privatization. This in turn explains the constitution of a private sector that was accustomed to state subsidies and protection and did not necessarily support neoliberalism. Conversely, the delay in the privatization process, especially in the case of the biggest firms, helped to maintain a strong segment of state ownership in the financial and competitive sectors, thus preventing the formation of a stronger pro-neoliberal business base in the 1990s, while continued state ownership in the noncompetitive sector provided a constant demand for subsidies and state protection. Privatization accelerated at the end of the 1990s, providing grounds for a renewed neoliberal project. However, enduring state presence in the country's biggest companies (especially, but not only, in the noncompetitive sector) helped to maintain the demand for subsidies and the possibility of an alternative social bloc—if not fully replacing neoliberalism with a more developmental project like that in Argentina, at least significantly impairing its consolidation.

The creation of support through privatization not only strengthened neoliberal blocs and weakened the possibility of forming alternative alliances, it also circumscribed the policy space and therefore the options of elected governments to the preferences of neoliberal businesses. The threat of capital flight—that is, the wielding of business structural power—generated fear among Estonian authorities willing to make monetary and exchange rate policy more responsive to the demands of their constituencies, particularly in the mid and late 1990s (see chapter 7). In the case of Chile, a combination of structural and instrumental power blocked a more developmental industrial policy in the 1990s and 2000s. In sum, by increasing the power of businesses with neoliberal preferences, support creation through privatization decreased the responsiveness of elected governments and, therefore, contributed to the erosion of representative democracy.

6

Blocking Opposition

POLITICAL REPRESENTATION AND
LIMITED DEMOCRACY

AS WE SAW IN CHAPTER 5, the creation of support among financial and competitive business sectors generated a business base that favored the continuity of neoliberalism. In this chapter, I investigate how neoliberal social blocs used political institutions to block the representation of adversaries in formal politics.

During the processes of economic and political liberalization in Latin America and Eastern Europe, economic reforms were expected to bring immediate costs to the population and positive results only in the long term. Opening these countries' polities to democratic competition was expected to derail the process of sustained economic reform, reduce the legitimacy of democratic procedures, and eventually undermine new democracies, impeding their consolidation (as we saw in chapter 2). This paradox produced a wide range of scholarly opinion on the optimal design and sequencing of free-market and democratic institutions during the transition period. It also resulted in several constraints on the capacity of political parties, particularly those on the left of center, to represent the desires of majorities for economic security and influence policy design.

Far from a temporary fix, key aspects of these limited political democracies or *democraduras* (O'Donnell and Schmitter 1986)—justified in the context of fragile economies and democracies—were perpetuated over time, permitting the resilience of neoliberalism through what I call *opposition blockade*.

Opposition blockade affected the political expression and representation of interests opposed to neoliberalism through key aspects of the institutional design of the new polities. These included, among others, electoral rules, executive-legislative relations, and the establishment of veto powers. A fourth source, typical of postcommunist countries, was lustration: the screening and banning of candidates running for relevant public positions because of their possible or perceived collaboration with the communist secret service. I analyze the operation of these sources of *opposition blockade* in detail, providing evidence demonstrating their effects on the resilience of neoliberalism and, more specifically, on the kinds of institutional constraints that were most effective at blocking opposition to it.

The evidence reveals that the design of electoral laws was the most successful way of limiting the power of political and societal actors opposing neoliberalism. It limited the power resources of the left in Chile and Estonia, blocking its capacity to form governments or change existing policies. Although Argentina and Poland also sought to limit the electoral representation of the political left, for several reasons, ranging from the weakness of actors making the attempt to miscalculations in institutional design, these efforts were less effective.

A second source of opposition blockade, the design of executive-legislative relations to empower specific actors expected to shelter economic reforms, was more pervasive in the cases of neoliberal discontinuity—Argentina and Poland—although not insignificant in Chile and Estonia. Increasing the power of executives—or for that matter, veto players able to block policy changes—proved effective while office holders remained neoliberal, but given the more open electoral possibilities, it backfired when office fell in the hands of political actors and parties less willing to support neoliberalism. As will become clear, while relevant politically, lustration in Eastern Europe was not directly linked to neoliberalism's resilience.

Research on business-party relations in Eastern Europe has shown that increased competition for office—and political alternation—has tended to create differentiated patterns of competition for business support, and therefore, diverse business-party coalitions (Schoenman 2014). In other words, opposition blockade not only contributed to neoliberal resilience by reducing political representation and policymaking influence; it also reinforced support creation by affecting the competition for business support among political parties.

If opposition blockade is, in fact, a causal factor of neoliberal resilience, we should find that:

1. Key political institutions had a clear partisan bias: that is, political institutions that defined who can participate in the political arena and who can influence policy have a systematic bias,
2. This bias was against political forces representing the losers of reform or actors challenging neoliberalism, and
3. Realistic counterfactuals can be made about the ability of those groups affected by opposition blockade to actually challenge neoliberalism if the mechanism had not been in place.

In order to construct these counterfactuals, I rely on the paired comparisons of countries presenting the most similar configuration (Argentina-Chile, Estonia-Poland). To be consistent across cases, opposition blockade should be either absent or have one of the above links missing in the cases of neoliberal discontinuity.

Designing *Democraduras* in the South and the East

At the beginning of their countries' transition, political elites in Latin America and Eastern Europe took into account a variety of experiences as they worked to design political institutions that restricted representation and access to policymaking. They considered strategic concerns in the conditions surrounding transitions, lessons from the characteristics of previous democratic regimes perceived as having led to democratic breakdowns in the first place, and foreign models of "good practice" (Elster, Offe, and Preuss 1998, 80; Haggard and Kaufman 1995, 230). Their quest coincided with the professionalization of institutional political science and the belief that political institutions were prime determinants of economic performance and political stability (Franzese 2002; Haggard and McCubbins 2001; Shugart and Carey 1992). In this context, research on political institutions gave concrete answers for constitutional engineering.

Generally, the tasks for constitutional engineers were three (see Haggard and Kaufman 1995): 1) to moderate extremist (i.e., leftist or populist) parties; 2) to reduce programmatic allegiances in favor of broad-based catchall parties; and 3) to reduce constraints on executives to expedite, pass, and/or sustain economic reforms. Analysts saw two decisions as the most important in constitutional design: electoral laws (including franchise extension and electoral systems) and the form of government (including executive powers and the relationship between executive and parliamentary powers) (Haggard and

Kaufman 1995; Haggard and McCubbins 2001; Lijphart 1991; Sartori 1994; Shugart and Carey 1992). Of course, political institutions were not only designed for efficiency; there were also distributive considerations regarding which groups would or should be favored, which patterns of policymaking would be followed through, and how reformers perceived threats and opportunities for future democratic consolidation. In this sense, reformers' interpretations of the situation and their ideas about how institutions better met their preferences determined their choices.

Electoral laws were central to these tasks. They transformed voting preferences into "democratically legitimized political power," shaped party systems, and managed sociopolitical cleavages and divisions (Carey 2018; Cox 1990; Elster, Offe, and Preuss 1998, 109–11; Sartori 1994, 35–36). Moreover, electoral laws were found to affect a number of relevant policy outcomes such as government spending, redistribution, and income equality (Iversen 2008, 612), and were considered key to reducing the polarization of votes and the fragmentation of party systems (see Haggard and Kaufman 1995). Not least, as Sartori recognized, electoral systems were seen as "the most specific manipulative instrument of politics" (cited in Lijphart 1991, p. 73), thus highly amenable to constitutional engineering. For these reasons, the choice of electoral system was seen as "arguably, *the* most important—of all constitutional choices that have been made in democracies' "(Arendt Lijphart cited in Kaminski 2002, 350).

A second dimension of institutional design was the form of government: more specifically, the power of the executive and its relationship with the legislative. Where electoral laws did not prevent parliaments from becoming more diverse and representative (i.e., potentially fragmenting and polarizing), countries could block opposition and overcome reform stalemates by empowering executive authority (Haggard and Kaufman 1995, 227). A number of prerogatives were used to bypass parliaments, including the frequent use of executive decrees, plebiscitarian appeals, and emergency powers (Haggard and Kaufman 1995, 165). More generally, countries could devise different types of veto powers to block attempts at reform by parliamentary majorities.

Finally, lustration was a specific response of the postcommunist states as they decided what the role, if any, of former communist intelligence officers should be in the newly-gained democracies (Horne 2009; Misztal 1999; Szczerbiak 2002a). Governments screened relevant individuals for their possible participation in the communist secret services before they were allowed to take office. A related process, decommunization, limited the ability of high-ranking communist officials to occupy public office in new democracies.[1] Lustration and decommunization had a moral as well as political background: they represented the need to deal with transitional justice, but also, with the support and loyalty of high-ranking authorities, and public administrators in general, to democratic procedures and the rule of law. In practice, however, lustration and the related decommunization process implied the reduction of representation of those who longed for the stability and economic protection of the former communist regimes, and the consequent capacity of former communists to present a democratic left political alternative. Jozef Oleksy, former Polish prime minister ousted from government in 1995 under lustration pressures, defined lustration as the "brutal action of the right attempting the elimination of the left from political life" (cited in Misztal 1999, 42).

Table 6.1 shows different features of constitutional design during democratization in the four countries under study. They are distinguished by whether they blocked the representation of portions of the electorate, or blocked influence in the policymaking process. In turn, I describe these political-institutional characteristics in the countries under study and their success in blocking oppositions.

In Latin America, the most important rationale behind the design of new constitutional provisions was the need to isolate and reduce the representation of the losers of economic reform and their potential political representatives in leftist and populist parties. A wide literature pointed at the fragmentation and polarization of these countries' political systems, particularly in Argentina and Chile, as one of the main reasons leading to the democratic breakdowns of the 1970s (Collier and Collier 1991; Haggard and Kaufman 1995). The Chilean left, represented by the Communist and the Socialist Parties and their many offshoots, had represented the working class and popular masses during the twentieth century, holding a permanent one-third of the votes (Collier and Collier 1991; Scully 1996; Valenzuela 1978). In Argentina, polarization had come not so much from established parties but from splinter groups that had turned into active subversive organizations. This said, unlike Chile, the pattern of social mobilization by the populist Justicialista Party had long given conservative parties and the military a constant motivation for breaking democracy (Cavarozzi 1986; O'Donnell 1973).

---

1. Lustration and decommunization are concepts that are often difficult to separate analytically, and even more so in political practice (Misztal 1999).

TABLE 6.1. Political Institutions and Opposition Blockade

	Representation			Policymaking process	
	Electoral laws	Lustration	Executive powers	Non-elected veto players	Legislative thresholds
Argentina	Yes (representation of provinces)	No	Yes (use of decree powers; re-election)	Yes (Supreme Court)	No
Chile	Yes (vote/seat bias)	No	Yes (exclusive initiative and control of budget)	Yes (tutelary role for military; Constitutional Tribunal; non-elected senators)	Yes (for key legislation)
Estonia	Yes (restricted franchise)	No	No	No	No
Poland	Yes (different results)	Yes	Yes (strengthen president, "fast-lane" congress approval)	No	No

Source: Author's elaboration.

The Chilean military junta was exceptional in its ability to bind the democratization process through restrictive political institutions. In their comparative work on democratization in Latin America and Europe, Linz and Stepan regard the Chilean arrangements as "the most constraining constitutional formula for a new democratic government" (Linz and Stepan 1996, 206). The provisions were enshrined in the 1980 Constitution, passed during the military dictatorship under a fraudulent referendum, and accepted by the more moderate opposition parties grouped in the center-left *Concertación* coalition as part of the democratization process. As its main ideologue bluntly put it, the 1980 Constitution was arranged in a way that:

> if the adversaries were to govern, they were constrained to take actions not so different from those that one would desire, or to use a metaphor, ... the room of maneuver the field imposes to those who play in it [is] so reduced ... to make the contrary extremely difficult (Guzmán 1979, 19 my translation).

The Gordian knot of this architecture was a unique system for congressional elections, combining proportional representation with the lowest possible district magnitude: two. In practice, this "binominal system," as it became known, forced the majority to outperform its closest competitor by a two-to-one margin to get the second seat. It was engineered taking into account the "three-thirds" dynamic of electoral representation prevalent during most of twentieth-century Chile: one-third for the right, one-third for the center, and one-third for the left (see Scully 1996; Valenzuela 1978). The idea was to force the convergence of the center and the left into one political block in their quest for the second seat, thereby moderating the left and boosting the representation of the right from its historical one-third, to 50 percent. Moreover, following the results of the 1988 referendum that ousted Pinochet, the political engineers of the dictatorship gerrymandered electoral districts to boost the representation of those districts where Pinochet had a higher vote (Polga-Hecimovich and Siavelis 2015).[2]

In terms of executive-legislative relations, the constitutional provisions established under the dictatorship favored a strong executive with full agenda-setting powers and a number of prerogatives over the legislative, exclusive law initiative in several key domains and absolute control over the budgetary process (see Baldez and Carey 2001). In fact, the Chilean Congress could only modify the destination of expenditure; it was prohibited from proposing new expenditure targets or increasing any expenditure, with the exception of specific items and only if it provided new sources of funding.

Military authorities, wary that after democratization the executive branch could be dominated by the left, devised a series of counter-balances inside and outside Congress. In addition to the expected increased weight of the right thanks to the electoral system, the dictatorship established 9 unelected senators in addition to the 38 democratically elected ones. These senators would be designated by independent state powers: four by the military-controlled Council of National Security (COSENA; see below), two by the outgoing president, and another three by the Supreme Court. In addition, it set the rule that outgoing presidents would become lifelong senators after finishing their term in office, except for the president immediately following the return to democracy. This meant that when the dictatorship fell, Pinochet was able to remain at the head of the military for another ten years, directly nominate six

2. The 1988 plebiscite showed a strong correlation between size of regions, in terms of population, and vote for Pinochet, reflecting the historically higher support for the right in less populated rural areas. This outcome was used to gerrymander electoral districts in the new electoral law (Londregan 2000, 85–93). As a result, while the most populated and left-leaning district of West Santiago, elected one senator for every 1.5 million inhabitants, the least populated and right-leaning Aysén district elected one senator for only 45.000 inhabitants (Siavelis 2010, 33).

out of nine unelected senators (as former president and as member of the COSENA), and eventually become life-long senator after retiring from the military.

The dictatorship also established a number of veto players who were expected to defend neoliberalism if adversaries were powerful enough to overrule the electoral system and the non-elected senators in Congress. The first were known as "authoritarian enclaves" and gave the military a tutelary role over the political system (Rabkin 1992). They included the inability of the president to remove the armed forces' commanders; the Council of National Security (COSENA), a body controlled by the military with the capacity to impugn and veto institutional reforms and legislation when they were perceived as hurting national security and sovereignty; and the Constitutional Tribunal, an independent agency that judged the constitutionality of new legislation. The final "blockade" protecting against any attempt at reform was the adoption in the Constitution of a set of supermajority thresholds for changing legislation (Fuentes 2012; Angell and Pollack 1990, 15).[3] Key aspects of this limited democracy—like the National Security Council, the unelected and life-long senators, and the binominal electoral system—were attached to the highest threshold for change: two-thirds majorities in both chambers. Other institutions such as the Central Bank and the Law on Mining Concessions were given "organic constitutional" status and attached to a four-sevenths threshold in both chambers (see chapter 7). It is not hard to see that, granted a high chance that the right would get close to 50 percent of seats in Congress, any change of this institutional configuration was close to impossible.

As if this were not enough, the outgoing military government established a series of additional measures to limit the exercise of authority by the incoming democratic government, including staffing of the Supreme Court (responsible for nominating non-elected senators and members of the COSENA[4]),

3. The 1980 Constitution includes four types of supermajority thresholds (Fuentes 2012, 40–41; Huneeus 2007): the milder one regulates "qualified quorum laws" (*leyes de quorum calificado*) and require absolute majority for changes. One example is the TV and Radio Council regulating censorship. The second threshold regulates the "organic constitutional laws" (*leyes orgánicas constitucionales*), and require four-sevenths of both Chambers. They apply to areas such as political parties, local and regional administration, the functioning of the Congress and the armed forces, and the Central Bank. The third supermajority relates to constitutional reforms and requires three-fifths approval in both Chambers. The final and most stringent one is the two-thirds threshold reserved for key institutional legacies of the Pinochet dictatorship.

4. For an account of the role of the Chilean Supreme Court as defender of neoliberalism and the Pinochet legacy, see Manzetti (2010, 222–27).

fixing the government payroll, and fixing the military budget (Huneeus 2007, 431–48; Siavelis 2010, 35–42).

In Argentina, due to the economic debacle identified with neoliberalism and the defeat in the Falklands (Malvinas) War, the outgoing military was not in a position to bind future democratic authorities in any way (Linz and Stepan 1996, 191; McGuire 1996, 197). However, before democratization in 1983, the caretaker government of general Bignone issued an ad hoc electoral law that could be seen as an attempt to bias representation in a similar, although much less explicit, way as in Chile. It reduced the threshold for obtaining representation in Congress from 8 percent to 3 percent of the vote, with the objective of favoring small provincial parties that had supported the military government (McGuire 1995, 190).

The most serious attempts at blocking opposition came, however, a decade later during the presidency of Carlos Menem. Menem sought to change executive-legislative relations, circumventing Congress and strengthening his presidential powers as the only actor capable of consolidating neoliberalism in the country (see Acuña 1995, 124). Due to the acute economic, social, and political crisis of 1989, Menem assumed office five months ahead of the official beginning of his term. He negotiated an agreement with the outgoing president, Raúl Alfonsín from the rival UCR party, that the sizeable UCR caucus in Congress allow a temporary increase of executive power in order to cope with the emergency situation.

The Decrees of Necessity and Urgency (DNUs) were a prerogative of the Argentine president not clearly sanctioned in the Constitution, but that had been used in a handful of situations in the past in contexts of extreme emergency.[5] Based on these decrees, two emergency laws were devised in 1989 that conferred extraordinary powers on the president to control the public budget and privatize state assets in order to confront the hyperinflationary chaos and the incipient popular revolt. Rubio and Goretti (1996, 445) report that Menem even considered the possibility of closing down Congress altogether, but the leak of the plan to the opposition and the press, and contrary voices inside his party, frustrated the operation.

The use of extraordinary powers through DNUs extended well beyond the 1989 emergency and throughout Menem's two consecutive mandates (1989–

5. Situations included civil wars, popular revolts, and acute economic crises (Rubio and Goretti 1996, fn. 24; 28). In most cases, the Congress ratified the decisions of the executive after the emergency situation had passed. For a comparison of similar actions in the United States and European countries, see Rubio and Goretti (1996, 450–51).

1994 and 1995–1999). Unlike the two emergency laws of 1989, the rest of the DNUs that Menem expedited were not founded on a delegation of powers from Congress to the executive; they consisted of a self-delegation of legislative power without approval or explicit consent of the Congress (Rubio and Goretti 1996, 448–49).[6] Menem's interpretation of the Constitution was that "the legitimacy and validity of these acts is founded on the basis of a manifest intention to submit them to legislative approval" (Rubio and Goretti 1996, 455). He considered the inclusion of a sentence to communicate the new norm to the Congress sufficient to establish their legitimacy.

Given the weak constitutional foundations of the use of DNUs, an important step in this strategy was control of the Supreme Court, the highest judicial tribunal and arbiter in cases of constitutional legitimacy. As soon as he took office, Menem sent to Congress a bill to increase the number of members from five to nine, so that he could gain a majority by appointing the new members. As justification, Menem resorted again to the assertion that there was a national emergency and the president needed to be able to count on a supportive Supreme Court, citing the similar court packing scheme attempted by Franklin D. Roosevelt during the U.S. New Deal.[7] After approval in the second half of 1989, two sitting judges resigned, allowing Menem to appoint six out of nine judges. The final move of the Menem administration—very much in the direction of a personalization of support for neoliberalism—was a successful proposal to amend the Constitution to be able to run for a second term in 1994, prolonging his period as Argentina's champion of neoliberalism.

In Eastern Europe, the design of electoral systems and other political institutions was premised on the need to prevent communists and their successor parties from gaining influence in the new democracies (Elster, Offe, and Preuss 1998, 112; Lijphart and Waisman 1996a, 6). Therefore, what in Latin America consisted of isolating and reducing leftist representation became, in Eastern Europe, isolating and reducing the representation of former communists and their successor parties (see Grzymała-Busse 2001).

6. In this sense, DNUs should not be confused with decree-laws which are a constitutional prerogative in several presidential democracies (Mainwaring and Shugart 1997, 44–47; Negretto 2004). As Rubio and Goretti (1996) clarify, even though Argentine presidents seem to have a tendency to undermine the institutional bases of their power, the concentration of executive power by the Menem administration through the use of DNUs was unprecedented in democratic times in Argentina.

7. In a live TV show, however, Menem confessed: "Why should I be the only Argentine President not to have my own Court?" (quoted in Helmke 2005, 144).

In Estonia, the identification of the communist past acquired the character of ethnic politics. This is also a reason why lustration did not loom large in the Estonian political landscape. As Steen has recognized, "[d]ue to the delicate ethnic situation, the first priority of the Estonian . . . indigenous elites was to oust Russians from power positions. Former CP [communist party] membership therefore became subordinate to the ethnic background of the new power elite" (Steen 1997, 100).[8] In this context, the electoral law was devised to exclude the large—mostly Russian-speaking—non-Estonian minority from voting. Discussions of the new citizenship law took place while Estonians were drafting a new constitution, restoring relations with Russia, and forcing the withdrawal of Russian troops from Estonian soil (completed only in mid-1994), all of which facilitated a harsh citizenship law. As Steen reckons, in these conditions "the democratic ideal of proportional representation of minority groups was perceived as a direct menace to national and cultural independence" (Steen 1997, 92).

The new citizenship law echoed the "legal restorationism" principle according to which the new nation state should be a restoration of the "illegally occupied" pre-1940 Estonian state and its nation base, meaning in practice that citizenship should be given only to those persons who were lawful citizens of Estonia prior to Soviet annexation and to their descendants while denying citizenship and voting rights to the sizable Russian minority, representing close to 40 percent of the population (see Pettai 2001; Pettai and Hallik 2002). The 1992 citizenship law not only excluded non-Estonians from voting in national elections,[9] it also banned them from running for office and from membership in political parties (Andersen 1997, 311), barred them from positions in the public administration in all but a few exceptions (D. Smith 2001, 74), and included a naturalization clause with language requirements which very few Russians were able to pass (D. Smith 2001, 74).[10] The new citizenship law did, however, give voting rights to Estonians living abroad.

8. In fact, one of the areas where ethnic Russians were overrepresented was public administration. Although the magnitude of public sector employment was much smaller than, e.g., industrial employment (ca. 20,000 versus 120,000), in relative terms Russians were slightly more concentrated in public administration with 46.6 percent participation of Russians in this sector versus 43.5 percent in industry (Mettam and Williams 1998, 381).

9. Noncitizens were allowed to vote and run for local elections from 1993. This was a necessary step since Russian-speaking authorities threatened secession in regions of the Northeast bordering with Russia where non-Estonians accounted for some 80 percent of the population (see D. Smith 2001, 88–89).

10. Grofman, Mikkel and Taagepera (1999) recount that in 1992 some 7,500 persons applied

Several other laws strengthened the harsh citizenship law and its regulation in the following years. The 1993 Law on Aliens established procedures and requirements for noncitizens to get permanent residency and work permits, and served in practice to intensify pressure on noncitizens to repatriate themselves to Russia (D. Smith 2001, 87; see also Pettai and Hallik 2002, 513; Andersen 1997, 312); in addition, naturalization requirements were tightened in 1995.[11] The lone attempt to universalize citizenship, promoted by a handful of pro-Russian MPs in 1997, was rejected (D. Smith 2001, 102). The 1992 electoral law further weakened the representation of minorities, setting high thresholds for gaining seats in Parliament and thus favoring large parties (see Grofman, Mikkel, and Taagepera 1999). The bar was raised even further in 1999 with a ban on electoral alliances, which forced smaller parties to converge with larger ones.

Finally, executive powers in Estonia were vested in the figure of the prime minister and their cabinet, the president being largely a figurehead. This decision was premised on the restoration of the highly parliamentarian Constitution of 1922, in contrast to the pre-war Constitution preferred by the ex-communists, which favored a strong presidential figure and was expected to benefit the visibility and popularity of some ex-communist authorities (Lauristin and Vihalemm 1997, 100–101). Reformers thus relinquished the direct election of the president (except for the first presidential election of 1992) and devised an indirect election by the Parliament. However, weak as the office was, the president still had one significant prerogative: he or she could mandate parties to conduct government talks, nominate the prime minister, and veto legislation—the last two, subject to confirmation by Parliament.

In Poland, electoral engineering was pervasive throughout the 1990s. Given the surprising results of the 1989 elections, which paved the way for democratization, political elites saw the need to devise an entirely new electoral system. The new scenario, which emerged in 1990–1991 during the compromise government of Solidarity figure Tadeusz Mazowiecki, reflected declining support for the Solidarity government, the related resurgence of deep-seated differences between liberal and conservative currents inside Solidarity, and the balkanization of post-Solidarity parties. Many splinter parties from the Solidarity

---

for citizenship; 5,400 were granted, among which close to three-fourths ethnic-Estonians that did not conform to the automatic pre-1940 citizenship rule.

11. New requirements included knowledge of the country's history and constitution, and had the practical effect of stalling naturalization applications (Pettai and Hallik 2002, 514; D. Smith 2001, 102).

camp, including those supporting the Mazowiecki government, feared the ambitions and authoritarian practices of the once leader of the movement Lech Wałęsa and the possibility that a majoritarian system would return him to power in a landslide (Benoit and Hayden 2004, 409; see Jasiewicz 1992). Similarly, given the overwhelming victory of Solidarity in the founding 1989 elections, ex-communists feared that a majoritarian system would wipe them off the political map completely. In this scenario, political elites devised an electoral system that adopted the most extreme form of proportional seat allocation, with no thresholds except for a 5 percent threshold for a 69-seat national list (out of a total 460 seats). The system changed again two years later ahead of the parliamentary elections of 1993, although in the opposite direction: favoring larger parties in an attempt to avoid fractionalization and political stalemate. In the end, during the 1990s every parliamentary election from 1989 on was preceded by a change in the electoral law and a concomitant struggle among the interested parties. Poland had a different electoral law for the 1989, 1991, 1993, and 1997 elections, each a battle prefigured by the need to increase one's own electoral strength and decrease that of opponents.

The second source of opposition blockade in Poland was lustration. Lustration debates have been a constant in the Polish political scene, most notably in 1992, during the SLD/PSL government in 1994–1997, and during the PiS-governments of 2005–2007 and 2015 to the present. Although the public—particularly at the beginning of the transition—was in favor of conducting some sort of lustration, its proper extent was a hotly debated topic (see Misztal 1999). The liberal camp of Solidarity favored what became known as a "thick line" with the past, that is, a broad division between past and present, national reconciliation, and the premise that former communists would be judged for their current activities and loyalty to democracy, not for their former allegiance to the communist regime. Conservatives in Solidarity, however, favored a clean break with the past, to the extent that scandals erupted when they made public extensive lists of names of supposed collaborators with the former secret services, even pointing the finger at Solidarity leader Lech Wałęsa at one point. Political elites rejected an extensive lustration effort led by this conservative-populist camp of Solidarity in 1992 and adopted a milder law in 1997, which set screening procedures for high-level public officers and created a Lustration Court. In 2005–2007 the populist Law and Justice Party, many of whose leaders had participated in the 1992 lustration attempt, proposed a new law that expanded the scope and transparency of the existing one. While the 1997 law required the screening of around 27,000 public offices, the 2005 version expanded it to roughly 700,000 people and released the information, formerly classified, on the internet (Horne 2009, 353–54).

Conversely, at the outset of the transition to democracy, heated discussions surrounded the proper place of the president in the emerging political system. Amid the uncertainty about outcomes of the 1989 elections following the roundtable negotiations, the communists re-introduced the presidency as a way to guarantee continued authority and oversight of the transition process (Jasiewicz 1997, 132–33; Howard and Brzezinski 1998, 136; Garlicki 1997, 82). The president was vested with significant legislative and executive powers, including the nomination of the prime minister and some ministers, responsibility for internal and external security as well as foreign relations, and the power to initiate and veto legislation, dissolve the Parliament, and establish martial law (Jasiewicz 1997, 136–37; Garlicki 1997). Many of these prerogatives were deliberately left unspecified, leaving ample space for interpretation.

After the landslide victory of Solidarity in 1989, Lech Wałęsa saw in the office of the presidency a way to acquire a political role that could steer economic reforms. He saw that the commitment of prime minister Mazowiecki to carry out the transition process through strict observance of parliamentarian democracy was actually slowing the pace of reforms (Orenstein 2001, 32; see Jasiewicz 1997, 132). As Orenstein has argued, "Wałęsa seemed inclined to prove that only he could hold the diverse strands of Solidarity together and keep a political 'umbrella' over the technocratic reform program" (2001, 39). In order to do this, he pressed for the introduction of a direct popular vote for the president in 1990, ran for the office himself, and won. Because of this, the presidency acquired a higher legitimacy than the Parliament, which by then was still a "contract" Parliament (Jasiewicz 1997, 136; Howard and Brzezinski 1998, 139–40).

At the same time, Wałęsa tried to influence the discussions on the new Constitution in order to introduce a semi-presidential system granting extensive powers to the president. In his view, only a strong president could reinforce political support for continued economic reforms and maintain their coherence in the face of rising criticism (S. Johnson and Kowalska 1995, 208; Orenstein 2001, 38; Howard and Brzezinski 1998, 148). His proposals for the presidency were drastic: for example, the power to dissolve Parliament, nominate and dismiss the cabinet and the prime minister, and declare a state of emergency (Millard 2000, 50). Congress, meanwhile, preferred a parliamentary system with a weak president, mimicking the basic German law (Howard and Brzezinski 1998, 139–41). At an impasse, lawmakers finally opted for a short-term solution; they adopted a temporary legal corpus and maintained a constitutional commission working in parallel on a definitive text. The temporary 1992 text or "Small Constitution" was a compromise between Parliament and the president: it maintained most of the existing powers of the president plus additional ones for the executive (Howard and Brzezinski 1998, 144; 158; Jasiewicz 1997, 147). For example, as with the DNUs in Argentina, it left open the possibility that Congress would delegate special powers to government on pre-accorded areas and for specific durations, excluding some key elements of governance like international agreements, social benefits, personal freedoms, and political rights. The provision was justified as necessary to prevent deadlock in public policymaking, especially in the area of economic reforms (Howard and Brzezinski 1998, 146).

From Transient to Permanent *Democraduras*: The Effects of Opposition Blockade on Neoliberal Resilience

Many of those who thought it necessary to insulate economic reforms during the initial stages of democratization came to the see the need to prolong that insulation from popular demands. They considered economic stability all-important for the long-term stability of democracy (Haggard and Kaufman 1995, 325). In this context, they worried about what would happen to neoliberal reforms when the temporal institutional constraints on opposition were lifted (Haggard and Kaufman 1995, 306). In many countries the second phase of political liberalization never arrived, and democracies remained *democraduras* as they sought to sustain neoliberalism. In other words, the very institutions devised to protect democratic consolidation ended up blocking democratic representation in order to protect neoliberalism.

In this section I analyze the effects of the institutional provisions described above as opposition blockade mechanisms. I show whether they had a clear representation bias, and whether this representation bias affected the capacity of alternatives to neoliberalism to express themselves politically and to influence policymaking. I also analyze which of these dispositions had the strongest effects.

Estonia: Blocking Opposition on the Basis of Ethnic Politics

In Estonia, the effects of opposition blockade on neoliberal resilience depended on the superposition of the ethnic cleavage between national Estonians and the mostly Russian minority, with the socioeconomic cleavage di-

TABLE 6.2. Estonia, Population and Elections 1990–2011

	Population				Vote	
	Total (A)	Voting age (B)	Registered (C)	Eligible (%) (C/B)	Total (D)	Turnout (%) (D/B)
1990	1,571,000	1,162,540	1,163,683	100.1	910,000	78.3
1992	1,544,000	1,142,560	689,319	60.3	467,629	40.9
1995	1,490,000	1,117,500	791,957	70.9	545,770	48.8
1999	1,415,236	1,071,447	857,270	80.0	492,356	46.0
2003	1,415,681	1,040,400	859,714	82.6	500,686	48.1
2007	1,315,912	1,039,335	897,243	86.3	555,463	53.4
2011	1,282,963	1,046,458	913,346	87.3	580,264	55.5

Source: Author's elaboration based on data from International Institute for Democracy and Electoral Assistance (International IDEA). http://www.idea.int/vt/countryview.cfm?CountryCode=EE.

viding winners and losers of reform. In effect, excluding ethnic Russians from voting silenced those who would have voted against the continuation of market reforms (for a similar argument, see Nørgaard 1996, 149; Pettai 2009). This in turn, influenced a party politics dynamic that prevented the formation of a more powerful left bloc, since parties did not have to worry about representing the interests of the losers of neoliberal reforms.

A quick look at the representation biases of Estonian political institutions shows the importance of the electoral law and the disenfranchisement of the Russian minority. It looms large when considering that the law defined eligibility to vote for the referendum on the new Constitution in June 1992, not to mention the first free parliamentary elections after more than fifty years under Soviet rule in September 1992. The effect seems evident in the electoral registry: before the new citizenship law persons eligible to vote were close to 1.2 million, a figure that dropped to less than 700,000, a dramatic drop of 40 percent (Pettai and Hallik 2002, 513).

Table 6.2 shows the effects of the 1992 Estonian citizenship law in terms of eligibility to vote between 1990 and 2011. For the founding 1992 elections only around 60 percent of those of voting age were allowed to vote. The number grew in 1995 and 1999 to 70 percent and 80 percent respectively and increased gradually during the 2000s. Still, in 2011 around 13 percent of the Estonian population—mostly ethnic Russians—was banned from participating in national elections.[12]

12. Estonian authors have complained that by focusing in individual rights, Western accounts of Estonian citizenship laws have been too critical and have not understood the nature of the challenges to the building of the new nation state that a more liberal law would have

In terms of the electoral system, evidence by Grofman, Mikkel, and Taage-pera (1999) suggest a strong bias against smaller parties possibly representing minorities. In fact, due to a 5 percent threshold, in 1992 some 20 percent of the vote went to candidates that were not elected. However, the authors also stress that this had no visible partisan bias. In fact, the law constituted a compromise between representatives of virtually all major currents of Estonian politics at the time—including ex-communists—and was so complex that electoral re-sults were almost impossible to trace, much less calculate in advance (see also Kaminski 2002, 350). Similarly, the 1999 ban on electoral alliances followed the divide between smaller and larger parties rather than left and right; there-fore, even small rightist parties were forced to merge with larger ones (see also D. Smith 2001, 105).

Indirect election of the president by parliament did, it seems, bias represen-tation and access to policy, even though the office's power was nominal. The 1992 presidential election is telling, since it was the only one where a popular vote was allowed. Ex-communist Arnold Rüütel, a popular figure related to the old regime and founder of the agrarian and protectionist Country People's Union party, had 43 percent of the votes (Lauristin and Vihalemm 1997, 100–101, 106). Second with 29.8 percent came Lennart Meri, minister of foreign affairs during the postcommunist Popular Front government in 1990–2; he was responsible for Estonia's free trade policy and was close to the right-wing Pro Patria Party (Feldmann and Sally 2002, 90–91). Since no candidate received the absolute majority, the right-wing-dominated Congress defined the elec-tion. It eschewed the nomination of Rüütel and elected Meri instead. In spite of his titular power, as Pettai recalls, Meri was "eager to set precedents and determine the full scope of his powers" (Pettai 2001, 131). He was confirmed again by a center-right cabinet after the 1995 parliamentary elections.

The Effects of Opposition Blockade in Estonia

The claim for opposition blockade in Estonia is as follows: if noncitizens with permanent residence in Estonia had had the right to vote in Congressional elections throughout the 1990s, they would have elected parliaments less sym-

---

entailed. In this sense, they underscore that Estonian citizenship law is not much different from Western European ones, and that the status of Russian-speakers was not different than Turkish *Gastarbeiter* in Germany or Arabs living in Israel, who only got citizenship rights after almost twenty years (D. Smith 2001, 75; Grofman, Mikkel, and Taagepera 1999, n. 4).

pathetic to neoliberalism (see Pettai 1997, 2009).[13] Is this true? To be specific, would Russian-speakers have voted the left? And how much was the Estonian center-left willing to promote an alternative to neoliberalism? I argue that this was a likely scenario, for three reasons: first, non-ethnic Estonians were concentrated among the losers of reform; second, they were discontented with existing economic and political institutions and showed a propensity to vote for left-leaning parties; and third, when these parties were in government, they did try to alter existing neoliberal policies.

I have already demonstrated (see chapter 4) that Russians were overly concentrated in industry, the sector that bore the costs of economic reforms. Regional disparities further demonstrate the concentration of hardship on the Russian minority. Russian-speakers have historically been concentrated in northeastern Estonia, especially in Ida-Viru County, the second-largest in the country, holding around 15 percent of its population. The percentage of non-ethnic Estonians, mainly Russian-speakers, living in Ida-Viru County was about 80 percent throughout the 1990s, which is equivalent to about a third of the entire non-ethnic population of Estonia.[14] Table 6.3 shows employment and production data for the three largest counties of the country, including Russian-dominated Ida-Viru. These three counties contain around two-thirds of Estonia's population and close to 70 percent of its economic activity. Counties with a high concentration of Russian-speakers experienced systematically worse industrial production and unemployment figures. In other words, they were harder hit by market reforms. In terms of industrial production, Russian-dominated Ida-Viru was in 1998 still well below the 1995 level at a time when the country was on average some 17 percent higher. Unemployment in 1993 in this county was 3.4 percent higher than the national level, while in 1998 the difference had risen to 5 percentage points. Non-Estonians were also at a disadvantage in employment (Russian speakers were concentrated in unskilled and elementary occupations) and earnings (Russian speakers earned consistently less than ethnic Estonians) (Titma, Tuma, and Silver 1998; Pettai and Hallik 2002, 517).

Russian-speakers not only bore the costs of market reforms; they were also more prone to vote their pocketbooks (Ehin 2007, 15). Opinion polls show that, while 65 percent or more of ethnic Estonians were prone to accept the

13. Several scholars interviewed supported this view.
14. Data from Statistics Estonia population database, "Statistics Estonia," http://pub.stat .ee/px-web.2001/dialog/statfile1.asp.

TABLE 6.3. Estonia, Unemployment and Industrial Production in Three Largest Counties 1995–1998

	1993		1994		1995		1996		1997		1998	
	A	B	A	B	A	B	A	B	A	B	A	B
Estonia	6.6	—	7.6	—	9.7	100	9.9	96.9	9.6	113.0	9.8	117.5
Harju County	5.3	—	6.6	—	8.4	100	8.5	97.4	8.5	112.2	9.1	117.8
Tartu County	7.9[a]	—	9[a]	—	12[a]	100	11.6[a]	97.1	11a	116.6	10[a]	162.6
Ida-Viru County	10	—	10	—	14.6	100	14.6	94.1	13.3	103.2	14.7	97.8

Source: Author's elaboration using data from Statistics Estonia database, http://pub.stat.ee/px-web.2001/dialog /statfile1.asp.
Note: A= Unemployment (percentage) B= Industrial production (index 1995=100).
[a]Includes Jõgeva, Põlva, Tartu, Valga, Viljandi, and Võru counties.

costs of economic reforms during the first half of the 1990s, a majority of Russian-speakers (70 percent in 1995) were ready to try alternatives if reforms did not quickly deliver (Lauristin and Vihalemm 1997, 125). Eventually, difficult socioeconomic conditions led them to distrust political institutions and throw their support behind authoritarian alternatives (Ehin 2007; see also Titma, Tuma, and Silver 1998). As late as the year 2000, 25 percent of Russian-speakers still supported a return to communism (Ehin 2007, 10; Lauristin and Vihalemm 1997, 122).

All this led Russian speakers to support left-leaning political alternatives—especially the Center Party. Table 6.4 shows that according to a representative poll conducted in 2003, two parties concentrated the vote of poorer constituencies: the agrarian Country People's Union and the Center Party. The People's Union was mostly supported by Estonians, while close to 30 percent of supporters of the Center Party were noncitizens—the highest share among Estonian parties. Data from Lauristin (2007, 54) confirms that a plurality of Russians preferred the Center Party. Interestingly, electoral results have also revealed that Estonians living abroad, who were allowed to vote under the 1992 citizenship law, had more rightist views than Estonians living in the country (Raun 1997, 355 n. 68).

Opposition blockade in Estonia was not only institutionalized as an exclusion of the Russian-speaking minority from participation in national elections. It was also reinforced by the emergence of a party system and political culture that prevented the constitution of more consistent left-wing political alterna-

TABLE 6.4. Estonia, Support Basis of Main Parties in 2003 (%)

	All	Centre Party	People's Union	Moderates	Reform Party	Pro Patria	Res Publica
Nationality							
Estonians	85	71	93	89	90	98	93
Non-Estonians	15	29	7	11	10	2	7
Income[a]							
< 113 USD	49	58	58	38	35	33	43
> 339 USD	5	1	0	1	12	9	15

Source: Lagerspetz and Vogt (2004, 65).
[a]Columns do not sum 100 because of omitted middle income ranges.
Note: Values converted to current USD using data from the International Monetary Fund (IMF).

tives. Some authors have actually claimed that the maintenance over time of a two-cleavage political space—institutionalized in Estonia by citizenship laws—prevents the formation of a credible left-wing alternative (Kitschelt et al. in O'Dwyer and Kovalčík 2007, 10). There is evidence that this was actually the case in Estonia.

As Raun has observed, "[f]ollowing the collapse of communism the left was so discredited that no party with any serious ambitions for electoral success would have dared to associate itself with that side of the political spectrum" (1997, 360). In 1995, Estonia became the first ex-communist country where the direct successor of the communist party was not represented in Parliament. This is partly explained by the party label it used on the ballot: "Left-Opportunity" (D. Smith 2001, 82). But ethnic Estonians were also reluctant to vote for the left-leaning Center Party because they saw it as "overly compliant toward Russian-speaking settlers" (D. Smith 2001, 82; see O'Dwyer and Kovalčík 2007, 15). An Estonian scholar explained to me: "You can't vote for the Center party if you are a good Estonian. You would maybe like their policies, but you can't vote them."[15] In sum, Estonians do not vote for the left-leaning Center Party, and other political parties are unwilling to represent the Russian minority. In fact, local analysts observe that "most Estonian politicians . . . view the Russians as a largely peripheral force, to be used when a few extra votes were needed, but not to be relied upon for the longer term" (Pettai and Hallik 2002, 514).

Recall that the few moments when left-leaning parties participated in government in Estonia were characterized by attempts at policy changes, espe-

15. Estonia, Interview 1.

cially efforts to make industrial policy more developmental. This was true during the participation of the agrarian People's Union in the 1995–1998 cabinet and, most notably, that of the Center Party in 2005–2007. Due to opposition blockade, they were not able to exert a greater influence on changing neoliberalism.

This was more strongly felt in 1995, when electoral results showed a turn to the left. The formation of the new government, however, became contentious. The highest electoral preferences went to the center-left KMÜ alliance (especially the agrarian parties in it) whose program included protective tariffs and subsidized support for ailing economic sectors. These and other policies were more closely affiliated with the left-leaning Center Party than with other parties represented in Congress. However, the Center Party's image as a pro-Russian party affected both its chances within the Estonian electorate (it placed only third in the election) and its effectiveness as a coalition partner in the new government (see Baltic News Service 1995c). The neoliberal Reform Party—the second majority—predicated its participation in government on the elimination of protective tariffs and subsidies from the government's program (Baltic News Service 1995e).[16] The formation of a KMÜ-Reform Party government effectively implied that electoral promises of higher protections and tempered neoliberalism had to be dropped (see D. Smith 2001, 95–96).

During this period, center-left parties also raised doubts about the functioning of the currency board, especially its suitability for different goals ranging from tackling inflation to increasing social spending. While prime minister Vähi of the centrist Coalition Party hinted at the possibility of establishing a floating exchange rate regime allowing the Central Bank to use active monetary policy to bring inflation down (Baltic News Service 1995d), the agrarian and more protectionist Country People's Union intended to merge the Central Bank reserves with those of the Treasury in order to allow higher public spending (Baltic News Service 1997a). The Center Party even asked Central Bank authorities to outline possible routes for devaluation (Baltic News Service 1998b). Once again the Reform Party, together with officials from the Bank of

16. The final composition of the government came as a result of three rounds of coalition talks. In the first round, the neoliberal Reform Party rejected participating in a government with the agrarian parties altogether. In the second round, KMÜ reluctantly turned to the Center Party and formed a short-lived government that fell after a political scandal, eliminating the Center Party as a government member. In the third round, the Reform Party agreed to participate in the government, but only at the expense of a written commitment that protectionist policies would be excluded.

Estonia, defended the currency board and criticized any attempt at changing it. They remained confident that the need for a parliamentary majority to change the exchange rate, together with their effective opposition in Parliament, would prevent any change (see more in chapter 7).

The citizenship laws and their effect on the party system erected a blockade that prevented coalition formation, and this blockade was made even stronger by several interventions of the Estonian president using the few resources at his disposal. When in office, right-wing Lennart Meri used his powers for opposition blockade at least two times. After the 1995 parliamentary elections, Meri maneuvered to break up a possible center-left KMÜ-Center Party government. He forced the Center Party chairman and interior minister Edgar Savisaar to resign under accusations of having wiretapped private coalition talks, thereby forcing a new government including the right-wing Reform Party (Pettai 2009, 83–84, 2001, 133). In 1999, the Center Party campaigned on a protectionist platform promising increased expenditures and progressive taxation, becoming the biggest party in Parliament, 7 percent ahead of its closest rival but falling short of an absolute majority. Commentators saw the Center Party's victory as yet another sign of the rejection of neoliberalism and the disintegration of the consensus over economic reforms that had prevailed (D. Smith 2001, 141). President Meri, however, used his prerogative to mandate coalition talks, and asked, not the Center Party, but the rightist Pro Patria Union—runner-up in the election—to form a new government. It did so in a coalition with other center-right parties (Reform Party and Moderates), maneuvering the Center Party out and leaving it—the party with the first electoral majority—in the opposition (Pettai 2009, 84; D. Smith 2001, 105–6).[17]

The Center Party remained the second-largest party in Parliament throughout the 2000s but was consistently left outside of government coalitions. As shown in chapter 4, the few and sporadic moments when it formed part of government, it showed a willingness to eschew the existing neoliberal policy regime. This was most notable in 2005–2007 when it introduced a developmental industrial policy framework centered on the Development Fund. In response to this, the Reform Party worked to sideline the Center Party from government, even forming highly unusual coalitions to do so if necessary.

---

17. Pettai (2009, 83–84) notes that much of this also had to do with personalities. After the alleged wiretapping scandal, Center Party chairman Edgar Savisaar became increasingly hostile to the full spectrum of political parties.

Chile: A Highly Constrained Polity and Multiple Sources of Blockade

There is a protracted controversy over whether the Chilean electoral system did in practice achieve the objective it was conceived for, that is, to boost the results of the electoral right at the expense of the left. Critiques of the Chilean political system argue it did (Munck 1994; D. Pastor 2004; Polga-Hecimovich and Siavelis 2015; Siavelis 2010). The electoral system successfully boosted the historical one-third of votes of the right, to well over 40 percent in terms of seat allocation in both chambers, particularly in the Senate (see table 6.5). This implied in practice that the electoral system forced the three-thirds (right-center-left) political dynamic, in place before the military dictatorship, into a two-bloc political space with increased representation of the right and reduced representation of the left. Moreover, despite consistently achieving at least 5 percent of the votes, the parties on the far left of the political spectrum remained without parliamentary representation during the entire decade, and well into the 2000s.[18] In other words, throughout the 1990s and the first half of the 2000s, this system maximized the vote-per-seat ratio in the districts that supported Pinochet in 1988, inflating the seat allocation of the right and shrinking that of the left, especially the parties that remained outside the center-left *Concertación* bloc.

Less critical voices argue that, at most, this binominal system benefited the two largest coalitions at the expense of minor parties, and that this is a normal feature of electoral systems around the world that cannot be dismissed as antidemocratic (Navia 2010; Zucco 2007). Thus, for Navia "the binominal system should be considered an authoritarian enclave because of its origin, not because of its effects" (Navia 2010, 308).

While it is true that the two biggest conglomerates were favored, the political significance of their size differs in important ways (see table 6.5 above). In all elections (except the 2001 election for deputies) the center-left *Concertación*

18. Considering only the coalition formed by the Communist Party, the vote shares for legislative elections in 1989, 1993, and 1997 are: 5.4 percent, 6.4 percent, and 7.5 percent (deputies), and 4.2 percent, 4.3 percent, and 8.5 percent (senators). The Communist Party managed to enter parliament only in 2009 thanks to a negotiation whereby the *Concertación* omitted presenting candidates in certain districts in order to support the communist candidate. The negotiation stemmed from the crucial support the communists gave to *Concertación* presidential candidates Lagos and Bachelet in the 1999 and 2005 runoffs against the Right. Data from "Servicio Electoral Chile," www.servel.cl.

TABLE 6.5. Chile, Vote and Seat Distribution for Two Main Coalitions in Congress (1989–2010)

Election year	Alianza (Right)				Concertación (Center-left)			
	Chamber		Senate		Chamber		Senate	
	Votes (%)	Seats (%)	Votes (%)	Seats (%)	Votes (%)	Seats (%)	Votes (%)	Seats (%)
1989	34.2	40	34.9	42.1 / 52.3[a]	51.5	57.5	54.6	57.9 / 46.8[a]
1993	36.7	41.7	37.3	50 / 54.3[a]	55.4	58.3	55.5	50 / 45.7[a]
1997	36.3	39.2	36.6	47.4 / 51.1[a]	50.5	57.5	49.9	52.6 / 48.9[a]
2001	44.3	47.5	44	50 / 50[a]	47.9	51.2	51.3	50 / 50[a]
2005	38.7	45	37.2	44.7[b]	51.8	51.7	55.7	52.6
2009	43.4	48.3	45.1	50[a]	44.4	47.5	43.3	50[a]

Source: Navia (2010, 307).
[a]Including nonelected senators.
[b]Not including one senator elected as independent.

received 50 percent or more of the votes. This result rose by a few points over the initial majority in terms of seats in some elections (1989 for deputies and senators, 1993, 1997, and 2005 for deputies), but decreased by a few points in others (1993 and 2005 for senators). Importantly, when the electoral system worked to increase the center-left's seats in parliament, this did not alter the majorities needed to pass or reject key reforms. On the contrary, the right's vote/seat relation improved in all elections, and in some of them (such as 1993 and 1997 for senators) it got nearly 50 percent of the seats with just over one-third of the vote. As we will see, this effectively gave the right the power to veto all reforms requiring higher thresholds to pass.

Beyond this quantitative argument, there is also a qualitative one related to the types of candidates that remained in or out of Parliament because of the incentives of the binominal system. For example, in the senatorial district of Western Santiago in the key 1989 congressional elections the right managed to get 32.5 percent of total votes against "only" 61.9 percent of the center-left *Concertación* (D. Pastor 2004, 46–47). As a result, the two elected candidates were the moderate Christian Democrat Andrés Zaldívar (31.3 percent of votes) for the *Concertación*, and the conservative Jaime Guzmán (17.2 percent of votes) for the right, leaving the socialist Ricardo Lagos (30.6 percent of votes) out of

Parliament. With his nearly 400,000 votes, Lagos had been the third candidate with more votes than any candidates in the 1989 election, but he did not get elected because he ran in the same list as the first majority in his district. Acute commentators on Chile, such as Angell and Pollack (1990), underscore the importance of this electoral result. It not only left one of the leaders of the Socialist Party, which was strongly resisted by the business community, outside of Congress, it also elevated the father of the 1980 Constitution and staunch defender of the Pinochet legacy, Jaime Guzmán.

Conversely, if one looks at the effects of the electoral system on the party system, even impartial accounts recognize the success of the initial intentions of electoral engineers: to reduce competition by forcing the center and the left to coalesce into one block, thereby forcing part of the left to moderate its demands and muting the representation of more recalcitrant leftists (Navia 2010; see also Madariaga and Rovira Kaltwasser 2019). By reducing the competition for seats (because the right and the center-left were relatively sure to get one seat each), competition for votes over alternative policies shifted to a competition over the nomination of candidates inside each coalition (Flores-Macías 2012; Navia 2010; Siavelis 2010). As Navia recognizes, this effectively "undermined one of the essential components of democracy, competitive elections" (2010, 308).

Considering a second component in the formula, namely, the unelected senators, makes the blockade on policy influence in Congress all the more visible. As table 6.5 above shows, when unelected senators are added to the already biased seat allocation in the Senate, the correlation of forces changes dramatically. Seats in the Senate fall below 50 percent for the left throughout the period except in 2001, when there was a tie. Without a majority in both chambers, and far from the supermajority thresholds to change key aspects of this constrained political scenario, the center-left found its legislative mandate severely constrained.[19]

Chile's *sui generis* electoral system was changed in 2015 after 26 failed attempts since its inception in 1989 (Gamboa and Morales 2016, 127). The need to solve internal quarrels in the governing coalition over the nomination of candidates, the decreased power of the right in Congress and increased presence of independent MPs—who were favored by the higher chances of representation that the reform gave them—are among the explanations for the

19. For a more detailed analysis of whether and how political institutions actually limited elected governments' decision making in Chile, see Madariaga (2020).

success of reform. Although it has revitalized the Chilean political scene, with the postreform formation of new parties and their successful contestation of congressional and even presidential elections, other mechanisms have taken their place in restricting the responsiveness of governments to their constituencies in the policymaking arena notably, the Constitutional Tribunal. (see Madariaga 2020).

Analyzing the Effects of Opposition Blockade in Chile

What are the policy implications of representation bias and its effect on the party system? Existing data show a high probability that, in the absence of the above-mentioned institutions, policy outcomes in Chile would have been quite different. These institutions—particularly the electoral system and the non-elected senators—have severely reduced the possibility to craft reform coalitions representing non-neoliberal sentiments (Huneeus 2007, 451; Barrett 1999, 19–22; see, e.g., Aninat et al. 2008).

Although strict support for non-neoliberal exchange rates or industrial policy alternatives among the population is difficult to prove, there are indications of fervent policy preferences contrary to neoliberalism. In fact, from the end of the 1980s and throughout the 1990s, opinion polls showed a marked preference for protectionist policies and state intervention among the population. An opinion poll at the beginning of the 1990s in Santiago found that 70 percent of respondents favored protection of domestic industry even if this meant increasing the cost of imported goods (Haggard and Kaufman 1995, 229). Further research has shown that, in general, the views of the Chilean population on issues such as market versus state, privatization, and so forth have been consistently more to the left than those of parliamentary elites (see Huneeus 2003; Ortega Frei 2003). In this sense, by biasing the representation of these preferences in Congress, the electoral system blocked the formation of anti-neoliberal reform coalitions in the political arena.

Opposition blockade in Chile also worked by preempting forces actually represented in Congress from passing more progressive legislation. In the first place, certain reforms were just not sent to Parliament; politicians knew they would be blocked. For example, despite the stated intention to change the Central Bank law "as soon as the new government was elected" (Alejandro Foxley cited in Bianchi 2008, 15), once in power the *Concertación* dropped the plan. One policymaker at the Central Bank later admitted: "we were convinced that we couldn't [change the law] because we lacked the majority in the senate, and we knew that we would lose" (Ffrench-Davis in Boylan 1998, 457). As we saw in chapter 4, the preeminent target on inflation enshrined in the Central Bank charter was used to justify the rolling over of the temporary progressive exchange rate policies attempted at the beginning of the 1990s. Another chance to change the Central Bank Law came in 2006 when a group of *Concertación* senators offered a bill to change the Central Bank's mandate to include employment and external competitiveness in addition to inflation control, and to increase its accountability to Congress (more details in chapter 7). The incorporation of competitiveness as a Central Bank goal was particularly important in the effort to adopt a more developmental exchange rate regime. But the proposed changes did not even make it to a floor vote. Unlike regular legislation—went the argument—under the 1980 Constitution only the executive had the prerogative of modifying "Organic Constitutional Laws" like the Central Bank Law. Therefore, the *Concertación* senators' proposal was declared unconstitutional.[20]

The experience of blockade eventually generated strategic actions from the part of forces inside Congress wanting to modify neoliberalism. Convinced that the only way to change certain things was to negotiate key reforms with the right, *Concertación* policymakers relinquished reforms that were perceived as non-negotiable. The thinking was that engaging in harsh negotiations over these more contentious areas would jeopardize reforms in other areas where a consensus could be reached. One such area was industrial policy. As a *Concertación* policymaker explicitly reckons:

> additional things that we wanted to do but we couldn't do: industrial development policies. It was vetoed. If we talked about that, we had everybody upon us, all the press and the neoliberal extremism, the UDI, etc. And this would have kept us from doing other things. . . . [21]

In other words, electoral and veto-player sources of opposition blockade in Chile effectively constrained the representation of progressive forces in Congress, reducing their ability to influence exchange rates and industrial policy throughout the 1990s and 2000s. Other possible influences of the institutions in place, such as their effects on the convergence of political parties toward

20. See Diario de Sesiones del Senado, República de Chile. Legislatura 354ª Sesión 36ª, Ordinaria. Miércoles 19 de julio de 2006.

21. Chile, Interview 2.

centrist alternatives, are harder to test but contribute to the diagnosis of reduced alternatives to carry forward left-wing policies once in government (see
Aninat et al. 2008; Flores-Macías 2012; Navia 2010).

This argument, however, falters during the second half of the 2000s. As
table 6.5 above shows, the center-left *Concertación* managed to get 50 percent
or more of the seats in both chambers during the Lagos[22] and Bachelet administrations, having enough votes to make changes to laws requiring simple
thresholds such as tax reforms or those involving increased public expenditure, whose design was heavily controlled by the executive. This is precisely
what happened with the tax on mining operations devised under the Lagos
presidency that was used to fund the new industrial policy scheme. While the
tax was rejected in Congress when presented as a modification to the Mining
law requiring supermajority thresholds, it did pass when presented as a tax
on mining operations, thus requiring only a simple majority (Napoli and
Navia 2012).

However, even with a majority in parliament—and after the elimination of
most "authoritarian enclaves" in 2005, clearing many of the prevailing institutional constraints (except for the electoral system and the Constitutional Tribunal)—the *Concertación* was not able to institutionalize a new industrial
policy framework. The coalition's failure was most visible when it tried to establish the National Council for Innovation and Competitiveness (CNIC), in
charge of managing the new mining tax and implementing the new industrial
policy based on regional clusters. As Bril-Mascarenhas and Madariaga (2019)
have shown, the opposition in Congress came from a cross-partisan coalition
of legislators representing mining regions, including *Concertación* Christian
Democrats and Socialists. Recent research on campaign finance scandals has
shown that competitive mining companies such as the privatized SQM and
those pertaining to the Luksic group made massive campaign contributions
across the political spectrum, particularly to Christian Democratic and Socialist candidates in mining regions (Matamala 2016).

In other words, the lifting of institutional constraints only partly opened
the door to changes in established neoliberal policies. Moreover, during the
negotiations to reform the existing institutional constraints, the right managed

22. While initially the Lagos administration counted with only 50 percent of the seats in the
Senate, the *Concertación* found itself with an absolute majority for almost the full two first years
of government given the temporary impeachment of two right-wing senators (Pinochet and
Errázuriz). See Madariaga (2020).

to strengthen others—particularly the Constitutional Tribunal which, according to critics, has increasingly acted as a "third chamber" blocking or severely modifying legislation (see Fuentes 2012; Madariaga 2020).

Delegative Democracy and Opposition Blockade in Argentina

Opposition blockade was less developed in Argentina and thus less successful in stopping the formation of alternative blocs that twice challenged the resilience of neoliberalism (see chapter 4). The electoral system devised shortly before the return to democracy in 1983 did not stop such blocs. Those supposedly harmed by the system—that is, bigger parties, and in particular, the populist PJ—did not in fact object to it (McGuire 1995, 190), and election returns confirmed that these parties were not threatened by this attempt at electoral engineering. For example, in 1983 the two biggest parties, the populist Justicialista Party (PJ) and the center-left Radicals (UCR), received a combined 84 percent of the vote for legislative elections, equivalent to 94.5 percent of the seats in Congress.

Until 1994, elections for the lower chamber were based on a closed-list proportional system with districts of different magnitude, while the Senate was elected by provincial governors with each province electing two seats (M. P. Jones 1997). In the case of the chamber, these dispositions reinforced the dominance of the two biggest parties, PJ and UCR, providing seats and resources for distributing policy and pork (M. P. Jones 1997; Mustapic 2002; Negretto 2004, 556). In the case of the Senate, although indirect election benefitted small provincial right-wing parties (M. P. Jones 1997, 266), it also reinforced the machines of the PJ, with their dependent clients, in the provinces (Spiller and Tommasi 2008, 78; 82–83; 90–94; cf. Levitsky 2003). Moreover, in the 1990s, when the PJ turned to neoliberalism under the leadership of President Menem, it was the UCR that increased its share of governorships—and therefore its representation in the Senate—and not the PJ (M. P. Jones 1997, 280–81; see Negretto 2004, 555). In sum, the Argentine electoral system did not serve as an opposition blockade mechanism because it did not have a clear partisan effect blocking the representation of those against neoliberalism or favoring its supporters.

Conversely, when the law regarding the ability of presidents to run for re-election was changed, it did result in representational bias but not necessarily in the expected direction. Re-election was not permitted under the Argentinean Constitution, and the PJ fell short of the two-thirds quorum needed to pass the reform in Congress. Thus, Menem's aspirations to be re-elected were eventually watered down by the need to negotiate with the opposition.[23] While he got the chance to be re-elected as well as an explicit declaration of Decrees of Necessity and Urgency (DNUs) as constitutional, the opposition UCR extracted several concessions that improved its bargaining position, including closer supervision on DNUs and limitations on their scope (see Rubio and Goretti 1996, 470),[24] and the sharing of nominations to the Supreme Court (Negretto 2013). Perhaps the most important was the inclusion of a third seat per district in Senate elections, a measure known to favor the second-largest party, the UCR. According to Negretto (2013, 158) "compared to the status quo, these reforms improved the institutional position of the opposition in general and the UCR in particular."[25] In fact, despite being comprehensively defeated in the 1995 presidential elections, the UCR managed to reverse a gradual yet sustained trend of declining representation in Congress and become a staunch opponent to Menem (Novaro 2009, 524).

The most consistent attempts at opposition blockade made during the Menem administration came along with efforts to increase the power of the executive. Increased executive power and the bypassing of Congress and the Constitution, allowed Menem to engage in full-fledged *decretismo*. He signed 162 DNUs in his first term and another 93 in his second term, far above the 35 DNUs used in the previous 135 years (Spiller and Tommasi 2008, 207; Negretto 2004, 554).[26] Of these decrees, only 14.1 percent were ratified by Congress and another 4.3 percent amended, while in 78.8 percent of the cases congressional response was merely "inaction" (Negretto 2004, 554).[27] In this context,

---

23. The biggest opposition party, the UCR, was forced to negotiate under Menem's threat of passing the reform without its approval. In the view of UCR leaders, this involved the risk of having an even less favorable result. The accord known as "Pacto de Olivos" was signed by Menem and ex-president Alfonsín (see Negretto 2013; M. P. Jones 1997; especially Acuña 1995).

24. From now on, no DNUs could be decreed in matters related to taxes, electoral issues, political parties, and penal law.

25. For a different view, see M.P. Jones (1997, 295–96).

26. Presenting a more extensive interpretation, Rubio and Goretti (1996, 451–52) argue that another 170 decrees were dispatched without recognizing them as DNUs, although "without doubt" sharing their characteristics, i.e., a self-delegation of legislative power not authorized or approved by the Congress.

27. According to Negretto (2004, 556–57), the existence of a PJ congressional majority was crucial to sustain this practice. In many cases PJ legislators explicitly abstained from deliberating on a DNU in order to balance on the one hand, their support for a president who controlled

Menem's staffing of the Supreme Court gave him an "automatic majority" that validated the president's irksome use of decree powers (Helmke 2005, 144; M. P. Jones 1997, 284). Reflecting this lack of accountability, O'Donnell famously coined the concept of "delegative democracy" (O'Donnell 1994).[28]

The Personalization of Opposition Blockade and Its Defeat in Argentina

The importance of DNUs for the success of economic reform in Argentina is unmistakable. As the father of the currency board, Minister of Economy Domingo Cavallo himself recognized in 1993 that "without them [the DNUs] 'not more than a 20 percent of economic reforms would have been possible'" (cited in Rubio and Goretti 1996, 446). Figures 6.1 and 6.2 illustrate that the overwhelming majority of DNUs were used to pass economic reforms that would be otherwise opposed in Congress. About 39 percent of those reforms were related to matters of fiscal policy; another 21 percent to labor market deregulation, wage restraint, and pension reform; and another 16 percent to matters related to public debt. As expected, the Supreme Court pronounced itself repeatedly in favor of both the form and content of Menem's DNUs. This automatic favor of the Supreme Court served as a constitutional backup for the rest of the Menem administration (see Rubio and Goretti 1996, 466–69).

This temporary "success" notwithstanding, opposition blockade during the Menem administration depended on a newly empowered executive, a position that could be taken by any partisan concern, not just supporters of neoliberal reform. In fact, the two elected presidents after Menem—De la Rúa, who grudgingly continued neoliberalism and Kirchner, who abandoned it—made extensive use of DNUs. With Congress weak and fragmented, the left-leaning Kirchner (president from 2003 to 2007) used DNUs to implement his "new developmentalist" project. He enacted 232 DNUs at a rate of 4.3 per month, comparable only to Menem's 4.4 per month (Levitsky and Murillo 2008, 19). As in the case of Menem, DNUs and other decree powers were used for flagship initiatives in economic reform, although of the opposite sign. One initiative was the tax on exports with which Kirchner extracted resources from the

significant political and material resources and, on the other, that of their potentially affected constituencies.

28. For a more nuanced assessment of the Argentine experience of democratic consolidation under Menem, and a critique of the "delegative democracy" argument, see Peruzzotti (2001).

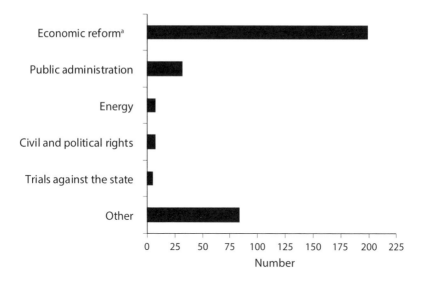

FIGURE 6.1. Argentina, Decrees of Necessity and Urgency (DNU) by topic 1989–1994
Source: Rubio and Goretti (1996, 453).
[a]Decrees in this category are most probably under-estimated. Several other categories (e.g., Public administration and Other) also include decrees related to economic reforms such as deregulation, fiscal retrenchment, and wages policy.

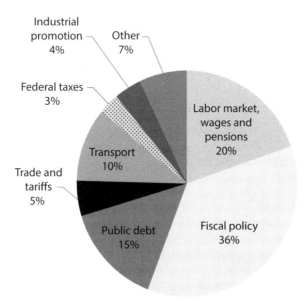

FIGURE 6.2. Argentina, Composition of Economic reform DNUs
Source: Rubio and Goretti (1996, 453).

competitive agricultural producers, subsidized wage goods, and got support from urban low and middle classes (see Richardson 2009). While Kirchner made several advances towards honoring the autonomy of the Supreme Court (like reducing its members from nine to seven, thereby withdrawing the possibility of appointing two loyal judges), he increased control over the bodies in charge of judge nominations (Levitsky and Murillo 2008, 19; see also Spiller and Tommasi 2008, 102).

In other words, although Menem used institutional means as a source of opposition blockade, the mechanism tended to personalize, rather than institutionalize, the support for neoliberalism, making it dependent on the political success of a handful of neoliberal individuals. Conversely, the need to negotiate constitutional reforms to increase opposition blockade in terms of presidential re-election and constitutional legitimacy of DNUs, meant making significant concessions to the opposition. In stark contrast with Chile, these concessions strengthened rather than weakened the opposition—especially the biggest opposition party, the UCR. Moreover, the provision of presidential re-election that was passed under Menem served to re-elect a president from the opposite camp, Kirchner's wife Cristina Fernández in 2011.

Delegative Democracy and Opposition Blockade in Poland

As in Argentina, opposition blockade proved a difficult task for neoliberals in Poland. The constant turnover of electoral laws during the 1990s is a sign of active partisan attempts to favor certain groups over others through electoral engineering. However, electoral calculations produced only short-term and inconsistent party alliances, as well as unintended side effects that made parties eventually discard election law as a relevant strategy. Each reform process had two characteristics that decreased their efficacy as a source of opposition blockade (Benoit and Hayden 2004; Kaminski 2002). First, parties tried to maximize their own vote-share irrespective of that of other parties holding similar policy views. Increasingly, the divide between big and small parties became more important than the difference between right and left. Second, parties participating in electoral engineering were unable to identify the electoral rule that would actually maximize their vote share.

The clearest manifestation of electoral miscalculation was the 1993 parliamentary election. Wary of the fragmentation effects that the highly proportional 1991 electoral law had produced, the largest parties in Parliament favored a less proportional system featuring the introduction of several thresholds for representation (Benoit and Hayden 2004, 412; see Jasiewicz 1992). Supporters included, notably, the parties representing the liberal wing of Solidarity (Benoit and Hayden 2004, 412). The fragmented antiliberal Solidarity camp was split between maintaining the status quo and supporting the reform proposal (Benoit and Hayden 2004, 414–15). The new law was approved and, in fact, decreased the proportionality of the electoral system with the introduction of thresholds for individual parties (5 percent), coalitions (8 percent), and another 7 percent for a national seat list. The results of the election, however, were a complete surprise: the election brought not the liberal Solidarity parties, but the postcommunist SLD and PSL parties back into power, leaving the post-Solidarity formations heavily underrepresented in Congress. Thanks to the decreased proportionality of the new system, with little more than one-third of the votes the ex-communists were able to control almost two-thirds of the Parliament. The miscalculation by conservative and neoliberal parties benefited the ex-communists, who pulled Poland out of the fast lane of orthodox neoliberalism (see chapter 4).

Lustration, a second source of opposition blockade, failed in Poland, since those who pushed it were not necessarily identified with neoliberal reforms. Despite its success in preventing left-leaning Jozef Oleksy from assuming office in 1995, the law did not prevent other prominent ex-communists from assuming the highest offices. Moreover, lustration was not necessarily aligned with market reform, as the most ardent neoliberals tended to support lustration only in its most minimal effects. In fact, the lustration law of 1997 that was supported by neoliberals in Parliament has been characterized as rather mild and "civilized" (see Szczerbiak 2002a), even receiving support from the PSL and from ex-SLD leader and President of the Republic Aleksander Kwaśniewski. Ex-communists wanted to present themselves as having made a clean break with the past, as well as forestall the possibility of a more extensive or "wild" lustration law (Szczerbiak 2002a; Misztal 1999, 45). The implementation of this law has been considered incomplete and nonsystematic, characterized by the unwillingness of courts to advance lustration cases (Horne 2009, 352).

Those who backed lustration more fiercely—the conservative-populist post-Solidarity parties—were not advocates of neoliberalism, and as a result some lustration episodes launched by these parties tended to work against the resilience of neoliberalism. For example, during the PiS-led process that implied an increase in scope and extension of lustration (and which was declared unconstitutional in 2007), a review of previous privatization processes found that companies privatized in connection with communist networks or under suspicious circumstances should return to the state—thus reversing instead of supporting neoliberalism (Horne 2009, 357).

In David Ost's (2005) famous formulation, the lustration agenda and its permanence in political discourse, although not successful from a legislative point of view, did serve the purpose of blocking opposition to neoliberalism. It managed to channel worker anger not into a socioeconomic divide (and therefore into the arms of left-wing parties) but instead into fractious cultural politics. Lustration, according to this view, ended up supporting right-wing populists and diminishing the transformative power of workers' protest. However, right-wing populists did criticize neoliberalism and the continuation of market reforms, delegitimizing continued reform efforts along orthodox neoliberal lines. As I have demonstrated in chapter 4, this criticism was an important factor explaining the increased representation of antireform sentiments in politics, and the rise of a competitive center-left alternative at the beginning of the transition process. In fact, Ost himself has recognized that although not providing a full departure from neoliberalism, the 1993–1997 center-left SLD/PSL government "was able to make . . . small but meaningful changes" (2005, 81).

The clearest source of opposition blockade in Poland, as in Argentina, came from attempts to increase the power of those actors seen as more conducive to market reform. In Poland this took the form of empowering Solidarity's Lech Wałęsa. However, in his quest to increase personal power, Wałęsa alienated the more democratic neoliberals, as well as his own support base. Eventually, the office passed to the opposition hands, just as happened in Argentina.[29]

The Polish reform path, like the Argentinean one, was accelerated by pressing political and economic circumstances and launched under the imperative of quick reforms. In this context, Solidarity leader Lech Wałęsa attempted over and over to increase executive power in order to insulate reformers from social pressures. As early as 1989, Wałęsa vowed to grant the government extraordinary powers to embrace, at one stroke, the whole set of economic reforms envisaged in the Balcerowicz Plan, including privatization and state restructuring (Kowalik 2011, 132; 165). The plea was rejected, but in return the govern-

---

29. To be sure, neither Wałęsa nor Menem were outright neoliberals. They both came from labor-based organizations, and combined market reforms with a populist political style. This, in fact, made them subject to constant suspicion from the true neoliberals. See Weyland (1999a).

ment got a "fast lane" congressional revision of all the relevant legislation. The most important legislation backing the Balcerowicz Plan was passed in only a few days and with no parliamentary or public debate (Kowalik 2011, 132; Orenstein 2001, 32).

After winning the presidency, Wałęsa tried to use decree power to overcome the parliamentary deadlock and accelerate reforms. During the promarket Bielecki government, Wałęsa backed government-sponsored legislation—eventually rejected—that aimed to get temporary special powers to enable the government to pass all outstanding market-reform-related legislation before the congressional election of October 1991 (Orenstein 2001, 40–41). During the 1993 Suchoka government, Wałęsa made a last attempt, again rejected in Parliament, to get decree powers to pass outstanding pro-market legislation (Orenstein 2001, 51). Wałęsa's proposals for breaching the stalemate in Congress and continuing the path of reforms included nominating himself as prime minister, which produced renewed fears of authoritarianism and parallels with other government takeovers by political strongmen in Polish history (Orenstein 2001, 44; Jasiewicz 1997, 139).

In the years that followed, Wałęsa promulgated a "maximalist" interpretation of his presidential powers (Millard 2000, 51), most notably during the government of the center-left SLD/PSL in 1993–1997. According to one observer, "Wałęsa's general strategy sought the greatest possible discomfiture for the government," making presidential veto "almost a routine part of the legislative process" (Millard 2000, 51). Even if the postcommunists were able to wield their large majority in Congress to override presidential vetoes, Wałęsa still sent legislation for revision to the Constitutional Tribunal, thus significantly delaying policymaking. An important veto target—eventually leading to the ousting of prime minister Pawlak in 1994—was the government's tax increase bill and a budget law involving spending increases (Jasiewicz 1997, 153). Wałęsa constantly threatened to dissolve the Parliament, attacked the cabinet and the prime minister, and had an active role in the downfall of two prime ministers between 1993 and 1995 (see Millard 2000, 50–52; Jasiewicz 1997, 148–54). In fact, the relative policy moderation of the SLD/PSL government can be at least partly explained by Wałęsa's constant pressure (see Jasiewicz 1997, 149–50).

In 1995, however, Wałęsa lost the presidential election to the ex-communist SLD candidate, Aleksander Kwaśniewski. This not only produced a reversal of the president's behavior; it also changed the pro-parliament nature of the drafts for the new constitution under an SLD-dominated constitutional commission (Garlicki 1997). During Wałęsa's term in office, drafts for the new constitution had been deeply influenced by the fear of a strong presidency, made worse by Wałęsa's behavior. However, wary of the possibility that his party might lose the next election, Kwaśniewski decided to re-introduce several presidential powers that were later approved (Millard 2000, 42–53; Garlicki 1997, 84–88; cf. Zubek 2001). More significantly, the president remained elected by popular vote, which gave the office a legitimacy of its own independent of Parliament—as well as a space to formulate policy. The president also maintained legislative initiative (although not exclusively) and veto power over legislation.

As in Argentina, the same institutional weapon under different partisan concerns yielded different results in terms of the resilience of neoliberalism. Kwaśniewski did not hesitate to use his renewed veto power in spite of his image as a relatively passive and compromising president, especially when sharing power with the right-wing AWS/UW government in 1997–2001. During this time Kwaśniewski made 14 vetoes (compared to none while his mandate coincided with the SLD/PSL government) (Zubek 2001, 216; Millard 2000). According to some commentators, legislative delays attributable to his vetoes decreased the efficiency of the AWS/UW government, intensifying its internal quarrels and contributing to its eventual breakup (see also Szczerbiak 1998, 2004).

Conclusion

In this chapter I have analyzed how opposition blockade permitted the resilience of neoliberalism through the reduction of representation and policy influence. Four sources of opposition blockade have been identified and analyzed: electoral rules, executive-legislative relations, veto players in general, and lustration (in Eastern Europe).

Electoral engineering was most notable in Chile, where an "innovative" electoral system boosted the representation of the right and shrunk that of the left throughout democratization. A number of arrangements increased this representation even more in Congress, such as non-elected senators and several veto points devised to block any attempt at change. In Estonia, the contrasting socioeconomic fates of ethnic groups during transition made possible the direct exclusion of the losers of reform from political participation, as governments repeatedly restricted the voting rights of the sizable Russian-speaking minority. This not only prevented the representation of this group, but also hindered the emergence of political parties aiming to represent them.

Failed attempts to manipulate electoral laws in Argentina and Poland serve as counterfactuals that help us understand the efficacy of "electoral" opposition blockade as a mechanism of neoliberal resilience. In Chile, an authoritarian government and an expected democratization process forced the center-left opposition to validate restrictive electoral laws as a lesser evil against the chances of re-gaining democracy after years of dictatorship; in Estonia, the ethnically-charged independence process disenfranchised about one-third of the population. In Argentina, weak military actors (hampered by economic crisis and the defeat in the Falkland Islands' War) were not able to institutionalize a political framework favorable to the maintenance of the status quo; in Poland, electoral engineering proved useless as a way to improve certain groups' power. Here, the power of the ex-communists and the inability to calculate results produced self-defeating strategies among rightist political parties. Moreover, self-oriented rather than policy-oriented motives for electoral manipulation generated electoral alliances that ran across existing cleavages instead of isolating those with higher chances of impugning neoliberalism.

Electoral sources of opposition blockade thus depended on specific contextual conditions for their activation. Effective experiences in Chile and Estonia suggest neoliberal coalitions in these countries were able to clearly identify the groups to block and thus to institutionalize a highly exclusionary democracy restricting the representation of these groups. At the same time the identification of these groups was policy-oriented (that is, blocking those who would support certain policies over others) instead of partisan-oriented (that is, blocking or privileging specific political parties). It is noteworthy that in both cases, electoral laws changed the party dynamic by blocking the representation of existing socioeconomic cleavages and generating patterns of political competition unrelated to these. The extent of misrepresentation by electoral laws, and the existence of strong veto points preventing access to policy from significant segments of society, has led to the definition of Chilean and Estonian democracies as "tutelary" (Pettai 2009; Rabkin 1992).

Argentina and Poland considerably strengthened the power of specific institutional players that became the bulwark of neoliberalism. In both countries this meant increasing the executive power of presidents in opposition to parliaments where opponents to neoliberalism were more strongly represented, thereby projecting a "delegative" type of democracy (O'Donnell 1994). As a mechanism of neoliberal resilience, however, this was effective only as long as office holders remained committed to neoliberalism. The time of the neoliberals in office proved too short, however, to entrench neoliberalism more deeply, especially in the case of Poland. Most significantly, the mechanism backfired when opponents managed to get hold of the same veto positions. The limited impact of this source of opposition blockade appears therefore related to a sort of *personalization* of the chances of neoliberal resilience instead of their *institutionalization*. For example, beyond the maintenance of Pinochet as a recurring political player, the veto players who were installed by the Chilean dictatorship relied on institutional counterbalances to the possible representation of opponents. This reflects the interaction between electoral and veto player sources of opposition blockade: without electoral blockade (as in Argentina and Poland), veto powers could be wielded by different political coalitions, following changes in the government's partisan orientation and losing their capacity to block opposition to neoliberalism.

The inability of political institutions in Argentina and Poland to prevent changes in the partisan orientation of effective power holders and veto players over the policy trajectory, points to another way opposition blockade affected neoliberal resilience. This has been researched by Schoenman (2014) for the case of Eastern Europe, and is particularly relevant to the Polish case, but can also be extended to the Argentinean case. Political competition—and alternation in office—also translated into competition for business support. In Poland, this generated differentiated patterns of business-party alliances and networks of businesses identified with specific partisan interests. The patterns of business support for different economic projects in Argentina (as we saw in chapters 4 and 5), suggest that a similar effect came about. We can conclude therefore that when opposition blockade was effective in reducing representation, it affected neoliberal resilience through a second channel: the reinforcement of earlier support creation efforts. In other words, the elaboration of constraining political institutions solidified not only political representation patterns, but also patterns of business-party relations, in the process building or obstructing a business base supporting alternative development projects. This in turn reinforced previous support creation efforts and the existence of a business base in favor of continuing neoliberalism. The case of campaign finance scandals in Chile further strengthens this point.

Finally, venturing into the effects of opposition blockade in the respective democracies, I argue that both the resilience of neoliberalism and the current sliding of Latin American and Eastern European democracies towards illiberal populist alternatives can be traced to these mechanisms of opposition block-ade. By restricting political representation, opposition blockade mechanisms have eroded the capacity of opponents of neoliberalism to express themselves in the political arena. In Chile and Estonia, the cases of successful neoliberal resilience, this process consolidated a type of democracy where political com-petition was formally institutionalized, but where representation was severely restricted. Therefore, competition for office did not result in a competition between different development projects, but instead it resulted in the control of the trajectory of economic policy at the expense of democratic representa-tion. The lack of political forces representing popular majorities has led to a paradox: Chilean and Estonian democracies have strengthened institutionally all while their populations have increasingly repudiated political parties, and popular disaffection with the institutions of democracy has grown.

In Argentina and Poland, where neoliberal resilience failed due to traumatic neoliberal experiments, representation has blossomed in favor of populist par-ties and leaders who have sought to represent disaffected majorities by bypass-ing existing political institutions and attempting to erode political competi-tion—thereby undermining their stability. In other words, the different results of opposition blockade in the cases of neoliberal resilience and of neoliberal contestation has led to different paths of democratic erosion: maintaining for-mal democracy but without true representation (Chile, Estonia), or maintain-ing representation but reducing competition and basic freedoms (Argentina and Poland). I will come back to this argument in the conclusion, relating it to current research on the hollowing and backsliding of democracy and the rise of populism.[30]

30. As I will argue in more detail in the conclusion, the extent to which the Polish populists have threatened civil rights and basic constitutional prerogatives go well beyond the quarrels of Argentina's Cristina Fernandez with the press or her weakening institutions such as the sta-tistics office.

7

Locking-in Neoliberalism

INDEPENDENT CENTRAL BANKS AND
FISCAL SPENDING RULES

IN CHAPTERS 5 AND 6, I showed two mechanisms by which neoliberal social blocs managed to control the trajectory of public policy: the creation of business support and the blockade of opposition from political parties, usually on the left. Both mechanisms relied on the ability of neoliberal blocs to use structural as well as institutional resources to alter the balance of power between supporters and opponents of neoliberalism, preventing them from forming alternative coalitions and acquiring parliamentary representation.

But what happened when, contrary to expectations, opponents of neoliberalism managed to accumulate enough power to challenge established neoliberal policies? After all, political strategies and calculations may not yield the predicted results, and the underlying mechanism may end up producing unintended consequences. In this chapter, I formulate and test the operation of a third mechanism of neoliberal resilience: locking-in neoliberal policy alternatives through constitutionalization, that is, the embeddedness of exchange rates and industrial policies in institutional frameworks, often in the constitution itself, that made future changes and reforms more difficult. The delegation of policymaking authority to nonelected bureaucratic agencies that lies at the heart of constitutionalized lock-in is the main mechanism that the literature has identified as contributing to reduced democratic accountability and, ultimately, a "post-democracy" scenario (Crouch 2004; Mair 2013; see also Stasavage 2003; Haan and Amtenbrink 2000). In this chapter I demonstrate, however, that this mechanism mostly reinforced the operation of the other two. The evidence emphasizes the importance of the other two mechanisms—support creation and opposition blockade—in reducing both representation and the agency of unelected bureaucrats in policymaking (see also Adolph 2013; Clark, Golder, and Golder 2002; Stasavage 2003; Vaubel 1997).

As we shall see, the four countries under study attempted to lock-in neoliberalism through the establishment of independent central banks and fiscal policy rules, attaching them to institutional rules of the greatest possible constitutional range. These lock-ins were indeed helpful in preventing exchange rate fluctuation in the case of central bank Independence (CBI), but only impacted fiscal spending rules in a handful of situations. Only in Estonia was the impact directly linked to industrial policy.

More importantly, the successful operation of this mechanism, particularly in the case of CBI, led political actors to try to modify the institutional lock-in in attempts to change established neoliberal policies. In this context, constitutionalization interacted with the other two mechanisms of neoliberal resilience, support creation and opposition blockade. Once lock-ins were established, the chances for altering them depended heavily on the correlation of political forces in government and Parliament, thus linking lock-ins with opposition blockade. As the Estonian and Chilean cases show, this interaction proved strongest in preventing policy reversals. Conversely, the cases of neoliberal discontinuity (especially Argentina) show that in spite of the lock-in, and even in the absence of parliamentary majorities, when powerful business actors support alternative policies, political elites can maneuver to satisfy them regardless of the constitutionalization of neoliberalism. This is an indication that institutions do not have power independent of the societal actors that support them (see Amable 2003; Knight 1992; Pontusson 1995). In this sense, the illusion of institutional/constitutional constraints on policymaking masks the deeper reality of the hegemony of a dominant neoliberal social bloc over the rest of society.

In determining the influence that constitutionalized lock-in had over neoliberal resilience, I examine:

1. Whether central bank independence and fiscal spending rules were actually established with the explicit purpose of binding the hands of democratic authorities,
2. Whether independent central banks and fiscal spending rules actually prevented changes from neoliberal exchange rates and industrial policies in favor of more developmental alternatives, and

3. Whether groups opposed to neoliberalism tried to alter the underlying institutional bases of these agencies, and what was the outcome of these attempts.

Independent Central Banks in Latin America and Eastern Europe

Independent central banks emerged at the end of the 1980s and spread quickly throughout the world. From the early 1970s until 1989, only eight countries made statutory changes to their central banks, many of them strengthening the degree of control over monetary policy exercised by governments (Polillo and Guillén 2005, 1770–71). By contrast, during the 1990s as many as 17 countries in Eastern Europe and 11 countries in Latin America made statutory changes toward greater independence, while only one country in the world (Malta) reduced the degree of central bank independence (CBI).

Most scholars studying the politics of CBI in Latin America and Eastern Europe focus on explaining the adoption of independent central banks. They point to the role of international financial institutions and the opening of financial markets in empowering domestic reform coalitions (Maxfield 1998; R. A. Epstein 2008; see also Polillo and Guillén 2005). Others highlight the role of epistemic communities and their networks in diffusing common institutional models (J. Johnson 2016). Few authors have concentrated on the domestic politics side of the story: that is, how central banks have been fostered by coalitions willing to prevent the discretionary use of monetary policy by incoming authorities.[1] Conversely, while there is a large body of literature studying the economic effects of CBI, especially on inflation and growth (Neyapti 2001; Jácome and Vázquez 2008), the political effects of CBI have gone largely unexamined. Have independent central banks actually precluded the use of discretionary monetary policy? If they have, have actors with alternative policy preferences attempted reforms reducing CBI? As Adolph's (2013) path-breaking book has convincingly shown, partisan politics acts not only at the moment of establishing independent central banks but also in their operation.

I analyze to what extent independent central banks were used as devices constraining the available set of policy choices of future governments, especially in terms of exchange rates; the responses of those actors following alter-

---

1. For exceptions, see Goodman (1991) and Boylan (1998).

TABLE 7.1. Latin America and East Central Europe, Central Bank Independence and Reforms

		CBI Score[a]		
	Date of reform	ca. 1990	ca. 2000	ca. 2010
Argentina	1992, 2002, 2012	0.45	0.77	0.71 (2012)
Chile	1989	0.89	0.89	0.89
Latin American Average	—	0.45	0.66	0.68
Estonia	1992	0.77	0.77	0.79
Poland	1989, 1992, 1997	0.45	0.87	0.87
Eastern European Average	—	0.49 (1993)	0.69	0.82

Source: Bodea and Hicks (2015).
[a]Cukierman LVAW index. Regional averages include all countries belonging to each region in the database.

native policy courses but blocked by CBI; and the results in terms of policy continuity or change.

In the 1990s, Chile, Argentina, Estonia, and Poland all enacted reforms that gave a high degree of independence to their central banks, both in absolute terms and in comparison to their respective regions (see table 7.1). Following its tradition in the neoliberal *avant-garde*, Chile was one of the first countries in the world to institutionalize CBI in 1989. Poland and Estonia converted their former socialist monobanks into modern central banks early on in their reform processes. While Estonia established an independent central bank together with currency reform in 1992, Poland reformed its central bank in 1989 and 1992, but required a second reform process in 1997 in order to implement proper CBI. Only one of the countries studied here implemented reforms to reduce the independence of its central bank after increasing it: Argentina, in 2002 and in 2012. The first reform allowed the president to remove the central bank governor, while the 2012 reform restored the tutelage of the government over the Argentine BCRA.

The motives for implementing CBI have differed in the four countries. CBI was implemented in Chile and Poland as a way to bind the hands of future governments, while in Argentina it was implemented to show commitment to neoliberalism by a populist government, and in Estonia, as a mix between pragmatic and ideological considerations. The case analyses show that institutional lock-ins via CBI strengthened the resilience of neoliberalism only in very specific situations—usually when it was explicitly designed to bind the hands of future governments, as in Chile and Poland. However, the effects of

CBI were often mediated or aided by support creation and the blockade of opposition from political parties. In this sense, the lock-in mechanism depended on the underlying political and business bases of support for neoliberalism and the existence of political institutions preventing changes to CBI.

Chile

The constitutionalization of the Chilean Central Bank precluded the change of its objectives on at least one occasion, when parliamentarians from the center-left *Concertación* attempted to change the Central Bank's charter but were blocked by a combination of Chile's constraining political institutions and the high institutionalization of CBI.

The story of CBI in Chile goes back to the Chicago Boys in Pinochet's cabinet, who had already proposed an independent central bank by the mid-1970s (Fontaine 2001, 394–95). CBI was sanctioned in the 1980 Constitution, although leaving specific regulation for the future (Boylan 1998, 451). In 1986, a commission was formed to specify the Bank's "organic law." The purpose of this commission was explicit: to "isolate—as much as possible—the management of monetary policy from the political process" (Fontaine 2001, 397, translation is mine). The final law was promulgated together with a set of policy-binding regulations only a few days before the presidential elections of 1989 and was attached to one of the Constitution's supermajority thresholds requiring a four-sevenths (57 percent) approval in Congress for change (see Huneeus 2007, 439–42). In this sense, CBI was yet another way by which the dictatorship sought to constrain the policy options of the incoming democratic authorities (Boylan 1998).

The dictatorship's law fixed the central bank objective in price stability only, leaving the monetary policy council independent. Members of the council served for a period of ten years and could only be removed through accusations of not fulfilling the bank's mandate.[2] In 1989, outgoing military authorities sought to control the council by appointing four members loyal to the regime, plus another independent member. Leaders from the center-left *Concertación* criticized the content and timing of the project, and mounted intense public opposition (Bianchi 2008, 14). They complained that the military wanted to introduce "'a parallel economic team' that would destabilize the

---

2. In order not to renew the council entirely each time, the first council members were given staggered mandates of 2, 4, 6, 8, and 10 years.

economic policies of the new government" (Bianchi 2008, 15; Boylan 1998, 455), and threatened to change the law if they were elected.

The possibility that ongoing squabbles over the role of the new independent bank would undermine the bank's legitimacy prompted military authorities to come to the negotiating table. As a result, the final law incorporated a clause stipulating that in pursuing its price stability objective the bank should "have in mind the general economic policy orientation of the government." This "have in mind" [*tener presente*] clause was left purposefully ambiguous in order to satisfy the interests of the two negotiating parties (Fontaine 2001, 400). Negotiators also arrived at a new formula for the monetary policy council: the dictatorship would nominate two members, the *Concertación* another two, and another member would be independent (the 2-1-2 formula). Other concessions were also made in order to increase the legitimacy of the project in the eyes of the future democratic authorities. [3]

Once in government, the *Concertación* did not carry out the plan to change the bank's charter, allegedly because of the blockade of the rightwing opposition in Congress (Boylan 1998, 457). In exchange, the coalition tried to dominate the monetary policy council by staffing it with loyal officials. To be sure, the *Concertación* did not mean to overhaul the monetary policy council as such, nor openly contest the price stability mandate of the bank. The idea was to increase coordination between monetary and fiscal policy, as well as to use existing institutions to amp up the competitiveness goal of exchange rates. In the early 1990s, the center-left *Concertación* managed to alter the composition of the council and nominate three out of five members from its files (two Christian Democrats and one from the Party for Democracy PPD). This allowed the bank to conduct a less orthodox monetary policy: most significant, it strengthened the competitiveness goal in exchange rates to promote exports. Accordingly, the bank introduced exchange rate bands and imposed capital controls on short-term capital (the so-called *encaje*), allowing monetary authorities to actively manage the desired exchange rate level.

As economic growth improved and capital flowed into the country during the early 1990s, these changes allowed the government to smooth an otherwise powerful pressure toward exchange rate appreciation, thereby maintaining

3. Among them, the possibility for the finance minister to attend meetings of the monetary policy council with a right to speak (but not to vote), and some prerogatives like a 15-day temporary suspension of the council's resolutions and veto power on the imposition of exchange controls—both, however, could be overridden by the unanimous vote of the monetary policy council and have since then not been used.

export competitiveness throughout the period (Ffrench-Davis 2003, 284–85; Frenkel and Rapetti 2010; Fontaine 2001, 413–14). According to one Central Bank official, neoliberals pressured the bank to let the exchange rate float in order to use its appreciation to more rapidly control inflation.[4] The strategy of the heterodox council members, however, was a gradual control of inflation that allowed for the simultaneous management of price stability and competitiveness (see Bianchi 2008). These arrangements, however, ran potentially contrary to the bank's mandate of concentrating primarily on price stability. A former director of studies at the Central Bank wrote:

> The unwillingness to leave the [exchange rate] band despite the conflicts and pressures made the Central Bank look for different "second-best" options between 1990 and 1997. . . . All these measures were a sign of the increasing difficulty of resisting the tendency toward a more appreciated peso. Moreover, they reflected the secondary role of the exchange rate band between the objectives of the Central Bank, which concentrated its efforts on reducing inflation. Any conflict between the exchange rate band and the inflation target was always resolved in favor of the latter" (Morandé and Tapia 2002, 69; translation is mine).

Harmonization between price stability and the national competitiveness goals deteriorated during the Asian/Russian crisis in 1997. When the crisis erupted, the concern of the authorities was that a rapid capital outflow would produce significant exchange rate depreciation and threaten the inflationary targets for 1998 (Morandé and Tapia 2002, 70). They therefore suddenly tightened the band and increased interest rates. After the crisis, the bank established a free float and inflation-targeting framework and dropped capital controls. According to Morandé and Tapia "the free-floating exchange rate [regime] was perceived as much more coherent and immune to conflicts with the inflation targets than an exchange rate band" (2002, 71).

The free-floating exchange rate regime has been maintained ever since, without regard for its effects on competitiveness. This was most visible during the period of steep exchange rate appreciation that followed the boom in commodity prices in the mid-2000s (see Fazio and Parada 2010; Lüders 2010). Discontented with the actions of the bank and the tight monetary conditions that followed the change to a free float system and a renewed fixation on price stability alone, members of the Socialist Party unsuccessfully tried to change

4. Chile, Interview 2.

the bank's charter on two occasions: shortly after the Asian crisis in 1999, and again in the context of the negotiation surrounding the Law on Fiscal Responsibility in 2006 (see below). Both times they proposed to include in the bank's charter the objectives of economic growth, employment, and competitiveness, and to increase the bank's accountability to elected authorities (El Mercurio 1999; Estrategia 2006). The initiative was closely related to the perceived need to change the exchange rate policy and counted on support from a handful of business associations in the tradable sector who were suffering from exchange rate appreciation.[5] However, the most serious attempt, in 2006, failed miserably. The intention to change the bank's goals was declared unconstitutional, whereas that of increasing its accountability was rejected in the Senate. As I described in chapter 6, the institutions of opposition blockade (high thresholds for change in Congress and exclusive executive initiative to change especial institutions like CBI) were key to preventing changes.

In sum, the institutional lock-in of neoliberal exchange rates through central bank independence in Chile seems to have prevented the consolidation of a more developmental exchange rate regime during the 1990s. Despite the attempts made by a *Concertación*-led Central Bank, the conflict between the price stability constitutional mandate of the bank, and the goal of authorities to increase exchange rate competitiveness to promote manufacturing exports was solved in favor of the former once they started to openly collide. From then on, price stability has been the bank's only preoccupation, despite a significant loss of competitiveness due to exchange rate appreciation and vocal complaints by business sectors suffering from this, especially natural-resource exporters that were otherwise strongly in favor of the Chilean neoliberal policy regime (see Díaz Cordero 2011). More important, attempts at reforming the bank's mandate in order to include a new objective failed in Congress due to the effects of opposition blockade.

Estonia

CBI was partly responsible for blocking more progressive policies in Estonia, although not necessarily exchange rates. These constraints made center-left and agrarian parties propose amendments to the Central Bank Law in order to increase room to maneuver in policymaking. In so doing, they entertained

5. Among them, ASOEX (exporters of primary products) and ASEXMA (exporters of manufactures). Chile, Interview Chile 9.

the idea of changing the exchange rate regime altogether. However, strict institutionalization preemptively blocked any such intention.

The concern over CBI in Estonia dates back to the fight for independence from the Soviet Union and the introduction of a new currency. Amid economic turmoil, shortage of currency, hyperinflation, and the emergence of alternative payment devices (checkbooks, local currencies), and given the lack of experience with running a central bank in the previous fifty years, Estonian authorities aimed for simplicity and credibility in the monetary environment (Kukk 2007; see Laar 2002, 118–19; Sörg and Vensel 2000, 114). Siim Kallas, governor of the Bank of Estonia during this period and considered the father of currency reform, drew on the country's interwar experience in favoring a monetary arrangement that could mimic the transparency and simplicity of the gold standard (Knöbl, Sutt, and Zavoiceo 2002, 6–7).

However, a special committee set up by Prime Minister Tiit Vähi at the beginning of 1992 worked on the opposite currency reform project (Knöbl, Sutt, and Zavoiceo 2002, 11). This implied an active central bank and the need to borrow large external funds to sustain currency convertibility. Under the leadership of Governor Kallas, the Bank of Estonia developed its own concept of monetary reform in parallel and received the support of a mission of foreign experts who came to Estonia in the middle of preparations for the reform. These experts had previously advised the governments of Poland and Slovenia, favoring fixed exchange rates that were oriented toward price-stability. They suggested the idea of a currency board to Kallas, who embraced it since it supported his own preferences. With this expert support, Kallas came out on top and announced the currency board as the chosen mechanism for currency reform as of June 1992. According to a close participant, the decision to limit credit to the government and to commercial banks was crucial in the decision in favor of the currency board (Kukk 2007, 18). After some hesitation, the IMF endorsed the proposal and helped in the preparations.[6]

The currency reform established the independence of the central bank and set the exchange rate parity by law at 8 Estonian kroons (EEK) for one deutsche mark (DM). The Bank of Estonia was banned from extending credit to the government and public companies, its assets had to be kept strictly separated from the state budget, and only the Parliament could modify the

6. The IMF's skepticism was due to the belief that it was unrealistic that Estonia would meet the harsh fiscal and monetary policy requirements of the currency board (see Knöbl, Sutt, and Zavoiceo 2002, 8, 12; also Laar 2002, 117).

exchange rate peg. Two instruments allowed the Bank of Estonia to intervene in the market, although only to restrict aggregate demand (Kukk 2007, 18): permitting a temporary fluctuation of the exchange rate peg (+/−3 percent) and tightening bank reserve requirements.

Support for the currency board was facilitated by a chronic economic situation in 1992, as well as by the connections between currency reform and the national cause. According to Kukk, in those years "own currency and national independence were synonyms" (Kukk 2007, 20; see also Knöbl, Sutt, and Zavoiceo 2002, 21). This intimate relationship also made it possible to separate the economic effects of the currency board—economic contraction and company bankruptcies—from active opposition to it, limiting the understanding of the full consequences of such restrictive arrangements. As former prime minister Mart Laar recognized:

> The fact that politicians who outwardly supported the currency board were at the same time sure that after monetary reform the central bank or government would continue to deliver "cheap credits" to inefficient factories and collective farms indicates that many politicians probably never understood exactly what they had supported (Laar 2002, 122).

This understanding was realized gradually when the effects of the currency board became apparent. The first such moment was an acute banking crisis just as the currency board was being introduced. The crisis was triggered by the dissolution of the Soviet Union and exploded at the end of 1992, when Russian banks froze the foreign exchange deposits of Estonian banks, creating a strong credit contraction and a chain of bank failures. In spite of the relatively small size of the domestic banking sector and the possibility of limited bailouts in the currency board law, Prime Minister Laar and Governor Kallas quickly announced that no bailouts would be provided—not even to distressed state companies—in order not to impede the ongoing disinflation process and fiscal discipline (Fleming, Chu, and Bakker 1996, 14; 20; Laar 2002, 179–81, 187–88). Most important, they stressed the need to set a precedent to discourage future risk-taking (Laar 2002, 185; see also Fleming, Chu, and Bakker 1996, 14; 20). The concurrence of this crisis with the process of independence limited criticism. In fact, since some banks were suspected to have ties with Russian mafias, authorities could easily resort to nationalist sentiments to justify their actions (Laar 2002, 188; 191–92).

Minor expressions of discontent started to appear in 1995, during the KMÜ/Reform Party government. Government parties criticized the currency board on different grounds: while members of the agrarian Country People's Union proposed merging Central Bank reserves with those of the treasury in order to allow for higher public spending to deliver on the coalition's promises of higher subsidies for ailing firms (especially in agriculture), members of the centrist Coalition Party advanced the idea of changing the staffing procedures at the Bank of Estonia in order to appoint more responsive officials (Baltic News Service 1995a; Baltic News Service 1997a). Criticism intensified as the turmoil of the Russian crisis of 1997–1998 spread rumors of a possible breakup of the currency board. MPs from the Center Party (which would become the biggest party in Parliament in 1999) formally consulted Central Bank officials on potential mechanisms of devaluation (Baltic News Service 1998b), and experts floated the possibility of leaving the currency board after the crisis had passed (Pautola and Backé 1998, 98).

In the face of uncertainty, Central Bank authorities and the liberal Reform Party (founded by Kallas) staunchly defended the currency board, arguing that there were both institutional and practical impediments to altering it. As Kallas himself explained, a hypothetical parliamentary debate would take several weeks, requiring the Bank of Estonia to stop circulating money altogether during that period in order to prevent speculation (Baltic News Service 1995f). The Reform Party went further, including "no-devaluation" in its electoral platform for the 1999 elections (see Baltic News Service 1999). With the rejection by President Lennart Meri of a Center Party-led government in 1999, the formation of a right-wing government coalition led by the Reform Party, and support from the European Union (EU) alongside the prospective process of EMU accession, the currency board remained safely in place during these turbulent times (Feldmann 2006).

EU accession provided another scenario to contest these monetary arrangements. The agrarian-*cum*-populist People's Union party (formerly the Country People's Party) proposed holding a referendum to decide on EMU accession, which in practice reopened the debate on the modification of the currency board (Baltic News Service 2005a). Given the extent of Euroscepticism in the population, particularly with regard to EMU, the chances for a no vote to prevail were not insignificant (see Feldmann 2008, 252). The demand, however, proved short-lived amid fierce opposition by officials from the Bank of Estonia and widespread political rejection, especially by the Reform Party (Baltic News Service 2005b). More important, over time these maneuvers proved to be more a strategy to win the vote of a fairly Eurosceptical electorate rather than a critique of the currency board itself (Mikkel and Kasekamp 2008;

Feldmann 2006, 2008). In fact, direct challenges to the currency board framework were largely absent even in the context of the steep 2007–2008 crisis. To
the contrary, the Reform Party-led government took the opportunity to enter
the EMU by resorting to the internal deflation mechanism built into the currency board (Raudla and Kattel 2011). With the adoption of the euro in 2011,
the establishment of an institutional framework fostering price stability and
binding the hands of elected authorities came to full circle.

In sum, CBI and the currency board have been practically uncontested in
Estonia. In those few moments where there has been criticism, their strict
institutionalization and the practical consequences of modifying the board,
the staunch defense of the liberal Reform Party when in government, and the
inability of more critical parties to win enough votes to change existing regulations in Parliament, have prevented any serious attempts at change.

Argentina

CBI did constrain the intentions of left-leaning authorities in Argentina to
change established exchange rate policies. However, despite strict institutionalization, it did not prevent them from changing the institutional bases of CBI
altogether, even when they lacked parliamentary majorities. Counting on the
backing of a strong social bloc in favor of more interventionist policies, governments took advantage of institutional lacunae to change central bank operations without the need to change the central bank law itself.

Upon assuming office, the populist-turned-neoliberal Menem government
proposed CBI as a way to contribute to monetary stabilization and show its
commitment to a neoliberal reform path (see Starr 1997; Acuña, Galiani, and
Tommasi 2007; Frenkel and Rapetti 2010; M. Pastor and Wise 2001; Heredia
2011). In fact, the possibility of using credit from the Central Bank to finance
fiscal deficits, as well as the poor state of the bank's accounts and patrimony,
were seen as among the main reasons for the hyperinflation of the late 1980s
and the failure of the numerous stabilization programs that preceded it (see
Starr 1997, 90–91).

CBI was implemented in March 1991 with the "Convertibility Plan," which
also introduced a currency board arrangement. The new regulations fixed the
exchange rate parity by law (1 peso=1 U.S. dollar), took decisions on monetary
policy away from the Ministry of Economy, and created a monetary policy
council subject to nomination by the president and approval by the Senate.
Council members, including its president, would serve for six years. A special

congressional commission and accusations of malfeasance were necessary to remove them. One important difference from a pure currency board was the possibility of freely setting the limits on reserve requirements for banks and to back up to 20 percent, later expanded to 30 percent, of the monetary base with public bonds. While these two provisions eased the constraints of a classical currency board, *de jure* giving the BCRA the possibility to conduct monetary policy as well as to finance fiscal deficits, in practice they actually set a limit on the ability of the government to take up debt in order to finance its deficit (Bonvecchi 2002; see Starr 1997, 88–89).

Spiller and Tommasi argue that in the context of several stabilization failures and a lack of confidence in the authorities, "credibility can be temporarily achieved only through very rigid mechanisms" (2008, 74). This is exactly what was done with the Convertibility Law in Argentina. A run on the Argentine peso when Minister of Economy Cavallo flirted with the idea of changing the exchange rate parity from the U.S. dollar to a basket of currencies made it clear that the fate of neoliberalism depended on the maintenance of the currency board (Starr 1997, 95; Frenkel and Rapetti 2010, 31–32). Moreover, its ability to deliver inflationary relief, produce an initial growth boom, and survive the Tequila Crisis in 1995–1996, helped confirm the commitment of the business community at large to the new policy regime and the figure of President Menem (Starr 1997; Novaro 2009, 476–77; see M. Pastor and Wise 1999).

The real challenge to CBI and the continuity of the currency board scheme came with the 1999 elections and the new government of the center-left *Alianza* coalition. The Argentine economy had started to show signs of stress, most notably exchange rate appreciation affecting export competitiveness and the connected effects in terms of high and sustained unemployment. Although the new minister of economy, José Luis Machinea, had been critical of the currency board, he saw no possible escape due to its strict institutionalization:

> that is one of the problems that *convertibility* clearly had; that it was a trap and we had thrown the key to the bottom of the sea. And I think that is exactly what you should not do in economic policy.[7]

The *Alianza* government was far from having the majority in Parliament needed to change the currency board. Additionally, even if it achieved a temporary majority, any change would have to pass the clearance of the pro-

---

7. Argentina, Interview 8.

Menem Supreme Court, which was able to reverse legislation (Cherny 2009, 210–13). Wary of these difficulties, *Alianza* authorities opted for a "wait and see" approach, trying to gain time through halfway measures during domestic and international economic turmoil in 2000. In fact, the government categorically rejected the option of strengthening the policy framework even further through a dollarization, hoping for a better external scenario to bring relief to the pressing economic situation. Dollarization had already been discussed and proposed by Menem to the IMF in his last months in office and enjoyed the support of the neoliberal bloc (Cherny 2009, 123; Novaro 2009, 546–47; Castellani and Schorr 2004, 69–71). Menem went as far as creating a special secretariat in charge of developing a series of political texts about the benefits of dollarization. However, according to a member of the Alianza government, this would have implied the definitive closing of all alternatives:

> we were already in there with convertibility [the currency board]. Now, to dollarize and close any future possibility, I thought it was just *too much*. At least there had to be an open door.[8]

In spite of the "straitjacket" provided by the currency board framework, as economic conditions hardened in 2001 an alternative business coalition emerged, demanding changes (see chapter 4). First it was the noncompetitive sector, which, despite its huge arrears denominated in foreign currency, proposed the need to exit the currency board mechanism; second, the increase in social protest showed that the population would not put up with the internal deflation that the currency board implied. In this sense, the prospects of neoliberal resilience turned from institutional lock-in, to an increasingly political problem. In other words, the formation of this alternative social bloc calling for the demise of neoliberalism, epitomized precisely in an exit from the currency board, ultimately set the limits of the lock-in mechanism.

In this scenario of increased business and popular demands for change, Argentine presidents used their prerogatives to overhaul the institutions that held Argentine neoliberalism together. Already during 2001, President De la Rúa used decree powers to reform the bank's organic law making it possible for the president to remove the bank's governor—at that time Chicago Boy Pedro Pou. The decree also directly established the monetary policy measures that the president was asking for, namely, a reduction in reserve requirements in order to inject liquidity to the economy (Bonvecchi 2002; Novaro 2009,

8. Argentina, Interview 8.

594). President De la Rúa used decree powers once more to change the parity from a peso-dollar to a relationship between dollar and euro, in an unsuccessful—and ill-conceived—attempt to depreciate the Argentine peso and regain competitiveness (Novaro 2009, 594). In January 2002, with the crisis unraveling and President De la Rúa having resigned, interim president Eduardo Duhalde managed to get Congress to pass a Public Emergency Law eliminating the exchange rate parity and the currency board altogether.

While it is true that these changes were made in the context of the acute emergency that the Argentine economy faced in 2001 and 2002, they do show the possibility of exiting a strict institutional mechanism if the right societal supports are in place. One former Central Bank governor and minister of economy during the Menem administration expressed his frustrations with this situation in the following terms:

> If someone proposes today something similar [to a currency board] I would say there is no such thing like an institution that cannot be destroyed by the incumbent government.[9]

Néstor Kirchner assumed office as president in 2003 with a highly antineoliberal rhetoric and the backing of trade unions and industrialists from Argentina's noncompetitive sector (see chapter 4). Although Kirchner did not further change the Central Bank Law, in practice he subsumed the formally independent Central Bank to the mandate of the minister of economy. Even more so than Chile in the early 1990s, the strategy was to staff the Central Bank with loyal collaborators. Without the necessary votes in Parliament, the government used a legal technicality to circumvent the needed Senate confirmation process for appointing monetary policy council members, nominating them instead on an interim basis. The underlying regulation, which had been introduced in 1999 before the government of De la Rúa took office, authorized the government to unilaterally nominate temporary members while the Senate went through the process of nominating formal members. The Kirchner government thus claimed the ability to fill vacant posts at its discretion and change them whenever necessary. This was, in fact, the expedient used with three of four Central Bank governors between 2002 and 2004.[10] Martín Redrado, nominated to the post of president of the council in 2004 and confirmed by

9. Argentina, Interview 15.

10. Roque Maccarone (January 2002), Aldo Pignanelli (November 2002) and Alfonso-Prat-Gay (September 2004). Mario Bléjer voluntarily resigned (April 2002), but because of deep disagreements with Minister of Economy Roberto Lavagna (Lavagna 2011).

the Senate, was the closest to finishing his constitutional term but was removed by decree only months before his appointment ended. His fault: refusal to capitalize the Treasury so that the government could pay down outstanding debt. The Supreme Court declared the decree invalid, and he returned to office, but ultimately resigned anyway under pressure from President Cristina Fernández. When Redrado resigned, half of the decision-making posts at the Central Bank, including its president, vice-president, and the supervisory board of financial institutions, were occupied by interim members.[11]

As we saw in chapter 4, the Kirchner governments—at least up until the 2009 crisis—were characterized by a radically different exchange rate policy: a managed float intended to maintain a high and stable exchange rate that would promote industrial exports. They also floated several ideas to formally change the Central Bank Law at the end of decade, which they achieved in 2012. According to one pro-government newspaper, the new law implied returning the Central Bank to "its historical role of promotion of productive credit, accompanying the policies formulated by the government" (Zaiat 2012).

Poland

In Poland, CBI effectively constrained changes in the country's exchange rate regime. This made it highly contested: political parties wanting to reform neo-liberalist policies sought to weaken CBI through a variety of means. As in Argentina, although governments could not alter CBI legally, they did so in practice, challenging the legitimacy of an independent central bank.

In 1989, the last Polish communist government passed the Banking Act, transforming the communist monobank into a modern central bank. It established a two-tier banking system comprising a set of commercial banks that were state-owned and slated for privatization, along with the National Bank of Poland (NBP) as a lender of last resort. Epstein (R. A. 2002, 7) claims that this law already included important independence measures and was influenced by strict advice from international experts. However, the NBP law retained the goal of cooperating with government economic policy and kept the formulation of monetary policy in the hands of the government and the lower chamber of Parliament (Leszczyńska 2011, 58–59). Even the 1992 law accompanying the so-called Small Constitution, which was said to increase the bank's

11. Argentina, Interview 8.

independence, kept monetary policy subject to several measures of government control (Leszczyńska 2011, 60). According to one account, the opinion
of the NBP on monetary policy was, in effect, symbolic (Leszczyńska 2011, 61).

CBI in this early stage was therefore not high by international standards. In
fact, CBI measures placed Poland among the reform laggards in East-Central
Europe (Cukierman, Miller, and Neyapti 2002, 242). However, the concentration of power in the hands of the Central Bank governor—as opposed to a
monetary policy council—made it possible for a neoliberalist governor to
wield significant power. Once policy guidelines were passed by the lower
chamber and introduced into the budget, the NBP governor was relatively free
to set interest and exchange rates (K. Kowalczyk 1995). In 1992, President Lech
Wałęsa nominated Hanna Gronkiewicz-Waltz as NBP governor. While initially not particularly sympathetic to the neoliberal project, Gronkiewicz-
Waltz quickly moved in that direction as she tried to use exchange rate policy
to combat inflation (R. A. Epstein 2008, 55–56). She diminished the rate of
devaluation of the existing crawling peg, thus forcing the exchange rate to appreciate (R. A. Epstein 2008, 55–56), and even put forward the idea of establishing a free float regime, to the delight of the emerging private financial sector
(Gazeta Wyborcza 1995b; Gazeta Wyborcza 1995c).

This led to quarrels over the role of monetary policy, interest rates, and
exchange rates, especially when the center-left SLD/PSL coalition came into
government in 1993. Contrary to the NBP's strategy, Minister of Finance
Grzegorz Kołodko had opposed the fixed exchange rate of the early 1990s and
advocated a managed regime, desiring increased competitiveness rather than
stabilization (see chapter 4). The government still legally held the monetary
policy reins, and Kołodko forced an agreement with the NBP. He agreed to
release the exchange rate in return for the introduction of flotation bands
(+/–7 percent), in order to guide intervention in the foreign exchange market.
Moreover, Kołodko forced the NBP to significantly reduce interest rates in
order to funnel cheaper loans to producers in the competitive and noncompetitive sectors and reduce incentives for capital inflows that would appreciate
the exchange rate (see Gazeta Wyborcza 1995a; Gazeta Wyborcza 1995b). Following this agreement, the SLD/PSL government was energetic in demanding
active management of the exchange rate (Gazeta Wyborcza 1995d).

Quarrels over monetary policy continued, causing the SLD/PSL government in 1995 to announce a law modifying decision-making arrangements
inside the Central Bank. The idea was to dilute the authority of the NBP governor and politicize the bank's decisions by introducing a monetary policy

council that would be nominated by the government, the lower chamber, and the banking industry—then still overwhelmingly in the hands of the state (Polish News Bulletin 1996). The law also reinforced the principle that the NBP should cooperate with economic and social policies set by the government. Neoliberal parties in Parliament, led by the Freedom Union (UW), and NBP officials presented an opposing piece of legislation, that would strengthen the bank's independence and exclusive focus on price stability.

The debate about the NBP law became enmeshed with broader discussions around the new constitution, which strengthened the position of the neoliberals. In fact, despite enjoying enough votes in Parliament to pass the Constitution on its own, the center-left SLD/PSL coalition was forced to negotiate with the strong parliamentary and extra-parliamentary post-Solidarity opposition, who were threatening to boycott the new constitution if they were not included in the process (Millard 2000, 50; Howard and Brzezinski 1998, 149; Osiatyński 1997, 66). Neoliberals were also firmly backed by international organizations as they unveiled the new NBP bill and prepared to defend it publicly (R. A. Epstein 2008, 57–58). Although no conditionality was attached, the European Commission made it known that the neoliberals' version of the bill was the one that conformed better to EU legislation, and therefore the one that would secure a steadier accession process (see R. A. Epstein 2008, 58).

In negotiations, the neoliberal UW party agreed to include the monetary council proposed by the SLD/PSL government to dilute the authority of the governor, in exchange for strengthening the independence of the NBP and its exclusive fixation on price stability.[12] Independence was accepted by the center-left SLD/PSL in anticipation of EU accession (Zubek 2006, 201); they expected, however, that the ability to appoint the monetary council would be enough to control an NBP that was now formally centered on price stability. The final bill, however, was very close to the original neoliberal one (R. A. Epstein 2008, 57–58). In fact, after the 1997 law, the NBP became the most independent central bank in East-Central Europe, and one of the most independent in the world (see Cukierman, Miller, and Neyapti 2002).

The first monetary council was elected in 1997 by a right-wing-dominated Parliament and Senate, with a rather "hawkish" composition (see Polish News Bulletin 2003). That hawkishness was reinforced by the election of the architect of shock therapy, Leszek Balcerowicz, to chair the NBP board in 2000.

---

12. Poland, Interview 6.

Shortly before, while Balcerowicz was still finance minister of the AWS/UW government, he and former governor Gronkiewicz-Waltz agreed to implement a free float / inflation-targeting exchange rate scheme.[13] This decision meant the return of an exclusive anti-inflationary goal in exchange rate policy, and was also intended to favor the growth of the financial sector (Polish News Bulletin 2000). The approaching EU accession date and the accompanying necessity to accelerate the reduction of inflation in order to secure a quick adoption of the euro also influenced this renewed focus on price stability (see Zubek 2006, 199). The new floating regime did not preclude exchange rate intervention, but restricted it to instances when inflation targets were under threat (Panbuła, Kozinski, and Rubaszek 2011, 293). Approaching EU accession and a contractive policy by the NBP produced increasing capital inflows and appreciation of the złoty under the free-floating regime, quickly reducing inflation at the expense of economic contraction and loss of competitiveness.

Soon, the SLD/PSL government realized that the results of the central bank bill had not been well calculated. One participant in the negotiations said, "We had the monetary council, but the result was not very exciting."[14] Two consecutive governments tried to alter the law: the center-left SLD/UP/PSL in 2001–2004 and the populist PiS/Self-Defense/LPR in 2005–2007. The prevailing idea was to politicize its decision-making structure, reducing its excessive independence, and force a closer cooperation with the government in pursuit of wider economic policy objectives.

Backed by managers of state-owned companies in the competitive and noncompetitive sectors, the SLD/UP/PSL government engaged in intense fights with the NBP for a more active management of the exchange rate. It even advanced plans for an outright change to a managed floating system in order to maintain a high and stable exchange rate.[15] It unsuccessfully tried to force an agreement with the NBP implying an exchange of spending cuts for a relaxation of monetary policy, meaning lower interest rates and exchange rate devaluation. Unable to reach an agreement, in 2002 the government tried to achieve their goal through legislation, sending a bill to Congress to incorporate into the NBP mandate the goals of fighting unemployment and promoting economic growth (R. A. Epstein 2002, 14–15). The proposal added six new

13. The złoty was *de facto* freely floating since the AWS/UW government took office, as the last NBP intervention had been in 1998 (Panbuła, Kozinski, and Rubaszek 2011, 285).

14. Poland, Interview 6.

15. Polish News Bulletin (2002a); Poland, Interview 8.

members to the NBP's monetary policy council, and proposed a return to the government-led monetary policy that existed in the early 1990s (Polish News Bulletin 2002b).

However, the NBP was now inscribed in the Constitution—it could not be changed. The interested actors acknowledged that any change through ordinary legislation would probably be ruled unconstitutional by the Constitutional Court, and the two-thirds support in Congress needed for constitutional changes did not exist (Zubek 2006, 202–3). There are indications, moreover, that both the IMF and the EU Commission strongly opposed such moves (Zubek 2006, 203). This had a crucial impact inside the SLD, the senior party in the governing coalition and the main actor responsible for steering the EU accession process. It ended up dropping its support for the bill (see Zubek 2006, 203; R. A. Epstein 2008).

The 2005–2007 period witnessed a renewed and fiercer assault on central bank independence. In 2006, the populist PiS/Self-Defense/LPR government rehashed the 2002 changes, submiting a bill proposing to reduce the independence of the NBP by altering its decision-making organs, giving authority over monetary policy to the government, and introducing among its objectives those of employment and growth (Maciejewicz 2006b, 2006a). While Self-Defense was strongly in favor of eliminating the monetary policy council *tout court*, after realizing it didn't have the votes to pass the high constitutional threshold, it proposed allowing an easier removal of council members and of the NBP governor. This prompted fierce criticism from the EU Commission, and allegations that the law did not comply with EU legislation helped defeat the proposal in Parliament.

As a second strategy, the government coalition vowed to change the NBP from the inside, staffing it with allies. The occasion presented itself when NBP governor Balcerowicz ended his term in office in 2007. After several months of delay, PiS leader and President of the Republic Lech Kaczynski nominated a close collaborator to the post, generating widespread criticism in financial and business circles (Polish News Bulletin 2007b).[16] The appointment of Sławomir Skrzypek was understood as a way to overcome the problems with the Central Bank Law. As the vice-president of the populist Self-Defense Party acknowledged, "if President Skrzypek will take care of the economy, as he said

16. New governor Skrzypek had worked under Kaczynski's orders at the National Audit Office and the Warsaw City Hall, and had been appointed by him to the management board of the state-owned Pekao Bank.

during the parliamentary oath, then maybe a change in the law will not be necessary"[17] (Grochal and Baj 2007).

Skrzypek proved loyal to the government even if this did not necessarily pay off in terms of policy outcomes. Between 2007 and 2010, when he died in a plane accident, Skrzypek was the only council member who always voted against interest rate hikes (see Polish News Bulletin 2008a). Most significantly, Skrzypek tried to increase his influence by controlling the NBP organs under his direct mandate (Polish News Bulletin 2008b). He forced the resignation of the two deputies on the NBP management board and installed loyal collaborators in the analytical departments in charge of producing technical documents to back the decisions of the monetary policy council. A battle broke out behind the scenes between Skrzypek and the monetary policy council over the constitutionality and legality of these changes. Members of the council complained that the new staff, at Skrzypek's direction, were providing biased information leading to interest rate cuts. Skrzypek even set up a parallel "Academic Council" to furnish him with scientific advice in order to countervail the opinions of the monetary policy council. Despite the woes and warnings that the NBP was losing credibility, these attempts did not manage to substantially change the policy direction of the NBP. On the contrary, they just antagonized the other monetary policy council members, who often voted against Skrzypek's preferences (see Polish News Bulletin 2008a). After Skrzypek's death, the new President of Poland Bronisław Komorowski, member of the center-right Civic Platform (PO) party, nominated Marek Belka, a former prime minister, finance minister and centrist technocrat, to the position in an attempt to calm the waters.

In sum, the institutionalization of price stability has been contentious in Poland. Significant advances in the formalization of central bank independence were achieved with the negotiations surrounding the 1997 Constitution and, at least on paper, the National Bank of Poland (NBP) became one of the most independent in the world. In practice, however, its independence remained subject to explicit attempts to curb its original purpose. In the end, the effects of independent central banking on exchange rates have rested more on the partisanship of the monetary policy council members and the NBP governor, rather than on the bank's mandate.

---

17. "Jeśli prezes Skrzypek będzie dbał o gospodarkę tak, jak powiedział w sejmowej przysiędze, to może zmiana ustawy nie będzie potrzebna."

Fiscal Spending Rules in Latin America and Eastern Europe

Fiscal rules have spread with surprising rapidity, partly because of their incorporation in transnational integration regimes such as the EU (see Kopits 2001; Price 2010). There are three types of fiscal rules (Darvas and Kostyleva 2011, 156–57): expenditure rules, which set limits on public expenditure; balanced budget rules, which try to keep the debt-to-GDP ratio in check, usually in the form of a headline balance or structural balance (also known as cyclically-adjusted balance); and debt rules, which set an explicit limit or target for public debt. We can identify a fourth "revenue rule," particularly relevant in non-advanced countries that are commodity exporters, that sets up a contingency or stabilization fund to save windfall revenues and thereby smooth expenditure over the cycle (Kopits 2001, 11; Budnevich 2003).

Tables 7.2 and 7.3 show a summary of the characteristics of fiscal rules in the countries studied here in comparison with their respective regions. Table 7.2 shows an index of budgetary institutions, which unfortunately relies on a different measure for each region. While the index for Latin America is an additive one and goes from 0 to 100, the one for Eastern Europe is a weighted average with values between 0 and 4. In both cases, the higher the value, the more responsible the budget institutions are. In spite of the lack of inter-regional comparability, we can draw some interesting conclusions from the data. The first column shows the respective indices for the preparatory phase of the budget, whereas the second column shows the overall index. In the case of Latin America, Chile figures way above the average, while Argentina is below the average.[18] However, the score for the preparation phase of the budget in Argentina makes up more than half of the index, implying that this phase had a higher relative weight on the budget rule. In Eastern Europe, both Estonia and Poland have above-average indices. While Estonia's index is stronger in the preparation phase, the Polish score is higher in later phases of the budget procedure.

Table 7.3 shows the characteristics of fiscal rules in the four countries, and their reform dates. The second column shows whether fiscal rules were formal (legally established and enforced) or corresponded only to informal commitments. The rest of the columns describe the type of fiscal rules applied. Eastern

---

18. The index was calculated in 1999, before Argentina and Chile introduced formal fiscal rules, in 2000 and 2006, respectively.

TABLE 7.2. Latin America and Eastern Europe, Budget Institutions Index

	Budget preparation score	Overall score
Argentina[a]	27.5	50.16
Chile[a]	29.16	73.32
Latin American Average[b]	—	56.21
Estonia[c]	2.84	2.67
Poland[c]	2.34	2.42
Eastern European Average[c]	2.30	2.18

Source: Alesina et al. (2001), Darvas and Kostyleva (2011, 163–64).
[a]Additive score.
[b]Average index for countries ranked in the medium group.
[c]Weighted average score.

TABLE 7.3. Latin America and Eastern Europe, Date of Reform and Type of Fiscal Rules

Country/year	Formality	Expenditure	Balanced budget	Debt	Stabilization fund
Argentina 2000	Formal		X		X
Argentina 2005	Informal				X
Chile 1990	Informal		X		
Chile 2001	Informal	X	X		X
Chile 2006	Formal	X	X		X
Estonia 1992	Informal		X		
Estonia 1998	Formal		X	X	X
Poland 1997/1998	Formal	X		X	
Poland 2003	Informal	X			
Poland 2005	Informal	X			

Source: Author's elaboration.

European countries adopted fiscal rules earlier than Latin American ones as they approached EU accession. In fact, the Stability and Growth Pact required that these countries establish balanced or in-surplus budgets in the medium term. EU members must also comply with deficit and debt thresholds (3 percent and 60 percent of GDP, respectively). Failure to meet these targets may trigger an "excessive deficit procedure" and ultimately lead to pecuniary sanctions (Schuknecht 2005, 71). As a result, only the two Eastern European countries have adopted debt rules. Conversely, the most frequent form of fiscal rules is budget deficit rules, followed by expenditure rules and stabilization funds; the latter is absent only in Poland—the country where the export of raw materials represents the lowest share of total exports.

Estonia

Fiscal policy rules were effective in constraining expenditure by left-leaning parties in Estonia, and at least once this directly affected industrial policy proposals. No significant attempt at change has been made, presumably due to opposition blockade.

The 1992 Estonian Constitution included a balanced budget provision. This was closely influenced by the adoption of the currency board and the need to keep fiscal accounts in check in order to strengthen its performance (OECD 2000a, 82), as well as the necessity to show commitment to fiscal discipline to the IMF, which had backed the currency board with a standby agreement (Knöbl, Sutt, and Zavoiceo 2002). According to one Central Bank official, the stringent requirements of the currency board in terms of fiscal policy, together with the prohibition against financing fiscal deficits, "came to mean that a government cannot run a deficit."[19] Governments have thereafter followed this informal balanced budget rule, reinforced by budgetary institutions that have required every new additional expenditure proposal to identify its own revenue sources (Raudla 2010).

Expressions of discontent with the currency board and its effects on public expenditure flared up during the KMÜ/Reform Party government in 1995. The KMÜ coalition, especially the left-leaning Country People's Party, had promised increases in subsidies to farmers and improvements in social policy and did not approve of the principle of a balanced budget. Prime minister Vähi from the Coalition Party, however, vociferously defended the balanced budget, invoking the IMF standby loan and its importance for monetary stability to justify rejecting increases in subsidies to farmers (D. J. Smith 2002, 96). Amid the 1997–1998 financial turmoil, relief for the ailing agricultural and food-processing sectors became a highly debated topic. In spite of the insistence by the Country People's Party, Prime Minister Tarand resisted calls for such relief, and proposals to increase tariffs and subsidies were declared unconstitutional.

The crisis, however, put paid to Estonian fiscal conservatism and its record fiscal surpluses. The fiscal deficit rose to 2.8 percent during the second half of 1998 and to 4.0 percent in 1999 (OECD 2000a, 97). In order to eliminate the possibility of another digression from fiscal conservatism, in 1998 the government set up a contingency fund—the Stabilization Reserve Fund (SRF)—to

19. Estonia, Interview 1.

finance long-term investments and attenuate the pro-cyclical effects of the currency board (OECD 2000a, 96–99; Bank of Estonia 1999, 14). The SRF was used, for example, to bank privatization proceeds, thus further restricting expenditure increases. While in 1998 half of the privatization proceeds were deposited in the fund, depositing all revenues from privatizations became mandatory from 2000 onward (OECD 2000a, 98–99). Only a few months after its establishment (March 1999), the fund already amounted to 3.5 percent of that year's projected GDP (OECD 2000a, 99). Moreover, a new fiscal law adopted in 1999 applied a rule for acquiring new public debt in an already strict fiscal environment. The new law stipulated that the total amount of public borrowing (through loans or bonds) should not exceed planned investment expenditures, with an upper limit of 10 percent of state budget revenues (Gleich 2003, 13).

Once again, when they came into government in 2005 the People's Union Party demanded the expansion of fiscal expenditure by utilizing excess revenue deposited in the stabilization fund. This time, however, the target was not necessarily subsidies to specific economic sectors but public investment more generally (Baltic News Service 2005c). This idea sank without enough support in Parliament. Most notably, it was rejected by the senior coalition partner in government, the neoliberal Reform Party.

Debates on fiscal policy resurfaced amid the 2007–2008 crisis. The Reform Party-led government saw in the dramatic downturn of economic activity the possibility to meet the criteria for the long-desired EMU accession. This entailed supporting the disinflationary adjustment process led by the currency board and enacting austerity measures to maintain a balanced budget. Against criticism from center-left parties in Congress, in 2009—when economic activity sank by 13.8 percent—successive austerity packages capped some 10 percent of planned expenditure (Raudla and Kattel 2011, 171). One conspicuous victim of these caps was the industrial policy development of the past few years, especially the Development Fund created in 2006 as a public investment fund and promotion agency. As part of the efforts to balance the budget, the Reform Party-led government sold many of the shares it still had of privatized SOEs. In 2009 it took back and sold the Telekom shares that had been allocated to the Development Fund and constituted its main source of funding, significantly impairing its activities (see chapter 4).

In sum, fiscal spending rules have been strongly respected in Estonia and have been used as a direct explanation for constraining expenditure in industrial policy. This was particularly the case amid the Russian crisis and in the

2007–2008 financial crisis. The inability of opposing parties to get enough support in Parliament to change these rules reflects the longstanding influence of neoliberal parties in Congress and the shadow of the opposition blockade mechanism.

Poland

Fiscal spending rules have not been effective at constraining expenditure in Poland. Polish governments have systematically violated the rule through different strategies and alternative interpretations, although there is no evidence that this has been done to support industrial policy proposals—nor has the rule been changed, presumably because it was devised to conform to EU standards.

Poland has made several attempts to institutionalize conservative fiscal spending rules. The 1997 Constitution already incorporated a 60 percent limit on public debt, anticipating, as in the case of central banking, the need for future compliance with EU legislation. This was also part of the negotiations between the majority center-left parties and the right-wing opposition that surrounded the 1997 Constitution (Howard and Brzezinski 1998, 151). The ceiling on public debt was the price paid in exchange for the left parties' willingness to introduce explicit economic rights into the Constitution.[20] According to one participant in the negotiation, this result was seen as highly beneficial for the left: "at this time, the relation of the public debt to GDP was some 38 percent, so 60 percent seemed practically inaccessible. Therefore, it was generally accepted."[21]

The Public Finance Act of 1998, passed under the conservative AWS/UW government, specified two further thresholds for public debt, at 50 percent and at 55 percent. Each threshold increased spending limitations in order to avoid reaching 60 percent. Above 60 percent, the government is banned from borrowing, which means public finance has to be in balance or surplus (Rutkowski 2007, 3). Two further attempts to limit public spending took place during the SLD/UP/PSL and the PiS/LPR/Self Defense governments in the

20. The right to social security, which was retained from the 1992 Small Constitution, had served in the past as the basis for decisions by the constitutional tribunal limiting cuts to social benefits (see Osiatyński 1997, 75). A participant in the negotiations on the part of the left suggested that the inclusion of social rights into the Constitution was also linked to the negotiation over Central Bank independence. See Bugaj (2014).

21. Poland, Interview 6.

context of pre- and post-EU accession and the obligation to meet the Maastricht criteria. The former implemented the Belka rule, which proposed that real expenditure could not grow more than 1 percent annually, while the latter proposed a so-called fiscal anchor, a four-year nominal ceiling on the public deficit of PLN 30 billion.

All these efforts have failed to limit public spending. According to one account, the latter two deficit rules have been too weakly institutionalized to be effectively binding (Rutkowski 2007). While the first was dismissed by a lack of political will, the second was subject to "creative accounting," transferring expenditures from one year to the other, and from central government institutions to independent agencies not covered by the rule. Even the debt ceilings enshrined in the Constitution have been subject to interpretation. In 2010–2011, the center-right PO/PSL government crossed the 60 percent boundary, which according to the Constitution would have triggered an immediate obligation to balance the budget for the upcoming year. However, the government managed to avoid the 60 percent threshold and its austerity consequences using two strategies. First, it lobbied the NBP to obtain the transfer of a higher amount of its annual profit to the Treasury.[22] Second, it changed the definition of public debt, excluding from its calculus the highly loss-making social security funds, thus improving the debt record.[23]

In sum, just like in central banking, fiscal rules have remained contested in Poland. Polish authorities have unsuccessfully tried to institutionalize fiscal austerity through fiscal spending and deficit rules. In this case, even center-right governments have used the possibility of circumventing institutionalized fiscal provisions in creative ways.

Chile

Fiscal rules effectively constrained the ability of Chilean authorities to increase expenditure. However, this affected industrial policy prospects only indirectly, through the need to raise extra revenues to fund more progressive proposals, which brought the need for parliamentary negotiations under opposition blockade conditions. Even so, there have been no attempts at changing these rules.

22. *Country Report Select* 2010. Poland, Interview 8.
23. This had been a longstanding dispute with the European Commission's Economic and Financial Affairs Directorate (ECOFIN). See Zubek (2006, 212).

Shortly after the return to democracy in 1990, Chilean authorities agreed to an unwritten balanced budget fiscal rule (Huber, Pribble, and Stephens 2010, 82–83). This reinforced the already conservative bias of the budget process enshrined in the Constitution (see Baldez and Carey 2001), making fiscal policy in Chile particularly constrained. In fact, the country was the only democratic regime in 1990s Latin America to produce constant fiscal surpluses (Baldez and Carey 2001, 105).

This changed after the Asian crisis. In 1999, the fiscal balance was in deficit for the first time in 13 years, putting pressure on the government of socialist Lagos, who took office in 2000, to quickly bring it back in check. Despite the record of fiscal prudence, analysts accused public expenditure of exacerbating the economic decline after the crisis, spurring demands to further bind public expenditure (see De Gregorio, Tokman, and Valdés 2005). More significantly, the business community pressed Lagos to commit to fiscal discipline, which went against his plans for redistribution and social policy reforms. One business leader warned: "Lagos must choose between the distributive illusion and the telluric power of growth, . . . between commanding a government which either slows down private sector or strategically allies with business" (cited in Bogliaccini 2012, 127). Caring more about satisfying business demands than reactivating the economy, Lagos further formalized the existing fiscal rule, combining structural balance and expenditure rules and forcing his own government to deliver a 1 percent surplus. Although supporters have celebrated this rule as conducive to counter-cyclical fiscal policy (Ffrench-Davis 2010), fiscal policy during the Lagos administration continued to be extremely contractionary, exacerbating the economic downturn and unemployment that started with the Asian crisis. In fact, in 2005, the last year of Lagos's term, public expenditure was 2 points lower than in 1999, whereas the primary fiscal balance went from 0.5 percent of GDP in 2000 to more than 5 percent of GDP in 2005.[24] The structural balance rule of the Lagos administration was further formalized and passed as the "Fiscal Responsibility Law" in 2006, which required an advisory board to set parameters annually for long-term fiscal income and define the spending figure compatible with this trend. All excess revenue would be deposited in stabilization funds. The administration of socialist Michelle Bachelet, who took office in 2006, complied with the new fiscal law and maintained the self-imposed 1 percent surplus rule despite the resistance of *Concertación* parties.

24. Author calculations based on data from ECLAC.

The cap on expenditure that this fiscal rule produced constrained any spending increases for industrial policy, even as the need to stimulate industrial policy became increasingly obvious (see e.g., Muñoz Gomá 2001, 2003). Additional expenditure thereafter depended on the generation of new revenues. In the mid-2000s, a good opportunity to expand industrial policy expenditure was presented when Parliament discussed the introduction of a royalty on copper extraction, a longstanding dream of the progressive wing of the *Concertación*. The project, sent to Parliament in 2004, created the Fund for Innovation and Competitiveness, accumulating its resources from the royalty to foster investment in R&D. However, its dispositions changed the Mining Law attached to one of the supermajority thresholds enshrined in the Constitution, making it difficult to change it. The business community and the right-wing opposition staunchly opposed the royalty project and managed to reject it in Congress. The government tried once again in 2005; in this new version, however, the law was significantly watered down (see Napoli and Navia 2012). The royalty had become a specific tax on mining activities including significant concessions for companies, such as a clause of tax invariability for the next 15 years. As shown in chapters 5 and 6, to a great degree this outcome resulted from the joint operation of support creation and opposition blockade.

In sum, center-left governments in Chile have seen fiscal rules as a way to show commitment to fiscal responsibility, thereby placating the discontent of the business community. This has constrained their ability to increase industrial-policy-related expenditure—albeit only indirectly. More importantly, it has subjected industrial policy to parliamentary negotiations where opposition blockade mechanisms and business power have precluded more progressive policies.

Argentina

In Argentina fiscal policy rules have not been effective. As with CBI, partisan considerations related to the fulfillment of alternative policy programs have overruled existing institutional constraints. Although the rule remained on paper, it was abandoned in practice and/or subject to other contingent policy objectives.

Argentina established a fiscal rule during the Menem presidency, just a few months before the center-left De la Rúa government took office, as a way to constrain the next government's room to maneuver. The law set a ceiling for the public deficit starting at its 1999 level and declining gradually until achiev-

ing a "zero deficit" in 2005. Most significantly, the outgoing Menem administration elaborated a budget for the new government under these premises,
including reductions in public employment and social policy funds (Novaro
2009, 565). The new authorities were forced to abide by it, given the critical
economic situation they inherited and the need to show commitment to fiscal
restraint in order to keep capital inflows and IMF borrowing alive (Novaro
2009, 565; Bonvecchi 2002). The limits were nevertheless repeatedly violated
and even ignored during 2001 crisis and later developments in the Argentine
economy.

The Law on Fiscal Responsibility also created a fund (*Fondo Anti-Cíclico
Fiscal*) to save fiscal revenue for countercyclical purposes.[25] It set minimum
floors for the contribution of Treasury resources to the fund (1 percent in 2000,
1.5 percent in 2001, and 2 percent in 2002) until the fund built the equivalent
of 3 percent of GDP. Resources thus accumulated could be used in cases of
economic downturns (with a maximum withdrawal of 50 percent of the fund)
and to pay external debt in the case that the fund exceeded 3 percent of GDP.
Resources could also be invested in foreign exchange and central bank instruments. However, the fund was suspended for the duration of the 2001 crisis.

In 2005, the Kirchner administration floated the idea again, with the aim of
depositing excess fiscal surpluses and withdrawing foreign exchange from the
market in an environment of economic recovery and strong foreign exchange
inflows. The purpose was to help reinforce the policy of a high and stable exchange rate as well as to control an already high level of public expenditure,
which could potentially create inflationary pressures and exchange rate appreciation. The fund was ephemeral, and in practice it died with the resignation of its proponent, Minister of Economy Lavagna, in late 2005. In fact, despite announcements by the government of Cristina Fernández that the fund
was in full operation and that it had accumulated thousands of U.S. dollars,
journalists found that it had actually been deposited in a special account of the
Treasury where the resources were made available to cover current expenses
(Donovan 2009).

In sum, as with the case of CBI, the existence of fiscal spending rules has
not prevented Argentine governments from circumventing them. Again, the
binding character of neoliberal institutions appears to be strongly related to

25. Ley 25.152, infoLEG database, Centro de Documentación e Información, Ministry of
Economy. http://infoleg.mecon.gov.ar/infolegInternet/anexos/60000-64999/60039/texact
.htm.

the underlying power equilibrium and the support for alternative development projects.

Conclusion

The delegation of policymaking authority to autonomous bureaucratic bodies has been identified as one of the central causes of less accountable and less representative democratic governments, and the consequent erosion of the canonical model of postwar representative democracy in the West (Crouch 2004; Crouch, della Porta, and Streeck 2016; Mair 2013). This chapter has shown that central bank independence (CBI) and fiscal rules have been an important part of neoliberal projects and have been used to increase the resilience of neoliberalism in all the analyzed countries, by taking decision-making authority on exchange rates and industrial policy away from democratically elected authorities. But have these institutions actually constrained the reform attempts of democratic authorities opposing the continuity of neoliberalism?

The answer is partly yes, partly no. Yes, CBI and fiscal rules have constrained possibilities for more progressive exchange rate and industrial policies in certain moments. But the ability of central banks and fiscal rules to do so has in most cases been mediated by the power of existing social blocs and the political institutions that control representation in Congress. In other words, the mechanisms of support creation and opposition blockade are crucial to the functioning of independent central banks and fiscal rules as lock-in mechanisms.

Central bank independence (CBI) seemed key to sustained neoliberal exchange rates in all countries. This happened in Chile in the context of the Asian crisis, when CBI triggered the necessity to refocus on price stability after a short heterodox interlude. In Estonia, the strict institutionalization of the currency board—and more generally, the development of a "price stability culture" and the strong cultural attachment to the national currency—prevented devaluation during an early banking crisis, during Russia's default in 1998, and once again during the 2007–2008 crisis. CBI also prevented changes in exchange rate policy in Argentina in 2000 when a new government took office and in Poland during the 2000s. The experiences of Argentina and Poland, however, show that the actual mechanism was not, strictly speaking, the lock-in that these institutions generated. In Argentina, the currency board tied the hands of governments while the powerful noncompetitive sector still sup-

ported it. As the business sector started to withdraw its support for the neoliberal policy regime, and as an alternative social bloc emerged, the once revered "Convertibility Law" and CBI became only words. Once a new social
bloc came to power, it was not even necessary to change the actual Central
Bank Law to promote more progressive exchange rate policies. In the case of
Poland, an alternative social bloc never really solidified, and therefore opponents to neoliberalism were not able to successfully change the free-floating
exchange rate established shortly after central bank reform in 1997. The constant quarrels over monetary policy, and the explicit attempts to circumvent
central bank laws and procedures, however, show the fragility of its institutional setup in the absence of a dominant neoliberal bloc.

At a second glance, the Chilean resilience story seems to be not so much
associated with the independent central bank per se, but with the inability of
the governing center-left *Concertación* coalition to change it in Parliament. In
fact, the virtual impossibility of changing the bank's law in Congress each time
that proponents of a more progressive exchange rate policy intended to do so
seems to go a long way towards explaining the resilience of this policy domain.
Beyond specific episodes, in the long run this continuity is explained not by
the constitutionalized character of central bank independence, but by the representation biases built into Chilean political institutions—what we have
called "opposition blockade." In Estonia, similarly, one should not overlook
the ability of the Reform Party to form part of nearly all governments since
1995 and the role of President Lennart Meri in rejecting a Center Party-led
government in 1999, thereby limiting the possibility of parliamentary changes
to the strictly institutionalized currency board and central bank laws. This, in
turn, is linked to the representation biases of Estonian political institutions
through opposition blockade, as analyzed in chapter 6.

A closer analysis of the two cases of neoliberal discontinuity provides further
clarification. In Poland, a country where opposition blockade did not take root,
attempts to change the Central Bank in Parliament failed; by contrast, in Argentina—also a country without opposition blockade—Central Bank reforms
(and circumventions of those reforms) were successful. Here, the difference
seems to stem from the availability of an alternative social bloc able to carry out
a development project distinct from neoliberalism. As we analyzed in chapter
5, the explanation for this, that is, the availability of business support for an alternative development project, is the mechanism of support creation.

The analysis of the effect of fiscal policy rules over industrial policy offers
a similar, if somewhat less clear, picture. The Chilean fiscal rule of the early

2000s, later transformed into law, did constrain the possibility of carrying out more progressive industrial policy although only indirectly, through the need of raising additional revenue. And given the need to ask Congress to pass revenue-raising laws—like the royalty-*cum*-tax on copper mining—the true constraint became, once again, opposition blockade. In the case of Estonia, fiscal rules were openly invoked in order to prevent the increase of subsidies amid the Russian crisis. Moreover, during the 2007–2008 crisis, progressive industrial policy developments were quickly scaled back in order to keep fiscal accounts in check.

Again, the cases of Argentina and Poland help to clarify the true mechanisms in operation. The strongest case for demonstrating this point is Poland, where fiscal rules were assumed only half-heartedly in the context of pre- and post-EU accession. Ever since, they have been subject to contingent interpretations by incumbent governments, allowing them to maneuver around them and minimize their potential effect. In this sense, institutional arrangements ultimately depended, not on their own endogenous operation, but on the political compromises that sustained them and made them possible in the first place. Similarly, in Argentina, fiscal policy rules were never really considered to be actually binding, and governments periodically curbed them in order to meet their own expenditure priorities.

This chapter shows that even the most stringent lock-in mechanism does not preclude a substantial challenge against neoliberalism when the right actors are able to coalesce for that purpose. The evidence affirms that neoliberal blocs have been able to perpetuate their preferred policies primarily by increasing the power of specific segments of the business community to exercise their influence in the decisions of democratically elected governments, and by precluding the representation of large portions of society in the political arena. In this sense, the resilience of neoliberalism has not just reduced partisan influences in specific policies in favor of technical decisions or the effectiveness of elected governments; it has significantly altered democratic politics and the principles of democratic legitimacy and representation.

8

Lessons

NEOLIBERAL RESILIENCE AND THE
FUTURE OF DEMOCRACY

[I]f it is to survive, democracy must recognize that it is not a fountainhead of
justice and that it needs to acknowledge a conception of justice which does
not necessarily manifest itself in the popular view on every particular
issue. . . . Those who endeavor to persuade majorities to recognize proper
limits to their just power are therefore as necessary to the democratic process
as those who constantly point to new goals for democratic action.

—HAYEK 1978, 117

[T]he beneficiaries of the status quo have in their favor powerful ideologies,
often dressed as a (pseudo) economic science, that tell us that the best we can
hope is for a very restricted, and ultimately depoliticized democracy.

—O'DONNELL 2007, IX

[W]e cannot regard these systems, centered on the goal of avoiding majority
control, as democratic.

—DAHL 1956, 32

I OPENED THIS BOOK with an analogy between the ability of General Augusto Pinochet to maintain his grip on political power in Chile in the face of
many challenges, and the history of neoliberalism in Latin America and Eastern Europe. The relationship between neoliberalism and constrained demo-

cratic rule is not just characteristic of the relatively well-known Chilean story but is a generalized pattern. It applies both to the establishment of neoliberalism, which was often pushed under outright authoritarian regimes and shock therapy conditions, and its continuity. In other words, neoliberalism survived where it was protected from democracy.

The contributions of studying neoliberal resilience over thirty years and in two very different world regions go beyond the specific political and institutional factors affecting neoliberal resilience. Some of the topics raised here offer lessons to help us understand the relationship between the resilience of neoliberalism, the hollowing out and backsliding of democracy and the threat of the populist radical right, in the advanced and developing worlds alike. I discuss two controversial issues in connection with this: whether the constrained democracy offered by neoliberals is the only alternative that we can hope for to prevent a more definitive challenge to democratic rule by the populist radical right, or whether—and to what extent—populism can offer a corrective to many of democracy's current representational ills (see Mudde and Rovira Kaltwasser 2013b; Rovira Kaltwasser 2014).

In this book, I studied two aspects of neoliberalism's resilience: its coalitional bases—the actors that supported and defended it over time; and the mechanisms that increased their power resources, allowing them to maintain their grip on policy and institutional changes. The four countries I studied all had a strong and growing financial sector controlling a significant share of domestic economies, as well as right-wing parties active and influential in domestic policymaking. Even in the cases where right-wing forces were weak, they were able to strike strategic compromises that allowed them to influence policymaking far beyond their share of the vote. My findings reveal a striking result: if financial-sector and right-wing forces have been present throughout the cases, they constitute a necessary but not sufficient condition for neoliberal resilience. What then are the decisive actor(s) explaining neoliberalism's resilience?

In addition to analyzing the actors that supported neoliberalism, it is crucial to look at those who opposed it and/or presented alternatives to it. Because we are dealing with capitalist political economies, if these alternative policies or outright development projects are to have any chances of success it is crucial that they include significant members of the business community. This study suggests that the most probable business support for alternative development projects came from firms in the noncompetitive sector, that is, firms that cannot compete with foreign companies on their own, and therefore are willing to demand substantial help from the state under the form of what we have called a "developmental" economic policy regime. However, evidence also shows that changing economic and political circumstances like economic crises and or the prominence of multinationals, economic strategies such as diversification into different sectors, or the availability of political allies, can also change these firms' policy preferences and political behavior.

Given the vagaries of business support, competitive businesses, particularly exporters, emerge as pivotal actors because of their capacity to lend support for progressive coalitions and solve the external economic constraints on domestic development. Under what conditions can competitive businesses be systematically attracted into an alliance with actors seeking a progressive development project—as has been successfully achieved in some small northern European states (Katzenstein 1985; Ornston 2012)? Or alternatively, to what extent can progressive social blocs be sustained without the foundation of competitive sectors? Ultimately, coalitions for progressive development projects need to be both politically viable and economically feasible.

With this in mind, the resilience of neoliberalism lies in two simultaneous sets of processes: (1) the conditions under which financial and competitive sectors perpetuate themselves and their political allies (whether left or right) in power, and influence the trajectory of economic policy, while (2) noncompetitive sectors are either co-opted into neoliberal dominant blocs or prevented from pursuing alternative development projects even when governments want to represent them. As I have shown, to a great extent these conditions inhere in the very functioning of democracy, a political regime where expressions of majoritarian will can find representation and where common societal projects can be discussed and carried out in the context of constant deliberation and accountability. On paper, democracy provides the means for political alternatives to compete for office and generates incentives for elected authorities to effectively respond to business and citizen demands. These dimensions of democracy, often compounded by economic downturns, are the source of the democratic process's "institutionalized uncertainty" as Przeworski (1991) aptly referred to it. At stake is the capacity of democracy to allow the representation of meaningful alternatives in the political contest without them undermining democracy's very bases due to the emergence of hegemonic projects (see Przeworski 2019). The question is therefore: why and when did this institutionalized uncertainty mutate into a certainty that, independent of elections and of who governed, neoliberalism could not be replaced?

A policy regime like neoliberalism, subjecting people and industries to enhanced competition and economic volatility, and generating increasing inequality and economic concentration, can only secure its endurance in two ways: either by convincing citizens and entrepreneurs that, despite the results, they are better off under these conditions or that there are no meaningful alternatives (that is, through legitimation and cultural hegemony); or, through coercion, which in a democratic setting means altering the polity to either reduce the space for competition from alternative projects, reduce the possibility that these get effective representation in state policies, or both. In this book I have shown how the resilience of neoliberalism in Latin America and Eastern Europe depended on neoliberalism's ability to constrain democratic procedures thus understood. Although this is not a uniquely neoliberal way of reducing the expression and representation of political alternatives, the neoliberal political project has had a significant role in theorizing reductions of the representative dimension of democratic institutions, and in justifying this perhaps dubious project in terms of the greater good of democracy and freedom (see chapter 2). I analyzed three mechanisms by which dominant neoliberal blocs managed to perpetuate themselves in power and maintain their grip over policy changes: strengthening their power resources (*support creation*), weakening the resources of actors likely to contest neoliberalism (*opposition blockade*), or closing off policy alternatives altogether (*constitutionalized lock-in*).

Support creation altered economic structures using privatization to increase the power resources of broad categories of business, particular economic sectors or individual companies actually or potentially supporting neoliberalism, for instance, foreign capital in Estonia, or the financial and competitive sectors in Chile. Privatization strengthened the business support base of neoliberal social blocs and as a result their power to influence the decisions of democratically elected governments. Put another way, by targeting allies for privatization neoliberals reinforced the encroachment of democratic governments in the "market prison" of capitalism (Lindblom 1982), at the same time leaving alternative development projects without a business support base. In Chile, privatization strengthened the core of the neoliberal bloc with different business sectors at different times, thereby constituting a robust multi-sector neoliberal business front. In Estonia, privatization served as a compromise with the transnationalization of the economy, and an invitation for external capital to fuel its future development. Domestic development policies had to adapt, therefore, and follow the dictates of international capital.

Businesses thus empowered not only used different forms and channels of power to bring public policy closer to their preferences, but also precluded more progressive alliances among actors challenging neoliberalism. From this perspective, the most interesting effect that support creation had is what I called the "silencing" of the demand for a more developmental project. In Chile, this was reinforced by the fact that some of the biggest state-owned companies in the noncompetitive sector were alienated to the very individuals that carried out market reforms during the Pinochet dictatorship; in Estonia, silencing occurred because starting with privatization (but not restricted to it) competitive transnational companies represented a significant and increasing share of the domestic noncompetitive sector.

Argentina and Poland, by contrast, show the failure of this mechanism. In Argentina, privatization was used to entice support for neoliberal reforms from a strong noncompetitive sector opposing them. The resulting support was only short term and conditional on the performance of neoliberalism. In the long term, however, it served to increase the power resources of companies that were quick to support alternative social blocs when neoliberal policies stopped delivering. In Poland, privatization was heavily delayed and favored insiders who held preferences for continued state intervention. During the 2000s, privatization produced a broader base of support for neoliberalism, especially through external capital flows to the financial and competitive sectors. However, the Polish state maintained crucial stakes in all sectors, especially the noncompetitive one, becoming the target for attempts to reconstitute an alternative business base. Interestingly, as I concluded in chapters 5 and 6, this also had the effect of generating competition among political parties for the support of these different business bases.

Opposition blockade was used to alter democratic institutions, decreasing the representation of those actors opposing neoliberalism or directly blocking them through veto powers. The design of exclusionary political institutions appears to be the most directly strategic of all such mechanisms, as the cases of Estonia and Chile attest. There, specific political groups were identified and targeted for blockade, and the rules of electoral systems were biased to exclude them. In Estonia, neoliberals directly removed voting rights from the portion of the electorate that was most prone to vote for anti-neoliberal political alternatives: the Russian-speaking minority. In Chile, the *sui generis* binominal electoral system and district gerrymandering reduced the representation of left-wing parties in Parliament. In this case, the blockade was overdetermined by the array of "authoritarian enclaves" enshrined in the Pinochet-written

Constitution to protect neoliberalism from electoral majorities. Until very recently, neither of the two experiences was significantly contested by the affected parties, and both were highly successful owing to the specific contexts in which they were implemented: democratization and fears of an authoritarian reversal in Chile, and the transition from communism in ethnically-charged Estonia. The identification of these groups (the left and ethnic minorities) as potential menaces to the very democratization process helped to justify the mechanism as a necessary evil, if not as outright political responsibility. Thus, behind the apparent mask of democratic consolidation and success of these two countries, their closeness to a *democradura* or a "tutelary" form of democracy for most of the period here analyzed should not be downplayed (see Rabkin 1992; Pettai 2005).

Neoliberals in Argentina and Poland also tried to block opposition, but their successes came almost exclusively in strengthening the veto power of specific institutional players that became the bulwark of neoliberalism. The failure of this source of opposition blockade appears to be connected with the fact that it did not produce an institutionalization of opposition blockade *per se*, but a personalization of it. Neoliberalism in Argentina and Poland depended on the ability of presidents Carlos Menem and Lech Wałęsa to keep the technocratic policymakers and their neoliberal reform plans insulated. This brought these countries closer to the "delegative democracy" type of distortion, as was documented by O'Donnell (1994). However, the democratic bases of the office they occupied made them susceptible to removal by popular vote, as was eventually the case. As new incumbents of a different political stripe assumed office, they deactivated opposition blockade or used its provisions to pursue their own purposes and policy preferences.

Finally, neoliberals instituted a series of rules to defend their project even when they were not in power. The constitutionalization of neoliberalism— that is, enshrining neoliberal policy goals in strict laws and in the constitution itself—was supposed to make institutional changes and alternative interpretations of existing policies more difficult. The more neoliberals institutionalized, say, price-stability goals as main concerns of central banks, or monetary autonomy through central bank independence, and so forth, the less likely it was that monetary authorities could engage in heterodox exchange rate policy. In the case of fiscal policy, the more institutionalized were government expenditure procedures such as fiscal spending rules, sovereign funds to save budget surpluses, and so forth, the more constrained was the ability of governments to use fiscal spending (tax schemes, transfers) to support specific economic

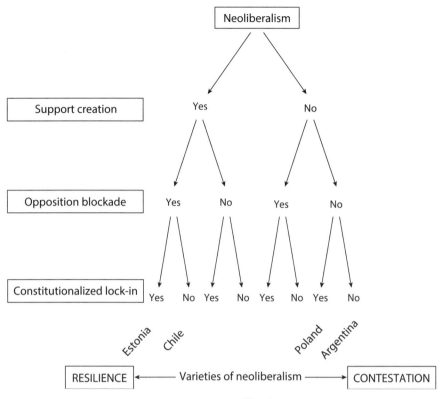

FIGURE 8.1. Varieties of Neoliberal Trajectories
Source: Author's elaboration.

sectors through industrial policy. My analysis shows that the effect of institutional lock-in via constitutionalization depended crucially on existing power balances and on the effect of other institutional constraints. This result supports a number of works on delegative institutions that show that their effects on constraining policy are mostly mediated by other structures (e.g., Clark, Golder, and Golder 2002; Stasavage 2003).

The cases under study do not represent two clearly distinguishable poles of neoliberal and nonneoliberal political economies, but variations on how the formation of social blocs and institutionalized democratic politics opened spaces for alternative projects, or shut them off. The operation of the three mechanisms mentioned above underpins variegated trajectories of neoliberal resilience and contestation (see figure 8.1).

On one end we have Estonia, where entrenched opposition blockade and constitutionalization, coupled with effective support creation, left little or no space for open contestation by the noncompetitive economic sector, the left, or labor—the actors most likely to impugn neoliberalism. On the other extreme is Argentina, where support creation strengthened rather than weakened the noncompetitive sector, opposition blockade strengthened rather than weakened the power of alternative political parties and labor, and because of this, constitutionalization through central bank independence and fiscal spending rules had only a temporary validity. In between, we find the cases of Chile and Poland. In Chile (towards the resilient neoliberalism end) support creation produced a broad business coalition, weakening noncompetitive-sector support for an alternative project; tight opposition blockade foreclosed a left-labor coalition despite democratization, although high popular support gave the center-left *Concertación* temporary chances to propose alternative policies; and constitutionalization helped to restrict the policy room for maneuver. As we discussed in chapter 7, however, the latter rested heavily on the other two mechanisms reinforcing policy consensus among the actors represented in the political arena. In this case, more research is needed to determine whether having a business support base for an alternative development project would have been enough to overcome the institutional hurdles enshrined in the Pinochet Constitution (see Madariaga 2020). This question becomes all the more important in the face of Chile's current events. Ever since Chile's "awakening" in October 2019 and the subsequent political accord that opened the way for a plebiscite on a new constitution, the business community has been extremely skeptical of the process with several voices agitating the fear of economic collapse should the current Pinochet-written constitution be replaced by another sanctioned by a democratically elected Constitutional Convention.

Conversely, in Poland (at a roughly similar distance from resilient and contested neoliberalism) support creation thwarted neoliberal business sectors during the 1990s, but benefitted them at the end of the decade, and opposition blockade was not able to reduce political opposition to neoliberalism but did have a partial effect on labor (especially toward the end of the 1990s). Here, the constitutionalization of neoliberalism, particularly in the case of central bank independence, seems key for fixing neoliberal policy alternatives and preventing opposing political actors from circumventing them. As I will discuss below, these varieties of neoliberalism have had remarkably diverse effects on the state of the underlying democracies, eroding them in different ways.

This general picture allows consideration of cases outside those here analyzed. For example, were the mechanisms of support creation, opposition blockade, and constitutionalized lock-in present or not in other countries such as Mexico, Colombia, or Peru in Latin America, and Bulgaria, Romania, and the other Baltic States in Eastern Europe? If yes, do they successfully explain these countries' neoliberal trajectories and the underlying dynamics of resilience or contestation?

Two additional reflections emerge going forward. The first is linked to the established relationship in the literature between policy regimes and institutions. It is a common understanding in comparative political economy that greater institutionalization is a synonym of greater coordination capacities and, therefore, of nonliberal variants of capitalism (Hall and Soskice 2001, 2001; Katzenstein 1985). However, when the continuity of neoliberalism prevails, this relationship is reversed. Stricter institutionalization makes resilient neoliberal regimes more likely because they impede the representation of alternative views in the arenas of political representation and policymaking, and restrict the policy room of maneuver of elected governments, while shallower institutionalization or no institutionalization at all makes discontinuities more likely (cf. Flores-Macías 2012). What is important therefore is not how institutionalized a political economy is, but the distributive character of those institutions and more precisely how they empower or disempower different groups of actors in society (see Amable 2003; Knight 1992; Pontusson 1995; Thelen 2014).

The second reflection is about the possible relationship between neoliberalism and the rise of populism, as has been increasingly analyzed in the literature. According to the now dominant view, populism is an ideology or discourse that separates the political space in a Manichean way between "the pure people" and "the corrupt elite," assigns "the corrupt elite" all the evils of the people's sufferings, and tries to truly represent "the pure people" by bypassing democratic institutions conceived as essentially serving the elite (Mudde 2004; Mudde and Rovira Kaltwasser 2017; Müller 2016).[1] The ascendance of radical right- and left-wing populist forces, their harsh nationalist rhetoric, and their assault on democratic institutions, is perhaps the most consequential political-economic phenomenon after the shocks and aftershocks of the 2007–2008 crisis.[2] Several authors have been tempted to build bridges between the Great Recession and the rapid rise of populist forces. The connection they usually trace, based on correlation rather than on mechanistic reasoning,

---

1. For different definitions of populism, see Hawkins and Rovira Kaltwasser (2017).
2. For the difference between mainstream and radical right populism, see Mudde (2013).

points from economic crises and demand stagnation to political dissatisfaction and the emergence of populism (see Dumas 2018; Eichengreen 2018).

If we apply this reasoning to this study's findings, we find a provocative if unexpected result: the resilience of neoliberalism appears to have shielded the accompanying democracies from the lure of populist movements. In fact, countries where neoliberalism has survived the longest are those that show the strongest democracies today, as reflected in all indicators of democracy for Chile and Estonia, while on the contrary, the cases of neoliberal discontinuity have been struck from early on by populist forces with varying consequences for the consolidation of their democracies. Thus, we might be tempted to equate Chile's and Estonia's relative success at taming the populists to neoliberalism's effect on constraining democracy: that is, it has safeguarded democracy's procedural dimension (the formal competition between political alternatives) against its normative dimension (its representativeness and responsiveness to the electorate). This resonates not only with the process of democratic hollowing in the advanced world (Crouch 2004; Mair 2013), but also and more importantly, with neoliberalism's secular political project.

In their book *Democracy in Deficit: The Legacy of Lord Keynes*, Buchanan and Wagner (1977) offered a candid if compelling reflection on the reforms necessary to shield democracies from their own perils. They wrote:

> The prudent person acts wisely when he imposes behavioral rules upon himself, rules that may bind his actions over a series of unpredictable future steps. Is it impossible to expect that prudent members of democratic assemblies of governance could do likewise? (J. M. Buchanan and Wagner 1977, 91).

More bluntly, in his *The Constitution of Liberty,* Hayek reasoned that "[t]hose who profess that democracy is all-competent and support all that the majority wants at any given moment are working for its fall" (Hayek 1978, 116–17).

Seen through this light, perhaps neoliberalism's best face presents itself as the savior of democracy and the universal values of cosmopolitanism and freedom, as appears in the case for saving the euro with the extremely damaging consequences this has for sovereign representative democracies (see Šumonja 2018). Does this provide a vindication for the neoliberal project of a limited democracy as the only way of defending democracy from its "excesses"? Is a limited democracy the only alternative to the growing pains of the populist *Zeitgeist*? Is this the best we can hope for the future of democracy?

My answer highlights the fact that economic ills do not directly translate into populism, just as neoliberalism's capacity to shield countries from populism by reducing representation does not directly translate into better democracies. To the contrary, following the findings of this book, I argue that we can find "varieties" of democratic erosion according to how countries reacted to the challenges to democracy that the different trajectories of neoliberal resilience posed.

Varieties of Neoliberal Resilience, Varieties of Democratic Erosion

Contrary to earlier accounts that associated populism with spendthrift governments, particularly in Latin America (Dornbusch and Edwards 1991), there is now agreement that, being an ideology in itself—and an extremely malleable one—populism can be coupled with the most different systems of economic policy. Far from considering populist forces as mere demagogues exploiting pressing social and economic problems, I follow more complex interpretations of this phenomenon that argue that while populism presents a threat to established democratic procedures, it also offers a corrective to many of democracy's current representational ills (Mudde and Rovira Kaltwasser 2013b; Rovira Kaltwasser 2014).

This is consistent with Peter Mair's incisive account of the process of democratic hollowing in the West. Mair (2013) saw two possible alternative scenarios to the crisis of democracy thus understood: the technocratic-*cum*-neoliberal scenario, which reduces even more the representative dimension of democracy while maintaining its competitive component (together with the infrastructure of basic freedoms), and the populist alternative, boosting the representative dimension of democracy at the expense of competition (and basic freedoms).

The findings of this book help establish more focused connections between the varied trajectories of neoliberal resilience and further varieties of democratic erosion that may or may not be related to the emergence of populist forces (Greskovits 2015; Przeworski 2019). Economic strain does not automatically translate into populist challenges, and countries' political institutions—in this case, strongly affected by different trajectories of neoliberal resilience and contestation—process existing challenges to democracy in different ways. A brief review of the more recent developments in Estonia, Poland, Argentina,

TABLE 8.1. Neoliberal Resilience and Democratic Erosion

		Neoliberalism	
		Resilience	Erosion
Democracy	Resilience	Estonia	Argentina
	Erosion	Chile	Poland

Source: Author's elaboration.

and Chile, and how the populist *Zeitgeist* has affected them, provides interesting insights.

Table 8.1 shows a summary of the trajectories of the four countries in terms of the resilience/contestation of neoliberalism, and the resilience/contestation of their democratic institutions, which reflects the myriad possible combinations between economic and political conditions in the aftermath of neoliberal development trajectories.

The two countries showing more resilient neoliberal trajectories, Estonia and Chile, have entered new political cycles that have led them to similar paths of neoliberal resilience, with incipient populist movements in their political systems, although they show different challenges in terms of their highly institutionalized and stable democracies. The new phase in Estonia is closely linked to its entrance to the Eurozone in 2011. In practical terms, Estonian policymaking did not actually change, having functioned for over twenty years with the intention of achieving this long-awaited milestone. Neither did Euro accession substantially alter existing policy debates, although supporters of hard money and small government did not have to work so hard to defend austerity any longer. The period, however, coincides with the erosion of the opposition blockade mechanism that affected ethnic minorities, therefore increasing the franchise on the side of the Russian-speaking minority, and the parallel emergence of a radical populist right alternative.

In 2016, the neoliberal Reform Party was left out of government for the first time since 1999, and the left-leaning Center Party became the head of a new government majority with the moderate Social Democrats and the conservative Res Publica. These parties proposed new policies in fields such as education and health, although they were constrained by EU and EMU rules. A new radical right-wing party, the Conservative People's Party of Estonia (EKRE), rapidly gained salience among the public and joined the government after winning the third place in the 2019 elections. Now, the fact that in a small country with a sizable ethnic minority, constant fears of loss of national identity, overt conflict and even threats of a military clash with Russia, and an economic crisis (2007–20008) eroding twenty years of economic growth such a party has emerged only in the last few years and still without a clear majority, seems to show that Estonian democracy is not under a substantive threat. In fact, the worrying nationalistic, anti-immigration, and homophobic overtones of EKRE have not implied a concomitant challenge to basic rights such as freedom of press and assaults on checks and balances as in other European countries with radical populist parties (see Cianetti 2018). Moreover, political participation and support for democracy in the country remain relatively high by comparative standards.

In Chile, by contrast, the rise of social movements and protest during the 2000s—then the most massive since democratization in 1990—signaled a significant degree of social discontent with the resilience of neoliberalism under the center-left *Concertación* coalition (Donoso and von Bülow 2017; Delamaza, Maillet, and Neira 2017; Rodriguez 2020). At first discontent was channeled institutionally to the right-wing opposition represented by Sebastián Piñera, while nonparty candidates and new party labels trying to better represent this discontent flourished (Luna and Mardones 2010; Donoso and von Bülow 2017). In 2013, socialist Michelle Bachelet achieved the presidency for the second time with a sizable parliamentary majority and a new coalition that included the hitherto sidelined Communist Party on the left, as a way to bring the protesters into the dynamics of institutionalized politics. With this "New Majority" coalition, Bachelet put forward a highly reformist agenda that intended to respond to citizen discontent by substantially changing different aspects of Chile's neoliberalism, including political reform, although it advanced much less than what was otherwise hoped (see Madariaga 2020). However, Bachelet did change the binominal electoral system for a moderately proportional one, which increased the chances of representation of alternative views and gave rise to a number of new political forces.

This political opening led to an explosion of new parties and political alternatives. Most notable was the rise of a new competitive alternative on the left (the Frente Amplio), composed of leaders of social movements (particularly former student representatives), the emergence of a new radical populist right represented by former UDI deputy José Antonio Kast's "Republican Action," and the erosion of the political center with the slump in support for the Christian Democrats.

Kast's movement not only shares the homophobic and xenophobic overtones of its European counterparts, but also, a worrying call to reconsider the place of Augusto Pinochet and his brutal dictatorship in Chilean history and the concomitant appeal to the right to shake off its "complexes." These are unequivocal signs of increasing representation of actors and demands hitherto sidelined from institutionalized politics but at the same time, of rapidly growing polarization and institutional instability in a country with comparatively low levels of economic strain and immigration problems. In fact, rapidly declining political participation and close to nil support for established political parties suggest that Chilean democracy is facing consequential challenges (see Luna and Altman 2011; Castiglioni and Rovira Kaltwasser 2016). The social explosion of late 2019 and the political responses to it presented a crucial crossroad for Chilean politics: to maintain the existing political institutions at the peril of further increasing the representation gap, or to change them altogether, hoping to rebalance the will of the people for greater political expression and socioeconomic inclusion. In between, the growing polarization of Chilean society and the re-emergence of extremist groups of right and left represents a serious threat even to the reformist political path.

The cases with more discontinuous policy trajectories also show different paths toward the erosion of democracy. After 2010, the dominance of radical right-wing populism deepened in Poland with the election of PiS to government in 2015 with an outright majority, the first since the return to democracy in 1989. This occurred at the same time as continued economic growth, rising employment, and stable inflation; in fact, Poland was the only European country to avoid recession during the aftershocks of the 2007–2008 financial crisis. Although PiS maintained its nationalistic and anti-neoliberal rhetoric, in practice it concentrated on using its parliamentary majority to deliver on its social-cultural proposals and unleashing its agenda of political hegemony following in the footsteps of Viktor Orban, the controversial Hungarian prime minister. PiS-led governments reduced civic freedoms (for example, reducing abortion rights) and conducted a crackdown on basic political liberties, making dangerous inroads into reducing press freedom, tampering with the TV and radio censorship bodies, staffing the constitutional court and justice tribunals, and advancing a new wave of lustration. However, PiS-led governments did not at the same time decisively roll back neoliberalism or significantly advance toward an alternative economic development model (see Shields 2015).

Argentina also saw an adversarial type of political discourse rise after the 2001–2002 economic and political collapse. The Kirchner governments successfully gave voice to the "que se vayan todos!" (all of them must go!) popular claim that followed the crisis and gave free rein to the populist "us versus them" discourse and to the polarization of Argentine society. This was particularly true after 2010. Following the first political defeats derived from the farmers' protests of 2008, the rise of inflationary pressures, and a new wave of capital flight, the government of Cristina Fernández increasingly blamed foreign capital (epitomized in judicial struggles against the "fondos buitres"—*vulture funds*),[3] domestic rentiers, and the press for the country's ills, but did not stage a crackdown on basic civic liberties and institutional checks and balances as in Poland. The new conditions brought by the international 2007–2008 financial crisis brought the previous alliances and policy compromises to an end, while ushering in a new period of economic instability.

Growing economic imbalances and citizen discontent with the government led to the victory of a new right-wing formation, Cambiemos, led by business tycoon Mauricio Macri. Macri promised to scale back the state-developmentalist project of the Kirchners and impose once again much-needed neoliberal discipline on the Argentine economy. However, Macri's liberalization of exchange rates and the capital account reinforced inflationary pressures and increased the vulnerability of the Argentine economy. In 2018, Macri had to call the IMF for help once again; it promised over US$50 billion in financial aid—the biggest loan in IMF's history—to stop capital flight in the context of a government not able to deliver on its promises of economic stability. In this scenario, the election in late 2019 of the Peronist party for a new presidential term augurs yet another swing to more developmentalist policies.

The contrast between the Polish and the Argentine stories is crucial for our understanding of the connection between the contestation of neoliberalism, populism, and democratic representation. As we saw above, despite the harsh rhetoric and economic patriotism, Poland's PiS did not in practice roll back neoliberalism nor present a viable alternative to it. In this sense, PiS deepened the script already captured in David Ost's (2005) masterful interpretation of the Polish trajectory: by giving free rein to the representation of nationalist and xenophobic sentiments—in great part fed by the inability of the Polish economy to deliver despite its continued high growth rate—PiS foreclosed the possibility of responding to the socioeconomic anxieties of the people,

---

3. In Argentina, the term "vulture funds" refers to the foreign investors who, amid the 2001 crisis, carried out moral hazard practices by lending funds to the Argentine government in distress at very high interest rates. After the crisis and default, they did not agree on the debt-restructuring plan offered by the government of Argentina—and accepted by the IMF—and sued it in U.S. tribunals hoping to realize the full value of their investments. See Roos (2019).

severely hurting the consolidation of traditional parties and party competition, and with it the consolidation of Polish democracy.

Unlike in Poland, in Argentina the Kirchners channeled discontent and representation back to the socioeconomic cleavage, thereby reducing the chances for the birth of radical right-wing populisms.[4] In fact, the emergence of the new right-wing alternative (Cambiemos) came to refresh and institutionalize programmatic representation in Argentina (Vommaro 2017). The responses of the political system to a new financial crisis are telling: apart from some dissonance on security issues, the extreme crisis situation has not fed right-wing populism, particularly of the more radical sort. In Chile, by contrast, significant openings to populist forces and political polarization have occurred amid a stable economy with low unemployment, gradually rising salaries, and no inflation. On the negative side, the renewal of political competition and representation in Argentina has not implied a concomitant strengthening of democratic institutions when it comes to checks and balances and mechanisms of horizontal accountability. Moreover, the inability of either of the two competing Argentine social blocs (progressive and neoliberal) to assert a hegemonic development project has led to acute dislocations, economic stop-go cycles, and a politics of serial institutional displacement (see Levitsky and Murillo 2013).

In sum, at the turn of the century countries with resilient neoliberalism started to slowly experience openings toward new political alternatives, as economic policy was finally institutionalized in Estonia, and as traditional parties reformed political institutions in an attempt to tame rapidly raising discontent in Chile. So far, these movements have been constrained by the dynamics of institutionalized politics and, therefore, have seen far weaker populist movements than their regional neighbors. However, democracy has not escaped significant challenges, some of which are directly related to the trajectory of suppressed representation, as the case of Chile blatantly attests. The latter case supports the idea that one can uphold the representative dimension of democracy or its "output legitimacy" only for a limited span of time without generating major dislocations and social pressures for democratization from below. Comparatively, the upcoming challenges seem therefore

4. For an interesting analysis of the relationship between market reforms, the alignment or disalignment of traditional political cleavages, and their effect on the continuity of party systems and neoliberalism, see Roberts (2015). For accounts relating the successes in representation of Latin American left-wing populist parties with their strong embeddedness in grassroots social movements, see Anria (2018), Etchemendy (2019).

far greater in this country than in Estonia. By contrast, Poland and Argentina show early appearances of populist forces due to the openness of their political systems, or, what is the same, the inability of their neoliberal elites to reduce democratic representation. The extent to which this led to offering alternatives to neoliberalism depended on the policy emphases posed by the populists. In this sense, the type of populism that emerged as a response to neoliberalism had important consequences for how it affected both existing democracies and the endurance of neoliberalism itself.

Putting Neoliberalism, Democracy, and Populism in Their Place

Peter Mair's anticipation of the populist *Zeitgeist* as a response to the hollowing of democracy resonates well with the trajectory of our two cases where neoliberalism failed to take root, and with the idea that populism can provide both a threat and a corrective to democracy. In these countries, the incapacity of neoliberals to twist democracy in order to perpetuate their project produced democratic responses in the form of higher representation. As mainstream politicians and parties of right and left turned neoliberal, eroding partisan differences, the openness of these democratic regimes generated a response from outside the political establishment: new movements and parties trying to represent those citizens and occupy the spaces abandoned on the right and left. This reinforces the belief that populism represents a complex phenomenon presenting both risks and opportunities for democracy, and this is precisely why it is attractive. As paradoxical as it gets, democracy's virtues—that is, enhancing representation in the context of a shrinking political space, and the emergence of populist solutions increasing representation by repoliticizing cultural or socioeconomic issues—are only overshadowed by the challenges that these very new contestants bring to the survival of that democracy. As Adam Przeworki (2019) insists, the key challenge lies therefore in how democracies allow for the meaningful expression and representation of alternatives, without these undermining the very bases of democratic competition.

Let's go back for a minute to our discussion of failed neoliberalism and populism. The effect of populist governments on the resilience of neoliberalism is not straightforward, and our analysis suggests it lies in how populists repoliticize either culturalist or socioeconomic issues (see Mudde and Rovira Kaltwasser 2013a). While many populists have certainly criticized neoliberalism and offered solutions in the form of higher economic nationalism, reduced economic globalization, and higher state intervention, one group, mainly from the right, has highlighted rather the cultural/nativist arguments, disregarding their economic proposals while in government. Although at a rhetorical level these countries have often entered a "post-neoliberal" era, in practice, populist leaders have relegated economic reform to second place. Even in Hungary, where the radical populist right has allegedly advanced the most, the roll-back-neoliberalism rhetoric has produced only very shallow changes (Bohle and Greskovits 2018; Fabry 2018; but see Appel and Orenstein 2018; Naczyk 2014). On the contrary, some of its flagship economic policies include the replacement of traditional welfare benefits for workfare programs, or the establishment of the so-called slave law eliminating working hour limits.

The case of Argentina is most interesting in this context. While the country is surely no paradise for democrats, inasmuch as the Kirchner governments re-aligned the right-left cleavage and did not erode democratic competition and basic freedoms to the extent that their Eastern European counterparts did, the country has been relatively immune to the siren chants of the radical populist right. In this sense, to the extent that right-wing populism does not respond to its economic plights and concentrates on cultural and nativist issues, giving free rein to "illiberal democracy" it seems to transform itself into "authoritarian neoliberalism" (Bruff 2014, 2016; Tansel 2017; Fabry 2019; for a discussion, see Ryan 2018). In a way, where neoliberalism has been more contested and failed to take root—and therefore, where more open democracies have allowed the entry of new populist contestants to the political game—neoliberals have successfully allied with them, as is evident in places like Hungary (Fabry 2019), Turkey (Tansel 2018), or, more recently, Brazil (Schipani and Leahy 2018; J. Epstein 2019). In other words, capital seems much too happy under populist leaders who despite their incendiary rhetoric, change little of the favorable status quo, or bend some of the rules-based governance practice promoted by neoliberalism only to favor powerful corporations even more. In fact, on the eve of the election in Brazil of the pro-torture, homophobic, and xenophobic candidate, Jair Bolsonaro, who openly defended the mass assassinations of Brazil's military dictatorship, the country's agribusiness elite gave Bolsonaro vociferous support (Betim and Olivera 2018), and even the Deutsche Bank felt no shame in stating that Bolsonaro was the financial market's *Wunschkandidat* (Schindler 2018). Therefore, it is important to note, as we have seen throughout this book and contrary to James Buchanan's candid warnings about democracy's self-inflicted ills, that despite their rhetoric true neoliberals and top businesses have never been that interested in competitive markets or consolidating democracy anyways.

In an early critique of the transition literature, Béla Greskovits (1998) pointed out that the effect of neoliberal reforms on democracy was the emergence of a "low-level equilibrium" characterized by "low-performing, institutionally mixed market economies and incomplete, elitist, and exclusionary democracies with a weak citizenship component" (Greskovits 1998, 184). With hindsight, this assessment was not only correct, but masterfully captured the beginnings of what I have shown in this book is the grim trajectory of democracy under neoliberalism. Would a radical left-wing populism constitute a true alternative to neoliberalism—either of the limited democracy or the authoritarian sort—and bring life again to today's threatened, if discredited, capitalist-democratic regimes? Perhaps the most important lesson that this book can leave is that the only sensible way to respond to the rise of populism is not to further curtail democracy, as rightists and the third-way left have long proclaimed, but rather to reclaim it. The Argentinean case here studied and the history of capitalism seem to suggest, however, that in this respect an excess of voluntarism should not trump a reasoned analysis. Will, alternatively, the logic of capital prevail—only if it is to dig its own grave, as proponents of the end of capitalism would have? Answers should combine economic stability and a strong drive toward developmental policy, with democracy's openness and quest for representation. In this case, democracy's ingrained capacity to produce swings in economic policy and development projects poses (once again!) formidable challenges.

Whether the future will bring a long and slow capitalist decline or a Polanyian movement revitalizing civil society's democratic protection against capitalism's auto-destructive forces, is still debatable. Although most commentators believe the latter is the less likely of the two scenarios given current developments, this is still an open question—and the future is by definition open-ended and based on imaginaries that are developed in present time (see Beckert 2016). Seen from this light, creativity and innovation are capitalist forces that can be used to turn capitalism's inextricable faith upside down. After all, if neoliberalism is more politics than economics, its demise and replacement for a more progressive regime falls into the domain of the possible. Thus, while a *pessimism of the intellect* is a most crucial skill to survive the vagaries of today and to analyze the turbulent ongoing processes of societal change, an *optimism of the will* may after all be democracy's best weapon.

INTERVIEWS

Argentina

1. Political science professor, San Martin University. Interview by the author (Buenos Aires, November 1, 2012).
2. Political science professor, Gino Germani Institute. Interview by the author (Buenos Aires, October 29, 2012).
3. Political science professor, San Martin University. Interview by the author (Buenos Aires, November 6, 2012).
4. Labor union leader (CGT/UOM). Interview by the author (Buenos Aires, November 5, 2012).
5. Advisor to Ministry of Economy (1980s). Interview by the author (Buenos Aires, November 13, 2012).
6. Economic sociology professor, CONICET. Interview by the author (Skype, February 28, 2013).
7. Labor union leader (FAECyS). Interview by the author (Buenos Aires, November 5, 2012).
8. Policymaker Ministry of Economy/Central Bank (1980s/2000s). Interview by the author (Buenos Aires, January 30, 2013).
9. Development economics professor, Di Tella University. Interview by the author (Buenos Aires, November 7, 2012).
10. Policymaker, Ministry of Economy (1980s/2000s). Interview by the author (Buenos Aires, November 15, 2012).
11. Policymaker, Ministry of Economy/Central Bank (2000s). Interview by the author (Buenos Aires, November 20, 2012).
12. Economics journalist at *El Clarín*. Interview by the author (Buenos Aires, November 22, 2012).
13. Juan José Llach, advisor to Ministry of Economy (1991–1994). Interview by Archivo de Historia Oral (AHO), two sessions.
14. José Alfredo Martínez de Hoz, minister of economy (1976–1981). Interview by Archivo de Historia Oral (AHO), three sessions

15. Roque Fernández, minister of economy (1996–1999). Interview by Archivo de Historia Oral (AHO), two sessions.

16. Juan Vital Sourrouille, minister of economy (1985–1989). Interview by Archivo de Historia Oral (AHO), three sessions.

Chile

1. Political science professor, University of Chile. Interview by the author (Santiago, October 16, 2012).

2. Policymaker, Central Bank (1990s). Interview by the author (Santiago, October 18, 2012).

3. Policymaker, Central Bank (1990s). Interview by the author (Santiago, October 24, 2012).

4. Policymaker, Ministry of Work (1990s–2000s). Interview by the author (Santiago January 17, 2013).

5. Development economics professor, University of Chile. Interview by the author (Santiago January 25, 2013)

6. Policymaker, Ministry of Economy (1990s). Interview by the author (Santiago, January 11, 2013).

7. Director local think tank. Interview by the author (Santiago, January 7, 2013).

8. Policymaker, Central Bank (2000s). Interview by the author (Santiago, November 27, 2012).

9. Policymaker, Ministry of Economy/Member of Parliament (1990s/2000s). Interview by the author (Santiago, January 28, 2013).

10. President, Business Association (2000s) / Board director. Interview by the author (Santiago, October 26, 2012).

11. CEO Business Association (2000s)/Board director. Interview by the author (Santiago, January 8, 2013).

12. Policymaker, Ministry of Economy/Central Bank (1990s). Interview by the author (Santiago, June 12, 2014).

13. Policymaker, Ministry of Economy/Ministry of Finance (1980s). Interview by the author (Santiago, June 13, 2014).

Estonia

1. Policymaker, Central Bank (2000s). Interview by the author (Tallinn, November 11, 2013).

2. Development economics professor, Tallinn Technical University. Interview by the author (Tallinn, November 13, 2013).

3. Political science professor, Tallin University. Interview by the author (Tallinn, November 13, 2013).

4. Policymaker, Ministry of Economy (1990s)/Development Fund. Interview by the author (Tallinn, November 14, 2013).

5. Political science professor, University of Tartu. Interview by the author (Tartu, December 3, 2013).

6. Policymaker, Ministry of Trade (1990s). Interview by the author (Tartu, December 3, 2013).

7. Political science professor, University of Tallinn. Interview by the author (Tallinn, December 6, 2013).

8. Advisor to prime minister (1990s/2000s). Interview by the author (Tallinn, December 9, 2013).

9. Policymaker, Central Bank (2000s). Interview by the author (Tallinn, December 10, 2013).

10. Advisor to minister of economy (1990s). Interview by the author (Tallinn, December 11, 2013).

11. Policymaker, Development Fund (2000s). Personal communication (January 18, 2014).

Poland

1. Researcher at local think tank. Interview by the author (Warsaw, October 7, 2013).

2. Policymaker, Ministry of Work and Social Affairs (1990s/2000s). Interview by the author (Warsaw, October 9, 2013, and January 9, 2014).

3. Policymaker, Ministry of Economy (1990s/2000s). Interview by the author (Cracow, October 24, 2013).

4. Advisor to prime minister (1990s). Interview by the author (Warsaw, October 30, 2013).

5. Policymaker, Ministry of Finance (1990s). Interview by the author (Warsaw, October 30, 2013).

6. Policymaker, Ministry of Finance (1990s)/Member of Parliament (1990s/2000s). Interview by the author (Warsaw, January 1, 2014).

7. Political science professor, Polish Academy of Sciences. Interview by the author (Warsaw, January 8, 2014).

8. Policymaker, Central Bank (2010s). Interview by the author (Warsaw, January 9, 2014).

9. Professor of economics and finance, Warsaw School of Economics. Interview by the author (Warsaw, January 13, 2014).

10. Policymaker, Ministry of Economy (1990s). Interview by the author (Warsaw, January 15. 2014).

BIBLIOGRAPHY

Acuña, Carlos H. 1995. "Algunas notas sobre los juegos, las gallinas y la lógica política de los pactos constitucionales (reflexiones a partir del pacto constitucional en la Argentina)." In *La nueva matriz poldítica argentina*. Edited by Carlos H. Acuña, 115–52. Buenos Aires: Nueva Visión.

———. 1996. "Las contradicciones de la burguesía en el centro de la lucha entre el autoritarismo y la democracia (1955–1983)." *Realidad Económica*, no. 138: 18–48.

Acuña, Carlos H., Sebastian Galiani, and Mariano Tommasi. 2007. "Understanding Reform: The Case of Argentina." In *Understanding Market Reforms in Latin America: Similar Reforms, Diverse Constituencies, Varied Results*. Edited by José María Fanelli, 31–72. Houndmills, UK: Palgrave Macmillan.

Adam, Frane, Primož Kristan, and Matevž Tomšič. 2009. "Varieties of Capitalism in Eastern Europe (with Special Emphasis on Estonia and Slovenia)." *Communist and Post-Communist Studies* 42 (1): 65–81.

Adolph, Christopher. 2013. *Bankers, Bureaucrats, and Central Bank Politics: The Myth of Neutrality*. New York: Cambridge University Press.

Agosín, Manuel. 2001. "Reformas comerciales, exportaciones y crecimiento." In *Reformas, crecimiento y políticas sociales en Chile desde 1973*. Edited by Ricardo Ffrench-Davis and Barbara Stallings, 99–131. Santiago, Chile: LOM/CEPAL.

Agosín, Manuel, Cristian Larraín, and Nicolás Grau. 2009. "Industrial Policy in Chile." Working Paper 294. Santiago de Chile: Department of Economics, University of Chile.

Ahumada, José Miguel. 2019. *The Political Economy of Peripheral Growth: Chile in the Global Economy*. Houndmills. UK: Palgrave Macmillan.

Alanen, Ilkka. 1999. "Agricultural Policy and the Struggle over the Destiny of Collective Farms in Estonia." *Sociologia Ruralis* 39 (3): 431–58.

Alesina, Alberto, Ricardo Hausmann, Rudolf Hommes, and Ernesto Stein. 2001. "Budget Institutions and Fiscal Performance in Latin America." IADB Working Paper Series 394. Washington, DC: Inter-American Development Bank.

Alesina, Alberto, and Roberto Perotti. 1999. "Budget Deficits and Budget Institutions." In *Fiscal Institutions and Fiscal Performance*. Edited by James Poterba and Jürgen von Hagen, 13–36. Chicago: University of Chicago Press and NBER.

Alesina, Alberto, and Lawrence H. Summers. 1993. "Central Bank Independence and Macroeconomic Performance: Some Comparative Evidence." *Journal of Money, Credit and Banking* 25 (2): 151–62.

Allsopp, Christopher, and David Vines. 2015. "Monetary and Fiscal Policy in the Great Moderation and the Great Recession." *Oxford Review of Economic Policy* 31 (2): 134–67. doi.org
/10.1093/oxrep/grv022.

Alt, James E., Jeffry A. Frieden, Michael J. Gilligan, Dani Rodrik, and Ronald Rogowski. 1996.
"The Political Economy of International Trade Enduring Puzzles and an Agenda for Inquiry."
Comparative Political Studies 29 (6): 689–717.

Amable, Bruno. 2003. *The Diversity of Modern Capitalism.* New York: Oxford University Press.

———. 2011. "Morals and Politics in the Ideology of Neo-Liberalism." *Socio-Economic Review*
9 (1): 3–30. doi.org/10.1093/ser/mwq015.

———. 2017. *Structural Crisis and Institutional Change in Modern Capitalism: French Capitalism
in Transition.* Oxford: Oxford University Press.

Amable, Bruno, and Stefano Palombarini. 2009. "A Neorealist Approach to Institutional Change
and the Diversity of Capitalism." *Socio-Economic Review* 7 (1): 123–43. doi.org/10.1093/ser
/mwn018.

Amsden, Alice H. 1992. *Asia's Next Giant: South Korea and Late Industrialization.* Rev. ed. New
York: Oxford University Press.

———. 2001. *The Rise of "The Rest": Challenges to the West from Late-Industrializing Economies.*
New York: Oxford University Press.

Amsden, Alice H., and Takashi Hikino. 2000. "The Bark Is Worse than the Bite: New WTO Law
and Late Industrialization." *The ANNALS of the American Academy of Political and Social
Science* 570 (1): 104–14.

Andersen, Erik André. 1997. "The Legal Status of Russians in Estonian Privatisation Legislation
1989–1995." *Europe-Asia Studies* 49 (2): 303–16.

Angell, Alan, and Benny Pollack. 1990. "The Chilean Elections of 1989 and the Politics of the
Transition to Democracy." *Bulletin of Latin American Research* 9 (1): 1–23.

Aninat, Cristóbal, John Londregan, Patricio Navia, and Joaquín Vial. 2008. "Political Institutions,
Policymaking Processes, and Policy Outcomes in Chile." In *Policymaking in Latin America
How Politics Shapes Policies.* Edited by Ernesto Stein and Mariano Tommasi, 155–98. Wash-
ington, DC: Inter-American Development Bank (IADB).

Anria, Santiago. 2018. *When Movements Become Parties: The Bolivian MAS in Comparative Perspective.* New York: Cambridge University Press.

Appel, Hilary, and Mitchell A. Orenstein. 2016. "Why Did Neoliberalism Triumph and Endure
in the Post-Communist World?" *Comparative Politics* 48 (3): 313–31.

———. 2018. *From Triumph to Crisis: Neoliberal Economic Reform in Postcommunist Countries.*
Cambridge: Cambridge University Press.

Ardito Barletta, Nicolás, Mario I. Bléjer, and Luis Landau. 1984. *Economic Liberalization and
Stabilization Policies in Argentina, Chile, and Uruguay: Applications of the Monetary Approach
to the Balance of Payments.* Washington, DC: World Bank.

Arellano, José Pablo. 1983. "De la liberalización a la intervención. El mercado de capitales en
Chile: 1974–83." Colección Estudios CIEPLAN 11. Santiago de Chile.

Armingeon, Klaus, Virginia Wenger, Fiona Wiedemeier, Christian Isler, Claudia Knöpfel, David
Weistanner, and Sarah Engler. 2018. "Comparative Political Data Set 1960–2016." Institute of
Political Science, University of Berne.

Arriagada Herrera, Genaro, and Carol Graham. 1995. "Chile: Sustaining Adjustment during

Democratic Transition." In *Voting for Reform: Democracy, Liberalization, and Economic Adjustment*. Edited by Stephan Haggard and Steven B. Webb, 242–88. New York: Oxford University Press/World Bank.

Åslund, Anders. 1994. "The Case for Radical Reform." *Journal of Democracy* 5 (4): 63–74.

Auty, Richard M. 1994. "Industrial Policy Reform in Six Large Newly Industrializing Countries: The Resource Curse Thesis." *World Development* 22 (1): 11–26.

Azpiazu, Daniel, Eduardo Basualdo, and Miguel Khavisse. 1986. *El nuevo poder económico en la Argentina de los años 80*. Buenos Aires: Siglo XXI.

Baccaro, Lucio, and Chris Howell. 2017. *Trajectories of Neoliberal Transformation: European Industrial Relations Since the 1970s*. Cambridge and New York: Cambridge University Press.

Baer, Werner. 1972. "Import Substitution and Industrialization in Latin America: Experiences and Interpretations." *Latin American Research Review* 7 (1): 95–122.

Baker, Andy. 2009. *The Market and the Masses in Latin America: Policy Reform and Consumption in Liberalizing Economies*. New York: Cambridge University Press.

Balassa, Bela A. 1987. "Public Enterprise in Developing Countries: Issues of Privatization." Discussion paper. Development Research Department 292. Washington, DC: World Bank.

Balcerowicz, Leszek. 1994. "Poland." In *The Political Economy of Policy Reform*. Edited by John Williamson, 153–77. Washington, DC: Institute for International Economics.

———. 1995. *Socialism, Capitalism, Transformation*. Budapest: Central European University Press.

Baldez, Lisa, and John M. Carey. 2001. "Budget Procedure and Fiscal Restraint in Posttransition Chile." In *Presidents, Parliaments, and Policy*. Edited by Stephan Haggard and Matthew D. McCubbins, 105–47. New York: Cambridge University Press.

Baltic Business News. 2009a. "Estonian Development Fund—Great Boast, Small Roast," March 30, 2009.

———. 2009b. "Estonia Should Strain for Euro," August 18, 2009.

Baltic News Service. 1995a. "Estonia's Monetary System Continues to Give Rise to Polemic," March 8, 1995.

———. 1995b. "Industrial, Banking Leaders Voice Hope That Reform Will Continue in Estonia," June 3, 1995.

———. 1995c. "Coalition Talks to Be Difficult in Estonia," July 3, 1995.

———. 1995d. "PM Once Again Calls Estonia's Monetary Policy Primitive," July 20, 1995.

———. 1995e. "Estonia's Parties Form New Coalition," October 23, 1995.

———. 1995f. "Bank of Estonia President: Kroon's Exchange Rate Might Hold for 10 Years," December 1, 1995.

———. 1996a. "Rural Parties in Estonia's Ruling Coalition Renew Calls for Farm Tariffs," June 5, 1996.

———. 1996b. "Estonian Cabinet Avoids Supporting Selected Branches," June 19, 1996.

———. 1996c. "Estonian Industry Association to Sign Cooperation Agreement with Rural Parties," July 23, 1996.

———. 1996d. "Head of Estonian Employers' Association Says Agreement with Farm Parties Non-Political," December 8, 1996.

———. 1997a. "Estonia's Central Bank Council Head Accuses Rural Union of Retreating from Strict Monetary Policy," April 24, 1997.

Baltic News Service. 1997b. "The Economist Warns Baltics of Currency Crisis," October 20, 1997.

———. 1998a. "Ruling Coalition's Farm Party Signs Accord with Centrists," January 22, 1998.

———. 1998b. "Estonian Kroon Not under Threat of Devaluation—Central Banker," December 15, 1998.

———. 1999. "Twelve Parties Vying for Seats in Estonian Parliament," June 3, 1999.

———. 2005a. "Estonia's New Finance Minister Wants Referendum on Euro," April 13, 2005.

———. 2005b. "Bank of Estonia Governor: Popular Vote on Adoption of Euro Has Already Taken Place," April 28, 2005.

———. 2005c. "Estonian People's Union against Reserving Surplus Revenue," December 29, 2005.

Ban, Cornel. 2016. *Ruling Ideas: How Global Neoliberalism Goes Local.* New York: Oxford University Press.

Bank of Estonia. 1999. "Monetary System and Economic Developments in Estonia." In Seminar on the Currency Boards in the Context of Accession to the EU, Brussels, November 25, 1999.

Barrett, Patrick S. 1999. "The Limits of Democracy: Socio-Political Compromise and Regime Change in Post-Pinochet Chile." *Studies in Comparative International Development* 34 (3): 3–36.

Barro, Robert J., and David G. Gordon. 1983. "Rules, Discretion and Reputation in a Model of Monetary Policy." *Journal of Monetary Economics* 12 (1): 101–21. doi.org/10.1016/0304 -3932(83)90051-X.

Baruj, Gustavo, Bernardo Kosacoff, and Adrián Ramos. 2009. "Las políticas de promoción de la competitividad en la Argentina. Principales instituciones e instrumentos de apoyo y mecanismos de articulación público-privada." Project documents 38. Buenos Aires: CEPAL.

Basualdo, Eduardo. 2006. *Estudios de Historia Económica Argentina.* Buenos Aires: Siglo XXI.

Bearce, David H. 2003. "Societal Preferences, Partisan Agents, and Monetary Policy Outcomes." *International Organization* 57 (2): 373–410.

Beck, Nathaniel, and Jonathan N. Katz. 1995. "What to Do (and Not to Do) with Time-Series Cross-Section Data." *American Political Science Review* 89 (3): 634–47.

———. 1996. "Nuisance vs. Substance: Specifying and Estimating Time-Series-Cross-Section Models." *Political Analysis* 6: 1–36.

Becker, Joachim, and Johannes Jäger. 2010. "Development Trajectories in the Crisis in Europe." *Debatte: Journal of Contemporary Central and Eastern Europe* 18 (1): 5.

Beckert, Jens. 2016. *Imagined Futures: Fictional Expectations and Capitalist Dynamics,* Cambridge, MA: Harvard University Press.

Beissinger, Mark R., and Gwendolyn Sasse. 2014. "An End to 'Patience'? The Great Recession and Economic Protest in Eastern Europe." In *Mass Politics in Tough Times: Opinions, Votes, and Protest in the Great Recession.* Edited by Nancy Bermeo and Larry M. Bartels, 334–69. Oxford and New York: Oxford University Press.

Bekerman, Marta, and Federico Dulcich. 2013. "The International Trade Position of Argentina. Towards a Process of Export Diversification?" *CEPAL Review,* no. 110 (August): 151–74.

Beltrán, Gastón. 2006. "Acción empresaria e ideología. La génesis de las reformas estructurales." In *Los años de Alfonsín: el poder de la democracia o la democracia del poder?* Edited by Alfredo R. Pucciarelli, 199–244. Buenos Aires: Siglo XXI.

————. 2011. "Las paradojas de la acción empresaria. Las asociaciones del empresariado argentino y la persistencia de las reformas estructurales." In *Los años de Menem. La construcción del orden neoliberal*. Edited by Alfredo R. Pucciarelli, 221–62. Buenos Aires: Siglo XXI.

————. 2014. "El empresariado argentino frente a la crisis." In *Los años de la Alianza: la crisis del orden neoliberal*. Edited by Alfredo Pucciarelli and Ana Castellani, 295–344. Buenos Aires: Siglo XXI Editores.

Benoit, Kenneth, and Jacqueline Hayden. 2004. "Institutional Change and Persistence: The Evolution of Poland's Electoral System, 1989–2001." *The Journal of Politics* 66 (2): 396–427. doi.org/10.1111/j.1468-2508.2004.00157.x.

Berdiev, Aziz N., Yoonbai Kim, and Chun Ping Chang. 2012. "The Political Economy of Exchange Rate Regimes in Developed and Developing Countries." *European Journal of Political Economy* 28 (1): 38–53.

Berend, Ivan. 1996. *Central and Eastern Europe, 1944–1993: Detour from the Periphery to the Periphery*. New York: Cambridge University Press.

Berg, Andrew, and Elliot Berg. 1997. "Methods of Privatization." *Journal of International Affairs* 50 (2): 357–90.

Bermeo, Nancy. 1990. "Rethinking Regime Change." *Comparative Politics* 22 (3): 359–77.

Bernhard, William, J. Lawrence Broz, and William Roberts Clark. 2002. "The Political Economy of Monetary Institutions." *International Organization* 56 (4): 693–723. doi.org/10.1162/0020 81802760403748.

Betim, Felipe, and Regiane Olivera. 2018. "A euforia de investidores que normalizam o risco do extremista Bolsonaro." *El País*, October 3, 2018. https://brasil.elpais.com/brasil/2018/10/02 /politica/1538432558_436000.html.

Bhagwati, Jagdish N., and T. N. Srinivasan. 1978. "Trade Policy and Development." In *International Economic Policy: Theory and Evidence*. Edited by Rudiger Dornbusch and Jacob A. Frenkel, 1–38. Baltimore, MD: Johns Hopkins University Press. https://books.google.com/books /about/International_economic_policy.html?id=3NS6AAAAIAAJ.

Bianchi, Andrés. 2008. "La Autonomía Del Banco Central de Chile: Origen y Legitimación." Central Bank of Chile Economic Policy Papers No. 26. Santiago.

Biebricher, Thomas. 2015. "Neoliberalism and Democracy." *Constellations* 22 (2): 255–66. doi .org/10.1111/1467-8675.12157.

Biglaiser, Glen. 1999. "Military Regimes, Neoliberal Restructuring, and Economic Development: Reassessing the Chilean Case." *Studies in Comparative International Development* 34 (1): 3–26.

Błaszczyk, Barbara. 1999. "The Changing Role of the State and Privatization Policies in Poland." In *Spontaner oder gestalteter Prozeß?: Die Rolle des Staates in der Wirtschaftstransformation osteuropäischer Länder*. Edited by Hans-Hermann Höhmann, 198–220. Baden-Baden: Nomos.

Blatter, Joachim, and Markus Haverland. 2012. *Designing Case Studies. Explanatory Approaches in Small-N Research*. Houndmills, UK: Palgrave Macmillan.

Blazyca, George, and Ryszard Rapacki. 1996. "Continuity and Change in Polish Economic Policy: The Impact of the 1993 Election." *Europe-Asia Studies* 48 (1): 85–100.

Bléjer, Mario I., and Fabrizio. Coricelli. 1995. *The Making of Economic Reform in Eastern Europe: Conversations with Leading Reformers in Poland, Hungary, and the Czech Republic*. Aldershot, UK: Edward Elgar.

Block, Fred. 1984. "The Ruling Class Does Not Rule: Notes on the Marxist Theory of the State."

The Political Economy: Readings in the Politics and Economics of American Public Policy. Edited by Thomas Ferguson and Joel Rogers, 32–46. Armonk, NY: Sharpe, 1984.

Blom, Raimo, Harri Melin, and Jouko Nikula. 1996. "The Green Banana of the Baltic States—Obstacles to Capitalist Development." In *Between Plan and Market: Social Change in the Baltic States and Russia*. Edited by Raimo Blom, Harri Melin, and Jouko Nikula, 7–25. Berlin: Walter De Gruyter.

Blyth, Mark. 2002. *Great Transformations: Economic Ideas and Institutional Change in the Twentieth Century*. Cambridge: Cambridge University Press.

———. 2013. *Austerity: The History of a Dangerous Idea*. Oxford and New York: Oxford University Press.

Boas, Taylor C., and Jordan Gans-Morse. 2009. "Neoliberalism: From New Liberal Philosophy to Anti-Liberal Slogan." *Studies in Comparative International Development* 44 (2): 137–61.

Bodea, Cristina. 2010. "Exchange Rate Regimes and Independent Central Banks: A Correlated Choice of Imperfectly Credible Institutions." *International Organization* 64 (3): 411–42.

———. 2014. "Fixed Exchange Rates, Independent Central Banks and Price Stability in Postcommunist Countries: Conservatism and Credibility." *Economics and Politics* 26 (2): 185–211. doi.org/10.1111/ecpo.12030.

Bodea, Cristina, and Raymond Hicks. 2015. "Price Stability and Central Bank Independence: Discipline, Credibility, and Democratic Institutions." *International Organization* 69 (1): 35–61. doi.org/10.1017/S0020818314000277.

Bodea, Cristina, and Masaaki Higashijima. 2017. "Central Bank Independence and Fiscal Policy: Can the Central Bank Restrain Deficit Spending?" *British Journal of Political Science* 47 (1): 47–70. doi:10.1017/S0007123415000058.

Bogliaccini, Juan A. 2012. "Small Latecomers into the Global Market. Power Conflict and Institutional Change in Chile and Uruguay." PhD dissertation, Chapel Hill: University of North Carolina at Chapel Hill.

Bohle, Dorothee, and Béla Greskovits. 2007. "Neoliberalism, Embedded Neoliberalism and Neocorporatism: Towards Transnational Capitalism in Central-Eastern Europe." *West European Politics* 30 (3): 443–66.

———. 2009. "Poverty, Inequality, and Democracy. East-Central Europe's Quandary." *Journal of Democracy* 20 (4): 50–63.

———. 2012. *Capitalist Diversity on Europe's Periphery*. Ithaca, NY: Cornell University Press.

———. 2018. "Politicising Embedded Neoliberalism: Continuity and Change in Hungary's Development Model." *West European Politics* 42 (5): 1069–93. doi.org/10.1080/01402382 .2018.1511958.

Boix, Carles. 2000. "Partisan Governments, the International Economy, and Macroeconomic Policies in Advanced Nations, 1960–93." *World Politics* 53 (1): 38–73.

Boltanski, Luc, and Eve Chiapello. 2005. *The New Spirit of Capitalism*. London: Verso.

Bonamo, Mark J. 1997. "Poland's Privatization Process: A View from the Inside." *Journal of International Affairs* 50 (2): 573–80.

Bönker, Frank. 2001. "Initiating and Consolidating Economic Reform: A Comparative Analysis of Fiscal Reform in Hungary, Poland and the Czech Republic, 1989–99." In *Successful Transitions: Political Factors of Socio-Economic Progress in Postsocialist Countries*. Edited by Jürgen Beyer, Jan Wielgohs, and Helmut Wiesenthal, 120–38. Baden-Baden: Nomos Verlag.

Bonvecchi, Alejandro. 2002. "Estrategia de supervivencia y tácticas de disuasión. Los procesos políticos de la política económica después de las reformas estructurales." In *El derrumbe politico en el ocaso de la convertibilidad.* Edited by Marcos Novaro, 107–93. Buenos Aires: Norma.

Boyer, Russell S. 2011. "Johnson's Conversion from Keynesianism at Chicago." In *Perspectives on Keynesian Economics.* Edited by Arie Arnon, Jimmy Weinblatt, and Warren Young, 135–67. New York: Springer. https://link.springer.com/chapter/10.1007/978-3-642-14409-7_7.

Boylan, Delia M. 1998. "Preemptive Strike: Central Bank Reform in Chile's Transition from Authoritarian Rule." *Comparative Politics* 30 (4): 443–62.

Bradford Jr., Colin I. 1990. "Policy Interventions and Markets: Development Strategy Typologies and Policy Options." In *Manufacturing Miracles. Paths of Industrialization in Latin America and East Asia.* Edited by Gary Gereffi and Donald L. Wyman, 32–54. Princeton, NJ: Princeton University Press.

Bratkowski, Andrzej, and Jacek Rostowski. 2004. "Why Unilateral Euroization Makes Sense for (Some) Applicant Countries." In *Beyond Transition: Development Perspectives and Dilemmas.* Edited by Marek Dabrowski, Jaroslaw Neneman, and Ben Slay, 75–90. Aldershot, UK: Ashgate.

Bresser-Pereira, Luiz Carlos. 2006. "Foreword." In *Monetary Integration and Dollarization: No Panacea.* Edited by Matias Vernengo, xiii–xix. Cheltenham, UK: Edward Elgar.

———. 2011. "From Old to New Developmentalism in Latin America." In *The Oxford Handbook of Latin American Economics.* Edited by José Antonio Ocampo and Jaime Ros, 108–28. Oxford Handbooks. Oxford and New York: Oxford University Press.

Bresser-Pereira, Luiz Carlos, José María Maravall, and Adam Przeworski. 1993. *Economic Reforms in New Democracies: A Social-Democratic Approach.* Cambridge: Cambridge University Press.

Bresser-Pereira, Luiz Carlos, José Luís Oreiro, and Nelson Marconi. 2014. *Developmental Macroeconomics: New Developmentalism as a Growth Strategy.* London and New York: Routledge.

Bresser-Pereira, Luiz Carlos, and Fernando Rugitsky. 2018. "Industrial Policy and Exchange Rate Scepticism." *Cambridge Journal of Economics* 42 (3): 617–32. doi.org/10.1093/cje/bex004.

Bril-Mascarenhas, Tomás. forthcoming. "Modelos de Intervención del Estado en el financiamiento de la inversión vía política industrial: neo-desarrollismo en Brasil, neoliberalismo en Chile y neo-estatismo en Argentina." In *Balance del Ciclo de los Gobiernos de Izquierda en América Latina.* Edited by Jorge Lanzaro. Buenos Aires: Planeta.

Bril-Mascarenhas, Tomás, and Aldo Madariaga. 2019. "Business Power and the Minimal State: The Defeat of Industrial Policy in Chile." *The Journal of Development Studies* 55 (6): 1047–66. doi.org/10.1080/00220388.2017.1417587.

Bril-Mascarenhas, Tomás, and Antoine Maillet. 2019. "How to Build and Wield Business Power: The Political Economy of Pension Regulation in Chile, 1990–2018." *Latin American Politics and Society* 61 (1): 1–25. doi.org/10.1017/lap.2018.61.

Brown, Wendy. 2015. *Undoing the Demos: Neoliberalism's Stealth Revolution.* New York: Zone Books.

Broz, Lawrence, and Jeffry A. Frieden. 2006. "The Political Economy of Exchange Rates." In *The Oxford Handbook of Political Economy.* Edited by Barry R. Weingast and Donald A. Wittman, 587–98. New York: Oxford University Press.

Bruff, Ian. 2014. "The Rise of Authoritarian Neoliberalism." *Rethinking Marxism* 26 (1): 113–29.

————. 2016. "Neoliberalism and Authoritarianism." In *The Handbook of Neoliberalism*. Edited by Simon Springer, Kean Birch, and Julie MacLeavy, 107–17. London and New York: Routledge. https://www.research.manchester.ac.uk/portal/en/publications/neoliberalism-and-authoritarianism(71d67d6f-7cf6-4b32-aa2a-49cd830489af).html.

Bruszt, László, and Béla Greskovits. 2009. "Transnationalization, Social Integration, and Capitalist Diversity in the East and the South." *Studies in Comparative International Development* 44 (4): 411–34.

Bruszt, László, and Gerald A. McDermott. 2009. "Transnational Integration Regimes as Development Programmes." In *The Transnationalization of Economies. States, and Civil Societies*, Edited by László Bruszt and Ronald Holzhacker, 23–59. New York: Springer.

Bubula, Andrea, and Inci Ötker. 2002. "The Evolution of Exchange Rate Regimes Since 1990; Evidence from De Facto Policies." IMF Working Paper 02/155. Washington, DC: International Monetary Fund. https://ideas.repec.org/p/imf/imfwpa/02-155.html.

Buchanan, James, and Gordon Tullock. 1967. *The Calculus of Consent*. Ann Arbor: University of Michigan Press.

Buchanan, James, and Richard Edward Wagner. 1977. *Democracy in Deficit: The Political Legacy of Lord Keynes*. San Diego, CA: Academic Press.

Budnevich, Carlos. 2003. "Countercyclical Fiscal Policy: A Review of the Literature, Empirical Evidence and Some Policy Proposals." In *From Capital Surges to Drought*. Edited by Ricardo Ffrench-Davis and Stephany Griffith-Jones, 269–91. Studies in Development Economics and Policy. Houndmills. UK: Palgrave Macmillan. doi.org/10.1057/9781403990099_14.

Bugaj, Ryszard. 2014. Bugaj: Ni pies, ni wydra Interview by Jan Fusiecki and Bogumil Kolmasiak. Krytyka Polityczna. http://www.krytykapolityczna.pl/artykuly/opinie/20141005/bugaj-ni-pies-ni-wydra.

Bull, Benedicte. 2008. "Policy Networks and Business Participation in Free Trade Negotiations in Chile." *Journal of Latin American Studies* 40 (2): 195–224.

Burawoy, Michael. 1982. *Manufacturing Consent: Changes in the Labor Process Under Monopoly Capitalism*. Chicago and London: University of Chicago Press.

Bustillo, Inés, and Helvia Velloso. 2014. "De bonos Brady a bonos globales: el acceso de América Latina y el Caribe a los mercados internacionales desde la década de 1980." In *La crisis latinoamericana de la deuda desde la perspectiva histórica*. Edited by José Antonio Ocampo, Barbara Stallings, Inés Bustillo, Helvia Velloso, and Roberto Frenkel, 83–120. Santiago de Chile: Comisión Económica para América Latina y el Caribe (CEPAL)—Naciones Unidas.

Cahill, Damien. 2014. *The End of Laissez-Faire?: On the Durability of Embedded Neoliberalism*. Cheltehham, UK, and Northampton, MA: Edward Elgar Publishing.

Cahill, Damien, and Martijn Konings. 2017. *Neoliberalism*. Hoboken, NJ: John Wiley and Sons.

Campbell, John L., and Ove Kaj Pedersen. 2001. *The Rise of Neoliberalism and Institutional Analysis*. Princeton NJ: Princeton University Press.

Campello, Daniela. 2015. *The Politics of Market Discipline in Latin America*. New York: Cambridge University Press.

Campero, Guillermo. 1984. *Los gremios empresariales en el período 1970–1983: comportamiento sociopolítico y orientaciones ideológicas*. Santiago de Chile: Instituto Latinoamericano de Estudios Transnacionales.

————. 1993. "Los empresarios chilenos en el régimen militar y el post-plebiscito." In *El difícil camino hacia la democracia en Chile, 1982–1990*. Edited by Paul W. Drake and Ivan Jakšić, 243–304. Santiago de Chile: FLACSO.

Camyar, Isa. 2014. "Political Parties, Supply-Side Strategies, and Firms: The Political Micro-Economy of Partisan Politics." *The Journal of Politics* 76 (3): 725–39.

Canelo, Paula. 2004. "La política contra la economía: los elencos militares frente al plan económico de Martínez de Hoz durante el Proceso de Reorganización Nacional (1976–1981)." In *Empresarios, tecnócratas y militares: la trama corporativa de la última dictadura*. Edited by Alfredo R. Pucciarelli, 219–312. Buenos Aires: Siglo XXI.

Canitrot, Adolfo. 1980. "Discipline as the Central Objective of Economic Policy: An Essay on the Economic Programme of the Argentine Government since 1976." *World Development* 8 (11): 923–28.

Cardoso, Fernando Henrique, and Enzo Faletto. 1979. *Dependency and Development in Latin America*. Berkeley: University of California Press.

Carey, John M. 2018. "Electoral System Design in New Democracies." In *The Oxford Handbook of Electoral Systems*. Edited by Erik S. Herron, Robert J. Pekkanen, and Matthew Soberg Shugart. 85–111. New York: Oxford University Press. http://www.oxfordhandbooks.com/view/10.1093/oxfordhb/9780190258658.001.0001/oxfordhb-9780190258658-e-6.

Carroll, William K., and Jean Philippe Sapinski. 2016. "Neoliberalism and the Transnational Capitalist Class." In *The Handbook of Neoliberalism*. Edited by Kean Birch, Julie MacLeavy, and Simon Springer, 25–35. London: Routledge.

Casaburi, Gabriel. 1998. "Políticas comerciales e industriales de la Argentina desde la década de 1960." Santiago de Chile: Economic Commision for Latin America and the Caribbean (ECLAC)—United Nations.

Castellani, Ana. 2004. "Gestión económica liberal-corporativa y transformaciones en el interiod de los grandes agentes económicos de la Argentina durante la última década militar." In *Empresarios, tecnócratas y militares: la trama corporativa de la última dictadura*. Edited by Alfredo R. Pucciarelli, 173–218. Buenos Aires: Siglo XXI.

————. 2012. "Privileged Accumulation Spaces and Restrictions on Development of State-Business Relations in Argentina (1966–1989)." *American Journal of Economics and Sociology* 72 (1): 90–121.

Castellani, Ana, and Alejandro Gaggero. 2011. "Estado y grupos económicos en la Argentina de los noventa." In *Los años de Menem. La construcción del orden neoliberal*. Edited by Alfredo R. Pucciarelli, 263–92. Buenos Aires: Siglo XXI.

————. 2017. "La relación entre el estado y la élite económica." In *Los años del kirchnerismo: La disputa hegemónica tras la crisis del orden neoliberal*. Edited by Alfredo Pucciarelli and Ana Castellani, 175–208. Buenos Aires: Siglo XXI Editores.

Castellani, Ana, and Martín Schorr. 2004. "Argentina: convertibilidad, crisis de acumulación y disputas en el interior del bloque de poder económico." *Cuadernos del CENDES* 57: 55–81.

Castiglioni, Rossana, and Cristóbal Rovira Kaltwasser. 2016. "Challenges to Political Representation in Contemporary Chile." *Journal of Politics in Latin America* 8 (3): 3–24.

Cavarozzi, Marcelo. 1986. "Political Cycles in Argentina since 1955." In *Transitions from Authoritarian Rule: Latin America*. Edited by Guillermo O'Donnell, Philippe C. Schmitter, and Laurence Whitehead, 19–48. Baltimore, MD: Johns Hopkins University Press.

Chang, Ha-Joon. 1996. *The Political Economy of Industrial Policy*. Houndmills. UK: Macmillan Press.

Cherny, Nicolás. 2009. "¿Por Qué Cambia la Política Económica? El Gobierno del Cambio de la Política Cambiaria en Argentina (1995–2003)." Buenos Aires: Facultad Latinoamericana de Ciencias Sociales (FLACSO).

Chwieroth, Jeffrey M. 2009. *Capital Ideas*. Princeton, NJ: Princeton University Press.

Central Statistical Office (Główny Urząd Statystyczny GUS). 1998. Statistical Yearbook of the Republic of Poland. Warsaw, December.

Cianetti, Licia. 2018. "Consolidated Technocratic and Ethnic Hollowness, but No Backsliding: Reassessing Europeanisation in Estonia and Latvia." *East European Politics* 34 (3): 317–36. doi.org/10.1080/21599165.2018.1482212.

Clark, William Roberts, Matt Golder, and Sona Nadenichek Golder. 2002. "Fiscal Policy and the Democratic Process in the European Union." *European Union Politics* 3 (2): 205–30.

Colclough, Christopher. 1993. "Structuralism versus Neo-Liberalism: An Introduction." In *States or Markets?* Edited by Christopher Colclough and James Manor, 1–24. Oxford: Clarendon Press. https://books.google.com/books/about/States_Or_Markets.html?id=nIhuGpTazHkC.

Collier, David. 1979. *The New Authoritarianism in Latin America*. Princeton, NJ: Princeton University Press.

———. 2011. "Understanding Process Tracing." *PS: Political Science and Politics* 44 (4): 823–30.

Collier, David, and Ruth Berins Collier. 1991. *Shaping the Political Arena: Critical Junctures, the Labor Movement, and Regime Dynamics in Latin America*. Princeton, NJ: Princeton University Press.

Connell, Raewyn, and Nour Dados. 2014. "Where in the World Does Neoliberalism Come From?" *Theory and Society* 43 (2): 117–38.

Copelovitch, Mark S., and Jon C.W. Pevehouse. 2013. "Ties That Bind? Preferential Trade Agreements and Exchange Rate Policy Choice." *International Studies Quarterly* 57 (2): 385–99.

Corrales, Javier. 1998. "Coalitions and Corporate Choices in Argentina, 1976–1994: The Recent Private Sector Support of Privatization." *Studies in Comparative International Development* 32 (4): 24–51.

Country Report Select. 2010. "Economic Policy: There Is Uncertainty over NBP Succession, but Disputes Ease," April 5, 2010.

Cox, Gary W. 1990. "Centripetal and Centrifugal Incentives in Electoral Systems." *American Journal of Political Science* 34 (4): 903–35. doi.org/10.2307/2111465.

Cox, Robert. 1987. *Production, Power, and World Order*. New York: Columbia University Press.

Crouch, Colin. 2004. *Post-Democracy*. London: Polity Press. https://books.google.com/books/about/Post_Democracy.html?id=FIkqmsn4O0QC.

———. 2011. *The Strange Non-Death of Neo-Liberalism*. Cambridge: Polity Press.

Crouch, Colin, Donatella della Porta, and Wolfgang Streeck. 2016. "Democracy in Neoliberalism?" *Anthropological Theory* 16 (4): 497–512. doi.org/10.1177/1463499616677904.

Crouch, Colin, and Wolfgang Streeck. 1997. *Political Economy of Modern Capitalism: Mapping Convergence and Diversity*. London: Sage Publications.

Crowley, Stephen. 2004. "Explaining Labor Weakness in Post-Communist Europe: Historical

Legacies and Comparative Perspective." *East European Politics and Societies* 18 (3): 394–429. doi.org/10.1177/0888325404267395.

Cukierman, Alex, Geoffrey P. Miller, and Bilin Neyapti. 2002. "Central Bank Reform, Liberalization and Inflation in Transition Economies—An International Perspective." *Journal of Monetary Economics* 49 (2): 237–64.

Culpepper, Pepper D. 2010. *Quiet Politics and Business Power: Corporate Control in Europe and Japan.* New York: Cambridge University Press.

Czarzasty, Jan, and Dominik Owczarek. 2012. *The Economic Crisis and Social Dialogue in Poland.* Warszawa: Instytut Spraw Publicznych.

Dahl, Robert A. 1956. *A Preface to Democratic Theory.* Chicago and London: University of Chicago Press. https://books.google.com/books/about/A_Preface_to_Democratic_Theory .html?id=tqJCN6_7NQcC.

———. 1972. *Polyarchy: Participation and Opposition.* New Haven, CT: Yale University Press.

———. 1989. *Democracy and Its Critics.* New Haven, CT, and London: Yale University Press. https://books.google.com/books/about/Democracy_and_Its_Critics.html?id=l1RQ ngEACAAJ.

Darvas, Zsolt, and Valentina Kostyleva. 2011. "Fiscal and Monetary Institutions in Central, Eastern and South-Eastern European Countries." *OECD Journal on Budgeting* 5 (11): 147–85.

De Gregorio, José, Andrea Tokman, and Rodrigo Valdés. 2005. "Flexible Exchange Rate with Inflation Targeting in Chile: Experience and Issues." IADB working paper series 540. Washington, DC: Inter-American Development Bank.

Delamaza, Gonzalo, Antoine Maillet, and Christian Martínez Neira. 2017. "Socio-Territorial Conflicts in Chile: Configuration and Politicization (2005–2014)." *European Review of Latin American and Caribbean Studies / Revista Europea de Estudios Latinoamericanos y Del Caribe* 104: 23–46.

Díaz Cordero, Rodrigo. 2011. "'Una Invitación a Pensar Chile': Competitividad y Crecimiento Armónico del País." Expediente Exportador 7. Santiago de Chile.

Diaz-Alejandro, Carlos. 1985. "Good-Bye Financial Repression, Hello Financial Crash." *Journal of Development Economics* 19 (1–2): 1–24.

Díaz-Bonilla, Eugenio, and Héctor E. Schamis. 2001. "From Redistribution to Stability: The Evolution of Exchange Rate Politics in Argentina, 1950–98." In *The Currency Game: Exchange Rate Politics in Latin America.* Edited by Jeffry A. Frieden and Ernesto, 65–118. Washington, DC: Inter-American Development Bank (IADB).

Dicken, Peter. 2010. *Global Shift: Mapping the Changing Contours of the World Economy.* Thousand Oaks, CA: Sage Publications.

Domínguez, Jorge I., ed. 1996. *Technopols: Freeing Politics and Markets in Latin America in The 1990s.* University Park: Pennsylvania State University Press.

Donoso, S., and M. von Bülow, eds. 2017. *Social Movements in Chile: Organization, Trajectories, and Political Impacts.* Basingstoke, UK: Palgrave Macmillan.

Donovan, Florencia. 2009. "Ahorrar En Tiempos de Vacas Gordas, Una Promesa Que No Se Cumplió." *La Nación,* August 2, 2009, sec. Economía.

Dornbusch, Rudiger, and Sebastián Edwards, eds. 1991. *The Macroeconomics of Populism in Latin America.* Chicago: University of Chicago Press.

Dornisch, David. 1999. "The Social Embeddedness of Polish Regional Development: Representative Institutions, Path Dependencies, and Network Formation." Working Paper 4–99. Brighton: Sussex European Institute.

Drahokoupil, Jan. 2009. *Globalization and the State in Central and Eastern Europe: The Politics of Foreign Direct Investment.* New York: Routledge.

Drake, Paul W. 1996. *Labor Movements and Dictatorships: The Southern Cone in Comparative Perspective.* Baltimore, MD: Johns Hopkins University Press.

Dumas, Charles. 2018. *Populism and Economics.* London: Profile Books.

Duménil, Gérard, and Dominique Lévy. 2011. *The Crisis of Neoliberalism.* Cambridge, MA: Harvard University Press.

Durán Lima, José E., and Mariano Álvarez. 2011. *Manual de Comercio Exterior y Política Comercial.* Santiago de Chile: Economic Commission for Latin America and the Caribbean (ECLAC)—United Nations.

Dyson, Kenneth, ed. 2006. "Euro Entry as Defining and Negotiating Fit: Conditionality, Contagion, and Domestic Politics." In *Enlarging the Euro Area: External Empowerment and Domestic Transformation in East Central Europe,* 7–43. Oxford and New York: Oxford University Press.

Eamets, Raul, Urmas Varblane, and Kaja Sostra. 2003. "External Macroeconomic Shocks and the Estonian Economy: How Did the Russian Financial Crisis Affect Estonian Unemployment and Foreign Trade?" *Baltic Journal of Economics* 3 (2): 5–24.

EBRD. 2000. *Transition Report 2000. Employment, Skills and Transition.* London: European Bank for Reconstruction and Development (EBRD).

———. 2005. *Transition Report 2005. Business in Transition.* London: European Bank for Reconstruction and Development (EBRD).

ECLAC. 1986. "La promoción industrial en la Argentina 1973–83." Buenos Aires: Economic Commission for Latin America and the Caribbean (ECLAC)—United Nations.

———. 2002. *Foreign Investment in Latin America and the Caribbean: 2001 Report.* Santiago de Chile: Economic Commission for Latin America and the Caribbean (ECLAC)—United Nations.

———. 2012. *Structural Change for Equality: An Integrated Approach to Development.* Santiago de Chile: Economic Commission for Latin America and the Caribbean (ECLAC)—United Nations.

The Economist. 1997. "Poland. An AWSome Future?" May 31, 1997.

Edwards, Sebastián. 1995. *Crisis and Reform in Latin America: From Despair to Hope.* New York: Oxford University Press.

Eesti Rahvusringhääling. 2005. "Arengufond Neelab 600 Miljonit Krooni," August 23, 2005.

———. 2009a. "Helenius: Arengufondi Asemel Tuleb Panustada Eksportijatele," September 24, 2009.

———. 2009b. "Raivo Vare: Valitsus Suretab Arengufondi Välja," September 25, 2009.

Egan, Patrick J.W. 2017. "The Political Economy of Exchange Rates in an Era of Global Production Chains." *International Interactions* 43 (3): 507–36. doi.org/10.1080/03050629.2016.11 95565.

Ehin, Piret. 2007. "Political Support in the Baltic States, 1993–2004." *Journal of Baltic Studies* 38 (1): 1–20.

Eichengreen, Barry. 2018. *The Populist Temptation: Economic Grievance and Political Reaction in the Modern Era.* Oxford and New York: Oxford University Press.

EIU Business Eastern Europe. 1997. "Poland: Ticks and Crosses," October 11, 1997.

EIU Newswire. 2003. "Poland Politics: Government Declares Victory in EU Talks," November 4, 2003.

Ekiert, Grzegorz. 1996. *The State against Society: Political Crises and Their Aftermath in East Central Europe*. Princeton, NJ: Princeton University Press.

Ekiert, Grzegorz, and Jan Kubik. 2001. *Rebellious Civil Society: Popular Protest and Democratic Consolidation in Poland, 1989–1993*. Ann Arbor: University of Michigan Press.

Elster, Jon, Claus Offe, and Ulrich Klaus Preuss. 1998. *Institutional Design in Post-Communist Societies: Rebuilding the Ship at Sea*. New York: Cambridge University Press.

Epstein, Rachel A. 2002. "International Institutions and the Depoliticization of Economic Policy in Postcommunist Poland: Central Banking and Agriculture Compared." EUI Working Papers 69. San Domenico di Fiesole: European University Institute (EUI).

———. 2008. *In Pursuit of Liberalism: International Institutions in Postcommunist Europe*. Baltimore, MD: Johns Hopkins University Press.

Epstein, Jim. 2019. "Libertarians Forged an Alliance with Brazilian President Jair Bolsonaro. Was It a Deal with the Devil?" *Reason*, July. https://reason.com/2019/06/01/deal-with-the-devil/.

Esping-Andersen, Gosta. 1985. *Politics against Markets*. Princeton, NJ: Princeton University Press. https://press.princeton.edu/titles/944.html.

———. 1990. *The Three Worlds of Welfare Capitalism*. Princeton, NJ: Princeton University Press.

Estrategia. 2006. "Condicionan Capitalización Del Central a Cambios En Ley Orgánica," July 11, 2006.

Etchemendy, Sebastián. 2001. "Constructing Reform Coalitions: The Politics of Compensations in Argentina's Economic Liberalization." *Latin American Politics and Society* 43 (3): 1–36.

———. 2012. *Models of Economic Liberalization. Business, Workers, and Compensation in Latin America, Spain, and Portugal*. New York: Cambridge University Press.

———. 2019. "The Politics of Popular Coalitions: Unions and Territorial Social Movements in Post-Neoliberal Latin America (2000–2015)." *Journal of Latin American Studies* 52 (1).

Etchemendy, Sebastián, and Ruth Berins Collier. 2007. "Down but Not Out: Union Resurgence and Segmented Neocorporatism in Argentina (2003–2007)." *Politics and Society* 35 (3): 363–401.

Etchemendy, Sebastián, and Candelaria Garay. 2011. "Argentina: Left Populism in Comparative Perspective, 2003–2009." In *The Resurgence of the Latin American Left*. Edited by Steven Levitsky and Kenneth M. Roberts, 283–305. Baltimore, MD: Johns Hopkins University Press.

Eyal, Gil, Iván Szelényi, and Eleanor R. Townsley. 1998. *Making Capitalism Without Capitalists: Class Formation and Elite Struggles in Post-Communist Central Europe*. London: Verso.

Fabry, Adam. 2018. "Neoliberalism, Crisis and Authoritarian–Ethnicist Reaction: The Ascendancy of the Orbán Regime." *Competition and Change*, November. doi.org/10.1177/1024529 418813834.

———. 2019. *The Political Economy of Hungary. From State Capitalism to Authoritarian Neoliberalism*. Basingstoke, UK: Palgrave Macmillan. www.palgrave.com/gb/book/9783030105938.

Fairfield, Tasha. 2015a. "Structural Power in Comparative Political Economy: Perspectives from Policy Formulation in Latin America." *Business and Politics* 17 (3): 411–41. doi.org/10.1515/bap-2014-0047.

Fairfield, Tasha. 2015b. *Private Wealth and Public Revenue in Latin America: Business Power and Tax Politics*. Cambridge: Cambridge University Press.

Faletto, Enzo. 1979. "La Dependencia y Lo Nacional-Popular." *Nueva Sociedad* 40 (January): 40–49.

Farrant, Andrew, Edward Mcphail, and Sebastian Berger. 2012. "Preventing the 'Abuses' of Democracy: Hayek, the 'Military Usurper' and Transitional Dictatorship in Chile?" *American Journal of Economics and Sociology* 71 (3): 513–38. doi.org/10.1111/j.1536-7150.2012 .00824.x.

Fazio, Hugo. 1997. *Mapa actual de la extrema riqueza en Chile*. Santiago de Chile: LOM.

———. 2000. *La transnacionalización de la economía chilena: mapa de la extrema riqueza al año 2000*. Santiago de Chile: LOM.

Fazio, Hugo, and Magaly Parada. 2010. *Veinte años de política económica de la concertación*. Santiago de Chile: LOM.

Feenstra, Robert C., Robert Inklaar, and Marcel P. Timmer. 2015. "The Next Generation of the Penn World Table." *American Economic Review* 105 (10): 3150–82. www.ggdc.net/pwt.

Feigenbaum, Harvey B., and Jeffrey R. Henig. 1994. "The Political Underpinnings of Privatization: A Typology." *World Politics* 46 (2): 185–208. doi.org/10.2307/2950672.

Feldmann, Magnus. 2006. "The Baltic States: Pacesetting on EMU Accession and the Consolidation of Domestic Stability Culture." In *Enlarging the Euro Area: External Empowerment and Domestic Transformation in East Central Europe*. Edited by Kenneth Dyson, 127–43. Oxford and New York: Oxford University Press.

———. 2008. "Baltic States: When Stability Culture Is Not Enough." In *The Euro at Ten: Europeanization, Power, and Convergence*. Edited by Kenneth Dyson, 243–56. Oxford and New York: Oxford University Press.

Feldmann, Magnus, and Razeen Sally. 2002. "From the Soviet Union to the European Union: Estonian Trade Policy, 1991–2000." *World Economy* 25 (1): 79–106.

Fernández, Roque B. 1991. "What Have Populists Learned from Hyperinflation?" In *The Macroeconomics of Populism in Latin America*. Edited by Rudiger Dornbusch and Sebastián Edwards, 121–48. Chicago: University of Chicago Press.

Ferry, Martin. 2007. "From Government to Governance: Polish Regional Development Agencies in a Changing Regional Context." *East European Politics and Societies* 21 (3): 447–74. doi .org/10.1177/0888325407303706.

Ffrench-Davis, Ricardo. 2003. *Entre el neoliberalismo y el crecimiento con equidad: tres décadas de política económica en Chile*. 3rd ed. Santiago de Chile: LOM.

———. 2010. "Macroeconomics for Development: From 'Financierism' to 'Productivism.'" *CEPAL Review* (102): 7–26.

Fish, M. Steven, and Omar Choudhry. 2007. "Democratization and Economic Liberalization in the Postcommunist World." *Comparative Political Studies* 40 (3): 254–82.

Fleming, Alex, Lily Chu, and Marie-Renée Bakker. 1996. "The Baltics: Banking Crises Observed." Policy Research Working Paper 1647. Washington, DC: The World Bank.

Flores-Macías, Gustavo A. 2012. *After Neoliberalism?: The Left and Economic Reforms in Latin America*. New York: Oxford University Press.

Fontaine Aldunate, Arturo. 1988. *Los economistas y el presidente Pinochet*. Santiago de Chile: Zig-Zag.

Fontaine, Juan Andrés. 2001. "Banco Central autónomo: En pos de la estabilidad." In *La transformación económica de Chile*. Edited by Felipe Larraín and Rodrigo Vergara, 393–427. Santiago de Chile: Centro de Estudios Públicos.

Fontevecchia, Agustino. 2018. "At Least $36 Billion Has Evaporated in Argentina: The Corruption Paradigm." *Forbes*, August 30, 2018. https://www.forbes.com/sites/afontevecchia/2018/08/30/at-least-us36-billion-has-evaporated-in-argentina-the-corruption-paradigm/.

Forys, Grzegorz, and Krzysztof Gorlach. 2002. "The Dynamics of Polish Peasant Protests under Post-Communism." *Eastern European Countryside* 8: 47–65.

Fourcade-Gourinchas, Marion, and Sarah Babb. 2002. "The Rebirth of the Liberal Creed: Paths to Neoliberalism in Four Countries." *American Journal of Sociology* 108 (3): 533–79.

Foxley, Alejandro. 1983. *Latin American Experiments in Neoconservative Economics*. Berkeley: University of California Press.

———. 1984. "Reconstrucción Económica para la Democracia." In *Después del monetarismo*, by Andrés Solimano, José Pablo Arellano, Alejandro Foxley, Patricio Meller, Oscar Muñoz, and Ricardo Ffrench-Davis, 13–94. Santiago de Chile: Editorial Aconcagua.

Fracchia, Eduardo, Luis Mesquita, and Juan Quiroga. 2010. "Business Groups in Argentina." In *The Oxford Handbook of Business Groups*. Edited by Asli M. Colpan, Takashi Hikino, and James R. Lincoln, 325–52. New York: Oxford University Press.

Franzese, Jr., Robert J. 2002. *Macroeconomic Policies of Developed Democracies*. Cambridge and New York: Cambridge University Press.

Frenkel, Roberto. 2003. "Globalization and Financial Crises in Latin America." *CEPAL Review* 80 (August): 39–52.

Frenkel, Roberto, José María Fanelli, and Juan Sommer. 1988. "El Proceso de Endeudamiento Externo Argentino." Documentos CEDES 2. Buenos Aires: Centro de Estudios de Estado y Sociedad (CEDES).

Frenkel, Roberto, and Martín Rapetti. 2008. "Five Years of Competitive and Stable Real Exchange Rate in Argentina, 2002–2007." *International Review of Applied Economics* 22 (2): 215–26. /doi.org/10.1080/02692170701880734.

———. 2010. "A Concise History of Exchange Rate Regimes in Latin America." Washington, DC: Center for Economic and Policy Research.

Frieden, Jeffry A. 1991a. *Debt, Development, and Democracy: Modern Political Economy and Latin America, 1965–1985*. Princeton, NJ: Princeton University Press.

———. 1991b. "Invested Interests: The Politics of National Economic Policies in a World of Global Finance." *International Organization* 45 (4): 425–51.

———. 2016. *Currency Politics: The Political Economy of Exchange Rate Policy*. Reprint ed. Princeton, NJ: Princeton University Press.

Frieden, Jeffry A., Piero Ghezzi, and Ernesto Stein. 2001. "Politics and Exchange Rates: A Cross-Country Approach." In *The Currency Game: Exchange Rate Politics in Latin America*. Edited by Jeffry A. Frieden and Ernesto Stein, 21–63. Washington, DC: Inter-American Development Bank (IADB).

Frieden, Jeffry A., David Leblang, and Neven Valev. 2010. "The Political Economy of Exchange Rate Regimes in Transition Economies." *The Review of International Organizations* 5 (1): 1–25.

Friedman, Milton. 1982. "Free Markets and the Generals." *Newsweek*, January 25, 1982.

Fuentes, Claudio. 2012. *El Pacto. Poder, constitución y prácticas políticas en Chile (1990–2010)*. Santiago de Chile: Ediciones UDP.

Gadomski, Witold. 2007. "Bank Wzięty." *Gazeta Wyborcza*, January 13, 2007, 297 edition, sec. Świateczna.

Gamboa, Ricardo, and Mauricio Morales. 2016. "Chile's 2015 Electoral Reform: Changing the Rules of the Game." *Latin American Politics and Society* 58 (4): 126–44. doi.org/10.1111/laps.12005.

Gans-Morse, Jordan, and Simeon Nichter. 2008. "Economic Reforms and Democracy Evidence of a J-Curve in Latin America." *Comparative Political Studies* 41 (10): 1398–1426.

Garlicki, Leszek Lech. 1997. "The Presidency in the New Polish Constitution." *East European Constitutional Review* 6: 81–88.

Garretón, Manuel Antonio. 2000. "Chile's Elections: Change and Continuity." *Journal of Democracy* 11 (2): 78–84.

Gazeta Bankowa. 1998. "Lista 500 Najwiekszych Przedsiebiorstw," 1998, 51/52 edition.

Gazeta Wyborcza. 1991a. "Dolar w górę, czy bez zmian," April 17, 1991, 559 edition.

———. 1991b. "Miło, ale mało," May 29, 1991, 593 edition.

———. 1991c. "Pełazjąca Devaluacja Złotowki," October 14, 1991, 709 edition.

———. 1995a. "Wolny złoty od 9 maja," April 26, 1995, 98 edition.

———. 1995b. "Złotówka pójdzie w górę," April 27, 1995, 99 edition, sec. Gospodarka.

———. 1995c. "Banki za płynną złotówką," April 29, 1995, 9 edition, sec. Gospodarka.

———. 1995d. "Złoty skok," December 22, 1995, 297 edition, sec. Gospodarka.

Geddes, Barbara. 1994. "Challenging the Conventional Wisdom." *Journal of Democracy* 5 (4): 104–18.

———. 1999. "What Do We Know About Democratization After Twenty Years?" *Annual Review of Political Science* 2 (1): 115–44.

Gelman, Andrew, and Jennifer Hill. 2006. *Data Analysis Using Regression and Multilevel/Hierarchical Models*. New York: Cambridge University Press.

George, Alexander L., and Andrew Bennett. 2005. *Case Studies and Theory Development in the Social Sciences*. Cambridge, MA: MIT Press.

Gerchunoff, Pablo, Esteban Greco, and Diego Bondorevsky. 2003. "Comienzos diversos, distintas trayectorias y final abierto: más de una década de privatizaciones en Argentina, 1990–2002." Serie Gestión Pública 34. Santiago de Chile: Comisión Económica para América Latina y el Caribe (CEPAL).

Gereffi, Gary. 1995. "Global Production Systems and Third World Development." In *Global Change, Regional Response: The New International Context of Development*. Edited by Barbara Stallings, 100–42. Cambridge: Cambridge University Press.

Gereffi, Gary, and Donald L Wyman. 1990. *Manufacturing Miracles: Paths of Industrialization in Latin America and East Asia*. Princeton, NJ: Princeton University Press.

Gerschenkron, Alexander. 1962. *Economic Backwardness in Historical Perspective*. Cambridge, MA: Belknap Press.

Gibson, Edward L. 1996. *Class and Conservative Parties: Argentina in Comparative Perspective*. Baltimore, MD: Johns Hopkins University Press.

Gibson, Edward L., Mariano Grondona, Armando Ribas, Juan Garcia, and Adelina Dalesio de

Viola. 1990. "Democracy and the New Electoral Right in Argentina." *Journal of Interamerican Studies and World Affairs* 32 (3): 177.

Gilejko, Leszek K. 2011. "Steel Industry: The Most Successful Example of the Sectoral Social Dialogue in Poland?" *Warsaw Forum of Economic Sociology* 2 (4): 67–76.

Gill, Stephen. 2002. "Constitutionalizing Inequality and the Clash of Globalizations." *International Studies Review* 4 (2): 47–65. doi.org/10.1111/1521-9488.00254.

Gleich, Holger. 2003. "Budget Institutions and Fiscal Performance in Central and Eastern European Countries." European Central Bank Working Paper Series 776. Frankfurt am Main: European Central Bank.

Glyn, Andrew. 2007. *Capitalism Unleashed: Finance, Globalization, and Welfare.* New York: Oxford University Press.

Gomułka, Stanisław. 1998. "Managing Capital Flows in Poland, 1995–98." *Economics of Transition* 6 (2): 389–96.

———. 2002. "Poland's Road to the Euro: A Review of Options." *CESifo Forum* 3: 39–44.

González, Felipe. 2015. "Micro-foundations of Financialization: Status Anxiety and the Expansion of Consumer Credit in Chile." PhD dissertation, Cologne: Universität zu Köln and Max Planck Institut for the Study of Societies.

González, Felipe, Mounu Prem and Francisco Urzúa (2020). "The privatization origins of political corporations" *The Journal of Economic History*. doi.org/10.1017/S0022050719000780.

Goodman, John B. 1991. "The Politics of Central Bank Independence." *Comparative Politics* 23 (3): 329–49.

Gorlach, Krzysztof, and Patrick H. Mooney. 1998. "Defending Class Interests: Polish Peasants in the First Years of Transformation." In *Theorizing Transition: The Political Economy of Post-Communist Transformations.* Edited by John Pickles and Adrian Smith, 262–83. London and New York: Routledge.

Gourevitch, Peter A. 1986. *Politics in Hard Times: Comparative Responses to International Economic Crises.* Ithaca, NY: Cornell University Press.

Grauwe, Paul De. 2017. *The Limits of the Market: The Pendulum between Government and Market.* Translated by Anna Asbury. Oxford: Oxford University Press.

Greeley, Brendan. 2012. "Krugmenistan vs. Estonia." *BusinessWeek*, July 20, 2012. http://www.businessweek.com/articles/2012-07-19/krugmenistan-vs-dot-estonia.

Greene, William. 2004. "The Behaviour of the Maximum Likelihood Estimator of Limited Dependent Variable Models in the Presence of Fixed Effects." *The Econometrics Journal* 7 (1): 98–119. doi.org/10.1111/j.1368-423X.2004.00123.x.

Greskovits, Béla. 1998. *Political Economy of Protest and Patience.* Budapest: Central European University Press.

———. 2007. "Economic Woes and Political Disaffection." *Journal of Democracy* 18 (4): 40–46.

———. 2015. "The Hollowing and Backsliding of Democracy in East Central Europe." *Global Policy* 6 (S1): 28–37. doi.org/10.1111/1758-5899.12225.

Grochal, Renata, and Leszek Baj. 2007. "Skrzypek objął rządy w NBP." *Gazeta Wyborcza*, December 1, 2007, 10 edition, sec. Gospodarka.

Grofman, Bernard, Evald Mikkel, and Rein Taagepera. 1999. "Electoral Systems Change in Estonia, 1989–1993." *Journal of Baltic Studies* 30 (3): 227–49.

Grugel, Jean, and Pía Riggirozzi. 2012. "Post-Neoliberalism in Latin America: Rebuilding and Reclaiming the State after Crisis." *Development and Change* 43 (1): 1–21. doi.org/10.1111/j.1467-7660.2011.01746.x.

Grzymała-Busse, Anna. 2001. "Coalition Formation and the Regime Divide in New Democracies: East Central Europe." *Comparative Politics* 34 (1): 85–104.

———. 2002. "The Programmatic Turnaround of Communist Successor Parties in East Central Europe, 1989–1998." *Communist and Post-Communist Studies* 35 (1): 51–66.

Guzmán, Jaime. 1979. "El Camino Político." *Realidad* 1 (7): 13–23.

Guzmán, Martín, José Antonio Ocampo, and Joseph E. Stiglitz. 2017. "Real Exchange Rate Policies for Economic Development." Working Paper 23868. National Bureau of Economic Research. Cambridge, MA. doi.org/10.3386/w23868.

———. 2018. "Real Exchange Rate Policies for Economic Development." *World Development* 110 (October): 51–62. doi.org/10.1016/j.worlddev.2018.05.017.

Haan, Jakob de, and Fabian Amtenbrink. 2000. "Democratic Accountability and Central Bank Independence: A Response to Elgie." *West European Politics* 23 (3): 179–90. doi.org/10.1080/01402380008425390.

Hachette, Dominique. 2001. "Privatizaciones: Reforma estructural pero inconclusa." In *La transformación económica de Chile*. Edited by Felipe Larraín and Rodrigo Vergara, 111–53. Santiago de Chile: Centro de Estudios Públicos.

Hacker, Jacob S., and Paul Pierson. 2002. "Business Power and Social Policy: Employers and the Formation of the American Welfare State." *Politics and Society* 30 (2): 277–325. doi.org/10.1177/0032329202030002004.

———. 2010. "Winner-Take-All Politics: Public Policy, Political Organization, and the Precipitous Rise of Top Incomes in the United States." *Politics and Society* 38 (2): 152–204.

Hagen, Jürgen von. 2002. "Fiscal Rules, Fiscal Institutions, and Fiscal Performance." *Economic and Social Review* 33 (3): 263–84.

Hagen, Jürgen von, and Ian J. Harden. 1995. "Budget Processes and Commitment to Fiscal Discipline." *European Economic Review*, Papers and Proceedings of the Ninth Annual Congress European Economic Association, 39 (3–4): 771–79. https://doi.org/10.1016/0014-2921(94)00084-D.

Haggard, Stephan. 1990. *Pathways from the Periphery: The Politics of Growth in the Newly Industrializing Countries*. Ithaca, NY: Cornell University Press.

Haggard, Stephan, and Robert R. Kaufman, eds. 1992. *The Politics of Economic Adjustment*. Princeton, NJ: Princeton University Press.

———. 1995. *The Political Economy of Democratic Transitions*. Princeton, NJ: Princeton University Press.

———. 2008. *Development, Democracy, and Welfare States: Latin America, East Asia, and Eastern Europe*. Princeton, NJ: Princeton University Press.

Haggard, Stephan, and Matthew D. McCubbins, eds. 2001. *Presidents, Parliaments, and Policy*. New York: Cambridge University Press.

Hajer, Maarten. 2003. "Policy without Polity? Policy Analysis and the Institutional Void." *Policy Sciences* 36 (2): 175–95. doi.org/10.1023/A:1024834510939.

Hall, Peter A. 1989. *The Political Power of Economic Ideas: Keynesianism across Nations*. Princeton, NJ: Princeton University Press.

―――. 1993. "Policy Paradigms, Social Learning, and the State: The Case of Economic Policymaking in Britain." *Comparative Politics* 25 (3): 275–96.

―――. 2003. "Aligning Ontology and Methodology in Comparative Politics." In *Comparative Historical Analysis in the Social Sciences*. Edited by James Mahoney and Dietrich Rueschemeyer, 305–36. Cambridge: Cambridge University Press.

Hall, Peter A., and Michèle Lamont. 2013. *Social Resilience in the Neoliberal Era*. Cambridge: Cambridge University Press.

Hall, Peter A., and David Soskice. 2001. "An Introduction to Varieties of Capitalism." In *Varieties of Capitalism: The Institutional Foundations of Comparative Advantage*. Edited by Peter A. Hall and David Soskice, 1–68. New York: Oxford University Press.

Hanke, Steve H. 2008. "Friedman: Float or Fix?" *Cato Journal* 28 (2): 275–85.

Hanley, Seán, and Allan Sikk. 2016. "Economy, Corruption or Floating Voters? Explaining the Breakthroughs of Anti-Establishment Reform Parties in Eastern Europe." *Party Politics* 22 (4): 522–33. doi.org/10.1177/1354068814550438.

Harvey, David. 2007. *A Brief History of Neoliberalism*. New York: Oxford University Press.

Hausmann, Ricardo, Jason Hwang, and Dani Rodrik. 2007. "What You Export Matters." *Journal of Economic Growth* 12 (1): 1–25. /doi.org/10.1007/s10887-006-9009-4.

Hawkins, Kirk A., and Cristóbal Rovira Kaltwasser. 2017. "The Ideational Approach to Populism." *Latin American Research Review* 52 (4): 513–28. doi.org/10.25222/larr.85.

Hayek, Friedrich A. 1973. "Economic Freedom and Representative Government." Occasional Paper 39. London: Institute of Economic Affairs.

―――. 1978. *The Constitution of Liberty*. Chicago: University of Chicago Press. https://www.goodreads.com/work/best_book/290255-the-constitution-of-liberty.

Hellman, Joel S. 1998. "Winners Take All: The Politics of Partial Reform in Postcommunist Transitions." *World Politics* 50 (2): 203–34.

Helmke, Gretchen. 2005. "Enduring Uncertainty: Court-Executive Relations in Argentina During the 1990s and Beyond." In *Argentine Democracy: The Politics of Institutional Weakness*. Edited by Steven Levitsky and María Victoria Murillo, 139–63. University Park: Pennsylvania State University Press.

Heredia, Mariana. 2004. "El proceso como bisagra. Emergencia y consolidación del liberalismo tecnocrático: FIEL, FM y CEMA." In *Empresarios, tecnócratas y militares: la trama corporativa de la última dictadura*. Edited by Alfredo R. Pucciarelli, 313–82. Buenos Aires: Siglo XXI.

―――. 2006. "La demarcación de la frontera entre economía y política en democracia. Actores y controversias en torno de la política económica de Alfonsín." In *Los años de Alfonsín: el poder de la democracia o la democracia del poder?* Edited by Alfredo R. Pucciarelli, 153–98. Buenos Aires: Siglo XXI.

―――. 2011. "La hechura de la política económica. Los economistas, la Convertibilidad y el modelo neoliberal." In *Los años de Menem. La construcción del orden neoliberal*. Edited by Alfredo R. Pucciarelli, 179–220. Buenos Aires: Siglo XXI.

Héritier, Adrienne. 2005. "Europeanization Research East and West: A Comparative Assessment." In *The Europeanization of Central and Eastern Europe*. Edited by Frank Schimmelfennig and Ulrich Sedelmeier, 199–209. Ithaca, NY: Cornell University Press.

Hexeberg, Barbro. 2000. "Implementing the 1993 SNA: Backward Revision of National Accounts Data." SNA News 11. Inter-Secretariat Working Group on National Accounts (ISWGNA).

Hirschman, Albert O. 1968. "The Political Economy of Import-Substituting Industrialization in Latin America." *The Quarterly Journal of Economics* 82 (1): 1–32.

Hooghe, Liesbet, Gary Marks, and Carole J. Wilson. 2002. "Does Left/Right Structure Party Positions on European Integration?" *Comparative Political Studies* 35 (8): 965–89.

Horne, Cynthia M. 2009. "Late Lustration Programmes in Romania and Poland: Supporting or Undermining Democratic Transitions?" *Democratization* 16 (2): 344–76.

Howard, A. E. Dick, and Mark F. Brzezinski. 1998. "Development of Constitutionalism." In *Transition to Democracy in Poland*. Second ed. Edited by Richard F. Staar, 133–61. New York: Palgrave Macmillan.

Huber, Evelyne, Jennifer Pribble, and John D. Stephens. 2010. "The Chilean Left in Power: Achievements, Failures, and Omissions." In *Leftist Governments in Latin America: Successes and Shortcomings*. Edited by Kurt Weyland, Raúl L. Madrid, and Wendy Hunter, 77–97. Cambridge and New York: Cambridge University Press.

Huneeus, Carlos. 2003. *Chile, un país dividido: la actualidad del pasado*. Santiago de Chile: Catalonia.

———. 2007. *The Pinochet Regime*. Boulder, CO: Lynne Rienner.

Hunya, Gábor. 1998. "Integration of CEEC Manufacturing into European Corporate Structures by Direct Investments." *MOCT-MOST: Economic Policy in Transitional Economies* 8 (2): 69–90.

Ilzetzki, Ethan, Carmen M. Reinhart, and Kenneth S. Rogoff. 2017. "Exchange Arrangements Entering the Twenty-first Century: Which Anchor Will Hold?" Working Paper 23134. National Bureau of Economic Research. Cambridge, MA. doi.org/10.3386/w23134.

Iversen, Torben. 2008. "Capitalism and Democracy." In *The Oxford Handbook of Political Economy*. Edited by Donald A. Wittman and Barry R. Weingast, 601–23. Oxford and New York: Oxford University Press. doi.org/10.1093/oxfordhb/9780199548477.003.0033.

Iversen, Torben, and David Soskice. 2019. *Democracy and Prosperity. Reinventing Capitalism through a Turbulent Century*. Princeton, NJ: Princeton University Press.

Jacoby, Wade. 2006. "Inspiration, Coalition, and Substitution: External Influences on Postcommunist Transformations." *World Politics* 58 (4): 623–51.

Jácome, Luis I., and Francisco Vázquez. 2008. "Is There Any Link between Legal Central Bank Independence and Inflation? Evidence from Latin America and the Caribbean." *European Journal of Political Economy* 24 (4): 788–801. doi.org/10.1016/j.ejpoleco.2008.07.003.

Jankowiak, Janusz. 2005. "Skutki opóźnienia przyjęcia euro." *Gazeta Wyborcza*, January 9, 2005, 203 edition, sec. Gospodarka.

Jasiewicz, Krzysztof. 1992. "From Solidarity to Fragmentation." *Journal of Democracy* 3 (2): 55–69.

———. 1997. "Poland: Wałęsa's Legacy to the Presidency." In *Postcommunist Presidents*. Edited by Raymond Taras, 130–66. Cambridge and New York: Cambridge University Press.

———. 2008. "The New Populism in Poland: The Usual Suspects?" *Problems of Post-Communism* 55 (3): 7–25.

Javorcik, Beata Smarzynska. 2004. "Does Foreign Direct Investment Increase the Productivity of Domestic Firms? In Search of Spillovers through Backward Linkages." *The American Economic Review* 94 (3): 605–27.

Johnson, Juliet. 2016. *Priests of Prosperity: How Central Bankers Transformed the Postcommunist World*. Ithaca, NY: Cornell University Press.

Johnson, Simon, and Marzena Kowalska. 1995. "Poland: The Political Economy of Shock Therapy." In *Voting for Reform: Democracy, Liberalization, and Economic Adjustment*. Edited by Stephan Haggard and Steven B. Webb, 195–241. New York: Oxford University Press and the World Bank.

Jones, Daniel S. 2012. *Masters of the Universe*. Princeton, NJ: Princeton University Press.

Jones, Mark P. 1997. "Evaluating Argentina's Presidential Democracy: 1983–1995." In *Presidentialism and Democracy in Latin America*. Edited by Scott Mainwaring and Matthew Soberg Shugart, 259–99. Cambridge: Cambridge University Press.

Kamiński, Bartlomiej. 1998. "Foreign Trade: Policies and Performance." In *Transition to Democracy in Poland*. Edited by Richard F. Staar, 2nd edition, 179–203. New York: Palgrave Macmillan.

Kaminski, Marek M. 2002. "Do Parties Benefit from Electoral Manipulation? Electoral Laws and Heresthetics in Poland, 1989–93." *Journal of Theoretical Politics* 14 (3): 325–58.

Kaplan, Stephen B. 2013. *Globalization and Austerity Politics in Latin America*. New York: Cambridge University Press.

Kattel, Rainer, Erik S. Reinert, and Margit Suurna. 2009. "Industrial Restructuring and Innovation Policy in Central and Eastern Europe since 1990." 23. Working Papers in Technology Governance and Economic Dynamics. Talinn and Oslo: The Other Canon Foundation and Tallinn University of Technology. http://spp.oxfordjournals.org/content/37/9/646.

Katz, Jorge, and Bernardo Kosacoff. 2001. "Technological Learning, Institution Building and the Microeconomics of Import Substitution." In *An Economic History of Twentieth-Century Latin America. Industrialization and the State in Latin America: The Postwar Years*. Edited by Enrique Cardenas, José Antonio Ocampo, and Rosemary Thorp, 3:36–57. Houndmills, UK: Palgrave Macmillan.

Katzenstein, Peter J. 1985. *Small States in World Markets: Industrial Policy in Europe*. Ithaca, NY: Cornell University Press.

Kaufman, Robert R. 1990. "How Societies Change Developmental Models or Keep Them: Reflections on the Latin American Experience in the 1930s and the Postwar World." In *Manufacturing Miracles*. Edited by Gary Gereffi and Donald L. Wyman, 110–38. Princeton, NJ: Princeton University Press.

Kaufman, Robert R., and Alex Segura-Ubiergo. 2001. "Globalization, Domestic Politics, and Social Spending in Latin America: A Time-Series Cross-Section Analysis, 1973–97." *World Politics* 53 (4): 553–87.

Keohane, Robert O., and Helen V. Milner. 1996. *Internationalization and Domestic Politics*. Cambridge and New York: Cambridge University Press.

Khan, Mushtaq H., and Stephanie Blankenburg. 2009. "The Political Economy of Industrial Policy in Asia and Latin America." In *Industrial Policy and Development: The Political Economy of Capabilities Accumulation*. Edited by Mario Cimoli, Giovanni Dosi, and Joseph E. Stiglitz, 336–76. New York: Oxford University Press.

King, Lawrence P., and Aleksandra Sznajder. 2006. "The State-Led Transition to Liberal Capitalism: Neoliberal, Organizational, World-Systems, and Social Structural Explanations of Poland's Economic Success." *American Journal of Sociology* 112 (3): 751–801.

Kingstone, Peter R. 2001. "Why Free Trade 'Losers' Support Free Trade Industrialists and the Surprising Politics of Trade Reform in Brazil." *Comparative Political Studies* 34 (9): 986–1010.

Kitschelt, Herbert. 1995. "Formation of Party Cleavages in Post-Communist Democracies Theoretical Propositions." *Party Politics* 1 (4): 447–72.

Klein, Michael W., and Jay C. Shambaugh. 2009. *Exchange Rate Regimes in the Modern Era.* 1 edition. Cambridge, MA: MIT Press.

Knight, Jack. 1992. *Institutions and Social Conflict.* Cambridge: Cambridge University Press.

Knöbl, Adalbert, Andres Sutt, and Basil B. Zavoiceo. 2002. "The Estonian Currency Board: Its Introduction and Role in the Early Success of Estonia's Transition to a Market Economy." IMF Working Paper 02/96. Washington, DC: International Monetary Fund.

Kohl, Heribert, and Hans-Wolfgang Platzer. 2004. *Industrial Relations in Central and Eastern Europe: Transformation and Integration: A Comparison of the Eight New EU Member States.* Brussels: European Trade Union Institute (ETUI).

Kołodko, Grzegorz W. 1993. "Strategy for Poland." Working Papers 40. Warsaw: Institute of Finance.

Kołodko, Grzegorz W., and Domenico Mario Nuti. 1997. "The Polish Alternative. Old Myths, Hard Facts and New Strategies in the Successful Transformation of the Polish Economy." Research for Action 33. Helsinki: UNU World Institute for Development Economics Research (UNU/WIDER).

Kopits, George. 2001. "Fiscal Rules: Useful Policy Framework or Unnecessary Ornament?" IMF Working Paper WP January 145. Washington, DC: International Monetary Fund.

Kornai, János. 1986. "The Soft Budget Constraint." *Kyklos* 39 (1): 3–30. doi.org/10.1111/j.1467 -6435.1986.tb01252.x.

Korpi, Walter. 1983. *The Democratic Class Struggle.* London and Boston: Routledge and Kegan Paul.

———. 1985. "Power Resources Approach vs. Action and Conflict: On Causal and Intentional Explanations in the Study of Power." *Sociological Theory* 3 (2): 31–45.

Kosacoff, Bernardo, ed. 1993. *El Desafío de la competitividad: la industria argentina en transformación.* Buenos Aires: Alianza Editorial.

Kosacoff, Bernardo, and Adrián Ramos. 1999. "The Industrial Policy Debate." *CEPAL Review* 68: 35–60.

Kotz, David M. 2015. *The Rise and Fall of Neoliberal Capitalism.* Cambridge, MA: Harvard University Press.

Kowalczyk, Anna. 2019. "Transnational Capitalist Classes and the State in Chile," New Political Economy, advanced online access. doi: 10.1080/13563467.2019.1664444.

Kowalczyk, Krzysztof A. 1995. "The NBP's Fortress." *Polish News Bulletin,* May 10, 1995, sec. Analyses and commentaries.

Kowalik, Tadeusz. 2011. *From Solidarity to Sellout.* New York: Monthly Review Press.

Krueger, Anne O. 1974. "The Political Economy of the Rent-Seeking Society." *American Economic Review* 64 (3): 291–303.

Kruk, Marynia. 2012. "Poland Continues Privatization Drive with Plan through 2013." 4-Traders.Com. 2012. http:// www.4-traders.com/POLISH-Oil-Gas-1413340/news/Poland -Continues-Privatization- Drive-with-Plan-through-14241207/.

Kubik, Jan. 1994. "Who Done It: Workers, Intellectuals, or Someone Else? Controversy over Solidarity's Origins and Social Composition." *Theory and Society* 23 (3): 441–66.

Kukk, Kalev. 2007. "Estonia's Way from Soviet Rouble to Own Kroon." Tallinn University of Technology Working Papers in Economics (TUTWPE) 163. Tallinn: Tallinn University of Technology.

Kuokštis, Vytautas, and Ramūnas Vilpišauskas. 2010. "Economic Adjustment to the Crisis in the Baltic States in Comparative Perspective." Prepared for 7th Pan-European International Relations Conference September, Stockholm.

Kurth, James R. 1979. "Industrial Change and Political Change: A European Perspective." In *The New Authoritarianism in Latin America*. Edited by David Collier, 320–62. Princeton, NJ: Princeton University Press.

Kurtz, Marcus J. 1999. "Chile's Neo-Liberal Revolution: Incremental Decisions and Structural Transformation, 1973–89." *Journal of Latin American Studies* 31 (2): 399–427.

———. 2001. "State Developmentalism Without a Developmental State: The Public Foundations of the 'Free Market Miracle' in Chile." *Latin American Politics and Society* 43 (2): 1–26.

Kurtz, Marcus J., and Sarah M. Brooks. 2008. "Embedding Neoliberal Reform in Latin America." *World Politics* 60 (2): 231–80.

Kuttner, Robert. 2018. *Can Democracy Survive Global Capitalism?* New York: W. W. Norton.

Kuusk, Kadri, and Anne Jürgenson. 2008. "Evaluation of Business Support Measures." Policy Analysis 10. Tallinn: Praxis Center for Policy Analysis.

Kydland, Finn, and Edward Prescott. 1977. "Rules Rather Than Discretion: The Inconsistency of Optimal Plans." *Journal of Political Economy* 85 (3): 473–91.

Laar, Mart. 2002. *Estonia: Little Country That Could*. London: Centre for Research into Post-Communist Economies.

Laclau, Ernesto. 1975. "The Specificity of the Political: The Poulantzas-Miliband Debate." *Economy and Society* 4 (1): 87–110.

Lagerspetz, Mikko, and Henri Vogt. 2004. "Estonia." In *The Handbook of Political Change in Eastern Europe*. Second ed. Edited by Sten Berglund, Joakim Ekman, and Frank H. Aarebrot, 57–93. Cheltenham, UK: Edward Elgar.

———. 2013. "Estonia." In *The Handbook of Political Change in Eastern Europe*. Edited by Sten Berglund, Joakim Ekman, Kevin Deegan-Krause, and Terje Knuten, 3d edition, 51–83. Northampton, MA: Edward Elgar Pub.

Larraín, Felipe, and Patricio Meller. 1991. "The Socialist-Populist Chilean Experience: 1970–1973." In *The Macroeconomics of Populism in Latin America*. Edited by Rudiger Dornbusch and Sebastián Edwards, 175–221. Chicago: University of Chicago Press.

Lauristin, Marju. 2007. "World-View and Support for Political Parties." In *Estonian Human Development Report 2006*. Edited by Mati Heidmets, 46–59. Talinn: Public Understanding Foundation.

Lauristin, Marju, and Peeter Vihalemm. 1997. "Recent Historical Developments in Estonia: Three Stages of Transition (1987–1997)." In *Return to the Western World: Cultural and Political Perspectives on the Estonian Post-Communist Transition*. Edited by Karl Rosengren, Marju Lauristin, and Peeter Vihalemm, 73–126. Tartu: Tartu University Press.

Lavagna, Roberto. 2011. *El desafío de la voluntad. Trece meses cruciales en la historia argentina*. Buenos Aires: ed. Sudamericana.

Lefort, Fernando. 2010. "Business Groups in Chile." In *The Oxford Handbook of Business Groups.* Edited by Asli M. Colpan, Takashi Hikino, and James R. Lincoln, 387–422. New York: Oxford University Press.

Leszczyńska, Cecylia. 2011. *An Outline History of Polish Central Banking.* Warsaw: National Bank of Poland.

Levitsky, Steven. 2003. "From Labor Politics to Machine Politics: The Transformation of Party-Union Linkages in Argentine Peronism, 1983–1999." *Latin American Research Review* 38 (3): 3–36.

———. 2005. "Crisis and Renovation: Institutional Weakness and the Transformation of Argentine Peronism, 1983–2003." In *Argentine Democracy: The Politics of Institutional Weakness.* Edited by Steven Levitsky and María Victoria Murillo, 181–205. University Park: Pennsylvania State University Press.

Levitsky, Steven, and María Victoria Murillo. 2008. "Argentina: From Kirchner to Kirchner." *Journal of Democracy* 19 (2): 16–30.

———. 2013. "Building Institutions on Weak Foundations." *Journal of Democracy* 24 (2): 93–107.

Levitsky, Steven, and Kenneth M. Roberts, eds. 2011. *The Resurgence of the Latin American Left.* Baltimore, MD: Johns Hopkins University Press.

Levitsky, Steven, and Daniel Ziblatt. 2018. *How Democracies Die.* New York: Crown.

Levy-Yeyati, Eduardo Levy, and Federico Sturzenegger. 2016. "Classifying Exchange Rate Regimes: 15 Years Later." SSRN Scholarly Paper ID 2820762. Rochester, NY: Social Science Research Network. https://papers.ssrn.com/abstract=2820762.

Lewandowski, Janusz. 1994. "Privatization in Poland: Organization, Methods, Results." Discussion Paper 36. Centre for European Studies, Nuffield College, Oxford.

Lijphart, Arend. 1991. "Constitutional Choices for New Democracies." *Journal of Democracy* 2 (1): 72–84. doi.org/10.1353/jod.1991.0011.

Lijphart, Arend, and Carlos H. Waisman. 1996a. "Institutional Design and Democratization." In *Institutional Design in New Democracies: Eastern Europe and Latin America.* Edited by Arend Lijphart and Carlos H. Waisman, 1–11. Boulder, CO: Routledge.

———, eds. 1996b. *Institutional Design in New Democracies: Eastern Europe and Latin America.* Boulder, CO: Routledge.

———. 1996c. "The Design of Democracies and Markets: Generalizing Across Regions." In *Institutional Design in New Democracies: Eastern Europe and Latin America.* Edited by Arend Lijphart and Carlos H. Waisman, 235–47. Boulder, CO: Routledge.

Lindblom, Charles E. 1982. "The Market as Prison." *Journal of Politics* 44 (2): 324–36.

Linz, Juan J. 1978. *The Breakdown of Democratic Regimes.* Baltimore, MD: Johns Hopkins University Press. https://books.google.com/books/about/The_Breakdown_of_Democratic_Regimes.html?id=_vfkp3sWAyIC.

Linz, Juan J., and Alfred Stepan. 1996. *Problems of Democratic Transition and Consolidation: Southern Europe, South America, and Post-Communist Europe.* Baltimore, MD: Johns Hopkins University Press.

Lipset, Seymour Martin. 1981. *Political Man: The Social Bases of Politics.* Expanded ed. Baltimore, MD: Johns Hopkins University Press.

Llanos, Mariana, and Ana Margheritis. 2006. "Why Do Presidents Fail? Political Leadership and the Argentine Crisis (1999–2001)." *Studies in Comparative International Development* 40 (4): 77–103.

Londregan, John B. 2000. *Legislative Institutions and Ideology in Chile*. Cambridge: Cambridge University Press.

Lora, Eduardo. 2012. "Structural Reform in Latin America: What Has Been Reformed and How It Can Be Quantified (Updated Version)." Inter-American Development Bank Working Papers 364. Washington, DC: Inter-American Development Bank (IADB).

Lüders, Rolf. 2010. "Rolf Lüders afirma que Chile ya sufre la enfermedad holandesa." *Diario Financiero*, December 28, 2010.

Luna, Juan Pablo, and David Altman. 2011. "Uprooted but Stable: Chilean Parties and the Concept of Party System Institutionalization." *Latin American Politics and Society*, 53: 1–28.

Luna, Juan Pablo, and Cristóbal Rovira Kaltwasser, eds. 2014. *The Resilience of the Latin American Right*. Baltimore, MD: Johns Hopkins University Press.

Luna, Juan Pablo, and Rodrigo Mardones. 2010. "Chile: Are the Parties Over?" *Journal of Democracy* 21 (3): 107–21.

Machinea, José Luis. 1990. "Stabilization under Alfonsín's Government: A Frustrated Attempt." Documento CEDES 42. Buenos Aires: Centro de Estudios de Estado y Sociedad (CEDES).

Maciejewicz, Patrycija. 2006a. "NBP według Samoobrony." *Gazeta Wyborcza*, March 30, 2006, 76 edition, sec. Gospodarka.

———. 2006b. "Projekt zmian w NBP jest zły." *Gazeta Wyborcza*, June 3, 2006, 55 edition, sec. Gospodarka.

MacLean, Nancy. 2017. *Democracy in Chains: The Deep History of the Radical Right's Stealth Plan for America*. Later printing. New York: Viking.

Madariaga, Aldo. 2017. "Mechanisms of Neoliberal Resilience: Comparing Exchange Rates and Industrial Policy in Chile and Estonia." *Socio-Economic Review* 15 (3): 637–60. doi.org/10.1093/ser/mww015.

———. 2019. "The Politics of Neoliberalism (in Europe's Periphery)." *Comparative European Politics* 17 (5): 797–811. doi.org/10.1057/s41295-018-0150-1.

———. 2020. "The Three Pillars of Neoliberalism: Chile's Economic Policy Trajectory in Comparative Perspective." *Contemporary Politics*. doi.org/10.1080/13569775.2020.1735021.

Madariaga, Aldo, and Cristóbal Rovira Kaltwasser. 2019. "Right-wing Moderation, Left-wing Inertia and Political Cartelisation in Post-Transition Chile." *Journal of Latin American Studies*. doi.org/10.1017/S0022216X19000932.

Mahoney, James. 2000. "Path Dependence in Historical Sociology." *Theory and Society* 29 (4): 507–48.

———. 2003. "Strategies of Causal Assessment in Comparative Historical Analysis." In *Comparative Historical Analysis in the Social Sciences*. Edited by James Mahoney and Dietrich Rueschemeyer, 305–36. Cambridge: Cambridge University Press.

———. 2005. "Combining Institutionalisms: Liberal Choices and Political Trajectories in Central America." In *Preferences and Situations: Points of Intersection Between Historical and Rational Choice Institutionalism*. Edited by Ira Katznelson and Barry R. Weingast, 313–34. New York: Russell Sage Foundation.

Mahoney, James, and Dietrich Rueschemeyer, eds. 2003. *Comparative Historical Analysis in the Social Sciences*. New York: Cambridge University Press.

Maillet, Antoine. 2015. "Variedades de neoliberalismo. Innovación conceptual para el análisis del rol del Estado en los mercados." *Revista de Estudios Políticos* 169: 109–36. doi.org/10.18042 /cepc/rep.169.04.

Mainwaring, Scott, and Matthew Soberg Shugart. 1997. "Presidentialism and Democracy in Latin America: Rethinking the Terms of the Debate." In *Presidentialism and Democracy in Latin America*. Edited by Scott Mainwaring and Matthew Soberg Shugart, 12–54. Cambridge: Cambridge University Press.

Mair, Peter. 2009. "Representative versus Responsible Government." MPIfG Working Paper 09/8. Cologne, Germany.

———. 2013. *Ruling the Void: The Hollowing of Western Democracy*. London and New York: Verso.

Mallon, Richard D., and Juan V. Sourrouille. 1975. *Economic Policymaking in a Conflict Society, the Argentine Case*. Cambridge, MA: Harvard University Press.

Maloney, John, Andrew C. Pickering, and Kaddour Hadri. 2003. "Political Business Cycles and Central Bank Independence." *The Economic Journal* 113 (486): C167–81.

Manzetti, Luigi. 1993. "The Political Economy of Mercosur." *Journal of Interamerican Studies and World Affairs* 35 (4): 101–41.

———. 2010. *Neoliberalism, Accountability, and Reform Failures in Emerging Markets: Eastern Europe, Russia, Argentina, and Chile in Comparative Perspective*. University Park: Pennsylvania State University Press.

Markowski, Radoslaw. 2002. "The Polish SLD in the 1990s: From Opposition to Incumbents and Back." In *The Communist Successor Parties of Central and Eastern Europe*. Edited by András Bozóki and John T. Ishiyama, 51–88. New York: M. E. Sharpe.

———. 2006. "The Polish Elections of 2005: Pure Chaos or a Restructuring of the Party System?" *West European Politics* 29 (4): 814–32.

———. 2008. "The 2007 Polish Parliamentary Election: Some Structuring, Still a Lot of Chaos." *West European Politics* 31 (5): 1055–68.

Maron, Asa, and Michael Shalev. 2017. *Neoliberalism as a State Project: Changing the Political Economy of Israel*. Oxford: Oxford University Press.

Martin, Cathie Jo, and Duane Swank. 2012. *The Political Construction of Business Interests: Coordination, Growth, and Equality*. New York: Cambridge University Press.

Martin, Roderick. 2013. *Constructing Capitalisms: Transforming Business Systems in Central and Eastern Europe*. Oxford: Oxford University Press.

Martínez, Javier, and Álvaro Díaz. 1996. *Chile: The Great Transformation*. Geneva and New York: United Nations Institute for Social Research (UNRISD) and Brookings Institution.

Martínez, Juliana, Maxine Molyneux, and Diego Sánchez-Ancochea. 2009. "Latin American Capitalism: Economic and Social Policy in Transition." *Economy and Society* 38 (1): 1–16.

Mason, Paul. 2017. *Postcapitalism: A Guide to Our Future*. Reprint edition. New York: Farrar, Straus, and Giroux.

Matamala, Daniel. 2016. *Poderoso Caballero: El Pe$o Del Dinero En La Política Chilena*. Fifth ed. (Tal Cual). Santiago de Chile: Catalonia: UDP.

Maxfield, Sylvia. 1998. *Gatekeepers of Growth: The International Political Economy of Central Banking in Developing Countries*. Princeton, NJ: Princeton University Press.

McDermott, Gerald A. 2002. "The Embedded Politics of Entrepreneurship and Network Restructuring in East-Central Europe." In *The New Entrepreneurs of Europe and Asia: Patterns of Business Development in Russia, Eastern Europe and China*. Edited by Victoria E. Bonnell and Thomas B. Gold, 214–54. Armonk, NY: M. E. Sharpe.

McGuire, James W. 1995. "Interim Government and Democratic Consolidation: Argentina in Comparative Perspective." In *Between States: Interim Governments in Democratic Transitions*. Edited by Yossi Shain and Juan J. Linz, 179–210. Cambridge: Cambridge University Press.

———. 1996. "Partidos políticos y democracia en la Argentina." In *La construcción de instituciones democráticas: Sistemas de partidos en América Latina*. Edited by Scott Mainwaring and Timothy Scully, 163–203. Santiago de Chile: CIEPLAN.

McKinnon, Ronald, and Sven Grassman. 1981. "Financial Repression and the Liberalisation Problem within Less-Developed Countries." In *The World Economic Order Past and Prospects*. Edited by Sven Grassman and Erik Lundberg, 365–90. London: Palgrave Macmillan. https://link.springer.com/chapter/10.1007/978-1-349-16488-2_11.

McMenamin, Iain. 2004. "Parties, Promiscuity and Politicisation: Business-Political Networks in Poland." *European Journal of Political Research* 43 (4): 657–76.

Meaney, Constance Squires. 1995. "Foreign Experts, Capitalists, and Competing Agendas Privatization in Poland, the Czech Republic, and Hungary." *Comparative Political Studies* 28 (2): 275–305.

Meller, Patricio. 1996. *Un siglo de economía política chilena (1890–1990)*. Santiago de Chile: Andrés Bello.

Melo, Alberto. 2001. "Industrial Policy in Latin America and the Caribbean at the Turn of the Century." IADB Working Paper 459. Washington, DC.

El Mercurio. 1999. "Recesión abre debate sobre institucionalidad del B. Central," September 12, 1999, sec. Economía y Negocios.

Mettam, Colin W., and Stephen Wyn Williams. 1998. "Internal Colonialism and Cultural Divisions of Labour in the Soviet Remblic of Estonia." *Nations and Nationalism* 4 (3): 363–88.

Mikkel, Evald, and Andres Kasekamp. 2008. "Emerging Party-Based Euroscepticism in Estonia." In *Opposing Europe? The Comparative Party Politics of Euroscepticism*. Edited by Aleks Szczerbiak and Paul Taggart, 1. Case Studies and Country Surveys: 295–312. New York: Oxford University Press.

Millard, Frances. 2000. "Presidents and Democratization in Poland: The Roles of Lech Wałesa and Aleksander Kwaśniewski in Building a New Polity." *Journal of Communist Studies and Transition Politics* 16 (3): 39–62.

Milner, Helen V. 1989. *Resisting Protectionism: Global Industries and the Politics of International Trade*. Princeton, NJ: Princeton University Press.

Mirowski, Philip. 2013. *Never Let a Serious Crisis Go to Waste: How Neoliberalism Survived the Financial Meltdown*. London and New York: Verso.

Mirowski, Philip, and Dieter Plehwe, eds. 2009. *The Road from Mont Pelerin: The Making of the Neoliberal Thought Collective*. Cambridge, MA: Harvard University Press.

Mishkin, Frederic S. 2007. "Is Financial Globalization Beneficial?" *Journal of Money, Credit and Banking* 39 (2–3): 259–94. doi.org/10.1111/j.0022-2879.2007.00026.x.

Misztal, Barbara A. 1999. "How Not to Deal with the Past: Lustration in Poland." *European Journal of Sociology / Archives Européennes de Sociologie* 40 (1): 31–55.

Monckeberg, María Olivia. 2001. *El saqueo de los grupos económicos al estado chileno*. Santiago de Chile: Ediciones B.

———. 2015. *La Máquina Para Defraudar: Los Casos Penta y Soquimich*. Santiago de Chile: Penguin Random House.

Montero, Cecilia. 1996. "Los empresarios en el desarrollo chileno." *Ensaios FEE, Porto Alegre* 17 (2): 152–81.

Morandé, Felipe, and Matías Tapia. 2002. "Política cambiaria en Chile: el abandono de la banda y la experiencia de flotación." *Economía Chilena* 5 (3): 67–94.

Morley, Samuel A., Roberto Machado, and Stefano Pettinato. 1999. "Indexes of Structural Reform in Latin America." Serie Reformas Economicas 12. Economic Commission for Latin America and the Caribbean (ECLAC)—United Nations. http://dag.un.org/handle/11176/357430.

Mudde, Cas. 2004. "The Populist Zeitgeist." *Government and Opposition* 39 (4): 541–63. doi.org/10.1111/j.1477-7053.2004.00135.x.

———. 2013. "Three Decades of Populist Radical Right Parties in Western Europe: So What?" *European Journal of Political Research* 52 (1): 1–19. doi.org/10.1111/j.1475-6765.2012.02065.x.

Mudde, Cas, and Cristóbal Rovira Kaltwasser. 2013a. "Exclusionary vs. Inclusionary Populism: Comparing Contemporary Europe and Latin America." *Government and Opposition* 48 (2): 147–74. doi.org/10.1017/gov.2012.11.

———., eds. 2013b. *Populism in Europe and the Americas: Threat or Corrective for Democracy?* New York: Cambridge University Press.

———. 2017. *Populism: A Very Short Introduction*. Very Short Introductions. Oxford and New York: Oxford University Press.

Mudge, Stephanie L. 2018. *Leftism Reinvented. Western Parties from Socialism to Neoliberalism*. Cambridge and London: Harvard University Press.

Mukherjee, Bumba, and David Andrew Singer. 2008. "Monetary Institutions, Partisanship, and Inflation Targeting." *International Organization* 62 (2): 323–58.

Müller, Jan-Werner. 2016. *What Is Populism?* University Park: University of Pennsylvania Press.

Munck, Gerardo L. 1994. "Democratic Stability and Its Limits: An Analysis of Chile's 1993 Elections." *Journal of Interamerican Studies and World Affairs* 36 (2): 1–38.

Münnich, Sascha. 2011. "Interest-Seeking as Sense-Making: Ideas and Business Interests in the New Deal." *European Journal of Sociology / Archives Européennes de Sociologie* 52 (2): 277–311.

Muñoz Gomá, Óscar. 2001. "La economía chilena en el cambio de siglo y la estrategia de desarrollo." In *Más allá del bosque: Transformar el modelo exportador*. Edited by Óscar Muñoz Gomá, 17–65. Santiago de Chile: FLACSO.

———. 2003. *Hacia un Chile competitivo: institutiones y políticas*. Santiago de Chile: Ed. Universitaria/FLACSO.

———. 2009. "El desarrollo institucional de CORFO y sus estrategias desde 1990." In *Desarrollo productivo en Chile: la experiencia de CORFO entre 1990 y 2009*. Edited by Óscar Muñoz Gomá, 11–51. Santiago de Chile: Catalonia.

Murillo, María Victoria. 2001. *Labor Unions, Partisan Coalitions, and Market Reforms in Latin America*. Cambridge: Cambridge University Press.

———. 2009. *Political Competition, Partisanship, and Policy Making in Latin American Public Utilities*. New York: Cambridge University Press.

Murillo, María Victoria, Virginia Oliveros, and Milan Vaishnav. 2010. "Dataset on Political Ideology of Presidents and Parties in Latin America." Columbia University.

Murillo, María Victoria, and Giancarlo Visconti. 2017. "Economic Performance and Incumbents' Support in Latin America." *Electoral Studies* 45 (February): 180–90. doi.org/10.1016/j.electstud.2016.10.007.

Mustapic, Ana María. 2002. "Argentina: la crisis de representación y los partidos políticos." *América Latina Hoy* 32: 163–83.

Myant, Martin, and Jan Drahokoupil. 2012. "International Integration, Varieties of Capitalism and Resilience to Crisis in Transition Economies." *Europe-Asia Studies* 64 (1): 1–33.

Myant, Martin, Jan Drahokoupil, and Ivan Lesay. 2013. "The Political Economy of Crisis Management in East–Central European Countries." *Europe-Asia Studies* 65 (3): 383–410.

Naczyk, Marek. 2014. "Budapest in Warsaw: Central European Business Elites and the Rise of Economic Patriotism since the Crisis." Centre d'études européennes; Sciences Po Paris—LIEPP. http://www.maxpo.eu/Downloads/Paper_MarekNaczyk.pdf.

Napoli, Enzo, and Patricio Navia. 2012. "La Segunda Es La Vencida: El Caso Del Royalty de 2004 y Del Impuesto Específico a La Gran Minería de 2005 En Chile." *Gestión y Política Pública* 21 (1): 141–83.

Navia, Patricio. 2010. "Living in Actually Existing Democracies: Democracy to the Extent Possible in Chile." *Latin American Research Review* 45: 298–328.

Negretto, Gabriel L. 2004. "Government Capacities and Policy Making by Decree in Latin America: The Cases of Brazil and Argentina." *Comparative Political Studies* 37 (5): 531–62.

———. 2013. *Making Constitutions: Presidents, Parties, and Institutional Choice in Latin America.* New York: Cambridge University Press.

Nelson, Joan M., ed. 1989. *Fragile Coalitions: The Politics of Economic Adjustment.* New Brunswick, NJ, and Oxford: Transaction Publishers.

———. 1993. "The Politics of Economic Transformation: Is Third World Experience Relevant in Eastern Europe?" *World Politics* 45 (3): 433–63.

Neyapti, Bilin. 2001. "Central Bank Independence and Economic Performance in Eastern Europe." *Economic Systems* 25 (4): 381–99. doi.org/10.1016/S0939-3625(01)00033-4.

Nölke, Andreas, and Arjan Vliegenthart. 2009. "Enlarging the Varieties of Capitalism: The Emergence of Dependent Market Economies in East Central Europe." *World Politics* 61 (4): 670–702.

Nørgaard, Ole. 1996. *The Baltic States after Independence.* Cheltenham, UK: Edward Elgar.

Novaro, Marcos. 2009. *Argentina en el fin de siglo. Democracia, mercado y nación (1983–2001).* Buenos Aires: Paidós.

Novaro, Marcos, and Vicente Palermo. 2003. *La dictadura militar, 1976–1983: del golpe de estado a la restauración democrática.* Buenos Aires: Paidós.

Nowakowska, Agata, and Dominika Wielowieyska. 2005. "PO-PiS o prywatyzacji." *Gazeta Wyborcza,* July 18, 2005, 165 edition, sec. Gospodarka.

Nuti, Domenico Mario. 1999. "Employee Ownership in Polish Privatizations." In *Reconstituting the Market: The Political Economy of Microeconomic Transformation.* Edited by Paul Hare, Judy Batt, and Saul Estrin, 81–97. Amsterdam: Harwood Academic Publishers.

———. 2000. "The Polish Zloty, 1990–1999: Success and Underperformance." *American Economic Review* 90 (2): 53–58.

Obinger, Herbert, and Reimut Zohlnhöfer. 2007. "The Real Race to the Bottom: What Happened to Economic Affairs Expenditure after 1980?" In *The Disappearing State?: Retrenchment Realities in an Age of Globalisation*. Edited by Francis G. Castles. Cheltenham, UK, and Northampton, MA: Edward Elgar.

Obstfeld, Maurice, Jay C. Shambaugh, and Alan M. Taylor. 2005. "The Trilemma in History: Tradeoffs Among Exchange Rates, Monetary Policies, and Capital Mobility." *The Review of Economics and Statistics* 87 (3): 423–38.

Ocampo, José Antonio, Barbara Stallings, Inés Bustillo, Helvia Velloso, and Roberto Frenkel. 2014. *La crisis latinoamericana de la deuda desde la perspectiva histórica*. Santiago de Chile: Comisión Económica para América Latina y el Caribe (CEPAL)—Naciones Unidas.

O'Connor, James. 1973. *The Fiscal Crisis of the State*. New York: St. Martin's Press.

O'Donnell, Guillermo. 1973. *Modernization and Bureaucratic-Authoritarianism: Studies in South American Politics*. Berkeley: University of California Press.

———. 1978. "Reflections on the Patterns of Change in the Bureaucratic-Authoritarian State." *Latin American Research Review* 13 (1): 3–38.

———. 1994. "Delegative Democracy." *Journal of Democracy* 5 (1): 55–69.

———. 2007. *Dissonances. Democratic Critiques of Democracy*. Notre Dame, IN: University of Notre Dame Press. https://undpress.nd.edu/9780268037284/dissonances.

O'Donnell, Guillermo, and Philippe C. Schmitter. 1986. *Transitions from Authoritarian Rule. Tentative Conclusions about Uncertain Democracies*. Vol. 4. Baltimore, MD: Johns Hopkins University Press.

O'Dwyer, Conor, and Branislav Kovalčík. 2007. "And the Last Shall Be First: Party System Institutionalization and Second-Generation Economic Reform in Postcommunist Europe." *Studies in Comparative International Development* 41 (4): 3–26.

OECD. 1996. *OECD Economic Surveys: Poland 1997*. Paris: Organisation for Economic Co-operation and Development.

———. 2000a. *OECD Economic Surveys: Baltic States: A Regional Economic Assessment*. Paris: Organisation for Economic Co-operation and Development.

———. 2000b. *OECD Economic Surveys: Poland 2000*. Paris: Organisation for Economic Co-operation and Development.

———. 2001a. *OECD Reviews of Foreign Direct Investment: Estonia*. Paris: Organisation for Economic Co-operation and Development. http://www.oecd.org/estonia/oecdreviewsof foreigndirectinvestmentestonia.htm.

———. 2001b. *OECD Economic Surveys: Poland 2001*. Paris: Organisation for Economic Co-operation and Development.

———. 2002. *Agricultural Policies in Transition Economies 2002: Trends in Policies and Support*. Paris: Organisation for Economic Co-operation and Development.

———. 2005. *Agricultural Policies in OECD Countries 2005*. Paris: Organisation for Economic Co-operation and Development.

———. 2009. *OECD Economic Surveys: Estonia 2009*. Paris: Organisation for Economic Co-operation and Development.

Offe, Claus. 1991. "Capitalism by Democratic Design? Democratic Theory Facing the Triple Transition in East Central Europe." *Social Research* 58 (2): 865–92.

Olson, Mancur. 1965. *The Logic of Collective Action: Public Goods and the Theory of Groups*. Cambridge, MA: Harvard University Press.

Orenstein, Mitchell A. 2001. *Out of the Red: Building Capitalism and Democracy in Postcommunist Europe*. Ann Arbor: University of Michigan Press.

Orłowski, Lucjan T. 1996. "The Path of Exchange Rates in the Polish Economic Transformation." Studies and Analyses 90. Warsaw: Center for Social and Economic Research (CASE).

Ornston, Darius. 2012. *When Small States Make Big Leaps: Institutional Innovation and High-Tech Competition in Western Europe*. Cornell Studies in Political Economy. Ithaca, NY: Cornell University Press.

Ortega Frei, Eugenio. 2003. "La Evolución Programática de Los Partidos Chilenos 1970–2009: De La Polarización Al Consenso." *Revista de Ciencia Política (Santiago)* 23 (2): 109–47. doi .org/10.4067/S0718-090X2013000200002.

Ortiz, Ricardo, and Martín Schorr. 2006. "La economía política del gobierno de Alfonsín: creciente subordinación al poder económico durante la 'década perdida.'" In *Los años de Alfonsín: el poder de la democracia o la democracia del poder?*. Edited by Alfredo R. Pucciarelli, 291–333. Buenos Aires: Siglo XXI.

Osiatyński, Wiktor. 1997. "A Brief History of the Constitution." *East European Constitutional Review* 6: 66–76.

Ost, David. 2005. *The Defeat of Solidarity: Anger and Politics in Postcommunist Europe*. Ithaca, NY: Cornell University Press.

Ostiguy, Pierre. 1990. *Los capitanes de la industria: grandes empresarios, política y economía en la Argentina de los años 80*. Buenos Aires: Legasa.

Ozkan, F. Gulcin. 2000. "Who Wants an Independent Central Bank? Monetary Policy-Making and Politics." *Scandinavian Journal of Economics* 102 (4): 621–43.

Palma, Gabriel. 2009. "Flying Geese and Waddling Ducks: The Different Capabilities of East Asia and Latin America to 'Demand-Adapt' and 'Supply-Upgrade' Their Export Productive Capacity." In *Industrial Policy and Development: The Political Economy of Capabilities Accumulation*. Edited by Mario Cimoli, Giovanni Dosi, and Joseph E. Stiglitz, 203–37. New York: Oxford University Press.

Palonen, Kari. 2003. "Four Times of Politics: Policy, Polity, Politicking, and Politicization." *Alternatives: Global, Local, Political* 28 (2): 171–86.

Panbuła, Piotr, Witold Kozinski, and Michał Rubaszek. 2011. "The Role of the Exchange Rate in Monetary Policy in Poland." BIS Papers 57. Basel: Bank for International Settlements (BIS).

PAP News Wire. 1993. "Situation Confused after Polish Devaluation," August 27, 1993.

Paster, Thomas. 2013. "Business and Welfare State Development: Why Did Employers Accept Social Reforms?" *World Politics* 65 (3): 416–51. doi.org/10.1017/S0043887113000117.

Pastor, Daniel. 2004. "Origins of the Chilean Binominal Election System." *Revista de Ciencia Política (Santiago)* 24 (1): 38–57.

Pastor, Manuel, and Carol Wise. 1999. "Stabilization and Its Discontents: Argentina's Economic Restructuring in the 1990s." *World Development* 27 (3): 477–503.

———. 2001. "From Poster Child to Basket Case." *Foreign Affairs*, November 1, 2001.

Paus, Eva. 2004. "Productivity Growth in Latin America: The Limits of Neoliberal Reforms." *World Development* 32 (3): 427–45.

Pautola, Niina, and Peter Backé. 1998. "Currency Boards in Central and Eastern Europe: Past Experience and Future Perspectives." Focus on Transition 1. Österreichische Nationalbank (ÖNB).

Pempel, T. J. 1998. *Regime Shift: Comparative Dynamics of the Japanese Political Economy*. Ithaca, NY: Cornell University Press.

Peruzzotti, Enrique. 2001. "The Nature of the New Argentine Democracy: The Delegative Democracy Argument Revisited." *Journal of Latin American Studies* 33 (1): 133–55.

Pettai, Vello. 1997. "Political Stability Through Disenfranchisement." *Transitions* 3 (6): 21–23.

———. 2001. "Estonia: Positive and Negative Institutional Engineering." In *Democratic Consolidation in Eastern Europe*.Vol. 1, *Institutional Engineering*. Edited by Jan Zielonka. Oxford University Press.

———. 2004. "The Parliamentary Elections in Estonia, March 2003." *Electoral Studies* 23 (4): 828–34.

———. 2005. "Understanding Politics in Estonia: The Limits of Tutelary Transition." 25. DEMSTAR Research Report. Aarhus: Aarhus University.

———. 2009. "Understanding Politics in Estonia: The Limits of Tutelary Transition." In *Pathways: A Study of Six Post-Communist Countries*. Edited by Lars Johannsen and Karin Hilmer Pedersen, 69–96. Århus: Aarhus University Press.

———. 2012. *Elections in Estonia, 1990–1992: Transitional and Founding*. Berlin: Sigma.

Pettai, Vello, and Klara Hallik. 2002. "Understanding Processes of Ethnic Control: Segmentation, Dependency and Co–Optation in Post–Communist Estonia." *Nations and Nationalism* 8 (4): 505–29.

Pierson, Paul. 2000. "Increasing Returns, Path Dependence, and the Study of Politics." *The American Political Science Review* 94 (2): 251–67.

———. 2004. *Politics in Time: History, Institutions, and Social Analysis*. Princeton, NJ: Princeton University Press.

Pion-Berlin, David. 1983. "Political Repression and Economic Doctrines: The Case of Argentina." *Comparative Political Studies* 16 (1): 37–66. doi.org/10.1177/0010414083016001002.

Plehwe, Dieter. 2009. "The Origins of the Neoliberal Economic Development Discourse." In *The Road from Mont Pelerin: The Making of the Neoliberal Thought Collective*. Edited by Philip Mirowski and Dieter Plehwe, 238–78. Cambridge, MA: Harvard University Press.

Pleines, Heiko. 2008. *Reformblockaden in der Wirtschaftspolitik*. Wiesbaden: VS Verlag für Sozialwissenschaften.

Polak, Jaques J. 2002. "The Two Monetary Approaches to the Balance of Payments: Keynesian and Johnsonian." In *The Open Economy Macromodel: Past, Present and Future*. Edited by Arie Arnon and Warren Young, 19–47. New York: Springer. www.springer.com/gp/book/9781 402071621.

Polanyi, Karl. 2001. *The Great Transformation*. 2nd ed. Boston: Beacon Press.

Polga-Hecimovich, John, and Peter M. Siavelis. 2015. "Here's the Bias! A (Re-) Reassessment of the Chilean Electoral System." *Electoral Studies* 40: 268–79. doi.org/10.1016/j.electstud .2015.09.006.

Polillo, Simone, and Mauro F. Guillén. 2005. "Globalization Pressures and the State: The Worldwide Spread of Central Bank Independence." *American Journal of Sociology* 110 (6): 1764–1802.

Polish News Bulletin. 1996. "Sejm to Look at Central Bank Bill," July 5, 1996, sec. Analyses and commentaries.

———. 2000. "The Zloty Unleashed," April 14, 2000.

———. 2001a. "SLD Economic Agenda Stuck Between a Rock of Voter Expectations and a Hard Place of Economies Realities," June 7, 2001.

———. 2001b. "Exports See Reasons for Panic," June 28, 2001.

———. 2002a. "RPP Cuts Rates by 50 Points, Rejects Suggestions to Amend Exchange Rate Regime," April 6, 2002.

———. 2002b. "SLD Support for New NBP Legislation Unclear after Parliament Sends Bills to Committees," May 28, 2002.

———. 2002c. "Weak Zloty a Remedy for Frail Business and Fearful Gov't," June 20, 2002.

———. 2002d. "Premier Meets Analysts to Discuss Strong Zloty, Economic Outlook," June 28, 2002.

———. 2003. "New RPP in 2004 Who Is Going to Replace the Hawks?" January 28, 2003.

———. 2004. "Giving Poland a Chance: Law and Justice Leader Explains Party's Agenda," November 25, 2004.

———. 2005. "The Euro Zone Advantages Outnumber Drawbacks," May 15, 2005.

———. 2006a. "Governing Party Takes Banks by Storm," January 23, 2006.

———. 2006b. "Sector Consolidations Government's Chief Method of Strengthening State-Owned Companies; Against Governmental Ideas," April 19, 2006.

———. 2006c. "KPP Calls for Long-Term Export Strategy," August 11, 2006, sec. Economy.

———. 2007a. "Two Portraits of Privatisation," May 15, 2007.

———. 2007b. "Slawomir Skrzypek? Controversial First Fiddler in Poland's Central Bank," September 1, 2007.

———. 2008a. "Skrzypek in NBP a Lesser Evil," May 2, 2008, sec. Comment and analysis.

———. 2008b. "Open War Behind Central Bank's Closed Doors," August 2, 2008.

Pontusson, Jonas. 1995. "From Comparative Public Policy to Political Economy Putting Political Institutions in Their Place and Taking Interests Seriously." *Comparative Political Studies* 28 (1): 117–47.

Pop-Eleches, Grigore. 2009. *From Economic Crisis to Reform*. Princeton, NJ: Princeton University Press.

Poznański, Kazimierz. 1996. *Poland's Protracted Transition: Institutional Change and Economic Growth, 1970–1994*. Cambridge: Cambridge University Press.

Prassad, Monica. 2006. *The Politics of Free Markets*. Chicago: University of Chicago Press. https://www.press.uchicago.edu/ucp/books/book/chicago/P/bo3641497.html.

Price, Robert W. 2010. "The Political Economy of Fiscal Consolidation." OECD Economics Department Working Papers 776. Paris: Organisation for Economic Co-operation and Development (OECD).

Przeworski, Adam. 1991. *Democracy and the Market: Political and Economic Reforms in Eastern Europe and Latin America*. Cambridge: Cambridge University Press.

———. 2019. *Crises of Democracy*. Cambridge: Cambridge University Press.

Purju, Alari. 1999. "The Political Economy of Privatization in Estonia." In *Reconstituting the Market. The Political Economy of Microeconomic Transformation*. Edited by Paul Hare, Judy Batt, and Saul Estrin, 199–235. Amsterdam: Harwood Academic Publishers.

Rabkin, Rhoda. 1992. "The Aylwin Government and 'Tutelary' Democracy: A Concept in Search of a Case?" *Journal of Interamerican Studies and World Affairs* 34 (4): 119–94.

Raig, Ivar. 2007. "Some Possible Negative Aspects of the EU Enlargement and the Impact for Estonia." Proceedings of the Institute for European Studies 3. Tallinn: International University Audentes.

Raudla, Ringa. 2010. "The Evolution of Budgetary Institutions in Estonia: A Path Full of Puzzles?" *Governance* 23 (3): 463–84. doi.org/10.1111/j.1468-0491.2010.01490.x.

Raudla, Ringa, and Rainer Kattel. 2011. "Why Did Estonia Choose Fiscal Retrenchment after the 2008 Crisis?" *Journal of Public Policy* 31 (2): 163–86.

Raun, Toivo U. 1997. "Democratization and Political Development in Estonia, 1987–96." In *The Consolidation of Democracy in East-Central Europe*. Edited by Karen Dawisha and Bruce Parrott, 334–73. Cambridge: Cambridge University Press.

Reinstein, Andrés, and Francisco Rosende. 2001. "Reforma Financiera en Chile." In *La transformación económica de Chile*. Edited by Felipe Larraín and Rodrigo Vergara, 341–90. Santiago de Chile: Centro de Estudios Públicos.

Reisman, David. 1990. *The Political Economy of James Buchanan*. London: Macmillan Press.

Richardson, Neal P. 2009. "Export-Oriented Populism: Commodities and Coalitions in Argentina." *Studies in Comparative International Development* 44 (3): 228–55.

Roberts, Kenneth M. 2008. "The Mobilization of Opposition to Economic Liberalization." *Annual Review of Political Science* 11 (1): 327–49. doi.org/10.1146/annurev.polisci.11.053006.183457.

———. 2011. "Chile: The Left after Neoliberalism." In *The Resurgence of the Latin American Left*. Edited by Steven Levitsky and Kenneth M. Roberts, 326–47. Baltimore, MD: Johns Hopkins University Press.

———. 2015. *Changing Course in Latin America: Party Systems in the Neoliberal Era*. New York: Cambridge University Press.

Robinson, William I., and Jerry Harris. 2000. "Towards a Global Ruling Class? Globalisation and the Transnational Capitalist Class." *Science and Society* 64(1): 11–54.

Rodríguez, Juan Pablo. *Resisting Neoliberal Capitalism in Chile. The Possibility of Social Critique*. Cham: Springer Nature.

Rodrik, Dani. 1996. "Understanding Economic Policy Reform." *Journal of Economic Literature* 34 (1): 9–41.

———. 2008. "The Real Exchange Rate and Economic Growth." *Brookings Papers on Economic Activity* 39 (2): 365–439.

Rogoff, Kenneth. 1985. "The Optimal Degree of Commitment to an Intermediate Monetary Target." *Quarterly Journal of Economics* 100 (4): 1169–89.

Roland, Gérard. 2002. "The Political Economy of Transition." *Journal of Economic Perspectives* 16 (1): 29–50.

Román, Enrique. 2003. "El fomento productivo en una economía de mercado: Lecciones del caso chileno." In *Hacia un Chile competitivo: instituciones y políticas*. Edited by Óscar Muñoz Gomá, 25–65. Santiago de Chile: Ed. Universitaria/FLACSO.

Roos, Jerome. 2019. *Why Not Default? The Political Economy of Sovereign Debt*. Princeton, NJ: Princeton University Press.

Rose, Shanna. 2006. "Do Fiscal Rules Dampen the Political Business Cycle?" *Public Choice* 128 (3/4): 407–31.

Rovira Kaltwasser, Cristóbal. 2011. "Toward Post-Neoliberalism in Latin America?" *Latin American Research Review* 46 (2): 225–34.

Rovira Kaltwasser, Cristóbal. 2014. "The Responses of Populism to Dahl's Democratic Dilemmas." *Political Studies* 62 (3): 470–87. doi.org/10.1111/1467-9248.12038.

Rozas, Patricio, and Gustavo Marín. 1988. *El mapa de la extrema riqueza*. Santiago de Chile: CESOC—PRIES—Cono Sur.

Rubio, Delia Ferreira, and Matteo Goretti. 1996. "Cuando el presidente gobierna solo. Menem y los decretos de necesidad y urgencia hasta la reforma constitucional (julio 1989–agosto 1994)." *Desarrollo Económico* 36 (141): 443–74.

Rueschemeyer, Dietrich, Evelyne Huber, and John D. Stephens. 1992. *Capitalist Development and Democracy*. Chicago: University of Chicago Press.

Rutkowski, Aleksander. 2007. "Ceilings and Anchors: Fiscal Rules for Poland." *ECFIN Country Focus* 4 (4): 6.

Rutland, Peter. 1997. "The Antinomies of Privatization in Eastern Europe." In *Restructuring Networks in Post-Socialism: Legacies, Linkages, and Localities*. Edited by Gernot Grabher and David Stark, 265–82. New York: Oxford University Press.

Ruutsoo, Rein. 1996. "The Emergence of Civil Society in Estonia 1987–1994." In *Between Plan and Market: Social Change in the Baltic States and Russia*. Edited by Raimo Blom, Harri Melin, and Jouko Nikula, 7–25. Berlin: Walter De Gruyter.

Ryan, Matthew D. J. 2018. "Interrogating 'Authoritarian Neoliberalism': The Problem of Periodization." *Competition and Change*, September. doi.org/10.1177/1024529418797867.

Saad-Filho, Alfredo. 2005. "From Washington to Post-Washington Consensus: Neoliberal Agendas for Economic Development." In *Neoliberalism: A Critical Reader*. Edited by Alfredo Saad-Filho and Deborah Johnston, 113–20. London and Ann Arbor, MI: Pluto Press.

Sachs, Jeffrey. 1990. "What Is to Be Done?" *Economist*, January 13, 1990.

———. 1994. *Poland's Jump to the Market Economy*. Cambridge, MA: MIT Press.

Sánchez, Gabriel, Inés Butler, and Ricardo Rozemberg. 2011. "Productive Development Policies in Argentina." IADB working paper series 193. Washington, DC: Inter-American Development Bank (IADB).

Sánchez-Ancochea, Diego. 2007. "Anglo-Saxon Structuralism versus Latin American Structuralism: Latin American Development Thought in Comparative Perspective." In *Ideas, Policies and Economic Development in the Americas*. Edited by M. Vernego and E. Perez Caldentey, 208–27. London: Routledge.

Santiso, Carlos. 2003. "Insulated Economic Policymaking and Democratic Governance: The Paradox of Second Generation Reforms in Argentina and Brazil." SAIS Working Paper Series WP/02/03. Washington, DC: School of Advanced International Studies.

Sartori, Giovanni. 1994. *Comparative Constitutional Engineering: An Inquiry into Structures, Incentives and Outcomes*. London: Macmillan.

Scapini, Juan Carlos. 2006. *Los gremios empresariales en Chile*. Santiago de Chile: Tajamar Editores.

Schamis, Héctor E. 1999. "Distributional Coalitions and the Politics of Economic Reform in Latin America." *World Politics* 51 (2): 236–68.

———. 2002. *Re-Forming the State: The Politics of Privatization in Latin America and Europe*.

Interests, Identities, and Institutions in Comparative Politics. Ann Arbor: University of Michigan Press.

Schamis, Héctor E., and Christopher Way. 2003. "Political Cycles and Exchange-Rate-Based Stabilization." *World Politics* 56 (1): 43–78.

Scharpf, Fritz. 1999. *Governing in Europe: Effective and Democratic?* Oxford: Oxford University Press. http://www.oxfordscholarship.com/view/10.1093/acprof:oso/9780198295457.001 .0001/acprof-9780198295457.

Schimmelfennig, Frank, and Ulrich Sedelmeier, eds. 2005. *The Europeanization of Central and Eastern Europe*. Ithaca, NY: Cornell University Press.

Schindler, Frederik. 2018. "Deutsche Bank über rechten Politiker: 'Wunschkandidat der Märkte.'" *Die Tageszeitung: taz*, October 16, 2018, sec. Politik. https://www.taz.de/!5543768/.

Schipani, Andres, and Joe Leahy. 2018. "Brazil's New Finance Minister Eyes 'Pinochet-Style' Fix for Economy." *Financial Times*, November 2, 2018. https://www.ft.com/content/1a2ba4f4 -de4e-11e8-9f04-38d397e6661c.

Schmidt, Vivien A., and Mark Thatcher, eds. 2013. *Resilient Liberalism in Europe's Political Economy*. New York: Cambridge University Press.

Schmitter, Philippe C. 1974. "Still the Century of Corporatism?" *The Review of Politics* 36 (1): 85–131.

Schneider, Ben Ross. 2004a. "Organizing Interests and Coalitions in the Politics of Market Reform in Latin America." *World Politics* 56 (3): 456–79.

———. 2004b. *Business Politics and the State in Twentieth-Century Latin America*. Cambridge: Cambridge University Press.

———. 2013. *Hierarchical Capitalism in Latin America: Business, Labor, and the Challenges of Equitable Development*. New York: Cambridge University Press.

Schneider, Martin R., and Mihai Paunescu. 2012. "Changing Varieties of Capitalism and Revealed Comparative Advantages from 1990 to 2005: A Test of the Hall and Soskice Claims." *Socio-Economic Review* 10 (4): 731–53.

Schoenman, Roger. 2005. "Captains or Pirates? State-Business Relations in Post-Socialist Poland." *East European Politics and Societies* 19 (1): 40–75.

———. 2014. *Networks and Institutions in Europe's Emerging Markets*. Cambridge: Cambridge University Press.

Schrank, Andrew, and Marcus J. Kurtz. 2005. "Credit Where Credit Is Due: Open Economy Industrial Policy and Export Diversification in Latin America and the Caribbean." *Politics and Society* 33 (4): 671–702.

Schuknecht, Ludger. 2005. "Stability and Growth Pact: Issues and Lessons from Political Economy." *International Economics and Economic Policy* 2 (1): 65–89. doi.org/10.1007/s10368 -005-0028-3-y.

Schvarzer, Jorge. 1981. *Expansión económica del estado subsidiario, 1976–1981*. Buenos Aires: Centro de Investigaciones Sociales sobre el Estado y la Administración (CISEA).

Schwartz, Herman. 1994. "Small States in Big Trouble: State Reorganization in Australia, Denmark, New Zealand, and Sweden in the 1980s." *World Politics* 46 (4): 527–55. doi.org/10.2307 /2950717.

Scully, Timothy. 1996. "Reconstrucción de la política de partidos en Chile." In *La construcción de instituciones democráticas: Sistemas de partidos en América Latina.* Edited by Scott Mainwaring and Timothy Scully, 83–112. Santiago de Chile: CIEPLAN.

Seawright, Jason, and John Gerring. 2008. "Case Selection Techniques in Case Study Research: A Menu of Qualitative and Quantitative Options." *Political Research Quarterly* 61 (2): 294–308. doi.org/10.1177/1065912907313077.

Shafer, D. Michael. 1994. *Winners and Losers: How Sectors Shape the Developmental Prospects of States.* Ithaca, NY: Cornell University Press.

Shields, Stuart. 2007. "From Socialist Solidarity to Neo-Populist Neoliberalisation? The Paradoxes of Poland's Post-Communist Transition." *Capital and Class* 31 (3): 159–78. doi.org/10.1177/030981680709300110.

———. 2015. "Neoliberalism Redux: Poland's Recombinant Populism and Its Alternatives." *Critical Sociology* 41 (4–5): 659–78. doi.org/10.1177/0896920513501349.

Shugart, Matthew Soberg, and John M. Carey. 1992. *Presidents and Assemblies: Constitutional Design and Electoral Dynamics.* New York: Cambridge University Press.

Siavelis, Peter M. 2010. *President and Congress in Postauthoritarian Chile: Institutional Constraints to Democratic Consolidation.* University Park: Pennsylvania State University Press.

Sikk, Allan. 2009. "Force Mineure? The Effects of the EU on Party Politics in a Small Country: The Case of Estonia." *Journal of Communist Studies and Transition Politics* 25 (4): 468–90.

Silva, Eduardo. 1996. *The State and Capital in Chile: Business Elites, Technocrats, and Market Economics.* Boulder, CO: Westview Press.

———. 2002. "Capital and the Lagos Presidency: Business as Usual?" *Bulletin of Latin American Research* 21 (3): 339–57.

———. 2009. *Challenging Neoliberalism in Latin America.* New York: Cambridge University Press.

Silva, Patricio. 1991. "Technocrats and Politics in Chile: From the Chicago Boys to the CIEPLAN Monks." *Journal of Latin American Studies* 23 (2): 385–410.

Simmons, Beth A., and Zachary Elkins. 2004. "The Globalization of Liberalization: Policy Diffusion in the International Political Economy." *American Political Science Review* 98 (1): 171–89.

Sirlin, Pablo. 1999. "Argentina's Industrial Specialization Regime: New-Generation Industrial Policy, or Merely a Transfer of Resources?" *CEPAL Review* 68 (August): 101–4.

Skalski, Ernest. 1992. "Za dolara 13 500 zł." *Gazeta Wyborcza*, February 26, 1992, 820 edition.

Sklair, Leslie. 2001. *The Transnational Capitalist Class.* Oxford: Wiley-Blackwell.

Skocpol, Theda, and Margaret Somers. 1980. "The Uses of Comparative History in Macrosocial Inquiry." *Comparative Studies in Society and History* 22 (2): 174–97.

Slobodian, Quinn. 2018. *Globalists: The End of Empire and the Birth of Neoliberalism.* Cambridge, MA: Harvard University Press.

Smith, David. 2001. *Estonia: Independence and European Integration.* London: Routledge.

Smith, David J. 2002. "Estonia." In *The Baltic States: Estonia, Latvia and Lithuania.* Edited by David J. Smith, Artis Pabriks, Aldis Purs, and Thomas Lane, 1–177. Postcommunist States and Nations. London: Routledge.

Smith, William C. 1990. "Democracy, Distributional Conflicts and Macroeconomic Policymaking in Argentina, 1983—89." *Journal of Interamerican Studies and World Affairs* 32 (2): 1–42.

Solvak, Mihkel, and Vello Pettai. 2008. "The Parliamentary Elections in Estonia, March 2007." *Electoral Studies* 27 (3): 574–77.

Sörg, Mart, and Vello Vensel. 2000. "The Currency Board in Estonia." In *Economic Policy in Eastern Europe: Were Currency Boards a Solution?* Edited by Iliana Zloch-Christy, 113–43. Westport, CT: Praeger Publishers.

Spiller, Pablo T., and Mariano Tommasi. 2008. "Political Institutions, Policymaking Processes, and Policy Outcomes in Argentina." In *Policymaking in Latin America How Politics Shapes Policies*. Edited by Ernesto Stein and Mariano Tommasi, 69–110. Washington, DC: Inter-American Development Bank (IADB).

Stallings, Barbara. 1978. *Class Conflict and Economic Development in Chile, 1958–1973*. Stanford, CA: Stanford University Press.

———. 1992. "International Influence on Economic Policy: Debt, Stabilization, and Structural Reform." In *The Politics of Economic Adjustment*. Edited by Stephan Haggard and Robert R. Kaufman, 41–88. Princeton, NJ: Princeton University Press.

Staniszkis, Jadwiga. 1990. " 'Political Capitalism' in Poland." *East European Politics and Societies* 5 (1): 127–41.

Stark, David, and László Bruszt. 1998. *Postsocialist Pathways: Transforming Politics and Property in East Central Europe*. Cambridge: Cambridge University Press.

Starr, Pamela K. 1997. "Government Coalitions and the Viability of Currency Boards: Argentina under the Cavallo Plan." *Journal of Interamerican Studies and World Affairs* 39 (2): 83–133.

Stasavage, David. 2003. "Transparency, Democratic Accountability, and the Economic Consequences of Monetary Institutions." *American Journal of Political Science* 47 (3): 389–402. doi .org/10.1111/1540-5907.00028.

Steen, Anton. 1997. "The New Elites in the Baltic States: Recirculation and Change." *Scandinavian Political Studies* 20 (1): 91–112.

Steger, Manfred B., and Ravi K. Roy. 2010. *Neoliberalism: A Very Short Introduction*. Oxford: Oxford University Press.

Steinberg, David A. 2010. "The Reversal of Political Parties' Support for Overvalued Exchange Rates." APSA 2010 Annual Meeting, Rochester, NY. http://papers.ssrn.com/abstract =1642066.

Steinberg, David A. 2015. *Demanding Devaluation: Exchange Rate Politics in the Developing World*. Ithaca, NY: Cornell University Press.

Stokes, Susan C. 2001. *Mandates and Democracy: Neoliberalism by Surprise in Latin America*. New York: Cambridge University Press.

Strassmann, W. Paul. 1976. "Development Economics from a Chicago Perspective." *Journal of Economic Issues* 10 (1): 63–80.

Streeck, Wolfgang. 1994. "Pay Restraint without Incomes Policy: Constitutionalized Monetarism and Industrial Unionism in Germany." In *The Return to Incomes Policy*. Edited by Ronald Philip Dore, Robert Boyer, and Zoe Mars, 118–40. London: Francis Pinter.

———. 2009. *Re-Forming Capitalism: Institutional Change in the German Political Economy*. New York: Oxford University Press.

———. 2014. *Buying Time: The Delayed Crisis of Democratic Capitalism*. London and New York: Verso.

———. 2016. *How Will Capitalism End?: Essays on a Failing System*. London: Verso.

Streeck, Wolfgang, and Kathleen Thelen. 2005. "Introduction: Institutional Change in Advanced Political Economies." In *Beyond Continuity: Institutional Change in Advanced Political Economies*. Edited by Wolfgang Streeck and Kathleen Thelen, 1–39. New York: Oxford University Press.

Šumonja, Miloš. 2018. "The Habermas-Streeck Debate Revisited: Syriza and the Illusions of the Left-Europeanism." *Capital and Class*, November. doi.org/10.1177/0309816818815257.

Sutela, Pekka. 2001. "Managing Capital Flows in Estonia and Latvia." BOFIT Discussion Papers 17. Helsinki: Bank of Finland Institute for Economies in Transition BOFIT.

Suurna, Margit, and Rainer Kattel. 2010. "Europeanization of Innovation Policy in Central and Eastern Europe." *Science and Public Policy* 37 (9): 646–64.

Swenson, Peter. 1991. "Bringing Capital Back In, or Social Democracy Reconsidered: Employer Power, Cross-Class Alliances and Centralisation of Industrial Relations in Denmark and Sweden." *World Politics* 43 (4): 513–44.

Szczerbiak, Aleks. 1998. "Electoral Politics in Poland: The Parliamentary Elections of 1997." *Journal of Communist Studies and Transition Politics* 14 (3): 58–83.

———. 2002a. "Dealing with the Communist Past or the Politics of the Present? Lustration in Post-Communist Poland." *Europe-Asia Studies* 54 (4): 553–72.

———. 2002b. "Poland's Unexpected Political Earthquake: The September 2001 Parliamentary Election." *Journal of Communist Studies and Transition Politics* 18 (3): 41–76.

———. 2002c. "The Political Context of EU Accession in Poland." 3. Briefing Papers. London: The Royal Institute of International Affairs.

———. 2004. "The Polish Centre-Right's (Last?) Best Hope: The Rise and Fall of Solidarity Electoral Action." *Journal of Communist Studies and Transition Politics* 20 (3): 55–79.

———. 2007. " 'Social Poland' Defeats 'Liberal Poland'? The September–October 2005 Polish Parliamentary and Presidential Elections." *Journal of Communist Studies and Transition Politics* 23 (2): 203–32.

Sznajder Lee, Aleksandra. 2006. "Effects of EU Accession on the Politics of Privatization—The Steel Sector in Comparative Perspective." In *Das Erbe des Beitritts: Europäisierung in Mittel- und Osteuropa*. Edited by Amelie Kutter and Vera Trappmann, 209–231. Baden-Baden: Nomos.

———. 2010. "Between Apprehension and Support: Social Dialogue, Democracy, and Industrial Restructuring in Central and Eastern Europe." *Studies in Comparative International Development* 45 (1): 30–56.

Taagepera, Rein. 1995. "Estonian Parliamentary Elections, March 1995." *Electoral Studies* 14 (3): 328–31.

———. 2006. "Meteoric Trajectory: The Res Publica Party in Estonia." *Democratization* 13 (1): 78–94.

Tansel, Cemal Burak, ed. 2017. *States of Discipline: Authoritarian Neoliberalism and the Contested Reproduction of Capitalist Order*. London and New York: Rowman and Littlefield International.

———. 2018. "Authoritarian Neoliberalism and Democratic Backsliding in Turkey: Beyond the Narratives of Progress." *South European Society and Politics* 23 (2): 197–217. doi.org/10.1080/13608746.2018.1479945.

Tavits, Margit, and Natalia Letki. 2009. "When Left Is Right: Party Ideology and Policy in Post-Communist Europe." *American Political Science Review* 103 (4): 555–69.

Teichman, Judith A. 2001. *The Politics of Freeing Markets in Latin America: Chile, Argentina, and Mexico*. Chapel Hill: University of North Carolina Press.

Terk, Erik. 2000. *Privatization in Estonia. Ideas, Processes, Results*. Tallinn: Estonian Institute for Future Studies.

Thelen, Kathleen. 1999. "Historical Institutionalism in Comparative Politics." *Annual Review of Political Science* 2 (1): 369–404.

———. 2014. *Varieties of Liberalization and the New Politics of Social Solidarity*. New York: Cambridge University Press.

Thies, Cameron G. 2014. "The Declining Exceptionalism of Agriculture: Identifying the Domestic Politics and Foreign Policy of Agricultural Trade Protectionism." *Review of International Political Economy* 22 (2): 1–21.

Thies, Cameron G., and Moises Arce. 2009. "The Politics of Exchange Rate–Based Stabilization Versus Structural Reforms in Latin America." *Comparative Political Studies* 42 (9): 1193–1216.

Tiits, Marek, Rainer Kattel, and Tarmo Kalvet. 2006. *Made in Estonia*. Tartu: Institute of Baltic Studies.

Tiits, Marek, Rainer Kattel, Tarmo Kalvet, and Rein Kaarli. 2003. *Competitiveness and Future Outlooks of the Estonian Economy*. Talinn: Research and Development Council.

Titma, Mikk, Nancy Brandon Tuma, and Brian D. Silver. 1998. "Winners and Losers in the Postcommunist Transition: New Evidence from Estonia." *Post-Soviet Affairs* 14 (2): 114–36.

Tsebelis, George. 1991. *Nested Games: Rational Choice in Comparative Politics*. Berkeley and Los Angeles: University of California Press.

Vachudova, Milada Anna. 2005. *Europe Undivided: Democracy, Leverage, and Integration after Communism*. New York: Oxford University Press.

Valdés, Juan Gabriel. 2003. *Pinochet's Economists: The Chicago School in Chile*. Cambridge: Cambridge University Press.

Valdivia, Verónica. 2003. *El golpe después del golpe: Leigh vs. Pinochet, Chile 1960–1980*. Santiago de Chile: LOM.

Valenzuela, Arturo. 1978. *The Breakdown of Democratic Regimes: Chile*. Baltimore, MD: Johns Hopkins University Press.

———. 1993. "Los militares en el poder: la consolidación de poder unipersonal." In *El difícil camino hacia la democracia en Chile, 1982–1990*. Edited by Paul W. Drake and Ivan Jakšić, 57–143. Santiago de Chile: FLACSO.

Vaubel, Roland. 1997. "The Bureaucratic and Partisan Behavior of Independent Central Banks: German and International Evidence." *European Journal of Political Economy* 13 (2): 201–24. doi.org/10.1016/S0176-2680(97)00004-9.

Végh, Carlos A., and Guillermo Vuletin. 2014. "The Road to Redemption: Policy Response to Crises in Latin America." *IMF Economic Review* 62 (4): 526–68.

Veigel, Klaus Friedrich. 2009. *Dictatorship, Democracy, and Globalization: Argentina and the Cost of Paralysis, 1973–2001*. University Park: Pennsylvania State University Press.

Viguera, Aníbal. 1998. "La política de la apertura comercial en la Argentina, 1987–1996." Presented at the Annual Meeting of the Latin American Studies Association (LASA), Chicago, September 24. http://lasa.international.pitt.edu/LASA98/Viguera.pdf.

Vogel, Steven K. 1999. "When Interests Are Not Preferences: The Cautionary Tale of Japanese Consumers." *Comparative Politics* 31 (2): 187–207. doi.org/10.2307/422144.

Vollrath, Thomas L. 1991. "A Theoretical Evaluation of Alternative Trade Intensity Measures of Revealed Comparative Advantage." *Weltwirtschaftliches Archiv* 127 (2): 265–80.

Vommaro, Gabriel. 2017. *La Larga Marcha de Cambiemos*. Buenos Aires: Siglo XXI Editores. http://www.sigloxxieditores.com.ar/fichaLibro.php?libro=978-987-629-778-3.

Wade, Robert. 1990. *Governing the Market: Economic Theory and the Role of Government in East Asian Industrialization*. Princeton, NJ: Princeton University Press.

Wallerstein, Immanuel, Randall Collins, Michael Mann, Georgi Derluguian, and Craig Calhoun. 2013. *Does Capitalism Have a Future?* Oxford and New York: Oxford University Press.

Walter, Stefanie. 2008. "A New Approach for Determining Exchange-Rate Level Preferences." *International Organization* 62 (3): 405–38.

Waterbury, John. 1989. "The Political Management of Economic Adjustment and Reform." In *Fragile Coalitions: The Politics of Economic Adjustment*. Edited by Joan M. Nelson, 39–55. Washington, DC: Transaction Publishers.

Way, Christopher. 2000. "Central Banks, Partisan Politics, and Macroeconomic Outcomes." *Comparative Political Studies* 33 (2): 196–224. doi.org/10.1177/0010414000033002002.

Wehner, Leslie. 2011. "Chile's Rush to Free Trade Agreements." *Revista de Ciencia Política (Santiago)* 31 (2): 207–26.

Weyland, Kurt. 1999a. "Neoliberal Populism in Latin America and Eastern Europe." *Comparative Politics* 31 (4): 379–401.

———. 1999b. "Economic Policy in Chile's New Democracy." *Journal of Interamerican Studies and World Affairs* 41 (3): 67–96.

Weyland, Kurt, Raúl L. Madrid, and Wendy Hunter, eds. 2010. *Leftist Governments in Latin America: Successes and Shortcomings*. Cambridge and New York: Cambridge University Press.

Williamson, John. 1990a. *Latin American Adjustment How Much Has Happened?* Washington, DC: Institute for International Economics.

———. 1990b. "What Washington Means by Policy Reform." In *Latin American Adjustment How Much Has Happened?* Edited by John Williamson, 7–38. Washington, DC: Institute for International Economics.

———. 2002. "The Evolution of Thought on Intermediate Exchange Rate Regimes." *Annals of the American Academy of Political and Social Science* 579: 73–86.

Woll, Cornelia. 2008. *Firm Interests: How Governments Shape Business Lobbying on Global Trade*. Ithaca, NY: Cornell University Press.

Wooldridge, Jeffrey M. 2002. *Econometric Analysis of Cross Section and Panel Data*. Cambridge, MA: MIT Press.

World Bank. 1993. *Estonia: The Transition to a Market Economy*. Country Studies. New York: The World Bank. http://elibrary.worldbank.org/doi/book/10.1596/0-8213-2351-2.

Wylde, Chris. 2012. *Latin America After Neoliberalism: Developmental Regimes in Post-Crisis States*. Basingtonstoke, UK, and New York: Palgrave Macmillan.

Zahler, Anrés, Claudio Bravo, Daniel Goya, and José Miguel Benavente. 2014. "Public-Private Collaboration on Productive Development in Chile." IDB Working Paper Series IDB-WP-502. Washington, DC: Inter-American Development Bank (IADB).

Zaiat, Alfredo. 2012. "Desmalezar." *Página/12*, March 4, 2012.

Zubek, Radoslaw. 2001. "A Core in Check: The Transformation of the Polish Core Executive." *Journal of European Public Policy* 8 (6): 911–32. doi.org/10.1080/13501760110098288.

———. 2006. "Poland: Unbalanced Domestic Leadership in Negotiating Fit." In *Enlarging the Euro Area: External Empowerment and Domestic Transformation in East Central Europe.* Edited by Kenneth H. F. Dyson, 197–213. New York: Oxford University Press.

Zucco Jr., Cesar. 2007. "Where's the Bias? A Reassessment of the Chilean Electoral System." *Electoral Studies* 26 (2): 303–14. doi.org/10.1016/j.electstud.2006.06.00

INDEX

Page references in italics indicate figures and tables.

ABA (*Asociación de Bancos Argentinos*), 101–2

ABIF (*Asociación de Bancos e Instituciones Financieras*) [Chile], 96, 151

accountability, 46, 49–50, 251; and Argentina, 204–6, 213–14, 254, 264; and central banks, 49–50, 202, 223; and checks and balances, 34, 37n, 38, 261, 263, 264; and Chile, 202, 223; and delegation of policy-making, 49, 216, 246; and democracy, 46, 50, 204–6, 208, 213–14, 216, 251, 246, 254, 264; and Estonia, 261, 262–63; and fiscal policy, 49–50, 246; and Hagen, Jürgen von, 49; horizontal, 264; and O'Donnell, Guillermo, 206; in Poland, 208–12, 213–14, 254, 263, and populism, 261–64; and presidential decrees, 205–6, and representation, 46; vertical, 46

AFPs (private pension fund administrators) [Chile], 150n8

AGD (business group), 157

Agency of Agriculture Market (Poland), 112

agriculture, 55, 64–66; and agricultural business interests, 86, 104, 117, 120, 121, 127, 158, 161–62, 173–74, 266; and anti-neoliberalism, 109–10, 119, 126, 131; and Argentina, 65, 86, 98, 102, 104, 154, 157, 158, 206–8; and Brazil, 266; and Chile, 65, 86, 86n, 173–74; and collective farms, 117, 162, 225; and Eastern Europe, 66, 131; and Estonia, 66, 108–9, 116, 117, 120, 121, 122–

23, 141, 161–62, 163, 166, 226, 239; and exchange rates, 86, 102, 131, 158, 170; and farmers, 109–10, 112, 115, 117, 119, 125–27, 131, 132, 161–62, 168–69, 239, 263; and industrial policy, 55, 104, 106, 108–9, 110, 112, 117, 120, 121, 122–23, 125, 126–27, 131, 158, 161–62, 166, 169, 170, 206–8, 226, 239; and liberalization, 86; and neoliberalism, 86, 141, 158, 169; nontraditional, 86; and Poland, 66, 106, 110, 112, 116, 126–27, 141, 169, 170; and privatization, 141, 161–62, 166, 168, 170, 173–74; and shock therapy, 116, 161; and state ownership, 141, 161

Ahumada, José Miguel, 94

AID (Agency for Industrial Development) [Poland], 112

Alanen, Ilkka, 162

Alfonsín, Raúl, 88, 90–92, 97, 132, 133, 153–54, 155, 155n, 184, 205n23

Allende, Salvador, 1, 87, 95, 139, 140, 143, 150

alternative political projects, 10, 14, 15, 22, 23, 36–37, 38, 47, 49–50, 52–53, 62, 77; and Argentina, 227–31, 244–46; business base for, 39–40, 53, 55, 77–80; and campaign funding, 39; and capital flight, 174–75, 262–63; and Chile, 201–2, 220–23; and coalition-building, 39–40, 53, 77; and contestation of neoliberalism, 4, 7, 10, 20, 24, 47, 52, 255–56; and constituencies, 39–40, 77, 174–75, 194; and constitutions, 93, 203, 203–4, 253–57; and corporatism,

315

public opinion: and alternative political projects, 105, 109–10, 193–94, 193, 201; and democracy, 43–44; and discontent, 105, 109–10, 193, 261, 263–64; and industrial policy, 201; and J-curve, 43–44; and neoliberalism, 14–15, 27, 43–44, 61, 105, 109–10, 193–94, 261; and neoliberalism by consent/legitimation, 14–15

public services, 138–39. *See also* public utilities

public utilities, 63n, 155, *172*, 173; and privatization, 92, 143, 146, *147*, 149–50, 156–57, *157*, 163, 168; 170–71, *171*; transnational public utility companies, 138

PZU, *129*, 171

R&D (research and development), 59–60, 244. *See also* innovation

radical market reform, 10, 22, 107–8, 116–17, 143

rationality, 26, 48

Raun, Toivo U., 195

RCA Index (Index of Revealed Comparative Advantages), 64, 64n7, 65–66. *See also* comparative advantage

redistribution, 58, 59, 50, 84, 104, 135, 179, 243

Redrado, Martín, 230–31

Reinhart, Carmen M., 67

rent-seeking: and the "corrupt elite," 257; and economic discretion of governments, 29–30; and development, 29–30; and government interventionism, 29–30, 31, 41; and industrial policy, 30; and Krueger, Anne, 29–30, 41; and privatization, 42; and "rent-seeking society theory," 29–30. *See also* clientelism; corruption; cronyism; patronage

Ricardo, David, 61

Richards (business group), *154*

The Road to Serfdom (Hayek), 32

Roberts Kenneth M., 16, 264n

Rodrik, Dani, 71

Romania, 172, 257

Röpke, Wilhelm, 28

Rosenstein-Rodan, Paul, 28

Rostowski, Jacek, 125n

Rubio, Delia Ferreira, 184–85, 184n, 185n6

ruble zone, 118

Rueschmeyer, Dietrich, 7n

Russia: and Estonia, 121, 123n34, 186, 160, 196, 225, 260–61; and Russian company managers, 107, 159–60, 173; and Russian crisis of 1997–1998, 51, 126–27, 163–64, 120, 122, 126, 162–64, 222, 226, 239, 240–41, 246, 248; and Russian migrant workforce in Estonia, 107, 117, 117n28; and Russian-speaking settlers, 195; and Russian-speaking minority in Estonia, 107, 107n22, 117, 117n29, 118–19, 173, 186–87, 190–92, 192–95, 212–13, 253–54, 260–61; and Russian military, 123n34, 186, 260–61

Rüütel, Arnold, 119, 192

SAPARD (Special Accession Programme for Agricultural and Rural Development), 106

Sapinski, Jean Philippe, 6

Sartori, Giovanni, 179

Savisaar, Edgar, 115–16, 118, 120, 122n, 123, 197

Schmidt, Vivien A., 6, 17–19

Schmitter, Philippe C., 12, 45–46

Schneider, Ben Ross, 79

Schneider, Martin, 64n7

Schoenman, Roger, 214

Schultz, Theodore, 28

Schwartz, Anne, 30

Schwartz, Herman, 12

SEB (business group), 164

Shaw, Edward, 30–31

shock therapy, 45; and agriculture, 116, 161; and alternative political projects, 45, 109–15, 119–20, 161; and Argentina, 85; and Balcerowicz plan, 107–13; and Chile, 85; and democracy, 45, 250; and dictatorships, 85; and employment, 116–17; and Estonia, 116–20, 161; and finance, 85–86,

A NOTE ON THE TYPE

This book has been composed in Arno, an Old-style serif typeface in the classic Venetian tradition, designed by Robert Slimbach at Adobe.